The Priestly Gift in Mishnah

BROWN UNIVERSITY
BROWN JUDAIC STUDIES

Edited by

Jacob Neusner
Wendell S. Dietrich, Ernest S. Frerichs,
Sumner B. Twiss, Alan Zuckerman

Number 20

The Priestly Gift in Mishnah:
A Study of Tractate Terumot

by Alan J. Peck

The Priestly Gift in Mishnah:

A Study of Tractate Terumot

by

Alan J. Peck

Scholars Press

Distributed by
SCHOLARS PRESS
101 Salem Street
Chico, CA 95926

The Priestly Gift in Mishnah:
A Study of Tractate Terumot

by
Alan J. Peck

Library of Congress Cataloging in Publication Data

Peck, Alan, 1953–
    The priestly gift in Mishnah.

    (Brown Judaic studies ; no. 20)
    Includes translation and commentary of tractate
Terumot in Mishnah and Tosefta.
    Bibliography: p.
    Includes index.
    1. Mishnah. Terumot–Commentaries. 2. Tosefta.
Terumot–Commentaries. 3. Terumah. I. Mishnah.
Terumot. English. 1981. II. Tosefta. Terumot.
English. 1981. III. Title. IV. Series.
BM506.T63P4   296.1'23   81-2764
ISBN 0-89130-488-6 (pbk.)   AACR2

Printed in the United States of America
1   2   3   4   5
Edwards Brothers, Inc.
Ann Arbor, Michigan 48106

For My

Parents

TABLE OF CONTENTS

This study systematically analyzes Tractate Terumot (heave-offering) in Mishnah and its corresponding document, Tosefta. My purpose is to investigate the nature of the world view revealed in these texts, that of nascent Rabbinic Judaism. This is accomplished through interpreting the laws which the framers of the tractate composed, and ultimately by ascertaining the meaning those rules had in the world in which they were promulgated. Study of Tractate Terumot thus is intended as basic in the work of interpreting Mishnah and the form of Judaism which that document richly represents.

My goals are reached through a fresh translation of and commentary to the tractate. This exegetical work aims at discerning how the men who produced the tractate understood the law of heave-offering. I claim to explain the meaning these laws conveyed to those who, in late-second-century Palestine, redacted them into the tractate before us. This goal excludes from consideration several possible questions. For example, while some of the tractate's rule might be older than their present redactional context, no attempt is made to identify such rules or to discover the sense they might have had prior to placement in that context. I likewise do not take into account the role which the laws of heave-offering played in the later history of Rabbinic Judaism. While valid in their own right, each of these tasks stands outside of the purpose of this study, discovery of the meaning of Tractate Terumot as an essay created in a particular historical setting, by a specific group of redactors.

My translation and exegesis are carefully designed to limit the meaning which I derive from the tractate's laws to that intended by their original framers. To do this, both translation and exegesis pay close attention to the disciplined mode of literary formulation which characterizes the tractate as a whole. My purpose in this is to show that the way in which the tractate's framers stated their laws offers an important key to the meaning they hoped those laws would convey. The translation, first, reproduces both the substance and the formal and syntactic traits of the Hebrew text. These features may then guide the actual interpretive work. The result is that I am able to specify the single legal point which each pericope is designed to emphasize. Careful literary analysis, combined with an understanding of the conceptual content of the law, thus leads us to the meaning of the pericope's rules.

A second step in interpretation is viewing as a whole the
larger structure of laws to which the individual pericope con-
tributes, and within which that pericope has its larger importance.
This work is carried out in introductions to the individual chapters of the tractate. These introductions delineate the underlying principle expressed in each of the tractate's several thematic
units, and indicate the role of individual pericopae in stating
and investigating that principle.

With the tractate's pericopae fully explained, it is possible
to identify the central issue addressed by the tractate as a whole.
This is the particular aspect of the topic of heave-offering which
generates the tractate's discussion. It therefore accounts for
the formulation of specific questions to be addressed, as well as
the selection and organization of particular themes. By identifying this issue we come to understand the chief concerns which
motivated and guided the formulators of the tractate. These concerns, in turn, may be viewed in light of the historical context
in which those redactors worked. This reveals the message which
they wished to convey in their own day, to their immediate
audience. This analysis, the result of my exegetical work, is
found in the introduction to the tractate. In this way the reader
may easily judge my larger conclusions against the data provided
by the individual pericopae of the tractate. Within that same
introduction, I provide a full account of the methods used in the
translation and commentary, and of the theoretical considerations
which determined those methods.

In addition to Mishnah, I have translated and discussed all
of Tosefta Terumot. Tosefta is an important tool in interpreting
Mishnah, for it is the only commentary which employs the tractate's
own formal characteristics and conceptual framework in elucidating
its individual rules. I therefore present the pertinent materials
from Tosefta after the pericopae of Mishnah to which they relate,
and indicate briefly how Tosefta's discussion deepens our comprehension of the central point or issue under discussion in the
tractate.

I gratefully acknowledge my debt to teachers and colleagues
who shared in the unfolding of this study. Foremost among these
is Professor Jacob Neusner, Brown University, under whose direction
this commentary was both conceived and written. Any merit this
work may have is due to his constant attention, criticism and

support. For his guidance and friendship, offered both inside and
outside of the classroom, I shall ever be thankful.

Fellow students in Professor Neusner's graduate seminar during the writing of this manuscript contributed important insights
and improvements. As a result of their careful scrutiny of my
work, this commentary is far better than it otherwise could have
been. They are: Professor Martin S. Jaffee, University of
Virginia; Professor Peter J. Haas, Vanderbilt University; Ms.
Maggie Wenig-Rubenstein; Mr. Leonard D. Gordon; and Mr. Abraham
Havivi. In 1977-79 Professor Richard S. Sarason, presently at
Hebrew Union College, Cincinnati, Ohio, also participated in that
seminar. I appreciate the suggestions he offered in that context,
as well as his guidance as a graduate instructor at Brown University.

Ms. Lisa Joy Avery kindly assisted me both in preparing the
original manuscript and in the arduous task of proofreading this
book. For her help in this, and in other ways too numerous for
me to count, I thank her.

Grants from the Max Richter Foundation and, in 1980-81, from
the Memorial Foundation for Jewish Culture, allowed me to devote
myself to the completion of this project. I appreciate these
foundations' gracious support of my work.

Ms. Winifred Bell, Providence, Rhode Island, carefully typed
this book for publication. I heartily thank her for her skill and
effort in creating this volume.

This book is dedicated to my parents, Richard W. and Eileen
S. Peck. Their constant love, understanding and support is the
source of all that I ever have done, and ever shall.

Alan J. Peck

Providence, Rhode Island
22 September 1980
12 Tishre 5741
*A present for my
grandfather, on
his seventieth
birthday.*

ABBREVIATIONS AND BIBLIOGRAPHY

Ah.	= 'Ahilot
Albeck	= H. Albeck, *The Six Orders of the Mishnah* (Jerusalem and Tel Aviv, 1957).
Ar.	= ^CArakhin
Aruch	= Alexander Kohut, ed., *Aruch Completum*, 8 vols. (Vienna, 1878-1892; second ed., 1926).
A.Z.	= 'Abodah Zarah
B	= Mishnah *Zera^Cim*, MS. Berlin 93; see Sacks-Hutner, pp. 43, 77-78.
b.	= *Babli*, Babylonian Talmud; *ben*, "son of."
B.B.	= Baba' Batra'
Bek.	= Bekhorot
Ber.	= Berakhot
Bert	= Obadiah b. Abraham of Bertinoro (fifteenth century), Mishnah Commentary in Romm ed. of Mishnah (Vilna, 1908, and reprints).
Bes.	= Besah
Bik.	= Bikkurim
B.M.	= Baba' Mesi^Ca'
B.Q.	= Baba' Qamma'
C	= Mishnah, early printed edition of unknown origin, probably Constantinople or Pisaro, c. 1516; see Sacks-Hutner, pp. 64, 82-83.
Ca	= Mishnah, MS. Cambridge 470, 1, printed in W.H. Lowe, *The Mishnah On Which the Palestinian Talmud Rests* (Cambridge, 1883; reprint: Jerusalem, 1967); see Sacks-Hutner, pp. 63, 67.
Dalman	= Gustav Dalman, *Arbeit und Sitte in Palastina*, 8 vols. (Guttersloh, 1928-42).
Danby	= Herbert Danby, *The Mishnah, translated from the Hebrew with introduction and brief explanatory notes* (London, 1933).
Dem.	= Dema'i
Donagan	= Alan Donagan, *The Theory of Morality* (Chicago, 1977).
Dt.	= Deuteronomy
E	= Tosefta, MS. Erfurt; see Lieberman, TZ, pp. 8-11.
Ed.	= 'Eduyyot
ed. princ.	= Tosefta, *editio princeps* (Venice, 1521).

Eissfeldt   = Otto Eissfeldt, *Erstlings und Zehnten im
                               Alten Testament* (Leipzig, 1917).

Epstein   = *Mekhilta d'Rabbi Šim'on bar Jochai*, ed.,
                               J.N. Epstein and E.Z. Melamed (Jerusalem,
                               1955).

Epstein, *Mabo'*   = Jacob Nahum Halevi Epstein, *Mabo' lenosah
                               hammišnah* [*Prolegomenon to the Text of
                               the Mishnah*], 2 vols. (Jerusalem and Tel
                               Aviv, 1948; second edition, 1964).

Epstein, *Mebo'ot*   = Jacob Nahum Halevi Epstein, *Mebo'ot
                               lesifrut hattanna'im* [*Prolegomena to the
                               Tannaitic Literature*], edited by Ezra Z.
                               Melamed (Jerusalem and Tel Aviv, 1957).

Erub.   = 'Erubin

Ex.   = Exodus

Feliks, *Agriculture*   = Yehudah Feliks, *Agriculture in Palestine
                               in the Period of the Mishna and Talmud*
                               (Heb.) (Jerusalem and Tel Aviv, 1963).

Feliks, *Plant World*   = Yehudah Feliks, *The Plant World of the
                               Bible* (Heb.) (Tel Aviv, 1957).

G   = Mishnah MS. fragments from the Cairo
                               Genizah, listed and numbered in Sacks-
                               Hutner, pp. 87-112.

Gen.   = Genesis

Gereboff, *Tarfon*   = Joel Gereboff, *Rabbi Tarfon: The Tra-
                               dition, The Man, and Early Rabbinic
                               Judaism* (Missoula, 1979).

Git.   = Gittin

GRA   = Elijah b. Solomon Zalman ("HaGa'on Rabbi
                               'Eliyahu," or "Vilna Gaon"; Lithuania,
                               1720-1797), Mishnah commentary, in Romm
                               edition of Mishnah (Vilna, 1908, and
                               numerous reprints); Tosefta emendations,
                               in Romm edition of Babylonia Talmud
                               (Vilna, 1886, and numerous reprints).

Gray   = George B. Gray, *A Critical and Exegetical
                               Commentary on Numbers* (New York, 1906)

Green, *Approaches*   = William S. Green, ed., *Approaches to
                               Ancient Judaism: Theory and Practice*
                               (Missoula, 1978).

Green, *Joshua*   = William S. Green, *The Legal Traditions of
                               Joshua ben Hananiah in Mishnah, Tosefta,
                               and Related Literature*. Brown University
                               doctoral dissertation. Dir. J. Neusner
                               (1974).

Green, "Techniques"   = William S. Green, "Redactional Techniques
                               in the Legal Traditions of Joshua B.
                               Hananiah," in J. Neusner, ed., *Christian-
                               ity, Judaism and Other Greco-Roman Cults*
                               (Leiden, 1975), vol. 4, pp. 1-17.

Güting = Beer, Georg, ed., *Die Mischna; Text,*
Übersetzung und ausführliche Erklärung
mit eingehenden geschichtlichen und
sprachlichen Einleitung. [Vol. 1:6:
Eberhard Güting, *Terumot*].

Haas = Peter Haas, *A History of the Mishnaic Law*
of Agriculture: Tractate Maaser Sheni
(Chico, 1980).

Hag. = Hagigah

Hal. = Hallah

HD = *Hasde David.* David Samuel b. Jacob Pardo
(Italy, Austria, Palestine, 1718-1790),
Sefer Hasde David [Tosefta commentary].
I. *Seder Zera'im* (Livorno, 1776; re-
print: Jerusalem, 1970).

Hor. = Horayot

Hul. = Hullin

HY = *Hazon Yehezqel.* Yehezqel Abramsky (1886-
1976), *Hazon Yehezqel* [Tosefta Commen-
tary]. *Sedar Zera^{c}im* (Vilna, 1925; second
ed.: Jerusalem, 1971).

Jaffee = Martin Jaffee, *Mishnah's Law of Tithes:*
A Study of Tractate Maaserot. Brown
University doctoral dissertation. Dir.
J. Neusner (1980).

Jastrow = Marcus Jastrow, *A Dictionary of the*
Targumim, the Talmud Babli and Yerushalmi,
and the Midrashic Literature, 2 vols.
(New York, 1895-1903; repr. New York,
1975).

JE = *The Jewish Encyclopedia,* 12 vols. (New
York and London, 1901-1906; repr. New
York, 1975).

K = Mishnah, MS. Kaufman A 50; photocopy:
Georg Beer, *Faksimile-Ausgabe des*
Mischnacodex Kaufmann A 50 (The Hague,
1929; reprint: Jerusalem, 1969); see
Sacks-Hutner, pp. 63, 65-66.

Kasovsky, *Mishnah* = C.Y. Kasovsky, *Thesaurus Mishnae:*
Concordantiae verborum etc., 4 vols. (Tel
Aviv, 1957, rev. 1967).

Kasovsky, *Tosefta* = C.Y. Kasovsky, *Thesaurus Thosephthae:*
Concordantiae verborum etc., 6 vols.
(Jerusalem, 1932-1961).

Kel. = Kelim

Ker. = Keritot

Ket. = Ketubot

Kil = Kila'yim

KM = *Kesef Mishnah.* Joseph b. Ephraim Karo
(1488-1575). Commentary to Maimonides'
Mishnah Torah, in standard editions of
the latter.

L   = Palestinian Talmud, MS. Leiden; see Sacks-
                       Hutner, pp. 63, 72.

Lehrman   = Isadore Epstein, ed., *The Babylonian
                       Talmud: Seder Zera^cim* II (London, 1948),
                       "Terumoth," tr. with notes by S.M.
                       Lehrman.

Lev.   = Leviticus

Levinthal   = Israel Levinthal, "The Jewish Law of
                       Agency," in E.M. Gershfield, ed. *Studies
                       in Jewish Jurisprudence* (New York, 1971).

Lieberman, *Light*   = Saul Lieberman, "Light on the Cave Scrolls
                       from Rabbinic Sources," *American Academy
                       for Jewish Research; Proceedings;* vol. 20
                       (1951), pp. 395-404.

Lieberman, TK   = Saul Lieberman, *Tosefta Ki-fshuta: A
                       Comprehensive Commentary on the Tosefta*,
                       I. *Order Zera^cim*, 2 vols. (New York,
                       1955).

Lieberman, TZ   = Saul Lieberman, ed., *The Tosefta Accord-
                       ing to Codex Vienna with Variants from
                       Codex Erfurt, Genizah MSS. and Editio
                       Princeps*, I. *The Order of Zera^cim* (New
                       York, 1955).

Löw, *Flora*   = Immanuel Löw, *Die Flora der Juden*, 4 vols.
                       (Vienna and Leipzig, 1926).

M   = Babylonian Talmud, Codex Munich 95; photo-
                       copy: Hermann L. Strack, *Talmud Babyloni-
                       cum Codicis Hebraica Monacensis 95*
                       (Leiden, 1912; reprint: Jerusalem, 1971);
                       see Sacks-Hutner, pp. 63, 69-70.

M.   = Mishnah

Ma.   = Ma^caserot

Maimonides   = (Moses b. Maimon, Spain and Egypt, 1135-
                       1204), *Kitah es-Siraj* [Mishnah commen-
                       tary]; in standard editions of the
                       Mishnah.

Maimonides, *Heave-* = *Hilkhot Terumot*, codification of laws of
offering   heave-offering in Maimonides' *Mishnah
                       Torah*.   This is the source of references
                       to Maimonides, *Tithes, Second Tithe and
                       Fourth Year Fruit, Seventh Year and
                       Jubilee*.

Mak.   = Makkot

Makh.   = Makhshirin

Mandelbaum   = Irving Mandelbaum, *A History of the
                       Mishnaic Law of Agriculture: Tractate
                       Kilaim, Translation and Commentary*. Brown
                       University doctoral dissertation. Dir.
                       J. Neusner (1980).

MB   = *Minḥat Bikkurim*. Samuel Avigdor b.
                       Abraham Karlin (nineteenth century),
                       Tosefta commentary (1842), in Romm edition
                       of Babylonian Talmud.

Me.	= Me^cilah
Meg.	= Megillah
Men.	= Menahot
Mid.	= Middot
Miq.	= Miqva'ot
M.Q.	= Mo^ced Qaṭan
MR	= *Mishnah Ri'šonah*. Ephraim Issac of Premysla (Poland, nineteenth century), Mishnah commentary (1882), in standard editions of Mishnah.
M.S.	= Ma^caser Šeni
MS	= *Meleket Šelomoh*. Solomon b. Joshua Adeni (Yemen and Palestine, c. 1600), Mishnah commentary, in standard editions of Mishnah.
MS.	= manuscript
Naz.	= Nazir
Ned.	= Nedarim
Neg.	= Nega^cim
Neusner, *Appointed Times*	= J. Neusner, *A History of the Mishnaic Law of Appointed Times*, 5 vols. (Leiden, 1981).
Neusner, *Cults*	= Jacob Neusner, ed., *Christianity, Judaism and Other Greco-Roman Cults: Studies for Morton Smith at Sixty*, 4 vols. (Leiden, 1975).
Neusner, "Current Events"	= J. Neusner, "New Problems, New Solutions: Current Events in Rabbinic Studies," *Studies in Religion*, vol. 8, no. 4 (1979), pp. 401-18.
Neusner, *Damages*	= J. Neusner, *A History of the Mishnaic Law of Damages*, 5 vols. (Leiden, 1982).
Neusner, *Development*	= J. Neusner, *Development of a Legend; Studies in the Traditions Concerning Yohanan ben Zakkai* (Leiden, 1970).
Neusner, *Eliezer*	= J. Neusner, *Eliezer ben Hyrcanus: The Tradition and the Man*, 2 vols. (Leiden, 1973).
Neusner, *Holy Things*	= J. Neusner, *A History of the Mishnaic Law of Holy Things*, 6 vols. (Leiden, 1978-79).
Neusner, *Judaism*	= J. Neusner, *Judaism: The Evidence of the Mishnah* (Chicago, 1981).
Neusner, *Life*	= J. Neusner, *A Life of Yohanan ben Zakkai* (Leiden, 1962; second edition, completely revised, 1970).
Neusner, *Method*	= J. Neusner, *Method and Meaning in Ancient Judaism* (Missoula, 1979).
Neusner, *Modern Study*	= J. Neusner, ed., *The Modern Study of the Mishnah* (Leiden, 1973).

Neusner, *Pharisees*

= J. Neusner, *The Rabbinic Traditions about the Pharisees before 70*, 3 vols. (Leiden, 1971).

Neusner, *Purities*

= J. Neusner, *A History of the Mishnaic Law of Purities*, 22 vols. (Leiden, 1974-1977).

Neusner, "Redaction"

= J. Neusner, "Redaction, Formulation and Form: The Case of Mishnah," *Jewish Quarterly Review* 70 (1980), pp. 1-22.

Neusner, *Tosefta*

= J. Neusner, *The Tosefta Translated from the Hebrew*, 5 vols. (New York, 1977-).

Neusner, "Transcendence"

= J. Neusner, "Transcendence and Worship Through Learning," *Journal of Reform Judaism* 25, 2 (1978), pp. 15-29.

Neusner, *Women*

= J. Neusner, *A History of the Mishnaic Law of Women*, 5 vols. (Leiden, 1979-80).

Nid.

= Niddah

Noth

= Noth, Martin, *Leviticus* (Philadelphia, 1963).

Num.

= Numbers

O^1

= Babylonian Talmud, MS. Oxford 366, Orders *Zera^{c}im* and *Mo^{c}ed*; see Sacks-Hutner, pp. 63, 68-69.

O^2

= Mishnah *Zera^{c}im*, MS. Oxford 393, with Maimonides' commentary, autograph; see Sacks-Hutner, pp. 63, 76-77.

Oh.

= 'Ohalot

Or.

= Orlah

P

= Mishnah, MS. Parma De Rossi 138 (photocopy: Jerusalem, 1970); see Sacks-Hutner, pp. 63, 66-67.

Pa

= Mishnah, MS. Paris 328-329 (photocopy: Jerusalem, 1970); see Sacks-Hutner, pp. 64, 79.

Par.

= Parah

Pe.

= Pe'ah

Pes.

= Pesaḥim

Pliny

= Pliny, *Natural History* [Loeb Classical Library], 10 vols. (London, 1938-63).

PM

= *Penei Moshe*. Moses Margolioth (eighteenth century), commentary to the Jerusalem Talmud, Zhitomir edition.

Popper

= William Popper, *The Censorship of Jewish Books* (New York, 1899).

Porter

= J.R. Porter, *Leviticus* (Cambridge, 1976).

Porton, "Dispute"

= Gary G. Porton, "The Artificial Dispute: Ishmael and Aqiba," in Neusner, *Cults*, vol. IV, pp. 18-29.

Porton, *Ishmael*

= Gary G. Porton, *The Traditions of Rabbi Ishmael*, 4 vols. (Leiden, 1976-).

Press   = Isaiah Press, *A Topographical-Historical*
                           Encyclopedia of Palestine, 4 vols.
                           (Jerusalem, 1955).

Primus, *Aqiva*   = Charles Primus, *Aqiva's Contribution to*
                           the Law of Zera^cim (Leiden, 1977).

Qin.   = Qinnim

R   = Jerusalem Talmud, MS. Vatican 133; Sacks-
                           Hutner, pp. 63, 73.

R.   = Rabbi

Rabad   = Abraham b. David of Posquieres (ca. 1120-
                           1198), glosses to Maimonides' *Mishnah*
                           Torah, in standard editions of the latter.

Rashi   = Solomon b. Isaac of Troyes (France, 1040-
                           1105), commentary to Babylonian Talmud,
                           in standard editions of the latter.

RDBZ   = David ibn Zimra (1479-1589), super-
                           commentary to Maimonides' *Mishnah Torah*,
                           in standard editions of the latter.

R.H.   = Roš Haššanah

Rosh   = Asher b. Yehiel (Germany and Spain, c.
                           1250-1327), Mishnah commentary, in stan-
                           dard editions of Babylonian Talmud.

S   = Palestinian Talmud, MS. British Museum
                           403, *Zera^cim*, with commentary of Solomon
                           of Sirillo (See Sirillo); see Sacks-
                           Hutner, pp. 63, 73-75.

Sa   = Mishnah *Zera^cim*, MS. Sassoon 531; see
                           Sacks-Hutner, pp. 63, 68.

Sacks-Hutner   = Nissan Sacks, ed., *The Mishnah with Variant*
                           Readings, Order Zera^cim, 2 vols. (Institute
                           for the Complete Israeli Talmud: Jerusa-
                           lem, 1972-75).

San.   = Sanhedrin

Sarason, *Demai*   = Richard S. Sarason, *A History of the*
                           Mishnaic Law of Agriculture: A Study of
                           Tractate Demai, Part One (Leiden, 1979).

Sarason, *"Zera^cim"*   = Richard S. Sarason, "Mishnah and Scripture:
                           Preliminary Observations on the Law of
                           Tithing in *Seder Zera^cim*, in W.S. Green,
                           ed., *Approaches to Ancient Judaism*, vol.
                           2 (Chico, 1980), pp. 81-96.

Segal   = M.H. Segal, *A Grammar of Mishnaic Hebrew*
                           (Oxford, reprint: 1970).

Sens   = Samson b. Abraham of Sens (France, late
                           twelfth-early thirteenth centuries),
                           Mishnah commentary, in Romm edition of
                           Babylonian Talmud.

Shab.   = Šabbat

Shav.   = Šabu^cot

Sheb.   = Šebi^cit

Sheq.   = Šeqalim

Sifra
= *Sifra debe Rab, hu' Sefer Torat Kohanim*, ed. I[saac] H[irsch] Weiss (Vienna, 1862; reprint: New York, 1946).

Sifré Dt.
= *Siphre ad Deuteronomium*, ed. L. Finkelstein, with H.S. Horovitz (Berlin, 1939).

Sifré Numbers
= *Siphre de'be Rab, Fasciculus primus: Siphre ad Numeros adjecto Siphre Zutta*, ed. H.S. Horovitz (Leipzig, 1917; reprint: Jerusalem, 1966).

Sirillo
= Solomon b. Joseph Sirillo (Spain, Balkans, Palestine, late fifteenth century, died c. 1558), commentary on Palestine Talmud, Order *Zera^cim* (Jerusalem, 1934-67). *Terumot* (1934).

Smith
= G.A. Smith, *Historical Atlas of the Holy Land* (London, 1936).

Snaith
= N.A. Snaith, *Leviticus and Numbers* (London, 1967).

Sot.
= Sotah

Strack
= Hermann Strack, *Introduction to the Talmud and Midrash* (Philadelphia, reprint: 1959).

Suk.
= Sukkah

T.
= Tosefta

Ta.
= Ta^canit

Tam.
= Tamid

Tem.
= Temurah

Ter.
= Terumot

Theophrastus, *Enquiry*
= Theophrastus, *Enquiry into Plants*, tr. Sir Arthur Hart, 2 vols. [Loeb Classical Library] (London, 1916).

TK
= see Lieberman, TK.

Toh.
= Tohorot

T.Y.
= Tebul Yom

TYT
= *Tosepot Yom Tob*. Yom Tom Lippmann Heller (Austria, Bohemia, Poland, 1579-1654), Mishnah commentary, in Romm edition of Mishnah.

TYY
= *Tip'eret Yiśra'el Yakin*. Israel b. Gedaliah Lipschutz (Germany, 1782-1860), Mishnah commentary, with supercommentary, *Tip'eret Yiśra'el Bo^caz*, by his son, Baruch Isaac b. Israel Lipschutz (1812-1877), in Romm edition of Mishnah.

Uqs.
= 'Uqsin

V
= Tosefta, MS. Vienna Heb. 20; see Lieberman, pp. 11-12.

Vc
= Babylonian Talmud, *editio princeps*, Venice, 1520-23 (photocopy: Jerusalem, 1967-72); see Sacks-Hutner, pp. 64, 83-84.

Weinfeld	= Moshe Weinfeld, *Deuteronomy and the Deuteronomic School* (Oxford, 1972).
White	= K.D. White, *Roman Farming* (Ithaca, 1970).
y.	= *Yerušalmi*, Palestinian Talmud.
Yad.	= Yadayyim
Yeb.	= Yebamot
Y.T.	= Yom Ṭob
Z	= Mishnah, MS. Paris 362, with commentary of Sens; see Sacks-Hutner, pp. 64, 79-80.
Zab.	= Zabbim
Zeb.	= Zebaḥim
Zuckermandel	= Moses Samuel Zuckermandel, *Tosephta, based on the Erfurt and Vienna Codices, with parallels and variants* (Trier, 1881-82; revised edition with supplement by Saul Lieberman, Jerusalem, reprint: 1970).

א	= '		ל	= l	
ב	= b		מ, ם	= m	
ג	= g		נ, ן	= n	
ד	= d		ס	= s	
ה	= h		ע	= c	
ו	= w		פ, ף	= p	
ז	= z		צ, ץ	= ṣ	
ח	= ḥ		ק	= q	
ט	= ṭ		ר	= r	
י	= y		שׁ	= š	
כ, ך	= k		שׂ	= ś	

ת = t

Transliterations represent the consonantal structure of the Hebrew word, with no attempt made to vocalize. I do not distinguish between the spirantized and non-spirantized forms of *b*, *g*, *d*, *k*, *p*, and *t*. Verbal roots are indicated by capitalization, e.g., *TRM*. When, on occasion, a word is vocalized, the following notation is used:

a = *qamaṣ, pataḥ*   i = *ḥiriq*
ei = *ṣere-yod*   o = *ḥolem, ḥolem ḥaser,*
e = *ṣere, segol, vocal šewa'*   *qamaṣ qaṭan*
          u = *suruq, qubbuṣ*

Quiescent *šewa'* is not represented. Proper names and commonly used words are reproduced in their most frequent English usage, e.g., Eleazar, Mishnah, etc.

INTRODUCTION

I. The Content of the Tractate

The topic of Tractate Terumot is heave-offering, one of the
several agricultural gifts which Mishnah requires Israelites to
set aside from produce grown in the Land of Israel.[1] This
particular offering is designated for the use of priests and
their households. Yet as we shall see in a moment, Mishnah is
little interested in the priests and their maintenance. Its
interest in heave-offering, rather, is from the point of view
of the Israelite householder who must give the offering. The
tractate prescribes how Israelites are to designate a portion
of their produce to be heave-offering, and outlines their responsibility to protect it from common use until they convey it
to the priest. In short, Tractate Terumot describes what it
believes all Israelites should know in order properly to pay
one of their required agricultural dues.[2]

Mishnah's concept of the specific agricultural gift which
it calls heave-offering derives from Scripture's priestly code.
If we are to make sense of what Mishnah, for its part, says
about this subject, we must begin with the passage on which it
depends. This is Num. 18:8-13, which reads:

> (8) Then the Lord said to Aaron, "And behold, I have
> given to you whatever is kept of the offerings made to me,
> all the consecrated things of the people of Israel; I have
> given them to you as a perpetual due.
> " (9) This shall be yours of the most holy things,
> reserved from the fire; every offering of theirs, every
> cereal offering of theirs and every sin offering of theirs,
> and every guilt offering of theirs, which they render to
> me, shall be most holy to you and to your sons. (10) In
> a most holy place you shall eat of it; it is holy to you.
> " (11) This also is yours, the offering of their
> gift (*trwmt mtnm*), all the wave offerings of the people of
> Israel; I have given them to you, and to your sons and
> daughters with you, as a perpetual due; every one who is
> clean in your house may eat of it. (12) All the best of
> the oil, and all the best of the wine and of the grain,
> the first of them (*r'šytm*) which they give to the Lord, I
> give to you. (13) The first ripe fruits (*bkwry*) of all
> that is in their land, which they bring to the Lord, shall
> be yours; every one who is clean in your house may eat of
> it."

The passage delineates those offerings which the people of
Israel contribute to the support of the Aaronide priesthood.
After discussing Temple-offerings, parts of which belong to the

1

priests, it turns to agricultural dues. It is difficult to determine the number and nature of the offerings listed in vss. 11-13.[3]
"The offering of their gift," vs. 11, appears to be a general term,
referring to all agricultural gifts which are eaten by the priests,
and including wave offerings (vs. 11), the best of the oil, wine
and grain (vs. 12) and first fruits (vs. 13). People who stand
behind Mishnah, however, have read "the offering of their gift" in
conjunction with vs. 12's "best of the oil, wine and grain, the
first of them." In this manner they identify a single agricultural gift, distinct from the "first fruits" of vs. 13.[4] In
Mishnaic parlance, this gift is called "heave-offering" (*trwmh*),
although it is also known by the term "first," suggested by vs. 12
(see M. 3:7).

The central facts which Mishnah knows about heave-offering
are taken from this passage. These are that heave-offering is
holy and the property of priests. In accordance with its sanctified status, it must be eaten in cultic cleanness and may be eaten
only by the priest and members of his household. These facts,
stated in Scripture, are basic to everything which Mishnah will
say about heave-offering. The tractate moreover completes the
priestly code's picture, by taking up specific questions which
must be answered if the priests indeed are to be supported, as
Scripture wishes. These are the issues which I stated at the outset, of how individual Insraelites are to separate and care for
the required offering, thereby assuring that the priest ultimately
will receive and consume it.

Yet this judgment about the relationship between Tractate
Terumot and Scripture is not entirely to the point. This is because at base the tractate uses the framework which I have described to discuss a question very different from the simple one
left open by Scripture, that is, of how Israelites are to pay the
priests their due. Mishnah's true interest, rather, must be expressed in terms of two separate, but related, issues. The first
is the process of sanctification. This is to say that the tractate asks how a certain quantity of produce grown on the Land of
Israel comes to be deemed holy. The second issue is the effect
which this produce, the heave-offering, has upon common food with
which it is mixed. This issue is expanded to include other situations in which heave-offering is used as if it were secular food,
for instance, cases in which it is eaten by a non-priest. These
problems must be dealt with, for they describe situations in which
the barrier that normally separates the distinct realms of the holy

and the secular is broken. In all, then, the tractate does not
dwell upon the priesthood and its needs, the issue so central in
Scripture. Rather, it uses laws governing the separation and disposition of heave-offering as a context in which to provide a
larger picture of its notion of sanctification and of the safe con-
duct of the holy through the profane world.[5] In order to understand the tractate's notion of the holy, let us therefore detail
the story of heave-offering as Mishnah Terumot tells it.

The first problem to be addressed is how a quantity of the
householder's produce becomes consecrated as heave-offering.
According to Tractate Terumot, this is accomplished by the thoughts
and deeds of the Israelite householder. That is to say, it is the
common Israelite -- the non-priest -- who, while forbidden to eat
holy produce, has the power to cause produce to be deemed holy.[6]
He does this, first of all, by formulating the intention to con-
secrate produce as the priestly gift. Then he pronounces a formula
by which he orally designates a portion of his produce to be heave-
offering. Finally, he effects his intention by physically separating that portion from the rest of the batch. Through these
thoughts and actions the householder determines what produce, and
how much of it, is to be deemed holy.

The main point, then, is that the common Israelite is central
in the process of sanctification. The holy heave-offering comes
into being only if man properly formulates the intention to
sanctify part of his produce, and indicates that intention
through corresponding words and actions. The centrality of human
intention in this process is illustrated by the fact that individuals deemed to have no understanding (e.g., imbeciles and
minors; M. 1:1), and therefore no power of intention, may not
validly designate heave-offering. It further is clear that by
his actions the householder is not simply removing from the batch
produce which already has a sanctified status. That no produce
is intrinsically holy is easily shown. An Israelite who has two
distinct batches of produce can designate and set aside from one
of them the heave-offering required of both.[7] The result is that
the liability of both batches to the separation of heave-
offering is fulfilled. This could not be the case if each batch
contained a quantity of already-holy produce which had to be removed. If that were so, what the householder did with one batch
could have no effect upon a different batch. According to
Tractate Terumot, therefore, it is the common Israelite who
imposes a status of sanctification on produce. This notion of

the centrality of the Israelite householder is further developed
in cases in which heave-offering is mixed with secular food, or
is used in some other way not fitting its sanctified status. To
such cases we now turn.

Once heave-offering has been designated and separated, a
new set of problems is encountered. These problems concern the
protection of heave-offering from misuse. For as long as the
consecrated priestly gift remains in the Israelite's domain, it
is liable to be used to some purpose other than its proper one,
the benefit of the priest. For example, the heave-offering
might be mixed or cooked with the Israelite's own common food.
Again, it might be eaten by the non-priest, or even planted as
seed. These are central points of danger in the passage of the
holy produce from the domain of the householder to that of the
priest. Tractate Terumot assumes that these problems will occur
and takes measures to correct them. It therefore asks of the
culpability of the non-priest for the mistreatment of the holy
offering. As we should expect on the basis of what we already
have seen, the answer to this question depends very much upon the
intentions and perceptions of the householder who allows the
heave-offering to become confused with his own food, or to be
eaten or planted.

Two brief examples will illustrate my point. The first is
the case in which heave-offering is cooked with an Israelite's
own common produce.[8] Through the cooking, the heave-offering
and profane produce are turned into a single dish. We might
therefore expect the tractate to rule that the whole dish, including the common produce, must thereafter be treated as if it
had absorbed the holiness of the heave-offering and is forbidden
to the Israelite. Otherwise the non-priest would use the consecrated produce to his own benefit. According to the tractate,
however, this is the case only if the Israelite perceives the
heave-offering to have improved his food. If so, he must refrain
from eating any of the produce, even if he succeeds in removing
the heave-offering from the dish. For even if the householder
removed the heave-offering from the dish, he still would view
himself as having benefitted from the flavor it imparted to his
food. What, on the other hand, if the householder does not
desire the flavor which the heave-offering imparted to his food?
Now he may simply remove the heave-offering from that food and
thereafter ignore the fact that heave-offering was cooked in it.
The actual flavoring-power of the heave-offering is not at issue,

but only the Israelite's personal likes and desires.[9] As long as
he does not perceive himself to benefit from the heave-offering,
he has maintained intact the barrier between the holy and profane. As we saw above, therefore, sanctification is not a
physical trait, but depends upon the intentions of the
Israelite.[10]

The case in which an Israelite plants heave-offering as seed
illustrates this same point.[11] We know that the Israelite should
not do this, for heave-offering is set aside for the use of the
priest alone. If the non-priest anyway plants the heave-offering, there are two possible outcomes. If he does so deliberately,
that is, with the full intention of using the priest's due as
his own, he is compelled both to allow the seed to grow and to
treat the crop which results as holy heave-offering. This constitutes a substantial loss to the Israelite. He both loses the
use of his field and may not eat the produce which grows from it.
If, however, the individual unintentionally plants the heave-
offering, he may plow it up. To be sure, he may not make
personal use of what is designated for the priest. But by the
same token, he is not held culpable for what he did unintentionally.[12]
Only by his intention does man encroach upon the holy, just as
it is only by his intention that he sanctifies produce in the
first place.

If we now recall Num. 18:8-13, upon which the tractate
depends, we may make two important observations. As I originally
said, Tractate Terumot indeed is indebted to Scripture for its
facts. Yet we also see that the tractate investigates a range
of questions which, while pertinent to the concerns of Num.
18:8-13, is quite different from what we might expect on the
basis of the priestly code. The central concern of Num. 18:8-13
is the maintenance of the priesthood. The tractate, for its
part, ignores questions which should be central in that context.
It does not ask how priests are to assure that Israelites in fact
pay the offering. Nor does it detail how the offering is
collected from those Israelites who do set it aside, or deal with
the question of which priests should receive it. In shifting
from the focus of the priestly code and speaking at length about
the centrality of the Israelite in calling into being and protecting the holy offering, the framers of Tractate Terumot have made
fundamental choices. The reasons for these choices must now be
specified.

An explanation is possible when we turn to the historical
context in which the Mishnah came into being. The Mishnah was
completed in Palestine in the late second century. Its central
authorities span the time period from immediately after the
destruction (in C.E. 70) of the Temple in Jerusalem,[13] to
approximately two generations after the failed Bar Kokhba revolt
of C.E. 132-5. As a part of the Mishnah as a whole, Tractate
Terumot thus speaks to a time at which the Temple, the visible
sign of God's presence and dominion, was gone. The cult, through
which the people of Israel acknowledged God's Lordship and
appealed to his mercies, had long ceased. The Land of Israel
was now under the hand of foreigners. There was little hope for
its return to Israelite sovereignty. For these reasons,
Israelites living during this time had good reason to believe
that God's lordship over and concern for the people and Land of
Israel indeed had come to an end. By speaking in this context
of the requirement to pay the priestly due, Tractate Terumot
makes the powerful statement that things have not changed so
much as the concrete events of history seemed to indicate.[14]
With the Temple in ruins, the priests no longer can function in
cultic service to God. Just as when the Temple stood, however,
the priestly due is to be separated and given to the priests.
Things go on as if, on the stage of history, nothing has happened.

The people who stand behind Tractate Terumot thus affirm
that the priests retain their special privileges. Despite the
loss of their cultic function, the priests remain God's repre-
sentatives on earth. For this reason they still must receive
the share which God mandated for them. This statement, however,
masks a deeper claim which the tractate's framers make. Through
their acknowledgment of the status of the priests, they affirm
that God still is owner of the Land and Lord over the people of
Israel. For these reasons alone the priests retain their status
and consequent claim upon produce of the Land of Israel.

For the framers of Tractate Terumot, the priesthood thus
serves as a symbol evoking God's Lordship and dominion. By
recognizing the privileges of the priesthood, the people acknowledge God's continued presence over the Land and people of Israel.
At the same time, for those who stand behind the tractate, the
priestly station can be nothing more than a symbol. This is
because, with the Temple and cult destroyed, the priests no
longer play a concrete role in the sanctification of Israelite
life. In focusing upon a specific locus and means of

sanctification to be operative in their day, the authorities of the tractate must turn their attention away from the priests. Accordingly, they concentrate upon the hopes and desires of the Israelite people as a whole.

Let me explain what I mean. According to the priestly source upon which Tractate Terumot depends, the earthly representation of God's power is in the cult of the priests. This power is seen in their capacity to lay on hands and designate sacrificial beasts as holy, in their service in God's Temple, and in their consumption of those parts of God's Holy Things which are not burnt on the altar. For the framers of Tractate Terumot these things are no more. Now there is no altar or sacrifice. The priests no longer eat sacrificial meat. Only one offering remains as a concrete reality. This is heave-offering, which the priests indeed still may eat. Yet in this offering the tractate's framers recognize an even stronger expression of God's continued power on earth. This expression lies in the fact that common Israelites designate heave-offering to be holy. In doing so, they exercise God's powers here on earth.[15] This is so even with the Temple in ruins. To make the claims of God's continuing presence, the tractate therefore focuses upon the actions and responsibilities of the Israelite who sets aside and protects the priestly due. By describing these actions and responsibilities, it makes the powerful point that even with the Temple gone, cultic sanctification remains. This means that God himself still rules over the people and Land of Israel. He moves in response to the intentions and perceptions of Israelites who separate the offering which he mandated. This message is poignant. For as is clear, with the Temple destroyed and the Land defiled, these intentions and perceptions were all that remained to deny the events of history and affirm God's Lordship.

II. *The Structure of the Tractate*

The preceding analysis depended on the claim that a single unifying principle underlies all of the diverse laws of Tractate Terumot. This principle, I argued, is that the intentions and perceptions of the common Israelite are central in the process of sanctification and in the maintenance of the holy in the profane world. The principle has been illustrated through several examples, referring specifically to the way in which heave-offering is designated, and to particular problems in the

maintenance of the priestly gift in the Israelite's domain. Let
us now go forward to prove that the tractate as a whole was intended by its framers to convey and explain this idea. Only if
we can show that this is the case, may we claim correctly to have
understood what those framers wished to say through their work
on the subject of heave-offering. To this end I now offer an
outline of the topics of Tractate Terumot. By describing these
topics as they unfold in the tractate as a whole, the outline
will show that the tractate is a sustained and cogent essay.
From beginning to end its topics have been chosen and organized
logically to develop the single idea which I argue is fundamental.

The tractate is in three parts. Each describes one stage
in the continuum through which heave-offering is 1) designated
and separated, 2) guarded in the Israelite's domain, and 3) conveyed to the priest. In each of these units, the tractate is
concerned with the actions and responsibilities of the Israelite
householder. It opens, Unit I, with a discussion of how produce
comes to be deemed holy. The practical question is how heave-
offering is designated and separated by the Israelite householder. Unit II turns to those mishaps which might occur after
the heave-offering is separated, but before it is conveyed to the
priest. Since it remains in the Israelite's domain, it might be
mixed or cooked with common food, or even eaten by a non-priest.
As in Unit I, the tractate here focuses upon the importance of
the actions and intentions of the Israelite. It asks of the role
these actions and intentions play in determining the effect which
the heave-offering has upon common produce with which it is mixed
or cooked. It further questions the parts these intentions play
in determining the culpability of the householder who allowed the
heave-offering to be misused. The final issue, Unit III, is that
of the proper disposal of heave-offering. This material clearly
addresses the priest, for it indicates what he may and may not do
with heave-offering. Yet closer examination reveals that even
here the tractate concentrates chiefly upon the Israelite. At
issue in the greater part of Unit III is the Israelite's responsibility to convey to the priest the heave-offering which he has
separated. The unit rules that small quantities of produce which
the householder himself perceives to be insignificant need not be
given to the priest. They may be eaten by the Israelite. Unit
III thus completes the picture drawn by Units I and II. It does
so by indicating circumstances in which the Israelite's responsibility to keep heave-offering in holiness has ended. As in the

previous units, these circumstances are determined on the basis
of the Israelite's own perceptions.

In all, Tractate Terumot unfolds in a straightforward and
logical manner. It tells the story of heave-offering, beginning,
middle and end. At each point it focuses upon the importance of
the actions and intentions of the Israelite householder who must
separate the priestly gift. The following outline depicts in
detail the structure of the tractate as I just have summarized
it. The comments at the end of each unit explain both what
subjects have been covered, and why they have been redacted in
their present order.

I. *How heave-offering is designated and separated. 1:1-4:6.*
  A. *Improper ways of separating heave-offering. 1:1-3:4.*
    1. *Improper ways of separating heave-offering which yield*
        heave-offering that is not valid. 1:1-5.
      1:1   Five sorts of people may not separate heave-
             offering; if they do so, it is not valid heave-
             offering.
      1:2-3 Expansion of two entries of 1:1's list.
      1:4   They may not separate olives as heave-offering for
             wine, nor grapes for oil; if they do so:
             Shammaites, It is valid; Hillelites, Not valid.
      1:5   They may not separate heave-offering + list of
             ten categories of produce; if they do so, it is
             not valid.
    2. *Improper ways of separating heave-offering which never-*
        theless yield valid heave-offering. 1:6-2:3.
      1:6   Five sorts of people may not separate heave-
             offering; if they do so, it is valid heave-
             offering.
      1:7   They may not separate heave-offering by measure,
             weight or count (+ complementary rules).
      1:8-9 They may not separate oil as heave-offering for
             crushed olives, nor wine for crushed grapes; if he
             did so, it is valid heave-offering (+ rule for
             preserved-olives and raisins.)
      1:10   Principle governing 1:8-9.
      2:1   They may not separate heave-offering from clean
             produce for unclean produce; if they do so, it is
             valid heave-offering (Eliezer: they may do so in
             the first place).

2:2   They may not separate heave-offering from unclean
        produce for clean produce; if he did so unin-
        tentionally, it is valid (intentionally, he has
        done nothing).

2:3   Two more examples of principle of 2:2.

3. *Special problems: Heave-offering separated from one kind*
    of produce for produce of a different kind. 2:4-6.

2:4A-E They do not separate heave-offering from produce
        of one kind for produce of a different kind; if he
        did so, it is not valid.

2:4F-G The priest should be given a type of produce he
        will be able to eat; Judah: he should be given
        produce of the highest quality, even if it will
        spoil.

2:5   Application of positions of 2:4F-G to concrete
        cases.

2:6M-P Expansion of Judah's view (stated anonymously).

2:6Z-X General principle coordinating 2:4A-E with Judah.

4. *Special problems: Cases of doubt whether or not heave-*
    offering was validly separated. 3:1-4.

3:1-2   In cases of doubt the heave-offering is valid, but
        heave-offering must be separated a second time.

3:3   Partners who both separated heave-offering from the
        same commonly owned batch of produce: Aqiba,
        sages and Yose dispute.

3:4   Qualification of Aqiba, 3:2.

B. *The rite of the separation of heave-offering. 3:5-4:6.*

  1. *The oral designation. 3:5-9.*

3:5   Dispute over proper language for designation:
        Simeon, sages, Eleazar Hisma, Eliezer b. Jacob.

3:6-7   Proper sequence for designation of heave-offering,
        first fruits, first tithe, second tithe (+ biblical
        proof text).

3:8   One who intends to say "Heave-offering," but says
        "Tithe" has not designated the offering.

(3:9   Heave-offering separated by gentiles and Samaritans
        is valid (+ cognate rules).)

  2. *The percentage of a batch of produce which is to be*
      designated and separated as heave-offering. 4:1-5.

4:1   One who separates a portion of the heave-offering
        required for a batch of produce may not thereafter

take heave-offering from that batch for a different
batch; Meir: he may.

4:2   Similar case--Meir: he may eat an amount of
        produce commensurate with the quantity of tithes
        he has separated; sages: he may not.

4:3   Statement of required measure of heave-offering
        (Shammaites dispute, Judah glosses).

4:4   An agent separates the quantity of heave-offering
        normally separated by the householder.

4:5   Dispute over how much of a batch of produce may be
        designated heave-offering: Eliezer, Ishmael,
        Tarfon and Aqiba.

3. *When the rite of separating heave-offering takes place.*
    4:6.

4:6   At three times in the year they calculate the
        quantity of produce in the storage basket in order
        to separate heave-offering (+ three methods of
        calculation).

The problem of Unit I is how the heave-offering required of
the householder's produce is designated within that produce and
then separated from it so that it can be given to a priest. These
are the first human actions involved with heave-offering and
therefore constitute the logical starting point for the tractate.
The central point which the unit makes is that, on the basis of
thoughts and deeds, the Israelite householder determines both what
produce, and how much of it, is to be deemed heave-offering. The
discussion takes place in two main parts. We begin by establishing who may separate heave-offering and what produce may be used
for that offering (Part A). This material is redacted first
because it contains the facts which the houlseholder will need to
know when he undertakes the actual designation and separation of
the offering. This is the subject matter of Part B. Let us now
examine the internal organization of each of these parts of
Unit I.

The main proposition of Part A is stated at A1-2. This is
that there are circumstances in which produce separated as heave-
offering in an improper fashion or by unfit individuals nonethe-
less may be considered valid heave-offering. In light of this
fact there are two possible outcomes of an improper separation
of heave-offering. These are that the produce which is separated
may not take on the status of heave-offering, the topic of A1, or

that it may, A2. In substance, these two sub-units are well
balanced with each other. Each is introduced with a list of five
individuals who should not separate heave-offering, and moves on
to improper methods of doing so. Only 1:7 is out of place,
lacking a statement of whether or not heave-offering separated
in the way it describes is valid *post facto*. Topically it belongs in B2, on the quantity of heave-offering to be separated.
I assume that it is placed here because of its use of the
formulaic, "They may not separate heave-offering..." This is
characteristic of all of the materials at A1-2, and is not used
at Part B. With the basic facts established at A1-2, A3-4 turns
to special problems, concluding Part A with cases of doubt. Such
cases commonly close topical segments within this tractate.

The order of sub-units in Part B presents no problem. B1
details how one designates heave-offering. B2 treats a question
secondary to that of B1. This is how much one should designate.
B3, finally, states when during the year one does so. This
issue is of relatively minor importance to the redactor, as is
indicated by the fact that it takes up only a single pericope.
The larger progression of ideas in Part B thus is from major concerns to minor ones, a fine redactional technique.

Among individual pericopae in Part B, only the placement of
4:3 requires discussion. This is the rule specifying the quantity of heave-offering which normally is separated. At first
glance it appears that this rule would be better situated at the
beginning of B2. There it would introduce the essentially
secondary rules of 4:1-2 and 4:4-5 by providing the principle
which is basic to them. This is that a set quantity of produce
normally is taken as heave-offering. Closer consideration reveals the logic of the redactor's organization. He begins with
the case of an individual who separates too little heave-
offering (4:1-2), follows with a statement addressed to householders who separate the proper quantity (4:3-4) and concludes
with rules for those who wish to separate more than is usual
(4:5). The ordering of pericopae thus shows a clear internal
logic and evidences careful redaction.

II. *The proper handling of heave-offering which has been separated*
     but not yet given to the priest. 4:7-10:12.
  A. *Heave-offering which is mixed with unconsecrated produce:*
      Neutralization. 4:7-5:9.
    1. *How heave-offering is neutralized. 4:7-13.*

4:7   Heave-offering is neutralized in one hundred and
       one parts of unconsecrated produce, so Eliezer;
       Joshua: slightly more; Yose b. Meshullam glosses.

4:8-9 Joshua: Black figs neutralize white ones and
       vice versa (+ two more examples); Eliezer: they
       do not; Aqiba offers mediating position.

4:10-11 Expansion of 4:8-9; further concrete cases under
       dispute.

4:12   Two bins of unconsecrated produce into one of
       which heave-offering fell--the unconsecrated
       produce joins together to neutralize the heave-
       offering (Simeon glosses).

4:13   Legal precedent involving Aqiba and Yose; Yose
       invokes principle of 4:12.

2. *Rules regarding the batch in which heave-offering was*
    neutralized and the produce taken to replace the heave-
    offering. 5:1-9.

5:1   Triplet: A *se'ah* of unclean heave-offering which
       fell into less than a hundred of unconsecrated
       produce--let it all rot. If the heave-offering
       was clean--sell the mixture to a priest. If the
       unconsecrated produce was unclean, the priest eats
       the mixture in small bits.

5:2-4 Triplet: A *se'ah* of unclean heave-offering which
       fell into a hundred of clean unconsecrated pro-
       duce--let a *se'ah* be raised up and burned, so
       Eliezer; sages: let it be eaten in small bits. A
       se'ah of clean heave-offering which fell into a
       hundred of unclean unconsecrated produce--raise up
       the *se'ah* and eat it in small bits. A *se'ah* of
       unclean heave-offering which fell into a hundred
       of clean heave-offering--Houses dispute.

5:5   Heave-offering which was neutralized and raised
       up and fell into other unconsecrated produce--
       Eliezer: it imparts the status of heave-offering
       like true heave-offering; sages: it does not.

5:6   A *se'ah* of heave-offering which fell into less than
       a hundred of unconsecrated produce and some of the
       mixture fell into other unconsecrated produce--
       same dispute as at 5:5.

5:7   A *se'ah* of heave-offering which fell into a

hundred of unconsecrated produce and one lifted it
out and more heave-offering fell into the same unconsecrated produce--the unconsecrated produce
remains permitted.

5:8   A *se'ah* of heave-offering which fell into a hundred of unconsecrated produce and was not lifted
out before more heave-offering fell in--the batch
now has the status of heave-offering; Simeon: it
does not.

5:9   A mixture of heave-offering and unconsecrated food
that is ground and the quantity of which increases
or diminishes--the proportion of heave-offering
to unconsecrated produce remains the same.

B.   *Heave-offering which is eaten by a non-priest.   6:1-8:3.*

   1.   *Unintentional consumption: payment of the principal and
added fifth.   6:1-6.*

6:1   A non-priest who unintentionally eats heave-
offering pays the priest the value of the heave-
offering (principal) and an added fifth.

6:2   The daughter of an Israelite who unintentionally
ate heave-offering and afterwards married a
priest--to whom does she pay the principal and
added fifth?

6:3   One who unintentionally gives his workers or
guests heave-offering to eat--who pays the principal and added fifth?   (Meir and sages dispute).

6:4   Triplet: One who steals heave-offering and does
not eat it, etc., if he unintentionally ate it,
etc., if it was heave-offering dedicated to the
Temple, etc.

6:5   They do not pay the principal and added fifth
with + list of six categories of produce, so Meir;
sages dispute.

6:6   They pay the principal and added fifth for heave-
offering of one kind with produce of a different
kind, so Eliezer; Meir: only with the same kind
(+ scriptural proof for each view).

   2.   *Intentional consumption: payment of the principal but not
the added fifth.   7:1-4.*

7:1   A non-priest who intentionally eats heave-offering
pays the principal but does not pay the added fifth.

7:2   The daughter of a priest who married an Israelite
and afterwards ate heave-offering pays the principal but not the added fifth, so Meir; sages:
she pays both.

7:3   Triplet of cases in which individual pays the
principal but not the added fifth.

7:4   General rule summarizing rules for cases in which
non-priests pay both principal and added fifth and
those in which they pay only the principal.

3.   *Cases of doubt concerning non-priest's liability for
eating heave-offering. 7:5-8:3.*

7:5-7 Two bins, one filled with heave-offering and one
filled with unconsecrated produce--if heave-
offering falls into one of them, but it is not
known which, we hold that it fell into heave-
offering. Triplet: If a non-priest ate the
produce in one of the bins, etc.; if produce from
one of the bins fell into unconsecrated produce,
etc.; if produce from one of the bins was sown as
seed, etc.

8:1-3 The wife of a priest who was eating heave-offering
and was told, "Your husband has died"--Eliezer:
she is culpable; Joshua exempts (+ five formally
and substantively parallel disputes).

C. *The cultic contamination of heave-offering. 8:4-12.*

8:4   Wine in the status of heave-offering which if left
uncovered is poured out, for fear that a snake
deposited in it venom.

(8:5-7 Rules governing produce which might contain snake
venom; irrelevant to Tractate Terumot, redacted
here to complete 8:4's discussion.)

8:8   A jug of wine concerning which there arose a
suspicion of uncleanness--Eliezer: one must still
protect it in cleanness. Joshua: let him make it
certainly unclean.

8:9   A jug of wine in the status of heave-offering
which broke in the upper vat and the lower vat is
unclean: Joshua and Eliezer, same positions as at
8:8.

8:10   Expansion of 8:9.

8:11   Restatement of Joshua's position + expansion of
8:9-10.

8:12   Women to whom gentiles said, "Give us one of your number so that we may rape her, or we will rape all of you," let them all be raped (= position of Eliezer, 8:8-9).

D.   *Heave-offering which is planted as seed.*   *9:1-7.*

9:1   The householder may not plow up heave-offering which he intentionally planted; unintentionally, he may plow it up.

9:2   Expansion of 9:1: a field planted with heave-offering is subject to offerings left for the poor.

9:3   Expansion of 9:1: the crop is subject to tithes.

9:4   What grows from heave-offering has the status of heave-offering (+ laws for the crops of seed in the status of seven other agricultural offerings).

9:5   Case of doubt concerning whether or not a field is planted with heave-offering: we rule according to whether or not the seed disintegrates.

9:6-7A-J Crop grown from untithed produce is subject to principle of 9:5 (+ other rules for untithed produce, and list of types of seed which disintegrate).

9:7K-N Status of fruit produced by saplings grown from seed in the status of heave offering (Judah glosses).

E.   *Heave-offering which is cooked or otherwise prepared with unconsecrated produce.*   *10:1-12.*

10:1   That which is flavored by heave-offering takes on the status of heave-offering (Judah glosses).

10:2A-C Dough leavened with heave-offering takes on the status of heave-offering.

10:2D-F Water tainted by barley in the status of heave-offering does not take on the status of heave-offering.

10:3   Unconsecrated bread which absorbs vapors from heave-offering-wine--Meir: it has the status of heave-offering; Judah: it does not; Yose: mediating position.

10:4   Bread baked in an oven fired with heave-offering-cumin remains unconsecrated.

10:5-6 Rules regarding produce flavored with fenugreek in the status of heave-offering; other rules for fenugreek.

10:7   Unconsecrated olives which are pickled with olives
        in the status of heave-offering--if they are
        flavored, they are forbidden.
10:8   Expansion of M. 10:7 for case of clean and unclean
        fish.
10:9   Expansion of M. 10:7 for case of locusts.
10:10   Only that which is pickled with leeks in the
        status of heave-offering is forbidden (vs. M.
        10:7).
10:11   Yose: only that which is boiled with beets is
        forbidden; Simeon: rule for cabbage; Aqiba:
        only that which is flavored by forbidden meat is
        forbidden (vs. 10:1-7); Yohanan b. Nuri: rules
        for liver.
10:12A An egg spiced with forbidden spices is forbidden.
10:12B-D Liquid in which heave-offering is cooked is
        forbidden.

Unit II discusses the householder's responsibility to protect from loss heave-offering which he has separated but not yet
given to the priest. Since this heave-offering remains in the
Israelite's domain, it is in danger of being used as if it were
his own common produce. It might, for instance, be mixed or
cooked with common food, or eaten by the non-priest. Such cases
are of central interest to the tractate, for they offer a context
in which to explore what happens when a sanctified offering is
used as if it were common produce. This constitutes the major
anomaly possible within the topic of heave-offering, because it
is the point at which the barrier between the holy and profane is
broken. Its adjudication, accordingly, takes up the longest unit
of the tractate. The unit endeavors to establish the effect
which holy produce has upon common produce with which it is
mixed. Does the mixture become holy because of the presence of
heave-offering in it? It further outlines the householder's own
culpability and concomitant responsibility to replace heave-
offering which, through his fault, is lost. The discussion takes
place in five parts. Each details rules for a particular hazard
which might befall heave-offering in an Israelite's domain.
These parts have been ordered so as to form logical transitions
with the materials of Unit I which precedes, and Unit III which
follows. The unit opens with the first problem the householder
might encounter after he designates and separates heave-offering.

It progresses through other problems and ends, finally, with
cases which introduce the specific concerns of Unit III.

Part A presents the first problem which might arise after
the heave-offering has been designated and separated. The householder has just separated the offering, and it falls back into
the batch from which it was taken, or into other produce on the
threshing floor. At issue is the status of the resultant mixture
of heave-offering and common produce. Is it to be deemed heave-
offering or secular food? As we might expect, this is determined
not only by the quantity of heave-offering in the mixture, but
also by the householder's ability to distinguish the heave-
offering from the common produce.

IIB-D present three other mishaps which might occur while
the priestly gift is in the Israelite's domain. The heave-
offering might be eaten by the non-priest (B), its cultic cleanness might be endangered (C), or it might be planted as seed (D).
These cases belong together because, in each, the householder's
culpability is determined by whether or not he intentionally
allows the heave-offering to be misused. I find, however, no
larger reason for the sequence of their presentation. This is not
the case as regards Part E, which concludes Unit II. Its topic
is cases in which heave-offering is cooked or otherwise prepared
with unconsecrated produce. It has been redacted at the end of
the unit in order to form a transition to Unit III which follows.
The topic of that unit is the priest's own preparation of heave-
offering.

The internal structure of Unit II's constituent parts is
straightforward. Part A begins with simple rules governing mixtures of heave-offering and common produce (A1). A2 moves to
derivative problems. Through these a theory of neutralization
is delineated. Part B likewise unfolds logically. It is
organized according to the restitution non-priests are required
to pay for eating heave-offering unintentionally (B1), intentionally (B2) and in cases of doubt (B3).

At IIC, the placement of 8:4-7 must be explained. These
pericopae fall outside of the specific topic of the unit to which
they belong. The unit is on the householder's responsibility to
protect heave-offering in cultic cleanness. 8:4-7, however,
gives rules for produce which may contain snake venom. Their
point is at 8:4, which states that heave-offering suspected of
containing snake venom is destroyed. It need not be given to a
priest. This rule has its present redactional setting in order

to signal the larger problem of 8:4-12. This is whether or not
the householder need preserve for the priest heave-offering which
is unclean. Such heave-offering is like that which contains
snake venom in that the priest may not eat it. In light of this
commonality of situations addressed, the two units clearly belong
together. Despite initial appearances, Part C thus evidences
careful organization and a clear redactional structure.

Part D discusses grain in the status of heave-offering which
a non-priest plants as seed. It addresses problems created by
such a situation in the same order as they will be encountered
by the Israelite householder. The first practical problem is
what the Israelite may and may not do with the field in which the
heave-offering is growing (9:1-3). As I noted above, this depends on whether or not he intentionally planted the field. 9:4
proceeds to the next logical question, the status of a crop grown
and harvested from such a field. At issue is whether or not this
crop is deemed to be heave-offering, like the seed from which it
grew. 9:5-6, finally, turn to cases of doubt and other special
problems, the usual concluding topics of discussion. While simple
in structure, Part E shows equal redactional care. It begins
with the principle which is central to the sub-unit as a whole
(10:1) and then presents cases which illustrate that principle
(10:2-12).

III. *The preparation and use of heave-offering by the priest.*
      11:1-10.

   A. *The proper preparation of produce in the status of heave-*
       offering. 11:1-3.

       11:1   Produce in the status of heave-offering must be
               prepared in the way that unconsecrated produce of
               its type normally is prepared.

       11:2   Expansion of 11:1: culpability of non-priest who
               eats heave-offering which was improperly prepared.

       11:3   Expansion of theory of 11:1 (+ four rules on
               liquids made from agricultural offerings).

   B. *Refuse from produce in the status of heave-offering.*
       11:4-8.

       11:4-5 Refuse which has food value or which the priest
               wishes to eat retains the status of heave-offering.

       11:6   A storage bin from which one emptied heave-offering
               --he need not sit and pick up every last kernel of
               grain.

11:7   Expansion of 11:6 for case of a jug of oil in the
        status of heave-offering.

11:8   Expansion of 11:7.

C. *Heave-offering which is not fit as human food, but has some
    other use. 11:9-10.*

11:9   Vetches in the status of heave-offering are used
        to feed the priest's cattle.

11:10   Unclean oil in the status of heave-offering may be
        kindled in the priest's lamp.

The tractate concludes with rules for the final disposition
of heave-offering. These rules make the point that the offering
should be used to the end for which it was designated. That is,
it must be eaten by a priest. This is the case as long as the
priestly due is considered food. If it is not, it no longer is
deemed to have a consecrated status. Then it may also be used
by non-priests, just like common produce. In light of these
facts, the unit asks when produce is or is not deemed to be food.
It is tightly organized logically to expound this problem. It
first discusses the normal preparation of food in the status of
heave-offering (IIIA). The next topic is refuse from such food
(IIIB). The final issue is the status of what is not deemed food,
but which has some other customary use (IIIC). The unit as a
whole thus shows careful organization. It plays out a single line
of inquiry from beginning to end.

Part A rules that heave-offering should be prepared in a way
in which as little as possible will be wasted. The priest thus
will eat almost all that was designated for his use. Parts B and
C turn to special problems. Part B, first, considers refuse left
from the normal preparation of heave-offering. It rules that
whether or not the refuse must be treated as food depends on the
attitude of the priest (11:5), or, importantly, the perceptions
of the Israelite householder himself (11:6-8). Just as the
Israelite consecrates heave-offering in the first place, so he
determines the point at which it no longer has a sanctified
status.

The produce at Part C cannot be used as food, but has some
other use. In order to allow the priest to use all that was
designated for him, the heave-offering may be put to its other
use. In such a case, further, it is of no concern that an
Israelite also benefits. This could occur, for example, if a
non-priest enjoys the light of a lamp kindled with heave-offering.

As at Part B, the unit thus describes situations in which heave-
offering becomes available for the use of Israelites. This is an
excellent conclusion to the tractate. It completes the circle of
events which began in Unit I, when the householder first designated and set aside produce for the use of the priest.

The topics of the tractate reveal the point which its
framers wish to make through their discussion of heave-offering.
These topics are, first, the role of the Israelite in the designation and separation of heave-offering; second, his responsibility to protect the priestly due for the priest; and, third,
the part he plays in the ultimate disposition of the offering.
The tractate as a whole thus speaks about common Israelites. It
proposes to delineate their responsibility as regards all aspects
of the designation and disposition of the priestly gift. Its
particular rules, moreover, make clear the centrality of the
Israelite's own intentions and perceptions. At each point these
determine the status of sanctification of produce which the
Israelite sets aside as the priest's share. Through the Israelite's powers of intention, produce first comes to be deemed holy.
Later, the holiness of the priest's gift may be encroached upon
only through actions which the Israelite performs purposely.
Finally, the offering no longer is considered holy when the
Israelite himself does not deem it to be edible. Through these
claims, the tractate argues that, even with the Temple in ruins,
the people of Israel continue to maintain the channels of holiness between heaven and earth. When the Temple stood, these
channels had been maintained both by the people, who paid agricultural dues, and through the work of the priests at the altar.
Now they are manifest only in the actions of the people of Israel.
They are seen in the people's labor on God's land, and in their
preparation of food for consumption in accordance with God's
principles of sanctity. The larger message is that things hardly
have changed from the time that the Temple stood. Holiness has
not disappeared from the earth. This is because God still is
owner of the Land and Lord over the people of Israel.

III. *The Task of Translation and Exegesis*

Conclusions about the larger meaning of Tractate Terumot
depend upon the interpretation of its individual laws. This work
occupies the translation and exegesis which follow. In order to
explain the specific goals and methods of this commentary, I must

now outline the central literary characteristics which have
shaped my approach to the tractate.

Tractate Terumot, with Mishnah as a whole, phrases all of its
laws in a small number of highly formalized and stylized linguistic patterns. These literary conventions occur both in anonymous
rules, and in the mouths of the tractate's named authorities,
early and late. This means that while the tractate cites
masters who lived over a period of almost two hundred years, the
form in which those citations appear is the work of a single
group of people, working at a single time. These are the final
framers of the tractate who, standing at the end of the law's
development, cast antecedent material into the form in which we
now have it.[16] By doing this they obscured the signs of literary
and legal development which would have occurred during the period
of the tractate's named authorities. While individual laws are
attributed to several generations of masters, Tractate Terumot as
we have it is a unitary creation of a single time and group of
people.

Two conclusions follow from these facts. The first is that
the meaning which we must discern in the laws of Tractate Terumot
is that imputed to them by their formulators and redactors.[17]
These individuals provided both the form and context in which
those rules make sense. The second conclusion, logically, is
that the very form and context of individual laws constitutes the
fundamental key to the meaning their formulators intended them to
convey. The redactors of the tractate used their talents to
create a cogent and pointed essay. They accomplished this by
employing literary conventions in a self-conscious and purposeful
manner.[18] The translation and commentary which follow are
designed to prove this fact. Each of these components of the
exegesis works toward uncovering the meaning of the tractate's
laws on the basis of the patterned language through which those
laws are expressed.

The goal of the translation, first, is to make available to
the English reader the formulaic character of the Hebrew text.
For this reason I do not aim at simplicity of English style, but
at close adherence to the linguistic structure of the Hebrew. In
cases in which the Hebrew is overly abstruse or otherwise difficult, I interpolate clarifying language or explanatory phrases.
These are placed in brackets to distinguish them from the content
of the Hebrew. Idiomatic Hebrew terms or phrases which elude
literal translation are transliterated in parentheses. This

provides access to the original text in cases in which compre-
hensibility of English precludes the accurate rendering of that
text. In cases of textual problems, parentheses also are used to
indicate the reading I have chosen, as well as other extant MS.
variants.[19] Throughout, then, the purpose of the translation is
to give the reader a clear picture of the substance and form of
the Hebrew text.[20] On the basis of both of these sense is to be
made of the laws of the tractate.

The translation plays a further role in allowing for interpretation of the tractate's laws. In it each pericope is divided
into its primary parts.[21] I identify these as the smallest
syntactic units of the pericope. Since these comprise the building blocks of each pericope, delineating them allows us to discern the formal traits of that pericope.[22] These traits are
indicated by the repetition of a single syntactic pattern in
several building blocks, or in the occurrence of an otherwise
stereotyped sequence of such blocks. Once these formal characteristics of the pericope are established, elements which are
secondary also can be identified. These are syntactic units
which break the formal pattern established in the pericope as a
whole. Only when seen as separate may these secondary elements
be properly interpreted. They may be discrete rules, with their
own particular point, or glosses intended in some way to impose
meaning upon the rest of the pericope.

We see that it is the task of the translation to highlight
those literary features which are central in the work of interpretation. Let me now indicate exactly how these traits guide
my exegesis. This will be illustrated for the forms most commonly found in Tractate Terumot, the dispute and the list.[23] Then
we may turn to the importance of formulaic language.

Disputes most usually are formed of a statement of case
(superscription) followed by two or more opposing legal positions.
By using this form, the redactor provides several types of information. The most obvious is that suggested by the superscription
itself. We must establish why the problem stated in the superscription should be an issue for the redactor. Second is the
assumption shared by the several parties in the dispute. This
common assumption most likely is that of the framer of the dispute himself. Finally we come to what perhaps is the most
interesting information as regards the redactor's own notions and
concerns. This is revealed by the two or more positions given to
resolve the problem stated in the superscription. This range of

choices, like the problem itself, is a key to the conceptions of
the redactor. For, we must assume that the solutions he offers
us are conceivable within, and therefore illustrate, the limits
of his own thinking.

The second form commonly found in the tractate is the list.
This consists of a series of entries brought together under a
single superscription. The superscription claims that all of the
items are subject to a single principle. The interpretative
task, accordingly, is to discern that principle. Yet the
exegete must also pay careful attention to the syntactic structure of individual entries in the list. A break in the formal
structure of these items indicates that the list juxtaposes
materials which do not necessarily belong together. They might,
for instance, illustrate diverse principles.[24] Ability to understand the point made by a list thus depends upon careful attention both to the use of this form in general, and to the
formulaic character of each list's individual entries.

Not all of Mishnaic discourse is cast in such forms as the
dispute and the list. Other large blocks of material simply make
use of a common and repeated syntactic pattern. In other words
several laws are stated within the bounds of a single linguistic
structure.[25] Like the dispute and list, the use of such a
formulary pattern offers a key to the larger point the redactor
hopes to make. By formulating a series of laws in a single
syntactic pattern, for instance, he indicates that those laws
must be viewed as a group, illustrating the same underlying principle. As with the list, the exegete must discern this principle.
A similar exegetical problem is presented by the case in which
there is a break in the formal patterning of individual rules.
A series of syntactically parallel protases may, for instance,
yield contrasting apodoses. Interpretation emerges from the
contrast between the several rules. Only by noticing the parallel
construction does the interpreter see that the point is not made
by each rule alone. The rules together, rather, provide the
parameters of a single larger principle of law.

An understanding of the meaning of individual pericopae is
only the first step in interpretation. As we have seen in the
outline of the tractate, pericopae do not stand in isolation, but
have a larger context provided by the thematic units of which
they are a part. A second step in interpretation, therefore, is
to view these thematic units as cogent wholes. We must identify
the issue they address, and point out the role of individual

pericopae in delineating, and, possibly, resolving, that issue.
Only when this is done do we fully understand the meaning which
the individual pericope has within the tractate. At this point
we likewise begin to discern the larger issue, or set of issues,
which the framers of the tractate address through discussion of
their topic.

Descriptions of thematic units are found in my introductions
to the chapters of the tractate. These chapters represent
divisions made by copyists and printers and therefore do not
invariably correspond to thematic units. Yet they offer con-
venient stopping points at which to draw an overview of the
material about to be discussed. I therefore use introductions
to the chapters of the tractate as a context in which to describe
the issue and content of the thematic unit(s) contained in the
chapter. If the chapter divides or encompasses more than one
thematic unit, I indicate this and describe the relationship
between the materials of the chapter under discussion and the one
preceding or following it. By placing these introductions before
the translation and commentary to the discrete pericopae of each
unit I give the reader the information necessary to discern the
full range of meaning contained in those pericopae. This, as I
said, is possible only when the pericopae are viewed in their
larger context.

Analysis of the thematic units of the tractate provides the
basis for the final step in interpretation. This is the work of
viewing the tractate as a cogent whole. My goal is to discern the
central issue which generated the tractate's discussion and
which, therefore, accounts for and ties together its several
themes. By doing this, we gain a clear perspective on exactly
what the framers of Tractate Terumot wished to say through their
discussion of the topic of heave-offering. This goal is reached
through an outline of the tractate as a whole. The outline
intends to uncover the single theme which encompasses all of the
questions addressed in the tractate's several thematic units.
When we have identified this theme, and the theory expressed
through it, we know the chief concern which motivated the framers
of the tractate in their work on the topic of heave-offering.
This concern, in turn, may be examined against the historical
context in which those redactors worked. At issue is how the
specific claims of the tractate relate to the human situation of
those who created it. Discerning that relationship allows us to
see clearly the message which the tractate's framers had for

their own day and audience. These issues already have been discussed in the first sections of this introduction. This intro-
ductory overview treats the tractate as a whole, and therefore
allows the reader to follow with understanding the exegetical
work which takes up the rest of the volume.

We see that the method of this commentary is to interpret
the tractate as an essay which, through it own stylistic conventions and within the boundaries of its own chapters, provides
important insight into the thought-world of its framers. In
selecting this approach, I believe that I have corrected the
principal shortcoming of previous interpretations of the tractate.
These commentaries, almost exclusively products of the rabbinic
tradition of exegesis,[26] consistently fail to read the tractate
as the product of a specific time and social context. They read
it, rather, as homogeneous with the entire corpus of rabbinic
documents, early and late.[27] All rules within this corpus are
read without regard to their origin and provenance, under the
assumption that together they comprise a single, transcendent,
Jewish law. The rules of individual documents are interpreted
within the framework of this artificial legal construct, and not
as components of the essays in which they have their redactional,
and therefore historical, meaning. In practical terms, this means
that the established rabbinic exegesis of the tractate is
atomistic, proceeding one rule at a time. Its goal is to discern
encompassing legal principles which link the tractate's discrete
rules with laws found elsewhere in Mishnah and in the rest of the
rabbinic literature.

The approach I have just described is antithetical to my own.
The rabbinic interest in the diverse laws of Tractate Terumot
ignores the intellectual framework within which those laws have
their historical meaning. While my use of rabbinic exegetes
accordingly is selective, the reader will find that their insights
appear often in this work. The reason is that for them, as for
me, exegesis of Mishnah consists of identifying and solving acute
problems of logic. Each statement of law has a number of interpretations possible within the bounds of its conceptual content.
This is the function of the nature of Mishnah itself.[28] Through
its language and substance Mishnah detaches its rules from any
concrete place or time. It therefore claims on the surface to
have no historical meaning, but rather to set out a diverse set
of interpretive potentials. These must be delineated in accordance with the exegete's own sense of logic and reason. It

therefore often happens that rabbinic exegetes already have
delineated the full range of interpretations plausible for a given
rule. I may claim to advance their work only in that I use the
formal and thematic traits of the tractate itself as guides in
selecting the meaning most probably intended by the framers of
the tractate. In this way I discern the original meaning of the
rule, and not the sense which it had in the later history of
Judaism.

One commentary to the tractate, Tosefta Terumot, deserves
special attention. Of the several tools which we have for the
interpretation of Mishnah, Tosefta is certainly the most important. It is the only commentary which takes seriously the
tractate's own formal characteristics and conceptual framework.
Indeed, it is phrased within the same linguistic patterns found
in Mishnah. Tosefta Terumot moreover cites the same authorities
found in Mishnah Terumot. For these reasons it constitutes an
especially important source for possible meanings of Mishnah's
laws. I therefore translate and comment on the whole of Tosefta
Terumot. My purpose is to discover the point which Tosefta
wishes to make about Mishnah's law and, of course, to use that
point to deepen our own insight into the law.

The methods which I use in translating and commenting on
Tosefta are the same as those applied to Mishnah. What differs
is that, in light of the specific importance of Tosefta, comments
on it are brief and have a narrow purpose. This is to state the
relationship between Tosefta and the relevant pericope of Mishnah,
and to describe the point which Tosefta makes about that pericope.
Where Tosefta supplements Mishnah, I indicate how the supplement
clarifies Mishnah's law. When Tosefta contradicts a rule of
Mishnah, I state the grounds for the disagreement. These
frequently arise from some unclarity in Mishnah's own reasoning
or in the relationships among several of Mishnah's rules. In
either case, understanding Tosefta advances our comprehension of
Mishnah's laws, and therefore constitutes an important element in
interpretation of the tractate.

IV. *Texts and Versions*

The translation of Mishnah Terumot is based on the text
found in standard editions of the Mishnah. In preparing the
translation I have referred also to the text published by
H. Albeck and pointed by H. Yalon, and to all MS. variants cited
in Sacks-Hutner. I indicate in parentheses all places in which I

diverge from the reading of the standard edition. The reasons
for my choices of reading are found in the body of the commentary
or in the footnotes, as appropriate to the particular case. The
English translations of Blackman, Lehrman and Danby have been of
benefit to me. Points at which my translation depends on their
work are indicated in brackets in the translation.

     For Tosefta Terumot I translate MS. Vienna, as reproduced
in Lieberman, TZ. Full consideration is given to variants found
in MS. Erfurt, and to the textual emendations suggested by
Lieberman in the notes to TZ and in TK.

TERUMOT CHAPTER ONE

M.'s first chapter presents rulings on two distinct issues:
1) individuals who are not fit to separate heave-offering
(M. 1:1-3, 6), and 2) ways in which heave-offering may not be
separated (M. 1:4, 5E-L, 7, 8-9, 10).[1] These two legal themes
articulate a single proposition, which will occupy the first two
chapters of M. This proposition is that there are circumstances
in which produce separated in an improper fashion, or by one who
is unfit, is nevertheless considered valid heave-offering. Given
this proposition, there are two possible outcomes to any improper
separation of heave-offering. On the one hand, even though a
separation of heave-offering is made improperly, or by one who is
unfit, it may be considered valid. In this case, the produce
which was separated as heave-offering will have the status of a
consecrated priestly gift. Alternatively, such an improper
separation of heave-offering may not be considered valid, even
post facto. In such a case, the fruit which was separated as
heave-offering retains the status of unconsecrated, untithed
produce, as does the produce from which it was separated. It is
in light of these two possibilities that the redactor has organized the discrete pericopae within the chapter. At M. 1:1-5 we
have examples in which a separation of heave-offering is not considered valid even *post facto*.[2] In contrast, M. 1:6-10[3] present
cases in which produce separated improperly is considered valid
heave-offering *post facto*.[4]

T. to this chapter is exceptionally long, offering material
supplementary to each of M.'s pericopae, and contributing several
essays of its own. These are on points only tangentially related
to M.'s issues. While M. contains few attributed lemmae (Judah
and Yose at M. 1:2, the Houses at M. 1:4), T.'s several attributions offer valuable attestations to specific pericopae in M.
and, moreover, to the chapter's larger legal concnerns. These
attestations indicate moreover that not all of the tractate's
attributions may be trusted. While the Houses are said to dispute
several problems related to improper manners of separating heave-
offering (M. 1:4, T. 3:14, 16), it appears that this issue, as
well as that of individuals who are not fit to separate heave-
offering, was still a topic of debate at Usha. It therefore is
unlikely to be authentic in the mouths of the Houses.

Specifically, Judah, T. 1:1A-B, and Simeon b. Gamaliel, T. 1:1G-I, relate to the issue of M. 1:1C1. Judah, T. 1:14A (as well as at M. 1:2), attests M. 1:1E-F. Simeon b. Gamaliel and Isaac, T. 1:15, attest M. 1:1E-F. M. 1:5G-H is attested to Usha by Eliezer b. Jacob, T. 2:8X. Judah, Yose and Simeon b. Eleazar, T. 3:4, attest M. 1:7. Simeon b. Gamaliel and Rabbi, T. 3:15, dispute an issue secondary to M. 1:19.

1:1-3

A. Five [sorts of people] may not separate heave-offering,

B. and if they separated heave-offering, that which they have separated is not [valid] heave-offering:

C. (1) a *heresh* (*hrš*), (2) an imbecile, (3) a minor,[5]

D. and (4) one who separates heave-offering from [produce] which is not his own.

E. (5) A gentile (*nkry*)[6] who separated heave-offering from [the pruduce of] an Israelite,

F. even with permission--

G. that which he has separated is not [valid] heave-offering.[7]

M. 1:1 (b. Shab. 153b, b. Yeb.
113a; D: b. Git. 52a)

H. A *heresh*

I. who speaks but does not hear

J. may not separate heave-offering,

K. but if he separated heave-offering, that which he has separated is [valid] heave-offering.

L. The *heresh* of which the sages spoke under all circumstances is one who neither hears nor speaks.

M. 1:2 (H-I: b. Ber. 15a; H+J:
y. Hag. 1:1, y. Yeb. 12:4; J:
b. Hag. 2b, b. Nid. 13b)

M. A minor who has not produced two [pubic] hairs--

N. R. Judah says, "That which he separates is [valid] heave-offering."[8]

O. R. Yose says, "If [he separated heave-offering] before he reached the age of vows (*ᶜwnt ndrym*), that which he has separated is not [valid] heave-offering.

P. "But [if he separated heave-offering] after he reached the age of vows, that which he has separated is [valid] heave-offering."

M. 1:3 (b. Nid. 46b; M-N: y. Yeb.

12:2)

The main point of the pericope is made by the repetition at
B of the claim stated at A. A notes that certain individuals may
not separate heave-offering. From this, B, which states that if
they do so anyway, their heave-offering is not valid, should be
obvious. This apparent redundancy introduces a distinction
central throughout the first two chapters of the tractate. M.
claims that the validity of heave-offering *post facto* (B) is not
in all cases controlled by the validity of the separation of
heave-offering *de jure* (A). The fact that certain individuals
should not separate heave-offering does not necessarily affect
the validity of heave-offering they have nevertheless separated.
As we shall see, M. 1:6, for instance, lists cases in which
heave-offering separated by unfit individuals is valid. A-B thus
constitute an acute, and important, introduction to the present
thematic unit.

The next problem is to explain the list's five entries. We
note, first, that the form of the items at C is distinct from that
of the entries at D and E-G. Whereas the items at C are substantives without modifiers, D and E are each composed of a noun and
relative clause. This means that C and D-G probably elicit
distinct principles of law. They must therefore be treated
separately from each other.

The *ḥeresh*, imbecile and minor, C, are distinguished from
other individuals in that they are not believed to understand the
implications of their actions (MR).[9] The injunction against their
separating heave-offering therefore indicates that this separation
is to be distinguished from the many other occasions on which an
individual takes a portion of produce for his own or someone
else's use. More is required than the simple setting aside of an
amount of food. The reason is that, in separating produce to be
heave-offering, the individual designates that produce to be holy.
He accomplishes this only if he is conscious of being engaged in
a sacred activity. The deaf mute, imbecile and minor, unable to
understand the implications of their actions, can not success-
fully do this.[10]

I already have noted that the form of the items at D and E-G
differs from that of the entries at C. It further is clear that
D and E-G belong together since G, which specifically glosses F,

also implies an important qualification of D. Yet D likewise
must be read with A-C, upon which it depends for sense. D thus
is a transitional step, a bridge between C and E-G. The importance in establishing this formal disjuncture is apparent when
we turn to interpret D and E-G. We immediately see that, unlike
C, these rules do not respond to the superscription at A. These
are not examples of individuals who may not separate heave-offering (TYY). (M. 3:9 explicitly states that a gentile may separate
heave-offering.) It is only in the present circumstance--when
they separate heave-offering from produce which is not their own--
that the heave-offering they separate is not valid. D-G thus
makes a point different from that of C. This point is that, as
M. Kil. 7:4-5 states, a person does not have the power to
sanctify property belonging to another. For this reason, an
individual may not separate heave-offering from produce which
does not belong to him (D, E). F introduces an important
qualification of this rule. Heave-offering separated from
produce which is not one's own will in fact be valid if the
owner of the produce previously has given permission. By making
another his agent the owner of the produce gives that person the
power to designate heave-offering on his behalf.[11] E-G's point,
then, is that a gentile may not act as the agent of an Israelite
(Bert, MR).[12] While we thus see that D-G makes a point quite
different from C, we also can discern the reason it is juxtaposed to C. This is because, with C, it illustrates the central
claim that produce separated as heave-offering must achieve a
status of sanctity.

   M. 1:2H-K continues M. 1:1's discussion of individuals who
may not separate heave-offering. It describes an individual, the
heresh who speaks but does not hear, whose heave-offering is
valid *post facto*.[13] By referring to a specific type of *heresh*,
H-K implies a distinction between that individual and other
hereshim. L underscores this distinction. It informs us that
the term *heresh* without further qualification, as at M. 1:1C,
always refers to a deaf-mute.

   My explanation so far depends on the assumption that H-K is
a unitary construction. This may not be the case. The question
which must be addressed is whether I in fact is integral to H-K
or, alternatively, whether it is an interpolation. If the former
is the case, there is no contradiction between the law of the
heresh at M. 1:1 and that of M. 1:2. The pericopae, rather,
refer to different individuals. If the latter is the case, both

pericopae originally referred to the same *heresh*, but disagreed
concerning the validity of heave-offering he separates. The
interpolation of I at the time the pericopae were juxtaposed will
have harmonized this contradiction. The fact that the items at
M. 1:1C are substantives without modifiers, while H-I consists of
a substantive + relative clause, constitutes formal grounds for
considering I an interpolation. This alone, however, is not
conclusive evidence that I is interpolated. The individuals at
M. 1:1D-E also are described by substantives + relative clauses.
We have no reason to believe that the modifiers in those cases
are glosses. Formal evidence therefore is not conclusive evidence of the character of I.

    Assuming, then, that I is not interpolated, the claim that
the pericopae were not originally contradictory still depends on
the assumption that, as L states, the term *heresh* without qualification indicates a deaf-mute. There is unfortunately little
evidence in M. or T. that may be used to ascertain the exact
sense of the term *heresh*. In all of M. and T., M. 1:2L stands
alone in alleging that a *heresh* is a deaf-mute. T. 1:2 on the
other hand defines a *heresh* as an individual who speaks but does
not hear. Since these statements are contradictory, they provide
no evidence as to the usual meaning of this term. The only other
evidence for the sense of the term *heresh* is at M. Meg. 2:4.[14]
The issue there is the fitness of the *heresh* to read in public
the scroll of Esther. That pericope therefore must refer to an
individual who can speak. Yet this single usage is not strong
evidence that the term *heresh* mentioned without qualification in
other contexts is not a deaf-mute. Like the formal evidence
referred to above, the contextual evidence for the meaning of the
term *heresh* is inconclusive.[15]

    In all, then, the evidence adduced does not offer a basis
for positing a state in redaction at which M. 1:1C and M. 1:2H+J-K
--contradictory statements of law--were harmonized by the interpolation of M. 1:2I. Whereas the distinction between the *heresh*
who is a deaf-mute and the one who is deaf is not made explicit
elsewhere in M. or T., there are no formal or contextual grounds
on which to conclude that it is artificial here. Let us now turn
to the substance of M. 1:2's rule.

    Heave-offering separated by M. 1:2's deaf person is valid.
It thus appears that that individual is deemed to have the powers
of intention required in the designation of produce to be holy.
Why, then, may he not separate heave-offering *de jure*?

B. Ber. 15a[16] states that the reason is his inability to hear the
blessing one must recite upon separating heave-offering. B.'s
reasoning, which establishes proper recitation of a blessing as
the *sine qua non* for separating heave-offering *de jure*, follows
the viewpoint of T. 3:1-2, which states that inability to recite
a blessing is the reason that a person who has had a nocturnal
emission, a mute, and a naked person, all mentioned in M. 1:6,
may not separate heave-offering *de jure*.[17] The deaf person's
blessing is disqualified since he cannot hear it; a person who
has had a nocturnal emission and a naked person are not allowed
to recite a blessing (M. Ber. 3:4, T. Ber. 2:14); the mute
obviously is incapable of reciting a blessing. In holding that
these individuals may not separate heave-offering *de jure*, M.
distinguishes between actions correlary to the separation of
heave-offering, and the more important requirement of proper
consciousness of the sacred character of the act. Individuals,
like the deaf person, who cannot perform the proper actions,
should not separate heave-offering. Yet if they do so anyway,
since they do so with proper understanding and commensurate
intention, that which they separate is valid heave-offering.

Like M. 1:1C3, M. 1:3 deals with the status of heave-offering
separated by a minor. The pericope does not, however, refer to
M. 1:1, or depend on it for its sense. This is important since,
as we shall see, Judah, M. 1:3N, cannot agree to the law of
M. 1:1C3.[18] M provides a topic sentence for both Judah's and
Yose's opinion. Its own interpretation, however, is problematic.
The growth of two pubic hairs is itself a sign of majority
(M. Nid. 6:11). The clause "who has not produced two pubic
hairs" therefore does not qualify the term "minor" in any way.
By definition a minor is someone who has not produced two pubic
hairs. This is a difficulty which the extant sources do not
allow us to solve.[19] Judah, N, states that even *de jure* a minor
may separate heave-offering. He would clearly disagree with the
rule of M. 1:1C2, which holds that heave-offering separated by a
minor is in no event valid.[20] Yose distinguishes between two
different types of minors, one who has reached the age of vows,
and one who has not. The age of vows is one year before the age
of majority.[21] At this age, the minor is considered capable of
understanding the nature of the rite of separating heave-offering
(MR). Once he has this understanding, even though he is a full
year from majority, the minor may validly separate heave-offering.

Yose's larger perspective on the requirements of the separation
of heave-offering thus is fully in line with that of M. 1:1C and
M. 1:2.

A.   R. Judah says, "A deaf-mute who separated heave-
offering--

that which he has separated is [valid] heave-offering."

B.   Said R. Judah, "$M^c\check{s}h$ b- The sons of R. Yohanan b.
Gudgada were deaf-mutes, and in Jerusalem all of the foods
requiring preparation in purity were prepared under their
supervision ($n^c\check{s}yn$ ^cl gbn)."

C.   They said to him, "Is that evidence [that a deaf-
mute may separate heave-offering]?

"For foods requiring preparation in purity do not require intention ($mh\check{s}bh$) and [therefore] may be prepared
under the supervision of a deaf-mute, imbecile or minor.
[But] heave-offering and tithes require intention [and
therefore may not be separated by such individuals]."

D.   R. Isaac says in the name of R. Eleazar, "The
heave-offering of a deaf-mute does not enter the status of
unconsecrated food (l' ts' $lhwlyn$) [even though it is not
valid heave-offering] because [there is] a doubt whether or
not he has understanding (d^ct)."

E.   What do they do for him?

[Since his understanding is in doubt, he may not
separate his own heave-offering. Yet since he may have
understanding, executors may not separate heave-offering for
him (Lieberman).]

F.   The court appoints him executors and he separates
heave-offering and they validate it ($mqyymyn$ $'wtw$)[22] at his
side.

[If the deaf-mute has understanding, the sanctity of
the heave-offering depends on him alone. If not, the action
of the executors is sufficient to make the heave-offering
valid.]

G.   Rabban Simeon b. Gamaliel says, "Who is the deaf-
mute [whose heave-offering is not valid, as at M. 1:1]?

H.   "Anyone who was a deaf-mute from birth ($mthyltw$).

I.   "But if he was of sound mind and became a deaf-mute
(pqh $wnthr\check{s}$),[23] he may write [indicating his intention to
separate heave-offering], and they validate [the document]
for him ($mqyymyn$ ^cl $ydyw$)[24] [but the sanctity of the

heave-offering depends solely on the deaf-mute]."

> T. 1:1 (A-C+F: y. Ter. 1:1; D:
> b. Shab. 153a, b. Yeb. 113a; G-H:
> b. Git. 71a, y. Git. 7:1)

The pericope is composed of three autonomous units, A-C,
D-F, G-I. A introduces the debate at B-C. D is glossed by E-F.
The material presented complements M. 1:1C1's discussion of the
deaf-mute's separation of heave-offering.[25]

Judah, A, states that heave-offering separated by a deaf-
mute is valid, contrary to the rule of M. 1:1C1. B gives the
basis for his opinion, a precedent which is actually irrelevant
to the issue of heave-offering.[26]   Sages, C, point this out.
They distinguish between foods requiring preparation in purity
and heave-offering. The preparation of foods in purity requires
only supervision, so that the foods do not come into contact with
a source of impurity. The separation of heave-offering, on the
other hand, requires understanding. Sages take for granted that
the deaf-mute, imbecile and minor, although perfectly capable of
supervising, do not have the understanding required in the
separation of heave-offering.[27]

Isaac (D-F) offers a middle ground between Judah and the law
of M. 1:1C1. He states that heave-offering separated by a deaf-
mute is in a status of doubt. Such heave-offering therefore may
not be eaten as unconsecrated food, although the produce from
which it was taken is still deemed untithed. According to F, the
sanctity of heave-offering may depend on an individual other than
the one who physically separates it.[28] This takes to an extreme
the distinction made in M. between the ritualistic aspects of
separating heave-offering (e.g., reciting a blessing) and the
required consciousness of the sacred character of the act. Human
intention alone is the critical factor in the valid separation of
heave-offering.

Simeon b. Gamaliel's point, G-I, is that only an individual
born a deaf-mute is not deemed to have the understanding required
to separate heave-offering. An individual who once possessed all
of his faculties, but later became a deaf-mute, remains in the
category of one who has understanding. Executors are needed only
to witness his document, thereby verifying the fact that produce
he is about to separate is intended as heave-offering.[29]

A.   [One who] hears but does not speak-- that is a mute.

B.   [One who] speaks but does not hear-- that is a
heresh.

C.   And each of these is equivalent to a person of
sound mind in every respect.

                    T. 1:2 (b. Hag. 2b, b. Git. 71s)

The pericope presents definitions of the mute and the
heresh in balanced declarative sentences. A is pertinent below,
at M. 1:6Cl. The definition of the *heresh*, B, is complementary
to M. 1:2H-I, yet contradicts M. 1:2L, as I have noted above.
B+C thus strengthens the distinction between the deaf-mute "of
which the sages spoke," M. 1:1Cl, and the deaf person, M. 1:2H-K.
As already stated, the distinction is between the individual who
does not have the understanding required to separate heave-
offering, and one who is "equivalent to a person of sound mind,"
that is, who has the required understanding.

A.   Who is an imbecile?

B.   (1) One who goes out alone at night, (2) who
sleeps in a graveyard, (3) who rips his clothing and (4) who
loses what is given him.

C.   [What if he is] at times an imbecile [and] at times
lucid (*hlwm*)?

D.   This is the general principle:[30]

E.   Whenever he is an imbecile, he is [deemed] an
imbecile in every respect.

But [whenever he is] sane, his is equivalent to a person
of sound mind in every respect.

                    T. 1:3 (y. Ter. 1:1, y. Git. 7:1;
                    A: b. Hag. 3b; C+E: b. R.H.
                    28a)

T.'s two parts, A-B and C-E, complement M. 1:1C2. Yet like
T. 1:2, they do not relate specifically to the issue of heave-
offering, or depend on M. in any way for sense. They simply
provide a definition of the imbecile mentioned anywhere in M. or
T.[31]

A.   R. Judah says, "[As regards] a minor whose father
placed him in a cucumber field--

"he [i.e., the minor] separates heave-offering
(*hw' twrm*)[32] and his father speaks (*mdbr*)[33] at his side
[indicating approval]. That which he separates is [valid]
heave-offering."

B. They said [to him], "It is not he [i.e., the minor]
who separated heave-offering, but rather his father who
confirmed [it] after him (ṧ'ymn 'hryw)[34]."

T. 1:4 (y. Ter. 1:1)

T. has Judah defend his position of M. 1:3N. He does this
by providing an example in which a minor validly separates
heave-offering. Sages, B, claim that the example does not prove
Judah's point. They differentiate between the one who physically
separates the heave-offering, and the one who, through his intention, validates the separation. They state that here the
sanctity of the heave-offering depends on the father. The minor
therefore cannot be said himself to have separated it.

A. How does one separate heave-offering from [produce]
which is not his own [as at M. 1:1D]?

B. [If one] went down to his fellow's field and picked
[produce] and separated heave-offering [from it] without
permission--

C. if he [i.e., the fellow, the householder] is apprehensive of robbery, that which [the other] has separated is
not [valid] heave-offering;

D. but if he is not apprehensive of robbery, that
which he has separated is [valid] heave-offering.

E. How does one know whether or not he is apprehensive
of robbery?

F. When (hry ṧ-) the householder came and found him
and said to him, "Go to the fine [produce to pick]"--

G. if there was fine [produce], [the householder meant
what he said (Lieberman) and thus] he is not apprehensive of
robbery;

H. but if not [i.e., if there was no fine produce]--
lo, this one is apprehensive of robbery [and his comment was a cynical one (Lieberman)].

I. If the householder should pick and add to them [i.e.,
to what the other already has picked], either way [i.e.,
whether or not there was fine produce], he is not apprehensive
of robbery.

T. 1:5 (y. Ter. 1:1, b. Qid. 52b,
b. B.M. 22a)

T. augments M. 1:1D by claiming that the validity of heave-
offering separated from produce belonging to someone else does
not depend on the owner's having given permission prior to the
actual separation. The owner's granting or withholding of

permission may be established after the fact, on the basis of his
attitude towards the individual found in his field. This being
the case, B-I ignores the question stated at A and explores the
problem of how to discern that attitude. The criterion offered
is whether or not the owner objects to the other person's taking
control of some of his produce. If he is "apprehensive of
robbery," the owner clearly would not have given the intruder
permission to take heave-offering from the produce.[35] Since he
does not agree to what the other has done, that individual's
separation of heave-offering is not considered valid. On the
other hand, the owner may show through words (D, G) or actions
(I) that he does not mind the other individual's taking some of
his produce. If this is the case, it may be assumed that, if
asked, the owner would have given the other person permission to
separate heave-offering from the produce. For this reason, that
which the other has separated is considered valid heave-offering.[36]

> A. [As regards] a thief, an extortionist (*'ns*)[37] and
> a robber--
>
> B. heave-offering they separate is [valid] heave-
> offering, tithes [they give] are [valid] tithes, and that
> which they dedicate [to the Temple] is [validly] dedicated.
>
> C. [But] if the [original] owners chased them [in
> order to recover their property]--
>
> D. heave-offering they separate is not [valid] heave-
> offering, tithes [they give] are not [valid] tithes, and
> that which they dedicate is not [validly] dedicated.
>
> E. Individuals who possess property confiscated from
> the original owners by the government (*bᵉly bty syqryqwn*)--
>
> F. heave-offering they separate is [valid] heave-
> offering, tithes [they give] are [valid] tithes, and that
> which they dedicate is [validly] dedicated.
>
> G. A son, a hired man, a slave and a wife (*'yšh*)
> separate heave-offering from that which they eat, but may not
> separate heave-offering from everything [i.e., from anything
> which is not specifically theirs to eat],
>
> H. since a person does not separate heave-offering from
> that which is not his own [see M. 1:1D].
>
> I. A son, from his father's [produce], and a wife from
> her dough, [even though they will not eat it all themselves]--
> these may separate heave-offering,

> J.   for they separate heave-offering with permission.
>
> T. 1:6 (A-D: y. Bik. 1:2;
>
> A-B: b. B.Q. 67a, 114a-b)

The pericope complements M. 1:1D by carrying forward the
issue introduced at T. 1:5, that of implied permission to
separate heave-offering. Each of its two parts, A-F and G-J,[38]
is carefully formulated. A-F's three rules are marked by the
apodosis which repeats at B, D and F. G-J's two rules, G-H and
I-J, bear their own exegetical glosses, H and J.

The individuals at A have taken property by force. Only on
the assumption that the original owners have given up hope of
recovering the property may these individuals separate heave-
offering. In such a case the property is deemed to belong to
the thieves. If the original owners protest (C), they show that
they still consider the property their own and do not consent to
anyone else's making use of it. In this case, heave-offering
separated by the thief, extortionist or robber is not valid. An
individual who holds property confiscated by the government (E)
is considered its legal owner (T. Git. 5:1).[39] For this reason
even if the original owner protests, heave-offering separated by
the present owner is valid (Lieberman).

G-H and I-J contradict each other. Each refers to a *son*
and *wife*, yet they do not agree as regards the right of these
individuals to separate heave-offering. Still, the contrasting
glosses at H and J indicate that the rules are to be read as a
unit. The point which emerges is that individuals assumed to
have permission to separate heave-offering may do so, even if the
permission has not been made explicit. This works as follows.
The individuals at G-H have no reason to separate heave-offering
from anything but what they eat, and therefore may not do so.
They are not presumed to have the householder's permission. The
individuals at I-J, on the other hand, must separate heave-
offering in order to complete tasks they are performing for the
householder. The wife must separate dough-offering before
completing work on the dough. The son is helping his father
harvest (Lieberman), or is doing some other task that requires
him to separate heave-offering. Since it may be assumed that the
householder expects the individuals concerned to separate heave-
offering and complete the tasks assigned to them, heave-offering
they separate is valid.

T. 1:7-8 are found below, after M. 3:4.

A. A householder is permitted to set aside ($lhqpyd$)[40]
[from his produce] a tithe which is liable to the separation
of agricultural offerings ($m^c\acute{s}r$ tbl), in the quantity of the
heave-offering of the tithe which is in the first tithe
[required from the same produce].

B. R. Yose says, "[As regards] a householder who
separated the heave-offering of the tithe ($\acute{s}trm$ $'t$ $hm^c\acute{s}r$)[41]--
"that which he has done is done [and valid]."

T. 1:9 (B: y. Ter. 1:1, see

b. Git. 30b-31a)

At issue is the householder's right to separate heave-
offering of the tithe. This offering usually is given to the
priest by the Levite, from the Levite's own first tithe. The
problem is addressed in two autonomous statements of law. While
set in the semblance of a dispute, each has its own operative
language. B further does not depend on A for sense. We therefore
must turn to each rule separately.[42]

A assumes that the householder may not separate heave-
offering of the tithe in place of the Levite. By doing so he
would arrogate to himself the exclusive right of the Levite. The
householder may, however, set aside an amount of produce for the
Levite to designate as heave-offering of the tithe. Lieberman
(TK, I, p. 300) gives the reason that the householder would wish
to do this. As its name implies, heave-offering of the tithe is
of the same high order of sanctity as heave-offering. It must be
consumed by the priest in purity. Since such stringency does
not apply to first tithe, however, the Levite is likely to
receive his portion--from which he must separate heave-offering
of the tithe--from unclean produce (see T. 3:12). Heave-offering
of the tithe separated by the Levite from this unclean produce
would not be usable. In order to alleviate this problem, the
householder sets aside a quantity of produce in a state of cleanness for the Levite later to designate as heave-offering of the
tithe for the unclean first tithe he receives.[43] Thus the priest
will receive heave-offering of the tithe in a state of cleanness.

Yose's concern is the householder who actually separates
(that is, designates as holy) heave-offering of the tithe. He
states that heave-offering of the tithe separated by the householder is valid. Yet this opinion implies that he, like A, holds
that, in general, the householder should not separate heave-
offering of the tithe and thereby arrogate to himself the right

of the Levite to do so.[44] This shared, but unstated, assumption
of A and B most likely accounts for their redactional juxtaposition.

A.   Executors (*'pytrwpym*) separate heave-offering and
give tithes [required of] the property of orphans.[45]

B.   They sell houses, fields and vineyards, cattle
[and] male and female slaves,

C.   in order to provide food for orphans [and] to
prepare for them a *sukkah*, *lulab* and show-fringes,

D.   and [to to perform for them] every obligation
(*mswwh*) which is stated in the Torah--

E.   to purchase for them a scroll of the Torah and
Prophets (ed. princ. adds: and Hagiographa),

F.   [that is,] a duty the scope of which is clearly
defined in the Torah (Jastrow, p. 1404, for *dbr hqswb mn
htwrh*).[46]

G.   But they may not redeem captives on their account
[i.e., with funds from these sales], nor, in the synagogue,
levy upon them charity to the poor,

H.   [that is, any] duty the scope of which is not
clearly defined in the Torah.

I.   (*w*) They are not permitted to set [the orphan's]
slaves free [by letting the slave pay his value], but they
may sell them to others in order that they set them free.

J.   Rabbi says, "I say that [the slave] may give him
[i.e., the executor] his value and redeem himself."

T. 1:10 (T. B.B. 8:14, b. Git.
52a; G: B.B. 8a; A: see
M. Git. 5:4)

K.   [Executors] may not sell [property of orphans] that
is at a distance in order to purchase[47] [property] that is
near; [nor may they sell] that which is of low quality in
order to purchase that which is of high quality.

L.   They may not litigate for the orphans [neither in
cases in which the orphans stand] to incur a liability nor
[in cases in which the orphans stand] to receive a benefit,
either to make a claim [against others] or [in cases of] a
claim being made [against the orphans] (*lhknys wlhwsy'*;
Lieberman, TK, I, p. 302), unless they have received permission from a court.

M.   "Executors must make account with the orphans [of
all business dealings they have engaged in] at the end [of

their tenure as executors]," the words of Rabbi.

N. Rabban Simeon b. Gamaliel says, "Orphans have
nothing other than that which the executors left them [i.e.,
no accounting need be made]."

O. [Executors] may sell slaves in order to purchase
landed property, but they may not sell landed property in
order to purchase slaves.

P. Rabban Simeon b. Gamaliel says, "[They may] not
even [sell] slaves in order to purchase landed property."

Q. A court may not make executors of woman and slaves
in the beginning [i.e., of its own accord].

R. But if their [i.e., the orphans'] father appointed
them during his lifetime, they may make them executors.

T. 1:11 (T. B.B. 8:14, b. Git.
52a; M-N: see M. Git. 5:4)

Only the superscription, A, relates T. 1:10-11 to the issue
of heave-offering, specifically, to the problem of separating
heave-offering from produce which belongs to someone else,
M. 1:1D. The term *executors*, at A, provides the antecedent of
the pronoun *they* throughout the well articulated essay which
follows. The construction is otherwise independent of that
stich and autonomous of M. Terumot.

A. R. Simeon b. Menasia[48] says, "Orphans who were
supported (*šsmkw*) by a householder--whether their father
[before his death], or a court [after the father's death]
made them dependent [on him]--

"he tithes [produce] and provides food for them [from
both the unconsecrated food and the tithe of the poor
(Lieberman)], for the sake of the social order
(*mpny tyqwn h^{c}wlm*, Jastrow, p. 1666; Danby (M. Git. 4:2):
as a precaution for the general good)."

B. And thus would R. Simeon b. Menasia say, "An
orphan, the son of a Levite, who was growing up under the
care of (*'sl*) a householder--

"he tithes [produce] and provides food for him [from
both the unconsecrated food and the first tithe (HD,
Lieberman)], for the sake of the social order."

C. If the son of his [i.e., the householder's] wife
[who the householder is not required to maintain] was a
priest or a Levite--

lo, this one [i.e., the householder] provides food for

him from his [i.e., the child's] portion (adding *mḥlqw*, as
at F) [i.e., feeds him tithe or heave-offering, alone].

T. 1:12 (A: see M. Git. 5;4)

D.   A minor who said to someone in the market place,
"Provide me tithe [of the poor] to eat"--

he provides him [tithe], for the sake of the social
order.

E.   If he [i.e., the householder] was raising (read
mgdl for *lgdl*; see Lieberman, TK, I, p. 305), a priest or a
Levite or a poor child [and is therefore responsible for the
child's maintenance][49]--

lo, this one provides food for them from his [i.e.,
the householder's] own [tithed, unconsecrated produce].

F.[50]   If the son of his wife was a priest, a Levite or
a poor child--

lo, this one provides food for him from his [i.e., the
child's] portion [alone] [=C].

G.   If [the householder] owed him [i.e., the child of
F] sustenance, or if [the child] worked with him for his
sustenance--

lo, this one [i.e., the householder] provides food for
him from his own [i.e., the householder's own tithed, unconsecrated food, but not from heave-offering or tithe, the
case being like that of E].

H.   And he makes for him [i.e., the child] an investment
of his portion [i.e., the householder may sell the heave-
offering or tithes he separates and save the money to be
given to the child at a time that the householder no longer
is in debt to him].

T. 1:13 (G-H: See b. B.M. 87b,
b. B.B. 52a)

The discussion of the proper treatment of orphans continues.
The issue now is the circumstances under which a householder may
use heave-offering or tithe to maintain orphans.   T. distinguishes
between children whom the householder is legally required to
maintain (E, G) and children who eat at the householder's table,
but who are not legally dependent on him (C, F).[51]   The householder may not support the former with heave-offering or tithe.
By doing so, he escapes providing for them at his own expense and
therefore uses heave-offering or tithes to his own benefit.   In
the case of children he is not required to feed, however, the

householder gains nothing by feeding them heave-offering or
tithe. It is as if he gave these things to any priest, Levite,
or poor person.

Simeon b. Menasia (A, B) disagrees with the rules of E and
G. He states that the householder may separate tithe and give
it, along with the now-tithed produce, to a Levite or poor child
for whom he is responsible. Lieberman suggests that this is for
the "general good" in that it assures that householders will not
refrain from taking in and maintaining orphans, who otherwise
would be supported solely from tithe.

D, finally, does not involve the householder's right to give
tithe to a child who eats at his table. It is redacted here
because it is a rule "for the sake of the social order," and,
moreover, because, like the rest of the pericope, it deals with
the proper distribution of tithe. Normally poorman's tithe is
not distributed in the market place. The case of the poor child
is an exception, legislated in order that a child might not go
hungry (Lieberman, TK, I, p. 304).

A. A householder may not separate [first] tithe
(l' $ytrwm$ $'t$ $hm^c\acute{s}r$)[52] [in order to make use of it himself
and later pay the Levite its value] and [only afterwards]
ask permission of a Levite.

B. Nor [may he take] the shoulder, two cheeks and maw
[referred to in Dt. 18:3] and [only afterwards] ask permission of a priest.

C. But he may make them [either the Levite or priest]
a loan, in order [later] to take ($lhywt$ $mpry\acute{s}$: ed. princ.,
HD, HY)[53] [repayment] for them from their portion.

D. Friends [of a householder] among the priesthood or
Levites ($mkry$ $khwnh$ $wlwyh$, reading with Rashi, b. Git. 30a,
Lieberman and HY; HD reads: friends of a particular priest
or Levite) are not permitted to do this [i.e., to borrow
money and allow the lender to collect from their portion
(Lieberman)].

E. But [in the case of] lost things [i.e., lost heave-
offering or tithe], it is permitted [i.e., either the householder at A may take them for his own use and only aferwards
ask permission (HY, HD), or a priest or Levite who has taken
a loan from a friend may allow that friend to use them as
repayment of the loan (MB)],

F. since [the finder] is equivalent to one who returns
a lost thing.

                      T. 1:14a (see M. Git. 3:7,
                      b. Git. 30a, T. Dem. 8:15)

T. 1:14a refers to individuals who wish to make personal use
of priestly gifts or the Levites' tithe. For this reason it refers to items that are not holy, and which may be used by non-
priests. Still, a non-priest may not generally take such things
for his own use (A, B), thereby arrogating the rights of the
priest or Levite. Matters are different, C, when a prior arrange-
ment with the priest or Levite exists.[54] Lieberman (TK, I,
p. 305-6) provides the reasoning behind D's qualification of this
rule. He states that by borrowing money and arranging for the
lender to take repayment from priestly gifts or tithe, priests
and Levites assure themselves of receiving a portion (or the value
thereof). Priests or Levites who always receive priestly gifts or
tithe from a particular householder gain no benefit from borrowing on their portion and for this reason may not do so.[55]

If E-F refers back to A-B, the point is that an individual
who finds lost priestly gifts or tithe may use them himself and
pay their value at his convenience. This is the dispensation
given to an individual who finds a lost thing (F). Alternatively,
E qualifies D, and the point is that since the finder of lost
priestly gifts or tithe normally is required to give them to the
first priest or Levite he encounters, there are no "friends among
the priests or Levites" as regards their distribution (Lieberman).
For this reason, even the individual who has made a loan to a
friend who is a priest or Levite may take them for his own use, as
repayment of that loan.

T. 1:14b is below, after M. 8:8-12.

A. *A gentile who separated heave-offering from [the*
produce of] an Israelite, even with permission--that which he
has separated is not [valid] heave-offering [= M. 1:1E-G].

B. $M^c \mathit{\check{S}} h$ b- In Pegah,[56] an Israelite said to a gentile,
"Separate the heave-offering [required] of [the produce on]
my threshing floor," and he separated it, and [afterwards]
the heave-offering fell back [into the unconsecrated food
still] on the threshing floor. (*w*) The case came before
Rabban Simeon b. Gamaliel [for judgement], and he ruled,
"Since a gentile separated the heave-offering [as an agent],
it is not [valid] heave-offering [which was mixed with the

produce on the threshing floor. Therefore all of the produce
remains in an untithed, unconsecrated status]."

    C. R. Isaac says, "A gentile who separated heave-
offering from [the produce of] an Israelite, and the owner
validated [it] at his side--

        that which he has separated is [valid] heave-offering."

                    T. 1:15 (A: b. Shab. 153b,

                    b. Yev. 113a, b. Git. 23b; C:

                    see y. Ter. 1:1, y. Dem 6:1)

A-B illustrates M. 1:1E-G's rule that a gentile acting as the
agent of an Israelite may not separate heave-offering. The
gentile's offering is not valid and therefore does not impart the
status of heave-offering to unconsecrated produce with which it
is mixed.[57] Isaac, C, applies to the case of the gentile the
principle of T. 1:1E-F and T. 1:4B. The validity of heave-
offering depends on the one who designates it, not on the one who
physically separates it.

    A. (1) One who sells produce to this fellow and says
to him [afterwards], "The produce I sold you is not tithed,"

        (2) "The meat [I sold you] is meat of a firstling,"

        (3) "The wine [I sold you] is wine for libations"--

    B. [in accordance with] the measure of the law
(*šwrt hdyn*), he is not believed [since he thereby shows himself purposely to have acted wrongly in making the sale].

    C. R. Judah says, "Israelites are not held suspect of
doing that [i.e., of lying about the status of produce they
have sold]. Rather, it is all [i.e., each case is judged]
in accordance with the character of the [particular] individual [and only a known liar is not believed]."

                    T. 2:1 (T. M.S. 3:12)

    D. [If] one was offering sacrifices with him [i.e.,
his fellow] and said to him, "They have been made refuse [by
my improper intention]," [or if] he was preparing with him
foods requiring preparation in cleanness and said, "They have
become unclean"--

    E. Israelites are not held suspect of doing that [i.e.,
of lying about the validity of Temple service, and therefore
he is believed].

    F. But [if] he said to him, "Sacrifices which I offered
with you on that [particular] day [in the past] were made
(Lieberman adds: refuse,) ["Foods requiring preparation in

cleanness which I prepared with you on that [particular] day
[in the past became] unclean"--

G. [in accordance with] the measure of the law, he is
not believed [since by admitting that he did not immediately
inform the other individual, he shows himself to have acted
wrongly].

H. R. Judah says, "Israelites are not held suspect of
doing that. Rather, it is all [i.e., each case is judged]
in accordance with the character of the [particular]
individual."

T. 2:2 (b. Git. 54b)

I. One who sacrificed the paschal lamb for the fellows
of his group (bny hbwrh; Jastrow, p. 416: "Those united for
eating the Passover lamb in company." See, e.g., M. Pes.
7:3) and said (that), "I did not sacrifice it for its own
name [i.e., with proper intention]"--

J. [in accordance with] the measure of the law, he is
(Lieberman adds with ed. princ. and T. Pes. 4:7: not)
believed.

K. R. Judah says, "[If it was] before they began [to
eat] it [that he made the statement], he is believed.

L. "But [if it was] after they began [to eat] it [that
he made the statement], he is not believed."

T. 2:3 (T. Pes. 4:3)

The pericopae are autonomous of M. and the topic of heave-
offering, marking the conclusion of T.'s unit of materials pertinent to M. 1:1-3.[58] The principle at A-B,[59] F-G and I-J is that
an individual's own testimony may not be accepted as evidence that
he is a wrongdoer.[60] Judah, at C and H, rejects this principle.
He says that, in general, an individual may be believed concerning
his own actions, even if he claims to have acted wrongly. Only in
cases in which the individual is a known wrongdoer may we assume
that he has some motive and therefore is lying.[61]

D-G distinguishes between a case in which the individual in
question acknowledges an error or mishap immediately (D-E), and
one in which he says nothing until, by his own words, he has
caused the cult to be profaned (F-G). In the former case, there
is no wrongdoing involved. Since he simply states that some mishap has occurred, there is no reason not to believe him. In the
latter circumstance (F-G), even if the individual were telling the
truth, his not having stated the facts immediately is incriminating.

His own words may not be taken as evidence that he is a wrongdoer,
and so he is not believed.

The individual at I states that, through his own misdeed, the
paschal lamb was improperly sacrificed (see M. Zeb. 1:1). According to J, even if he admits this at once, he shows himself to be
a wrongdoer and cannot be believed. Judah now makes a distinction such as the one made between the cases of D-E and F-G. If
the individual makes his admission immediately, Judah holds that
the case is like that of D-E. He simply acknowledges an error,
and there is no reason not to believe him. If, however, the individual waits until the others have begun to eat before making
his statement, he claims to have allowed them to eat of an unfit
paschal lamb. Since the individual thus shows himself to be an
evil doer, he may not be believed. In making this distinction,
Judah is inconsistent with his previously held opinion. He should
be expected to hold here, as he does at C and H, that each case
is judged in accordance with the character of the particular
individual involved.

1:4

A.   They may not separate olives as heave-offering for
[olive-] oil, nor grapes [as heave-offering] for wine.

B.   And if they separated [either olives as heave-
offering for both olives and oil, or grapes as heave-offering
for both grapes and wine (Maimonides, *et. al.*)]--

C.   The House of Shammai say, "Their [i.e., the grapes'
or olives'] own heave-offering is in it [i.e., in that which
they have separated; but that which they separated for the
wine or oil is not valid heave-offering]."

D.   And the House of Hillel say, "That which they have
separated is not [valid] heave-offering [in any respect]."

> M. 1:4 (y. Ter. 1:4, 5, 8; see
> also: T. Ter. 3:14, M. Ed. 5:2,
> y. Ma. 2:3, y. Git. 4:2; C: see
> y. Ter. 3:3, 4:4, Sifré Bammidbar
> #122, Horovitz, p. 147-48)

M. 1:10 states that heave-offering may not be separated from
produce the preparation for consumption of which has not been
completed for produce the preparation of which has been completed.
From this follows the rule at M. 1:4A, that heave-offering may
not be separated from olives or grapes for oil or wine (y. Ter.
1:4, Bert, TYY, Sens, Albeck).[62] At B-D the Houses dispute the

status of heave-offering separated in contradiction to this rule.[63]
On formal and, concomitantly, substantive grounds, the opinion of
the Shamaites is difficult. In light of the language operative
in the present thematic unit of the tractate, we would expect
them to state the logical opposite of the Hillelite opinion, viz.,
"that which they have separated is valid heave-offering."[64] In
order to make sense of the Shammaite opinion as it stands, we
must posit a case such as the one I have interpolated (following
all of the exegetes) at B. The individual separates grapes as
heave-offering for both grapes and wine, or olives as heave-
offering for both olives and olive-oil. The House of Shammai
state that even *post facto*, that which was separated for the oil
or wine is not valid heave-offering. Yet what about the grapes
which were separated as heave-offering for grapes, or the olives
which were separated as heave-offering for olives? The Shammaites
see no reason that these should not be valid heave-offering. They
do not deem probative the individual's original intention to
separate heave-offering for both grapes and wine, or olives and
oil. That which was separated for its own kind therefore may be
considered as valid heave-offering.

When understood apart from the context provided by the
opinion of the House of Shammai--which requires the interpolation
at B--the House of Hillel state simply that, even *post facto*,
heave-offering separated in contradiction to A's rule is not
valid.[65] In light of the Shammaite view--and the interpolation at
B--the opinion of the House of Hillel takes on a second level of
meaning. Unlike the Shammaites, the Hillelites take seriously the
individual's original intention. He intended to separate heave-
offering from olives for both olives and oil, or from grapes for
both grapes and wine. Since this cannot be accomplished, the
heave-offering he separates is in no way valid.[66]

1:5

    A. They do not separate heave-offering
I.   B. (1) from gleanings, or (2) from forgotten sheaves,
or (3) from [produce growing in the] corner of a field,
[which is left for the poor], or (4) from ownerless property;
II.   C. and (5) not from first tithe from which heave-
offering [of the tithe] has been removed;
    D. and (6) not from second tithe or [produce] dedi-
cated [to the Temple] which have been redeemed;
III. E. and[67] (7) not from that which is liable [to the

separation of heave-offering] for that which is exempt [from
the separation of heave-offering];

F. and not from that which is exempt for that which is
liable;

G. and[68] (8) not from that which is picked for that
which is not picked (*mhwbr*);

H. and not from that which is not picked for that which
is picked;

I. and (9) not from that which is new [viz., produce of
the present year] for that which is old [viz., produce left
over from a previous year (T. 2:6)];

J. and not from that which is old for that which is new;

K. and (10) not from produce of the Land [of Israel]
for produce from outside of the Land [of Israel];

L. and not from produce from outside of the Land [of
Israel] for produce of the Land [of Israel].

M. And if they separated heave-offering [from any of
the types of produce listed at B-D, or in any of the fashions
described at E-L]--

N. that which they have separated is not [valid] heave-
offering.

> M. 1:5 (A-B: y. Ter. 1:5; A-D:
> M. Hal. 1:3; G: b. Qid. 72a,
> y. Qid. 3:5; G-J: M. M.S. 5:11;
> I-J: T. R.H. 1:9, T. Bik. 7:1,
> Sifré Debarim 105 [Finkelstein,
> p. 164, ls. 1-3]; G-L: Sifré
> Bammidbar 120 [Horovitz, p. 147,
> ls. 4-9])

The list of ten entries is divisible into three formally distinct units of material, B, C-D and E-L. The items at B are described by unmodified substantives. C-D is slightly different,
substantives modified by relative clauses. Yet it is clear that
C-D belongs with B. This is indicated by the use of this same
series of items at M. Ter. 6:5 and M. Hal. 1:3. A major shift in
formulation occurs at E-L, which presents four balanced doublets
(E-F, G-H, I-J, K-L). Since it is likely that this shift in formal
pattern indicates a change in issue, the pericope will here be
treated in its two major parts, B-D and then E-L.[69]

Gleanings, forgotten sheaves and produce which grows in the
corners of a field are left by the householder for the poor. As
gifts which the householder is required to give up from his

produce, they are not liable to the separation of heave-offering.[70]
These things are like other types of sanctified offerings, which
stand outside of the system in which produce normally becomes
liable to the separation of heave-offering and tithes. Produce
which grows wild, or which is abandoned by its owner (B4) likewise
remains outside of this system. M. Ma. 1:1 stipulates that in
order to become subject to the separation of tithes, produce must
be owned.[71] Like the items at B1-3, first tithe and second tithe
(C-D) are agricultural offerings, and therefore not liable to the
separation of heave-offering. Even if they are redeemed, such
that they revert to an unconsecrated status, they do not take on
liability.[72] Since at the point at which liability normally is
incurred they stood outside of the system of tithes, they never
enter that system.[73]

At E-L, M.'s interest turns to unaccepable methods of
separating heave-offering. According to E-F, if a quantity of
fruit is to be separated from one batch of produce as heave-offering on behalf of another batch, each of the batches must be liable
to the separation of heave-offering. On the one hand, produce intended as heave-offering for produce which is not liable may not
be considered valid heave-offering. It is as if the heave-offering was taken from the exempt produce itself. On the other hand,
heave-offering separated from produce which is not liable (F) in
no event may be deemed valid heave-offering. G-H and K-L are
examples of these rules. Produce which is not yet picked, G-H, is
not liable to the separation of heave-offering, for it is not food.
Only produce of the Land of Israel, K-L, is subject to the separation of heave-offering and tithes.[74] The issue at I-J is
separate. Produce of all years of the sabbatical cycle is liable
to the separation of heave-offering. Yet M. takes seriously the
change of years in that cycle, and holds that produce of one year
is not homogeneous with produce of a different year. For this
reason, heave-offering may not be separated from the fruit of one
year of the sabbatical cycle on behalf of fruit of a different
year.

> A. *They may not separate heave-offering from new*
> [*produce*] *for that which is old* [= M. 1:5H]. How so?
> B. They may not separate heave-offering from produce of
> the present year for produce of the past year;
> C. and not from produce of the past year for produce of
> the present year.

D.   But [in the case of] a field [of trees (HD, Lieberman; see b. R.H. 15b)] which produces two crops (*brykwt*; E: *grnwt*) in one year.

E.   and so (*wkn*; E: *kgwn*)[75] an irrigated field [which gives produce continually throughout the year, M. B.B. 3:1]--

F.   they may separate heave-offering and give tithes from one [crop] for the other [within the same year (HY, Lieberman)].

G.   [If] he picked a vegetable on the evening of the new year before the sun set, and picked again after the sun set--

they (sic) may not separate heave-offering or give tithes from one for the other,

H.   since one is new, and the other is old.

I.   [If] it was the second [year of the sabbatical cycle when he picked the first vegetable] and the third [year] began [before he picked the second vegetable]--

the first [picked] is subject to second tithe [as required in the second year of the cycle] and the second [picked] is subject to tithe of the poor [as required in the third year of the cycle].

J.   [If] he picked an ethrog [which is like the fruit of a tree in all respects except that it is tithed in accordance with the year in which it is picked, M. Bik. 2:6] on the fifteenth of Shevat [the new year of trees, M. R.H. 1:1] before the sun set and picked again after the sun set--

they may not separate heave-offering or give tithes from one for the other,

K.   since one is new and the other is old.

L.   [If] it was the third [year of the sabbatical cycle when he picked the first ethrog] and the fourth [year] began [before he picked the second ethrog]--

the first [picked] is subject to tithe of the poor and the second [picked] is subject to second tithe.

T. 2:6 (T. R.H. 1:9, b. R.H. 15b)

M.   *They may not separate heave-offering from picked [produce] for unpicked [produce]* [= M. 1:5F]. How so?

N.   [If] he said, "This picked produce is designated heave-offering and tithes for this [other] unpicked produce,"

O.   or, "This unpicked produce is designated heave-offering and tithes for this [other] picked produce"--

P.   he has not said anything.

Q. But [if] he said, "This picked produce is designated heave-offering and tithes for this [other] unpicked produce as of the time that it will be picked"--

R. he may eat of it [i.e., of the picked produce] as a random meal, and he may designate it heave-offering and tithes for [produce of] another place [in his field] until [the unpicked produce] is picked.

S. [When] it is picked--

his designation becomes valid (*dbryw qyymyn*) [and the picked produce becomes heave-offering or tithes for what was originally unpicked produce].

                    T. 2:7 (b. Kid. 62b, y. Hal. 4:5)

T. In the same way:

U. [As regards] someone who was coming along the way, and a basket of untithed produce (*prwt š'ynn mtwqnym*) was in his hand, and he said, "Lo, this [basket of produce] is designated heave-offering and tithes for produce which I have in my home, as of the time I will reach the city"--

lo, this one eats from it [i.e., the basket] as a random meal, and designates it heave-offering or tithes for [produce of] another place [in his field] until he reaches the city.

V. [When] he reached the city--

his designation becomes valid [and the produce in the basket becomes heave-offering or tithes for the produce in his home].

W. [If] the produce [in his home] was eaten, stolen or lost--

[if this occurred] before he reached the city, the basket [remains] in its untithed, unconsecrated status;

[and if it occurred] after he reached the city, his designation is valid [since the produce in the basket became heave-offering or tithes before the other produce was eaten, stolen or lost].

X. Moreover, said R. Eleazar b. Jacob, "[If he said,] 'The produce of this garden bed--as of the time that it will become one third grown and be picked--is designated heave-offering and tithes for the produce of this [other] garden bed--as of the time that it will become a third grown and be picked,'

(HD adds with b. Qid. 62b: "and [each garden bed] became a third grown and was picked--

"his designation becomes valid.")

T. 2:8 (b. Kid. 62b)

Y. *They may not separate heave-offering from produce of*
the Land [of Israel] for produce from outside of the Land [of
Israel] [= M. 1:5J]. How so?

Z. They do not separate heave-offering from produce of
the Land of Israel on behalf of produce of Syria,

AA. and not from produce of Syria on behalf of produce
of the Land is Israel.

T. 2:9

As indicated by my use of italics, T. systematically cites
and enriches M. 1:5F-K. A-C, first, points out that the injunction against separating heave-offering from new for old, or old
for new, produce applies only to produce of differing years of the
sabbatical cycle. If a field produces two crops in the same year
(D-F) heave-offering may be separated from one on behalf of the
other. G-H now illustrates M. 1:5H-I's rule for the case of
vegetables, which become subject to the separation of heave-offering at the time they are harvested. If the new year intervenes
during a harvest, the produce is deemed to be of different years.
The rule of the ethrog is the same. Like a vegetable the ethrog
is subject to tithing as of the time it is picked (M. Bik. 2:6).
Yet since it grows on a tree, its new year is the fifteenth of
Shevat (M. R.H. 1:1). I and L follow logically from G-H and J-K
respectively. The point again is that a vegetable or ethrog is
subject to tithing in accordance with the year of the sabbatical
cycle in which it is harvested, not, for instance, the year in
which it is planted.

N-P restates M. 1:5F-G, cited at M. Q-S develops this theme,
noting that a designation of heave-offering may include a stipulation. Only when the terms of the stipulation are met does the
designation take effect. The rule of U-W is no different, except
that now the stipulation covers both the produce to be tithed and
that which is to be designated heave-offering.

Produce from Syria, Y-AA, is presumed to be from the field of
a gentile, and therefore not liable to the separation of heave-
offering and tithes (see M. Dem. 6:11). For this reason heave-
offering may not be separated from it for produce of Israel, which,
of course, is liable.[76]

A. An Israelite who purchased a field in Syria--

lo, he is like one who purchased [a field] in a suburb
of Jerusalem;

B.   he separates heave-offering and gives tithes for
[the produce which grows from] it.

C.   "An Israelite and a gentile who purchased together
a field in Syria--

D.   "lo, it [i.e., the produce they grow] is like un-
tithed (tbl) and tithed ($m^c w \acute{s} r$, see Lieberman, TK, I, p. 315;
b. Git. 47b reads: $hwlyn$) [produce] which are mixed together"--the words of Rabbi.

E.   Rabban Simeon b. Gamaliel says, "The Israelite's
portion [of the produce] is liable [to tithes and heave-
offering]; the gentile's portion is not liable."

>   T. 2:10 (A-B: M. Hal. 4:11,

>   T. B.Q. 1:5, b. Git. 8a;

>   C-E: y. Dem. 6:10, b. Git. 47a,

>   b. Hul. 135b, T. Ma. 2:22)

F.   An Israelite who purchased a field in Syria, even if
he sold it again to a gentile--

it [remains] subject to tithes and [to the law of] the
seventh [year],

G.   since it once has been made subject.

H.   But [in the case of] sharecroppers, tenant farmers,
hereditary land-tenants (Jastrow: $bty \ 'bwt$), or a gentile
who mortgaged his land to an Israelite, even though the
Israelite gave him final notice (E: $^c \acute{s} h \ lw \ y \acute{s} r 'l \ nymwswt$)
[that he was foreclosing on the loan and taking the field]--

[the field] is exempt from tithes and is exempt from the
sabbatical year [since it has never been the possession of an
Israelite].

>   T. 2:11 (A: b. Git. 47a; B:

>   b. Git 43b)

T. 2:10-11 continues the discussion of the laws of Syria,
begun in T. 2:9. Property owned by an Israelite in Syria is
liable to the separation of heave-offering and tithes (A); that
owned by a gentile is not. From this stems the dispute at C-E.
Rabbi (D) holds that the Israelite and gentile share in each piece
of produce. According to Simeon (E), we distinguish between the
portion of produce which the Israelite will eventually receive,
and that of the gentile. Only the former is liable to the separation of heave-offering and tithes. The point at F-H is that
once property in Syria is owned by an Israelite, even if it reverts to gentile ownership, it remains liable to the laws of tithes

and the sabbatical year. The farming of property in Syria without
actual ownership is not sufficient to make it liable to these
things (H). Unless the Israelite actually owns the property, it
remains in the status of property owned--and farmed--by a gentile.

A. What is [considered] the Land [of Israel] and what
is [deemed] outside of the Land [of Israel]?

B. All that slopes down from the Mountains of Amanah
(*twry smnyn*; E reads *twrws 'mnws*; for other readings see
Lieberman, TK, II, p. 316, and Jastrow, s.v., *'mnh*, p. 78)
and onward is the Land of Israel; from the Mountains of Amanah
and to the outside (E, T. Hal. 2:11, and parallels in y. and
b. read *wlhln*; V, ed. princ. read *wlpnym*) is outside of the
Land [of Israel].

C. Islands which are in the sea--
they view them as if there was a thread stretched from
the Mountains of Amanah to the Brook of Egypt.

From the thread and inwards is the Land of Israel;
from the thread and to the outside is outside of the
Land [of Israel].

D. R. Judah says, "All that is opposite the Land of
Israel, lo, it is like the Land of Israel,

E. as it is written [in Scripture], "For the western
boundary, you shall have the Great Sea and its coast" (Num.
34:6).

F. Islands which are on the borders (*sddyn*)--
they view them as if there was a thread [stretched] from
Kiflaria to the ocean, [and another] from the Brook of Egypt
to the ocean.

From the thread and inwards is the Land of Israel;
from the thread and to the outside is outside of the
Land [of Israel].

T. 2:2 (T. Hal. 2:11, y. Sheb.
6:1, y. Hal. 4:8, b. Git. 8a)

G. A ship which is coming from outside of the Land [of
Israel] to the Land [of Israel], and within it is produce
[the processing of which has not been completed (Lieberman)]--

H. from the [imagined] thread and to the inside, if it
touches [shore, the produce which is in] it is liable [to
heave-offering and tithes] according to a calculation [of how
much it grew from the time that it entered the territory of
the Land of Israel (MB, Lieberman)].

I.   But [a ship with produce in it] which is leaving the
Land [of Israel] is not liable[77] according to a calculation
[of how much the produce had grown in the Land of Israel,
since its processing will ultimately be completed outside the
Land of Israel (Lieberman)].

J.   R. Eleazar (E, ed. princ.: Eliezer) says, "Dirt (E,
ed. princ. add: of the Land of Israel) [with produce growing
in it (Lieberman), which was taken] outside of the Land [of
Israel] is liable according to a calculation [of how much the
produce had grown in the Land of Israel (MB)."

>   T. 2:13a (G-J: see M. Hal. 2:1-2,
>   b. Git. 7b)

T. continues to deal with issues tangentially related to
M. 1:5H-J. A-F gives an exact description of the borders of the
Land of Israel. This is required by M. 1:5H-J's statement that
heave-offering may not be separated from produce of the Land of
Israel for produce from outside of the Land of Israel, or *vice
versa*. G-J deals with the liability to tithing of produce which
is brought across these borders before its processing is completed. Since produce becomes liable to the removal of tithes at
the time its processing is completed, the important factor here is
where processing takes place. If processing takes place in the
Land of Israel, tithes must be removed for that portion of growth
which actually occurred in the Land of Israel (G-H). If processing
takes place outside of the Land of Israel, there is no liability
to tithes, even on that portion of produce which grew in the Land
of Israel (I). Eleazar qualifies this latter point. He states
that if produce is taken outside of the Land of Israel, but continues to grow in soil from the Land, tithes must be removed for
that amount of produce which grew in the Land of Israel.

T. 2:13b is found below, after M. 3:9.

A.   They may not separate heave-offering from produce
which has not reached one third [of its growth].

B.   How does one know whether or not it has reached one
third [of its growth]?

C.   If one plants it [i.e., plants a seed from the produce in question] and it sprouts (following E, ed. princ.:
wmsmht; V reads *wmsmsmht*), it is known that it has reached
one third [of its growth].

D.   But if one plants it [i.e., plants a seed] and it

does not sprout, it is known that it has not reached one
third [of its growth].

> T. 2:14 (A: see M. Hal. 1:3 and
> T. Hal. 2:5)

At issue is the point in its growth at which produce becomes
liable to the separation of heave-offering, a fitting conclusion
to T.'s unit of materials pertinent to M. 1:5.

1:6

A.   Five [sorts of people] may not separate heave-
offering,

B.   but if they separated heave-offering, that which they
have separated is [valid] heave-offering:

C.   (1) a mute, (2) a drunkard, (3) a naked person, (4)
a blind person, and (5) a person who has had a nocturnal
emission

D.   may not separate heave-offering.

E.   But if [any of these individuals] separated heave-
offering, that which they have separated is [valid] heave-
offering.

> M. 1:6 (see: y. Ber. 2:4, y. Ter.
> 1:1, y. Meg. 2:5)

By repeating the formal pattern of M. 1:1, the redactor introduces Chapter One's second set of materials. These deal with cases
in which heave-offering is improperly separated, yet is considered
valid. Through repetition of form the redactor also indicates
that M. 1:1 and 1:6 must be read in conjunction with each other.
As we shall see, the point here, as at M. 1:1, is that the validity of heave-offering depends on its having been separated by an
individual with requisite powers of intention. The five individuals listed here have those powers, and therefore heave-offering they separate is valid. There are, however, other factors,
in light of which they should not separate heave-offering in the
first place. A mute, naked person, or an individual who has had
a nocturnal emission may not recite the blessing which accompanies
the separation of heave-offering (see M. Ber. 3:4-5 and T. Ter.
3:1-2). A person who cannot see or who is drunk is not capable of
choosing the most choice produce to be designated as heave-offering (see M. 2:4, 6, and T. 3:1-2). The inability of these individuals to carry out these aspects of the separation of heave-
offering restricts them from separating heave-offering *de jure*.

Since they have the required understanding, however, heave-offering which they anyway separate is valid.[78]

 A. For what reason did they say [that] a mute does not
separate heave-offering (V: *twrm*; E, ed. princ.: *ytrwm* [as
at M. 1:6Cl]?

 B. [They said it] because he may not recite the
blessing.[79]

 C. For what reason did they say [that] a blind person
may not separate heave-offering [as at M. 1:6C4]?

 D. [They said it] because he cannot distinguish [pro-
duce which is of] good quality from that which is of bad
quality [in order to separate heave-offering from the more
choice, as required by M. 2:6].

 E. For what readon did they say [that] a drunkard may
not separate heave-offering [as at M. 1:6C2]?

 F. [They said it] because he has no understanding ($d^{c}t$)
[to separate heave-offering from the best of his produce
(y. Ter. 1:6, HY, Lieberman)].

 G. Even though he is drunk, (1) that which he buys is
[validly] bought, (2) that which he sells is [validly] sold,
(3) vows he makes are [valid] vows, (4) that which he dedicates [to the Temple] is [validly] dedicated, and (5) that
which he gives as a present is a [valid] present.

 H. [If] he committed a transgression for which he is
obligated [to bring] a sin-offering, they require him [to
bring] (E adds: a sin offering).

 I. [If he committed a transgression for which he is
liable] to execution by stoning, they require that he be
executed by stoning.

 J. The general principle in this matter [is that] a
drunk person, lo, he is equivalent to a person of sound mind
in every respect.

T. 3:1 (A-F: y. Ter. 1:6; G-J:
b. Erub. 65a)

 K. For what reason did they say [that] a person who has
had a nocturnal emission may not separate heave-offering [as
at M. 1:6C5]?

 L. [They said it] because he may not recite the blessing [see M. Ber. 3:4].

 M. For what reason did they say [that] a naked person
may not separate heave-offering [as at M. 1:6C3]?

N. [They said it] because he may not recite the blessing [see M. Ber. 3:5, T. Ber. 2:15].

O. But he covers himself with straw or with stubble or
with anything and recites the blessing.

T. 3:2 (E: T. Ber. 2:14)

T. cites each of the items at M. 1:6C and explains why the
individual in question may not separate heave-offering.[80] G-I+J
is autonomous, and, in fact, contradicts E-F. While F states that
the drunkard has no understanding ($d^c t$), G-I+J holds that he is
like a person of sound mind. y. Ter. 1:6, followed by HY and
Lieberman, resolves the contradiction by stating that at issue in
F is only the drunkard's ability to select choice produce, not
full soundness of mind. This interpretation does not take into
account the usual usage of the term $d^c t$ (see above, T. 1:1D-F).
It does however explain why heave-offering separated by a drunkard
may be considered valid. He has no understanding, but his powers
of intention equal those of an individual of sound mind.

A. [If] he was going to remove heave-offering, first
tithe or second tithe, at what point does he recite the
blessing?

B. [He recites it] once he has [actually] removed them
[T. Ber. 6:14: at the time he removes them].

C. [When] he has removed them--

D. if he is going to designate them [heave-offering,
first or second tithe by making an oral pronouncement (HY)],
[the status of] sanctity does not pertain to them until he
designates them.

E. But if he is not going to designate them [by making
such a pronouncement], when he has removed them, they have
become sanctified.

T. 3:3 (A-B: T. Ber. 6:14; C-E:
T. M.S. 4:14)

T. is autonomous of M., continuing the discussion of the
recitation of the blessing over heave-offering, T. 3:1A-B, 3:2K-O.
A-B states simply that the blessing over heave-offering is recited
after the heave-offering has been separated. The alternatives
would be that the householder recite the blessing either before he
actually separates the heave-offering, or, possibly, when he gives
the heave-offering he has separated to the priest (HY).[81] Whereas
C-E is dependent on A-B for its sense, its issue is separate.[82]
The problem is no longer that of reciting the blessing. Rather,

T. now asks, When does produce separated as heave-offering take on
the holy status of heave-offering? The controlling factor is
whether or not the householder plans to make an oral pronouncement
declaring that which he separates to be heave-offering.[83] If he
does not plan to do so, his actions in physically separating the
heave-offering from the rest of his produce are sufficient to mark
the sanctification of that which he separates (E). If, however,
the householder removes a portion of his produce, planning to declare it heave-offering at a later time, that which he separates
is not considered heave-offering until such time as he actually
makes the declaration (D).[84]

1:7

A. They do not separate heave-offering by (1) a measure
[of volume], by (2) weight, or by (3) a count [of the number
of pieces of fruit being separated as heave-offering].

B. But he separates the heave-offering of (1) [produce]
which has been measured, of (2) that which has been weighed,
and of (3) that which has been counted.

C. They do not separate heave-offering in a basket (sl)
or in a vessel (qph) which [hold a known] measure.

D. But he separates heave-offering in them [if they are]
one half or one third part [filled].

E. He may not separate heave-offering in [a basket
which holds one] $se'ah$, [if it is] one half part [filled],

F. since the half thereof is a [known] measure (Danby,
p. 52).

M. 1:7

The point is made through the carefully balanced but opposing
rules of A and B. As its verbal root (RWM) indicates, heave-
offering is a quantity of produce which literally is "heaved" up
from the householder's produce. This being the case, the householder may not designate as heave-offering a predetermined and
measured quantity of produce (A).[85] He may however use one of
several possible methods in order accurately to estimate the
quantity of produce he wishes to designate for the priest (B).
C-F refers to secondary problems. By using a basket which holds
a known measure, the individual ascertains the quantity of produce
he separates, even if he does not mean to. He may however use
such a basket without filling it completely, for then he has no
way of knowing how much produce he has taken. A basket which
holds exactly one $se'ah$ is an exception to this rule (E-F). Since

one half *se'ah* is an easily calculable and commonly used measure,
the individual may not separate heave-offering by filling such a
vessel half way.[86]

A. R. Judah says, (1) "A man measures [the volume of]
his untithed produce and brings it into his house, provided
that he does not separate heave-offering according to a
[fixed] measurement.

(2) "A man weighs his untithed produce and brings it
into his house, provided that he does not separate heave-
offering according to [a fixed] weight.

(3) "A man counts his untithed produce and brings it
into his house, provided that he does not separate heave-
offering, according to a [fixed] count" [see M. 1:7A-B].

B. R. Yose b. R. Judah says, (1) "[He does] not
[separate heave-offering] according to a measure [of volume],
nor from that which has been measured.

(2) "Not according to weight, nor from that which has
been weighed.

(3) "Not according to a count, nor from that which has
been counted."

C. They said to him, "$M^c\check{s}h$ w- We were gathering figs
behind your father, and he said to us, 'Count them.'"

D. Said R. Simeon b. Eleazar, "$M^c\check{s}h$ b- A certain old
man in ^{c}Ardascus[87] would weigh his basket when it was full
and then weigh it again when it was empty [in order to ascertain the exact weight of his produce], and R. Meir would
praise him."

E. One who separates the heave-offering of a basket [of
producd] and [afterwards] produce is discovered [hidden] in
the sides, lo, the heave-offering of this [produce] has [also]
been separated (*'lw trwmwt*),

F. since it was his intention to separate heave-offering for all [that was in the basket].

T. 3:4 (A: y. Ter. 1:7)

According to T., the rule of M. 1:7A-B is under debate in
Ushan times. It is attributed to Judah, T. 3:4A.[88] Yose disputes, holding that heave-offering must be separated wholly by
estimation. C and D offer legal precedents which support
M. 1:7A-B as against Yose. The named sages are clearly in favor
of having heave-offering separated from produce the quantity of
which previously has been ascertained.[89]

E turns to a separate issue, redacted here only because it
refers to a basket. The individual separates heave-offering from
a basket of produce which contains pieces of fruit of which he is
not aware. The individual's purpose, however, is to separate
heave-offering for all of the produce, and therefore his intention
is effective even over the fruit of which he is not specifically
cognizant (HD).[90]

    A.   [If] there were figs or pomegranates [lying in a
pile] before him, they do not require him to sit and calcu-
late (V, E, ed. princ. read $m\check{s}^c r$; other printings: $m^c\acute{s}r$)
[the difference in size] between the small and large [pieces
of fruit] (*byn bdqh byn bgsh*).

    B.   Rather, he separates heave-offering [for all of the
produce at once,] as is his way [*viz.*, according to the
quantity he normally separates; see M. 4:3], by [separating
produce of] average size (*bbynwny*).

T. 3:5

A householder who counts his produce in order to separate
heave-offering by an estimation of number need not distinguish
among variously sized pieces of fruit (A). By using medium sized
pieces of fruit as heave-offering (B), he compensates for the
presence of both larger and smaller produce.[91]

    A.   One who separates the heave-offering [required] of
the [produce on the] threshing floor must direct his intention
(*ykwyn 't lbw*) towards that [edible produce] which is in the
(1) chaff, and upon that which is in the (2) straw, and
towards that which is on the sides [of the threshing floor]
(E, GRA delete: and towards that which is on the (4) threshing floor [itself]).

    B.   One who separates the heave-offering [required] of
the [wine in the] tank (*bwr*; ed. princ.: *gt*) must direct his
intention towards that which is in the (1) seeds (*hrṣnym*) and
towards that which is in the (2) pomace.

    C.   One who separates the heave-offering [required of
the [oil in the] vat (*gt*; ed. princ.: *bwr*)[92] must direct his
intention towards that which is in the peels.

    D.   And if he did not direct his intention [towards
these things]--

    E.   it is a condition imposed by the court that he [in
all events] will have separated heave-offering for all [of
the produce].

T. 3:6

T. is autonomous of M., presenting three closely formulated
rules (A, B, C) all of which are glossed by D-E. The point in
each case is that when an individual separates heave-offering, he
must focus his intention upon all of his produce, even that which
normally is considered refuse. In this way, he insures that
heave-offering is separated on behalf of all that is edible. D-F
states that, as at T. 3:4E-F, even if he fails in this regard,
his separation of heave-offering is effective for all of the
produce.

A.   R. Yose (so E, Serilio; HD reads: Judah) says, "All
[of the wine in] a wine-press room (E: *byt hgtwt*; see
Jastrow, p. 1686) constitutes a single batch (*tpysh*) [and
therefore heave-offering may be separated from discrete
quantities of wine within the room]."

B.   How so?

C.   [If there was] one press for two tanks, two presses
for one tank, two presses for two tanks--

D.   when [the wine in] all of them constitutes a single
batch, they separate heave-offering and remove tithes from
[the wine in] one [tank] for [the wine in] another [tank].

E.   [If] one of them [i.e., one of the tanks] became
unclean, he separates heave-offering from the clean [wine]
which is in it [i.e., which is in the wine-press room] for
the unclean [wine] which is in it.

F.   [If] all [of the wine] does not constitute a single
batch, they do not separate heave-offering or remove tithes
from [the wine in] one [tank] for [the wine in] another [tank].

G.   [If] one of them [i.e., one of the tanks] became
unclean, he may not separate heave-offering or remove tithes
from the clean [wine] which is in it [i.e., in the wine-
press room] for the unclean [wine] which is in it.

H.   And so would R. Judah say, "All [of the oil in] an
olive-press room constitutes a single batch (E: *tpysh 'ht*;
V: *qwrh 'ht*)."

I.   How so?

J.   [If there was] a single beam [used for pressing]
for two tanks, two beams for one tank, two beams for two
tanks--

K.   when all [of the oil] constitutes a single batch,
they separate heave-offering and remove tithes from [the oil
in] one [tank] for [the oil in] another [tank].

L. [If] one of them [i.e., one of the tanks] became
unclean, he separates heave-offering from the clean [oil]
which is in it [i.e., in the olive-press room] for the unclean [oil] which is in it.

M. [If] all [of the oil] does not constitute a single
batch, they do not separate heave-offering or remove tithes
from [the oil in] one [tank] for [the oil in] another [tank].

N. [If] one of them [i.e., one of the tanks] became
unclean, he may not separate heave-offering from the clean
[oil] which is in it [i.e., in the olive-press room] for the
unclean [oil] which is in it.

T. 3:7 (A: y. Ter. 2:1)

T. complements M. 1:5's discussion of valid and invalid
methods of separating heave-offering. Its two units, A-G and
H-N, are formally identical. They differ only in that A-G refers
to a wine-press and its apparatus, and H-N to an olive-press.
The point in each case is that produce may not be separated from
one batch of produce as heave-offering for a different batch, unless both batches are contained in a single, circumscribed area
(see M. Bik 2:5). A and H state that a wine- or oil-press room
always constitutes such an area. The press-room therefore imputes
the status of a single batch upon all of the tanks of wine or oil
contained within it. C-G and J-N now take away what A and H have
granted. They hold that enclosure within a single press-room does
not necessarily meld discrete vats of wine or oil in a single
batch.[93] In some cases, possibly those in which the press-room
itself is divided into distinct parts, heave-offering may not be
separated from one tank on behalf of all of the tanks. In these
cases it must be separated individually from each tank. As regards E+G and L+N, see M. 2:1-2. Heave-offering is not ordinarily
separated from clean produce for that which is unclean, or *vice
versa*. As M. 1:1B-C states, this is permitted in the case of a
single batch of produce.

A. [If] he was gathering bunches of greens (ed. princ.:
'gdy yrq; V: *gpy yrq*) and placing them in a garden, he
separates heave-offering from one [bunch] for [the produce
contained in] all [of them].

B. [If] he placed a different kind (*myn 'ḥr*; see
Lieberman, TK, I, p. 326) [of greens] among them, he separates heave-offering from each [bunch] individually.

C. [If] he placed many [different] kinds in a vessel--

D.   [if there was] cabbage on top and cabbage on the
bottom and a different kind [of produce] in the middle,

E.   he may not separate heave-offering from that which
is on top (E, ed. princ.: $h^c lywn$; V reads $h^c lyh$) for that
which is on the bottom, unless he [first] brought them together.

T. 3:8 (C-E: y. Ter. 1:1)

F.   [If there were] five heaps [of produce] on a threshing floor, he separates heave-offering from one [of them] for
[the produce contained in] all [of them].

G.   Said R. Judah, "When [is this the case]?

"When most of [the produce of] the threshing floor ($^c yqr$
$hgwrn$) is still present [on the threshing floor].

"[If] most of [the produce of] the threshing floor is
not present, he separates heave-offering from each [heap]
individually."

T. 3:9

H.   One who places his produce inside of his house,

I.   even though it is scattered about,

J.   separates heave-offering from one [amount of pro-
duce] for all [of the produce].

K.   [If there were] two bins in one attic, he separates
heave-offering from each one individually [Maimonides,
Heave-offering 3:18, GRA, HY, MB: he separates heave-
offering from the one (bin) for (the produce in) both].

L.   (1) Bags of produce, and (2) circles of pressed figs,
and (3) jugs of dried figs--

[if they are] all in one area ($hqph$), he separates
heave-offering and removes tithes from [the produce in] one
[individual container] for [the produce in] another.

T. 3:10

T. 3:8-10 carry forward the topic of T. 3:7, exploring
several cases in which separate bunches, heaps or containers of
produce may or may not be deemed to comprise single batches for
purposes of separating heave-offering. A-E presents a single
formal unit, consisting of two cases, A+B and C-E. In the first,
an individual places in the open produce he has picked. As long
as only one type of produce is in the area, all of the produce is
held to comprise a single batch. This being the case, heave-
offering is separated from one bunch of produce for all of the
produce. As soon as a different kind of produce is placed
alongside the other bunches, the produce no longer comprises a

single homogeneous batch, for heave-offering may not be separated
from produce of one kind on behalf of produce of a different kind
(M. 2:4-6). The individual now must separate heave-offering
separately from each bunch. The case at C-E is different, in that
the vessel itself acts to unify into a single body of produce that
which it contains. As long as all of the produce of a single kind
is together within the basket, heave-offering may be separated
from it, as from a single batch of produce. The fact that there
are other kinds of produce in the same basket is of no concern.
Like the basket, the threshing floor (F) acts for purposes of
separating heave-offering to conglomerate into a single batch all
of the produce piled on it. According to Judah (G), this is the
case only at the beginning of the threshing, when all of the
produce of the harvest is present. Later, when most of the produce has been removed from the threshing floor and the rest has
been divided into distinct piles, the threshing floor does not
have this same effect. Like the basket (C) and the threshing
floor (F), a house melds into a single batch the produce scattered
in it (H-J). K states that an attic does not have the effect of
combining into a single batch produce contained in two separate
bins. Unable to explain the reason for the difference in law between a house and an attic, the commentators cited "correct" T.
to read that the attic does have that effect. The rule of L is no
different from those rules which precede.

> A. As of when may they separate the heave-offering
> [required] of [the produce on] the threshing floor?
>
> B. From the time that the fork [used for sifting the
> grain] is taken away.
>
> C. [If] he sifted some [of the produce], he separates
> heave-offering from that [portion] which has been sifted for
> that which has not [yet] been sifted.
>
> T. 3:11 (y. Ma. 1:6)
>
> D. As of when may they separate the heave-offering of
> the [wine in the] vat?
>
> E. From the time that they have trampled [the grapes]
> warp and woof.
>
> F. As of when may they render it [i.e., the vat] un-
> clean?
>
> G. The House of Shammai say, "After the first tithe has
> been removed."
>
> H. The House of Hillel say, "After second tithe has been
> removed."

I.   Said R. Judah (y. Ter. 3:4: R. Yose), "The law is
according to the words of the House of Shammai, but the
majority behave according to the words of the House of
Hillel."

J.   And sages say, "They take out heave-offering and
tithes (y. Ter. 3:4: heave-offering and heave-offering of
the tithe)and forthwith render the vat unclean."

> T. 3:12 (y. Ter. 3:4; see T. Toh.
> 11:4)

K.   As of when may they separate the heave-offering
[required] of olives?

L.   From the time that they have pressed them ($m\check{s}yt^c nw$).

M.   And R. Simeon says, "From the time that they have
been ground ($m\check{s}yythnw$)."

N.   R. Yose b. R. Judah says, "He brings olives in a
basket and places them in the press ($ltwk$ $hmml$; y. Ter. 3:4
reads: tht $hmml$) and presses them warp and woof [and then
separates heave-offering from them]."

O.   They said to him, "[The law of] grapes is not like
[that of] olives.

P.   "Grapes are soft and let their wine ooze out easily
($nwtqwt$).

"Olives are hard and do not let their oil ooze out
easily."

> T. 3:13 (y. Ter. 3:4; see T. Toh.
> 11:4)

T. is a singleton, marking the conclusion of T.'s unit of
material on the separation of heave-offering from discrete
batches of produce. It sets out to determine the point at which
heave-offering may be separated from produce on the threshing
floor, and from wine and oil in the press. The underlying principle is that heave-offering may not be separated from produce
the production of which is not completed (M. 1:10). Thus, in each
case, T. establishes the earliest point in the processing of the
produce at which its preparation is considered completed. As
regards produce on the threshing floor, this is when the fork used
to sift the produce has been taken away (B).[94] C contradicts
M. 1:10, which states that heave-offering may not be separated
from produce the preparation of which has been completed for produce the preparation of which has not been completed. T. next
turns to the question of when grapes being pressed for wine may

have their heave-offering separated. According to E, a single
trampling is sufficient.[95] G-J brings into play a secondary issue,
that of purity. Since many individuals are found in the vicinity
of the wine vat, it is likely that the wine accidentally will be
made unclean. In order to avoid a situation of doubt in this regard, the vat is purposely made unclean. At issue is the point at
which this may be done. Heave-offering will obviously have first
to be separated. The House of Shammai[96] state that beyond this,
first tithe alone need be separated in cleanness. This is because
heave-offering of the tithe will later be separated from the first
tithe. The House of Shammai thus hold that second tithe may be
separated from unclean produce. Its owner will redeem it and take
the money to Jerusalem, and there purchase clean produce for consumption as second tithe. The House of Hillel disagree, stating
that second tithe must be removed in a state of cleanness. The
opinion of sages (J), as recorded in the several MSS. and editions
of T., is no different from that of the House of Hillel.

While K-L begins by asking about olives, the dispute which
follows is clearly interested in the oil which results from their
processing. The disputing opinions are well balanced, $T^C N$ vs. THN.
The anonymous opinion (L) states that the initial pressing of
olives signifies the completion of the olives' processing.[97]
Simeon (M) chooses a later time. Yose (N) reverts to the schema
established for the separation of heave-offering from wine (D-E).
In intent, his opinion is the same as that of L. O-P disputes,
holding that, for the reason given, a single pressing does not
draw sufficient oil to allow the olives' processing to be deemed
complete.

1:8-9

A. They may not separate oil as heave-offering for
olives which have been crushed (hnktšyn) [but the processing
of which has not yet been completed (Albeck, TYT)],

B. nor wine [as heave-offering] for grapes which have
been trampled [but the processing of which has not yet been
completed].

C. But if he (sic) separated heave-offering [in either
of these fashions]--

D. that which he has separated is [valid] heave-
offering (trwmtw trwmh; seventeen MSS. and editions lack the
word trwmh).

E. But he must separate heave-offering again (yhzwr

wytrwm) [from the wine or oil which the grapes or olives eventually produce (Albeck, Bert)].

F.   The first [produce separated as heave-offering] imposes the status of heave-offering [upon other produce with which it is mixed (*mdm^c t*)], by itself [i.e., even if it falls into other produce apart from the second produce separated as heave-offering; cf., M. 3:1].

G.   And [non-priests who accidentally eat it] are liable to the [added] fifth on its account.

H.   But this is not the case as regards the second [produce separated as heave-offering].

M. 1:8

I.   But (S, Z, T³ lack: *w*) they may separate oil as heave-offering for olives which have been preserved (*hnkbšyn*),

J.   and wine [as heave-offering] for grapes which are being made into raisins (*l^c šwtn ṣmwqyn*).

K.   Lo (*hry*; fifteen MSS. and versions read: *my*), if (*š*) he separated oil as heave-offering for olives intended for eating (*l'kylh*) [i.e., olives the preparation of which has been completed],

L.   or olives [as heave-offering] for olives intended for eating,

M.   or wine [as heave-offering] for grapes intended for eating,

N.   or grapes [as heave-offering] for grapes intended for eating,

O.   and [afterwards] decided [instead] to press them [i.e., any of the produce which he originally intended for consumption as foods],

P.   he need not separate heave-offering [a second time].

M. 1:9 (y. Ter. 1:8)

The processing of olives or grapes is not considered complete until they have been pressed or crushed several times (see T. 3:12-13). Since, as we recall, heave-offering may not be separated from produce the preparation of which has been completed for produce the preparation of which has not been completed, wine or oil may not be separated as heave-offering for olives or grapes which have undergone only an initial pressing (A-B). Heave-offering separated from produce the processing of which is not completed for produce the preparation of which is completed is however valid *post facto* (M. 1:10). Thus, heave-offering

separated in either of the ways described at A-B is valid (C-D).
E concludes the declarative sentence begun at C-D with a somewhat
unexpected qualification of that rule. E's point is that in his
first separation of heave-offering, the individual will have set
aside as heave-offering wine or oil sufficient only for the
quantity of wine or oil which initially exuded from the grapes or
olives. In order to ensure that the priest receives the required
percentage of all of the produce, E therefore rules that the householder must separate heave-offering a second time, when he has
finished pressing the grapes or olives.[98] Only when he has separated heave-offering for all of the produce has he fulfilled his
obligation. F-H is a secondary expansion of E. It distinguishes
between the status of the two quantities of produce which the individual will have separated as heave-offering. It holds that by
his first actions, the householder indeed separated all of the
heave-offering required of his produce. This heave-offering is
subject to the stringencies normally accorded a priestly gift. If
it is mixed with unconsecrated produce in a ratio of more than one
part to one hundred, it imposes the status of heave-offering upon
that produce (see M. 4:7).[99] The second stringency is given at D.
As Lev. 22:10-14 states,[100] a non-priest who eats a holy thing
must repay its value and an additional fifth (see M. 6:1). The
second quantity of produce, H, was taken from food from which
heave-offering already was separated. It therefore does not have
the status of consecrated heave-offering. While it is given to a
priest as part of his share, it does not impose the status of
heave-offering upon other produce with which it is mixed, and a
non-priest who eats it is not required to pay the added fifth of
its value paid by one who unintentionally eats a holy thing.

I-J continues A-B's thought. Since neither olives which are
being preserved (I), nor grapes which are being made into raisins
(J) require further processing, heave-offering may be separated
for these things from oil and wine. K-P concludes the unit with
the usual ambiguous case. An individual has separated heave-
offering for either preserved olives or for grapes intended for
eating. Now he decides to press these things for oil or wine,
that is, to continue their processing. At issue is whether or not
his changed intention alters the grapes' or olives' liability to
the separation of heave-offering. P rules that his original intention is probative. Since he separated heave-offering validly
de jure, unlike at A-E, he need not separate heave-offering a
second time.

A.   *They do not separate oil as heave-offering for olives*
which have been crushed [but the processing of which has not
yet been completed],

B.   *nor wine [as heave-offering] for grapes which have*
been trampled [but the processing of which has not yet been
completed].

C.   *[But] if he separated heave-offering [in either of*
these fashions]--

D.   *that which he has separated is [valid] heave-*
offering.

E.   *But he must separate heave-offering again.*

F.   *The first [produce separated as heave-offering]*
imposes the status of heave-offering [upon other produce with
which it is mixed], by itself.

G.   *And [non-priests who unintentionally eat it] are*
liable to the [added] fifth on its account.

H.   *But this is not the case as regards the second*
[produce separated as heave-offering] [= M. 1:8A-H].

I.   And he must remove from it (E: *mhm;* V: *^{c}lyhn*)
[i.e., from the second produce separated as heave-offering]
tithes (so E; V reads: *trwmwt;* ed. princ. reads: *trwmh;*
Sens, HY read: *trwmt m^{c}śr*).

J.   R. Yose says, "The House of Shammai say, 'They may
separate heave-offering [in the ways decribed at A-B].'

K.   "And the House of Hillel say, 'They may not separate
heave-offering [in either of those ways].'

L.   "[But] they agree that if he separated heave-offering [in either of these fashions], that he must separate
heave-offering a second time."

M.   One who separates olives as heave-offering for
olives which are going to be crushed,

N.   or grapes [as heave-offering] for grapes which are
going to be trampled--

O.   that which he has separated is [valid] heave-
offering,

P.   but he must separate heave-offering again [when the
processing of the grapes or olives is completed].

Q.   The first [produce separated as heave-offering] imposes the status of heave-offering [upon other produce with
which it is mixed].

R. The second [produce separated as heave-offering] does not impose the status of heave-offering [upon other produce with which it is mixed].

S. The first [produce separated as heave-offering]-- [non-priests who eat it accidentally] are liable to the [added] fifth on its account.

T. The second [produce separated as heave-offering]-- [non-priests who eat it accidentally] are not liable to the [added] fifth on its account.

U. And he must designate it [heave-offering, by making an oral proclamation].

V. [If] he went and made the original olives [i.e., the ones that he had separated as heave-offering (MB, HY, PM)] into oil,

W. or the original grapes [i.e., the ones that he had separated as heave-offering] into wine--

X. that which he has separated is [valid] heave-offering,

Y. and he does not have to separate heave-offering a second time.

T. 3:14 (J-L: y. Ter. 1:8; M-P: y. Ter. 1:9)

T.'s several units cite and expand M. 1:8, drawing out the implications of M.'s rules and adding correlary material. As M. 1:8 stated, first, heave-offering taken from produce from which heave-offering already has been separated does not have the status of true heave-offering (H). For this reason, tithes must be separated from that heave-offering, just as from all untithed, unconsecrated produce (I).[101] According to Yose, J-K, the rule of M. 1:8A-B follows the opinion of the House of Hillel. The Shammaites, to the contrary, hold that oil or wine may be separated as heave-offering for olives which have been crushed or from grapes which have been pressed. The Shammaites thus should further reject the rule of M. 1:10, which states that heave-offering may not be separated from produce the processing of which has been completed for produce the preparation of which has not been completed.[102] According to L, both of the Houses agree to the rule of E. Yet just as the anonymous rule of M. 1:8A-B is represented as following the Hillelite position, so this lemma is consistent only with the Hillelite point of view. The House of Hillel hold that the individual's separation of heave-offering was

not valid *de jure*. It is not at all surprising, therefore, that
they should require the individual to separate heave-offering a
second time. The Shammaites, on the other hand, hold that the
individual separated heave-offering validly from the start. This
being the case, they should have no reason to require that he
separate heave-offering a second time. The fact that the Shammaites are made to concede to the Hillelite view indicates that
the unit derives from pro-Hillelite sources.

M-P makes the same point as M. 1:9J-P, that the householder's
intention at the time he separates heave-offering is probative.
Unlike in M.'s case, the householder here intends already at the
time he separates heave-offering to continue the processing of the
produce. His designation of heave-offering, therefore, is not
valid *de jure*, and he must separate heave-offering a second time,
once he completes the processing (see y. Ter. 1:9, followed by MB
and Lieberman). The rules of Q-T are the same as those at
M. 1:8F-H. U holds that since the second heave-offering is not
true heave-offering, the individual who separates it must designate it by making an oral proclamation. Y-Z notes that if the
householder himself presses the olives or grapes he separated as
heave-offering, they retain their consecrated status. Further,
since he now will give the priest produce the processing of which
is completed, he need not separate heave-offering a second time
(HY, MB).[103]

A. "*One who separates olive-oil* (so E, ed. princ., HD,
HY, Lieberman; V reads: olives) *as heave-offering for olives
intended to be eaten* [= M. 1:9K],

B. "lo, this one separates as heave-offering [a quantity of oil proper] for the [amount of] oil the olives are
fit to produce"--the words of Rabbi.

C. Rabban Simeon b. Gamaliel says, "They separate as
heave-offering [a quantity of oil proper] for the edible
produce which is in them, but not for the pits."

D. And they agree that in the case of hard olives
(*qwlpsyn*) [which are not fit to be pressed (HD)] that they
separate heave-offering for the edible produce which is in
them, but not for the pits.

T. 3:15 (y. Ter. 1:9)

T. explores an ambiguity in the rule of M. 1:9K, cited here
at A. The problem is how the householder is to determine the
amount of oil required as heave-offering for his olives. Rabbi,

B, and Simeon, C, give the two logical possibilities. Since the
heave-offering is to be given in oil, Rabbi, first, wants the
householder to treat the produce for which it is given as if it
too were oil. He does this by calculating the quantity of oil the
olives are capable of producing. Simeon b. Gamaliel, to the contrary, takes into account the intended use of the olives. They
will be eaten, and therefore the householder must separate heave-
offering from them in accordance with the quantity of food they
contain. Since the pits are not edible, he subtracts their
volume from the total. The case of hard olives, which yield no
oil, is problematic for Rabbi. The individual who has such olives
cannot separate heave-offering for them by the method suggested at
B. For this reason, in the case of hard olives, Rabbi must concede to Simeon's point of view and so reject his own theory.

    A.   One who separates the heave-offering [required] of
grapes (ed. princ., HY, Sens and Rosh to M. 1:10 lack:
"[which are being brought] to the market place," found in V)
which he is going to make into raisins,

    B.   figs, which he is going to make dried figs (grwgrwt),

    C.   pomegranates, which he is going to make split and
dried pomegranates (prd),

    D.   [that which he has separated is valid] heave-
offering,

    E.   and he does not need to separate heave-offering a
second time [after he completes the preparation of the
produce].

    F.   R. Eliezer says, "The House of Shammai[104] say, 'He
does not need to separate heave-offering a second time.'

    G.   "And the House of Hillel say, 'He must separate
heave-offering a second time.'

    H.   "Said the House of Hillel to the House of Shammai,
'Lo, it [i.e., Scripture] says [And your offering shall be
reckoned to you as though it were the grain of the threshing
floor and] as the fulness of the wine press (Num. 18:27).
This one has not separated heave-offering from the wine
press.'

    I.   "Said to them the House of Shammai, 'Lo, it [i.e.,
Scripture] says All the tithe [of the land, whether of the
seed of the land or of the fruit of the trees is the Lord's;
it is holy to the Lord] (Lev. 27:30). If you say that he
needs to separate heave-offering a second time, this one

still has not carried out *it is holy to the Lord.'"*
                    T. 3:16

T. supplements M. with yet another example in which heave-
offering is separated from produce the processing of which is not
completed. A-E contradicts M. 1:8A-E and T. 3:14M-P. We should
expect that the individual will have to separate heave-offering a
second time, after he completes the processing of his produce.
Eliezer, F-G, has the Houses dispute this very issue.[105] The view
of A-E is shown to be the opinion of the House of Shammai. As we
might expect, the Hillelites disagree and are consistent both with
M. 1:8A-E and T. 3:14M-P. They hold that the individual must
separate heave-offering again, when he finishes processing the
produce. In the debate which follows, H-I, the Houses argue from
Scripture about the requirements of the proper separation of
heave-offering. According to the House of Hillel, the householder
here has not yet separated heave-offering *from the wine press*,
that is, from produce the processing of which has been completed
(HY). Therefore he has not fulfilled his obligation and must
separate heave-offering again. In response, the House of Shammai
takes note of the statement in Leviticus that *all tithe is holy to
the Lord*. Their point seems to be that since *all tithe is holy to
the Lord*, the individual's first separation of heave-offering was
valid, and he need not separate heave-offering a second time. Yet,
since both of the Houses agree that the original separation of
heave-offering was valid, the Shammaite's statment *this one still
has not carried out it is holy to the Lord* does not seem to be the
point. I find no satisfactory way to interpret it.[106]

                    1:10

    A. They may not separate heave-offering

    B. from (1) produce (*dbr*) the preparation [for con-
sumption] of which is completed for produce the preparation
of which is not completed;

    C. nor from (2) produce the preparation of which is not
completed for produce the preparation of which is completed;

    D. (O^2, G^5, M, Z, T^3 lack:) nor from (3) produce the
preparation of which is not completed for produce the preparation of which is not completed.

    E. But if he separated heave-offering [in any of these
ways]--

    F. that which he has separated is [valid] heave-offering.
                M. 1:10 (y. Ter. 1:2)

The central notion of this tripartite construction is that of
M. 1:5E-F. Heave-offering may not be separated from produce which
is not liable to the separation of heave-offering. Produce the
processing of which is not completed is not deemed food and therefore is not liable to the separation of heave-offering or tithes
(M. Ma. 1:1). The present laws follow from this fact. As E-F
states, however, heave-offering separated from such produce is
deemed valid *post facto*. This is because the produce ultimately
will be made liable, when it is ready to be eaten. Prior to that
point it has an ambiguous status. While heave-offering should not
be separated from it, A-D, if it is, E-F, that heave-offering is
deemed valid.

 A. They separate heave-offering from [the produce in] a
heap (*^{c}rymh*; E: *hmws*) on behalf of [the produce in] a pile
(*kry*);

 B. but not from [the produce in] a pile for [the produce in] a heap.

T. 3:17

T. is autonomous of M, for the preparation both of produce in
a heap and in a pile is considered complete. The produce in a
pile, however, has had a longer time to dry out and therefore is
of higher quality (MB, HY, Lieberman). Since heave-offering
should be separated from produce of better quality for produce of
worse quality (M. 2:4), heave-offering may be separated from the
produce in the heap for the produce in the pile (A), but not *vice
versa* (B).

 A. One who brings kernels of grain into his house in
order to make them parched kernels of grain (*mlylwt*), lo,
this one separates [unparched] kernels of grain as heave-
offering [for all of the produce].

 B. A Levite who was assigned [as first tithe] (1)
kernels of grain, and plans to thresh them (*l^{c}swtn gwrn*),
(2) grapes, and plans to press them for wine, (3) olives, and
plans to press them for oil--

 C. just as (*škšm š-*)[107] the first heave-offering [i.e.,
the heave-offering which the householder separates from his
produce] is derived from the threshing floor and from the
wine press,

 D. so heave-offering of the tithe [which the Levite
separates must be taken] from the threshing floor and from

the wine press.

T. 3:18a (C-D: see b. Bes 13a-b)

T.'s two separate parts, A and B+C-D, ask of the applica-
bility of M. 1:10's rule to cases involving the processing of
specific kinds of food. According to A, parching is not an intrinsic step in the preparation for consumption of kernels of
grain. Even unparched, the kernels are ready to be eaten and so
are liable to the separation of heave-offering. The householder
therefore may separate unparched kernels as heave-offering for
parched ones.

B asks the same question regarding the threshing of grain
and the making of wine and oil from grapes and olives. It holds
that these are intrinsic steps in the processing of these foods.
A Levite who receives grapes, olives or kernels of grain as first
tithe and who plans to continue their preparation in any of these
ways therefore may not separate heave-offering of the tithe until
he has carried out these steps in processing. This is because, as
C-D explains, the rules for the separation of heave-offering of
the tithe are like those for the separation of heave-offering.

TERUMOT CHAPTER TWO

The chapter's two sections, M. 2:1-3 and M. 2:4-6, detail
rules governing the designation of produce found in one batch as
heave-offering on behalf of produce located in a different batch.
This is to say that M. does not expect the householder to separate heave-offering individually from each discrete quantity of
produce in his possession. Within certain limitations he may,
rather, use a single batch of produce as a source for the heave-
offering required of all of his produce. These limitations are
articulated at M. 2:4A-B, F-G+H, and are repeated as a "general
principle" at M. 2:6Q+R-T. They are: 1) heave-offering may not
separated from one genus of produce on behalf of produce of a
different genus, e.g., from olives for grapes; and 2) if the householder owns different species within the same genus of produce,
heave-offering should be separated from the species which is of
higher quality. These statements, found at M. 2:4-6, are
prefaced, at M. 2:1-3, with essentially derivative materials
dealing with the separation of heave-offering from clean produce
on behalf of unclean produce and *vice versa*. By placing these
secondary materials first, the redactor is able to leave
M. 2:6Q-T's well articulated general principle as a fitting conclusion to this chapter and to M.'s first larger thematic unit.
Let us now examine the significance of the two central notions of
this chapter.

The rule that heave-offering may not be separated from produce of one genus on behalf of another is an expression of M.'s
insistence that distinct kinds of produce be kept apart from one
another. In separating heave-offering, man may not violate the
taxonomic categories established by God at the time of creation.
Even *post facto*, heave-offering separated from produce of one
genus on behalf of produce of a different genus is not valid.
Both the produce for which heave-offering was separated and that
which was designated heave-offering retain the status of untithed,
unconsecrated food.

The rule that heave-offering is separated from the choicest
of the individual's produce is first expressed by Judah, M. 2:4H.
This view prevails at M. 2:4K-L and M. 2:5-6, in opposition to the
anonymous opinion of M. 2:4F-G. That rule distinguishes between
cases in which produce separated as heave-offering will immediately be given to a priest, and those in which it will be some time

before the priest will receive his portion. The claim is that
only in the former case must heave-offering be separated from
produce of the highest quality. If, however, it will be some time
before the heave-offering will be given to the priest, it should
be separated from whichever produce is not likely to spoil. This
ensures that the priest will be able to eat his offering. Since
it is clear from Judah's opinion that he does not share this concern, it follows that before us are two different notions of the
obligation to separate heave-offering. Judah's concern seems to
be that the individual designate as heave-offering that portion
of the produce which is most susceptible to sanctification. This
is the part of the produce which is of the highest quality. Without regard to the priest, therefore, the householder separates
heave-offering from the best of his produce. The anonymous
opinion, on the other hand, regards consumption of heave-offering
by the priest as an integral facet of the valid separation of
heave-offering. While this opinion agrees that if possible the
priest should be given quality produce,[1] it holds that this is
secondary to the more important consideration of the priest's
receiving heave-offering which he will, in fact, be able to eat.

As in Chapter One, M. supplies few attributions. While
Eliezer (b. Hyrcanus)[2] (M. 2:1J) attests to Yavneh the law of the
separation of clean produce as heave-offering for unclean produce,
it is clear that this issue, as well as the others in Chapter Two,
were still under debate in Ushan times. As I have noted, for instance, the rule regarding the separation of heave-offering from
produce of better quality on behalf of produce of worse quality
is attributed to Judah (M. 2:4H). T. adds further evidence that
this chapter's issues were still under debate at Usha. Specific
attributions are to 'Ila'i (in dispute with sages, T. 3:18H-L),
and Nehemiah (T. 3:19E), who disputes the rules of M. 2:2K-L.
While Isaac (T. 2:5) cites a Houses dispute on an issue secondary
to the separation of heave-offering from different species of a
single genus of produce, this same issue is raised by Simeon b.
Gamaliel (and Ishmael), T. 4:1b-2, and by Judah and Simeon b.
Gamaliel, T. 4:3-4. It therefore appears that while the major
issues under discussion here may date back to Eliezer, it is unlikely that they originate with the Houses. In all events the
bulk of the law was still being worked out at Usha.

2:1-3

A. They may not separate heave-offering from that
[produce] which is clean for that which is unclean.

B. But if they separated heave-offering [in that man-
ner], that which they have separated is [valid] heave-
offering.

C. However, (O^1, B, G^1, G^3, G^4, G^5, G^7, Ca, C, Pa, L,
M, O^2, S, P, Z, K, Sa read *b'mt*; printed edition: *b'mt 'mrw*):

D. [as regards] a circle of pressed figs, a portion of
which became unclean--

E. he separates heave-offering from the clean [produce]
which is in it for the unclean [produce] which is in it;

F. and so [in the case of] a bunch of greens;

G. and so [in the case of] a heap [of produce].

H. [If] there were two circles [of pressed figs], two
bunches [of greens], two heaps [of produce], one of which was
unclean and one of which was clean--

I. he may not separate heave-offering from one for the
other.

J. R. Eliezer says, "They separate heave-offering from
that which is clean for that which is unclean."

M. 2:1 (See M. Hal. 1:9, T. Bik.
1:6; C-D: see T. T.Y. 2:12)

K. They do not separate heave-offering from that
[produce] which is unclean for that which is clean.

L. And if he separated heave-offering   [in that
manner]--

M. [if he did it] unintentionally, that which he has
separated is [valid] heave-offering;

N. [but if he did it] intentionally, he has not done
anything (*l' ^{c}śh klwm*).

O. And so [in the case of] a Levite (*bn lwy*) who had
[unclean (TYY, MR, Albeck) first] tithe from which heave-
offering [of the tithe] had not been separated. [If he] was
removing from it [heave-offering of the tithe for other clean
first tithe which he possessed (TYY, MR, Albeck)] (*hyh mpryš
^{c}lyw whwlk*)--

P. [if he did this] unintentionally, that which he has
done is done [and valid];

Q. [but if he did it] intentionally, he has not done
anything.

R. R. Judah says, "If he knew about it [i.e., knew that
the produce was unclean] from the beginning, even though [he
forgot and his later actions were] unintentional, he has not
done anything.

M. 2:2 (K: y. Ter. 6:1; K-M:
b. Pes. 33a; K-N: b. Yeb. 89a,
b. Men. 25b)

I.   S.   One who immerses [unclean] utensils on the Sabbath--
     T.   [if he does so] unintentionally, he may use them;
     U.   [but if he does so] intentionally, he may not use
them.

II. V.   One who tithes [his produce], or who cooks on the
Sabbath--
     W.   [if he does so] unintentionally, he may eat [the
food he has prepared];
     X.   [but if he does so] intentionally, he may not eat
[the food].

III. Y.   One who plants [a tree] on the Sabbath--
     Z.   [if he does so] unintentionally, he may leave it
[to grow] (*yqyym*);
     AA. [but if he does so] intentionally, he must uproot
[it].

     BB. But in the seventh year [of the sabbatical cycle],
whether [he has planted the tree] unintentionally or intentionally, he must uproot it.

M. 2:3 (S-AA: see T. Shab 3:9-11;
S-X: b. Git. 54a; V-X: b. Bes.
17b, b. Shab. 38a, b. Ket. 34a,
y. Shab. 3:1, y. Erub. 4:1; Y-AA:
b. Git. 53b)

The central issue here is the validity of heave-offering
separated from clean produce on behalf of unclean produce and *vice
versa*. The pericope's primary elements are the contrasting rules
M. 2:1A-B and M. 2:2K-N. C-I is interpolated. This is clear
since *however*, C, is formulaic joining language, indicating a case
which does not follow a foregoing general rule.[3] D-I, moreover,
separates Eliezer's opinion, J, from A-B, with which Eliezer disputes. O-Q, likewise, is secondary to K-N. Both of these cases
are glossed by Judah, R. M. 2:3, finally, is substantively autonomous of this tractate, redacted here because its three cases make
the same point as is made by M-N and O-P.

We begin by concentrating on those elements of the pericope
which I have judged to be primary, A-B and K-N. They state that
heave-offering may not be separated from clean produce for that
which is unclean (A), or from unclean produce for that which is

clean (K). As regards the validity of heave-offering separated
in these ways, B holds that *post facto* clean produce separated as
heave-offering for what is unclean is valid. M-N holds that
produce separated as heave-offering from unclean produce on behalf
of clean produce may or may not be valid, depending on the prior
intention of the individual who separated it. As we presently
shall see, with one exception, these laws may fully be understood
on the basis of the general principle offered at M. 2:6S-T for the
separation of heave-offering from one species of produce for
produce of a different species within its same genus. According
to this paradigm a householder who has more than one species
within the same genus should separate heave-offering from the
species which is the choicest. If he separates heave-offering
from produce which is less choice for produce which is more choice,
however, the separation is considered valid. It is clear, first,
that clean produce is comparable to produce of better quality.
When designated heave-offering and given to a priest, such produce
may be eaten by the priest. This is not the case for unclean
produce, which the priest may not use. He must, rather, let it
rot.[4] In light of these facts, A, which states that clean produce
may not be separated as heave-offering for unclean produce is
problematic. It contradicts the paradigmatic rule I just have
outlined and is not, of itself, logical.[5] Contrary to A, we should
expect that a householder who has both clean and unclean produce
should separate heave-offering from that produce which is clean,
thereby providing the priest with heave-offering which he may eat.
This, in fact, is exactly the point which Eliezer makes at J. I
therefore find it impossible to determine either the reason for
the rule of A, or its force within M.'s larger corpus of law.
That A is anomalous is further emphasized by the rule at B, which
gives the ruling which our understanding of the laws of the separation of heave-offering leads us to expect. In stating that *post
facto* a separation of clean produce as heave-offering for unclean
produce is valid, it follows the expected paradigm for the separation of heave-offering from one batch of produce on behalf of
another.

K is consistent with the rule that heave-offering should not
be separated from produce of worse quality for produce of better
quality. *De jure* heave-offering should not be separated from
produce which is unclean for produce which is clean. The status
of such a separation of heave-offering *post facto* is complicated
by the fact that, as I have stated, a priest may not eat unclean

heave-offering. The householder who separates heave-offering from
unclean produce for clean produce does not simply give the priest
produce which is of low quality. Rather, he prevents him from eating his portion altogether. Accordingly M. does not rule, as it
normally does in cases in which heave-offering is separated from
produce of low quality for produce of better quality, that *post
facto* the separation is valid. Instead it holds that each case is
judged in light of the original intention of the person who separated the heave-offering. If he purposely separated heave-offering
in such a way as to prevent the priest from receiving edible produce, his separation is not valid (N).[6] By separating heave-offering from produce which is of no use to the priest, the householder
indicates that he did not perform the separation with proper intention. If, on the other hand, the householder was not aware that
the produce from which he separated heave-offering was unclean, we
cannot argue that he performed the separation with improper intention. In such a case the separation, performed with proper intention, is deemed valid (M).

We may now turn to the interpolation at C-I and to J, Eliezer's
dispute with A. According to C-I the injunction against separating
clean produce as heave-offering for unclean produce applies only in
a case in which the clean and unclean produce are located in different batches. If, however, there is both clean and unclean produce
in a single batch,[7] even *de jure*, clean produce may be separated as
heave-offering for all of the food. This rule takes into account
the fact that heave-offering normally is separated from a single
batch of produce for that same batch. A householder who separates
heave-offering in that way need not divide the produce into individual portions. As long as he separates heave-offering from that
which is clean and which, therefore, may be eaten by a priest, his
separation is considered valid *de jure* (D-G). H-I is obvious. It
restates A, using as examples the specific kinds of produce mentioned at D-G. Eliezer, J, rejects completely the notion that
clean produce may not be separated as heave-offering for unclean
produce. He would hold that clean and unclean produce simply should
be categorized as produce of better and worse quality, and so follows the general principle which states that heave-offering should
be separated from the better of the householder's produce.

The Levite's responsibility in separating heave-offering of
the tithe, O-Q, is the same as that of the householder who separates heave-offering. Like the individual at K-N, the Levite may
not purposely separate unclean first tithe as heave-offering of

the tithe for clean first tithe (Q). If he does so unintentionally,
however, his separation is deemed valid (P). Judah, R, holds that
only if the householder or Levite had no prior knowledge that the
produce was unclean may that produce be considered valid heave-
offering for clean produce. The point is that once the individual
is aware that his produce is unclean, even if he claims to have
forgotten, his subsequent actions in separating heave-offering
from that produce cannot be considered unintentional.

In each of M. 2:3's cases, the householder infringes upon the
restrictions of the Sabbath by performing a forbidden type of
work. As at L-M and P-Q we rule that if he has acted unintentionally, he may derive benefit from his actions.[8] This rule is
qualified only in the case in which the individual simultaneously
breaks the law of the Sabbath and of the seventh year of the
sabbatical cycle. Since in that case the continued growth of the
tree impinges upon the restrictions of the seventh year, the
householder is required to uproot it (BB).

E. *R. Eliezer says, "They separate heave-offering from
that which is clean for that which is unclean"* [= M. 2:1J].

F. Said R. Eliezer, *"M^{c}sh w-* There was a fire on the
threshing floors of Kepar Signa', and [afterwards] they
separated heave-offering from that which was clean for that
which was unclean."

G. They said to him, "Is that evidence?

"Rather, they separated heave-offering from each [type,
clean or unclean] for its own [type] (*trmw mhn ^{c}lyhn*)."

H. R. 'Il^{c}a'i says in the name of R. Eliezer, "They
separate heave-offering from that which is clean for that
which is unclean even in [the case of] wet [produce].

I. "How so?

J. "One who pickled his olives in a state of uncleanness and wished to separate heave-offering from them in
cleanness, brings a funnel the [smaller] opening of which
does not hold an egg's bulk, and rests it in the opening of
the jug [of pickled olives]. (*w-*) He brings [clean] olives
and places them in it [i.e., in the funnel] and separates
heave-offering [from these clean olives for the unclean
olives in the jug].

K. "The result (*nms'*) is that he separates heave-
offering from that which is clean for that which is unclean,
and separates from a single batch (*mn hmwqp*) [as required by
M. 2:1D-E]."

L. They said to him, "Only in the case of wine and oil
is the term *wet* applicable [and since the method you suggest
will not work in the case of either of these things, you have
not offered support for the rule of H]."

T. 3:18b (H-L: y. Hal. 4:1)

Eliezer, F, adduces a precedent in support of this opinion
of M. 2:1J. In the course of a fire at Kepar Signa' most of the
wheat on the threshing floor was made unclean. Eliezer claims
that in the aftermath of that fire clean produce was separated as
heave-offering for the rest of the unclean produce. Sages, G,
reply that this is not what occurred. They state that heave-
offering was separated from unclean produce for unclean produce
and from clean produce for clean produce (MB, HY). Such separations of heave-offering are valid.[9]

'Il^{c}a'i, J-K, understands Eliezer's view to be simply that
heave-offering may be separated from clean produce for unclean
produce within a single batch (= M. 2:1C-I). He offers in
Eliezer's name a means by which produce which is wet, and therefore susceptible to uncleanness, can be made into a single batch
with unclean produce. Under normal circumstances such a procedure
would cause the clean produce itself to be contaminated. Eliezer
suggests using a funnel to avoid this problem. Keeping the point
of contact between the clean and unclean produce to less than an
egg's bulk prevents the transfer of uncleanness,[10] yet creates a
single batch within which clean produce may be separated as heave-
offering for unclean produce. Sages (I) hold that the term *wet*
applies only to liquids, wine and oil. Since the procedure outlined at J will not facilitate the creation of a single batch
from clean and unclean quantities of these things, the example,
they hold, does not support the rule of H.

A. R. Yose says, "One who separates heave-offering from
that which is unclean for that which is clean [see M. 2:2K],
whether [he does so] unintentionally or intentionally--
"that which he has separated is [valid] heave-offering."
B. Said R. Yose, "How is this one different from (add
with E through *tithe* at C:) one who separates heave-offering
from that which is of low quality for that which is of high
quality [a separation which M. 2:6T holds is valid *post
facto*]?"
C. They remove heave-offering of the tithe (so V, E;

ed. princ. reads: *trwmwt wm^c śrwt* (1) from that which is unclean for that which is unclean,

    (2) and from that which is clean for that which is clean,

    (3) and from that which is clean for that which is un-
clean (so y. Ter. 2:1, b. B.Q. 115b, GRA, HY, Lieberman; V,
ed. princ., E read: *mn ḥtm' ^c l hthwr*).

    D. But [they do] not [remove it] from that which is un-
clean for that which is clean (so y. Ter. 2:1, b. B.Q. 115b,
GRA, HY, Lieberman; V, ed. princ., E. read: *mn hthwr ^c l
ḥtm'*) [see M. 2:2O-Q].

    E. R. Nehemia says, "They do not remove [heave-offer-
ing of the tithe] from that which is unclean for that which
is unclean except in the case of produce about which there
is a doubt whether it already was tithed (*'l' bdm'y blbd*)."

    F. They said to him, "Lo, it [i.e., Scripture] says,
[*So shall you also present an offering of the Lord from all
your tithes, which you receive from the people of Israel;*]
*and from it, you shall give the Lord's offering to Aaron the
priest* (Num. 18:28)."

T. 3:19 (y. Ter. 2:1; C-E

b. B.Q. 115b)

T. is composed of two autonomous units, A-B, supplementary to
M. 2:2K-N, and C-D+E-F, which complements M. 2:2/O-Q. Yose, A,
rejects M.'s claim that if a householder intentionally separates
unclean produce as heave-offering for clean produce, his separation is not valid. Like Eliezer, M. 2:1J, he holds that clean
and unclean produce are equivalent to produce of better and worse
quality (B). Just as a separation of produce which is less choice
as heave-offering for better produce is valid, so heave-offering
separated from unclean produce on behalf of clean produce must be
considered valid.

    The point of C-D is straightforward. The Levite may not un-
necessarily give the priest unclean heave-offering of the tithe
(D). This agrees with M. 2:2/O. Nehemiah (E) rejects the notion
of C1, that heave-offering of the tithe normally may be separated
from unclean first tithe on behalf of other unclean first tithe.
He claims that this may be done only in the case of produce which
may already have been tithed. Nehemiah, then, holds that except
in a case in which the priest may already have received his share,
he must be given as heave-offering of the tithe clean, and therefore edible, produce. Sages, F, quote Scripture as evidence

against this view. The offering *to the Lord*--heave-offering of
the tithe--is to be separated *from it*, that is, from any produce
which the Levite comes to possess, even if it is unclean.

A. One who separates heave-offering, and one who removes tithes on the Sabbath, whether [he does so] unintentionally or intentionally--

B. (T. Shab. 3:9 adds:) that which he has separated is
[valid] heave-offering and

C. the tithes he has removed are [valid] tithes.

D. One who immerses [unclean] utensils on the Sabbath,
whether [he does so] unintentionally or intentionally--

E. [the utensils] are counted to him as having been
immersed (*ᶜlw lw ydy tbylh*) [cf., M. 2:3].

T. 4:1a (T. Shab. 3:9-10)

T. supplements the law of M. 2:3, which states that an individual who purposely transgresses the laws of the Sabbath may not
derive benefit from his actions. T. states that however this may
be, his actions in removing the tithes from his produce or in
purifying unclean utensils are effective. The individual's
actions in performing these rituals are viewed as autonomous of
the context in which he performed them. His intentions to perform the rituals alone is central.

2:4-6

A. They may not separate heave-offering from [produce
of one] kind for [produce] which is not of its same kind.

B. And if he separated heave-offering [in this way]--
that which he has separated is not [valid] heave-
offering.

C. All kinds of wheat are [considered] one [species];

D. all kinds of figs, dried figs and [circles of]
pressed figs are [considered] one [species]--

E. so (*w*) he separates heave-offering from one [kind of
wheat, or figs] for another [kind].

F. Wherever (*kl mqwm*) there is a priest [to receive the
heave-offering at once],

[the householder] separates heave-offering from the
choicest [produce] (*hyph*).

G. Wherever there is not a priest [to receive the
heave-offering immediately],

he separates heave-offering from that which keeps
(*hmtqyym*).

H.   R. Judah says, "He always should separate heave-
offering from the choicest [produce]."

> M. 2:4 (A-B: b. Bek. 53b, b. Tem.
> 5a, see M. M.S. 5:11, Sifré
> Bammidbar 120, Sifré Zutta, *Qoraḥ*,
> 18:26; F-H: b. Ber. 39b; F-G:
> b. Men. 55a)

I.   They separate a whole small onion as heave-offering
[for other produce], but not half of a large onion.

J.   R. Judah says, "No, rather, they separate half of a
large onion as heave-offering [for other produce]."

K.   And so would R. Judah say, "They separate onions
from large towns (*mbny hmdynh*) as heave-offering for [onions]
from villages, but not [onions] from villages [as heave-
offering] for [onions] from large towns,

L.   "since they [i.e., the onions grown in large towns
(TYY)] are the food of city-people (*pwlytyqyn*, Jastrow, p.
1140) [and therefore of higher quality]."

> M. 2:5 (I-J: b. Ber. 39b)

M.   And (B, G^1, Ca, Z, Sa, M, O^2, lack *w*) they separate
olives for oil as heave-offering for olives for pickling;

N.   but not olives for pickling [as heave-offering] for
olives for oil.

O.   And [they separate] wine which has not been boiled
[as heave-offering] for that which has been boiled;

P.   but not that which has been boiled [as heave-offer-
ing] for that which has not been boiled.

Q.   This is the general principle:

R.   [in the case of] any [produce] which is a distinct
kind (*kl'ym*) in relation to another [type of produce]--
he may not separate heave-offering from one for the
other, even from the choicer [as heave-offering] for the less
choice.

S.   But [in the case of] any [produce] which is not a
distinct kind in relation to other [produce]--
he separates heave-offering from the choicer for the
less choice, but not from the less choice for the choicer.

T.   But if he separated heave-offering from the less
choice for the choicer--
that which he has separated is [valid] heave-offering.

U.   Except in the case of rye-grass (*znwnyn*) [separated
as heave-offering] for wheat,

    V. since it [i.e., rye-grass] is not a food.

    W. And (O^2, G^3, K, R lack: w) cucumber ($q\check{s}wt$) and squash ($mlppwn$) are a single kind.

    X. R. Judah says, "[They are] two [different] kinds."

                 M. 2:6 (O-P: see M. Ter. 11:1;

                         S-T: see b. Yeb. 89b; W-X, see

                 M. Kil. 1:2, T. Kil. 1:1)

In the pericopae before us, two distinct legal issues are introduced and, at Q+R-T, assimilated into a single statement of law. The first of these issues involves the separation of heave-offering from one genus of produce for another, distinct genus (A-B). The second deals with the separation of heave-offering from produce of one type on behalf of produce of a different type, but within the same genus. This problem is introduced at C-E, and is further articulated in the dispute between Judah and sages, G+H (+I-J). It is Judah's view which dominates at K-L and which is expressed in the general principle at R-T.

Heave-offering may not be separated from produce of one kind on behalf of produce of a distinct kind (A). Doing so would violate the taxonomic categories established by God himself at the time of creation (Gen. 1:11-12). Even *post facto* such a separation of heave-offering is not valid. The distinct kinds of produce do not combine with one another to form a single batch, but remain discrete entities. Produce taken from one kind therefore may not be considered the heave-offering required of a different kind. The householder's actions in separating such heave-offering are null (B).[11]

C-E carries matters forward with the next logical point. Different species within a single genus are not regarded as distinct kinds. Heave-offering therefore may be separated from one species for another. The problem in such a case is to establish which species should be the source of the heave-offering required of both. This issue is addressed in the dispute of F-G+H. On the one hand it seems clear that, if possible, the priest should be given the best of the householder's produce (see Num. 18:12, 29). At the same time, however, we must take into account the possibility that produce separated as heave-offering will spoil before it is given to the priest. In such a case he would lose his share completely. The anonymous rule of A-G therefore distinguishes between cases in which the householder will be able immediately to present a priest his portion, and cases in which it

will be some time before the heave-offering will reach the hands
of a priest. In the former case, heave-offering is separated from
that produce which is of the best quality (F). If, on the other
hand, the heave-offering will not be given to a priest for some
time, it is separated from the produce which is least likely to
spoil (G). Judah, H, rejects the distinction made at F-G. He
holds that heave-offering must always be separated from the best
of the produce, as required by Num. 18:12. The priest's being
able to consume the heave-offering accordingly is not an issue for
Judah.

I-J instantiates the dispute between Judah and G, referring
to a case in which it will be some time before the householder
will give to a priest heave-offering he has separated (TYY, MS).[12]
While large onions are of better quality, if they are cut in half
--to allow the householder to designate as heave-offering the
required quantity of produce--they will spoil quickly. The
anonymous opinion, I, therefore, holds that heave-offering is
separated from small onions which, although of lower quality, are
not liable to spoil. Judah, of course, disagrees. He holds, as
at H, that heave-offering must be separated from the more choice
of the householder's produce. K+L provides a further example of
Judah's view. Onions grown in large towns are of better quality
than onions grown in villages.[13] The individual who possesses
both of these types of produce must therefore separate heave-
offering from the onions grown in large towns. As far as I can
tell, however, neither of these types of produce is less subject
to spoiling than the other. It is clear therefore that while this
case is interesting from Judah's point of view, it stands outside
of the framework of Judah's dispute with the rule of F-G.[14] M-N
and O-P likewise do not know this dispute, but simply exemplify
Judah's opinion. Olives used for oil, and wine which has not been
boiled, are of better quality than olives intended for pickling,
and boiled wine.[15] Heave-offering therefore is separated from the
former for the latter, but not *vice versa*.

R-T now correlates the rule of A-B with Judah's opinion of
H. The only addition it makes to those rules is at T, which
states that if heave-offering is separated from less choice produce for better produce, it is deemed valid heave-offering. This
is because the two types of produce are homogeneous and therefore
combine to form a single batch. V-W+X glosses. Since rye-grass
is not a food, it is not liable to the separation of heave-offering for other produce, even of its same kind (see M. 1:5F). The
issue of W+X is clear.[16]

A. *They do not separate heave-offering from [produce]*
of one kind for [produce] which is not of its same kind
[= M. 2:4A].

B. But they said, *"All kinds of (1) wheat are [con-*
sidered] one [kind] [= M. 2:4C];

C. "all kinds of (2) beans (*'ypwlyn*), (3) walnuts
(*'gwzyn*),[17] (4) almonds (*šqdym*)[18] and (5) pomegranates are
[considered respectively] a single [kind],

D. "[and therefore] they separate heave-offering and
remove tithes from one [type of any of these things] for
another [type] [see M. 2:4E]."

T. 2:4

E. [If] there were [both] black and white figs in his
house,

F. and so two species of wheat--

G. they[19] separate heave-offering and remove tithes
from one for the other.

H. R. Isaac says in the name of R. Eleazar (b. Hul.
136b reads: 'Il^{c}a'i),[20] "The House of Shammai say, 'They
may not separate heave-offering [from one for the other].'

I. "And the House of Hillel say, 'They separate heave-
offering [from one for the other].'"

T. 2:5 (b. Hul. 136b)

A-D cites the rule of M. 2:4A+C+E and adds four further
examples of kinds of produce various species of which are considered homogeneous for purposes of separating heave-offering.
E-G is formally autonomous of what precedes, repeating the rule
that all kinds of wheat (F=M. 2:4C) and different types of figs
(E=M. 2:4D) are considered single kinds. This unit acts as a
superscription for the Houses dispute cited by Isaac, H-I. As is
standard, the anonymously states rules, E-G, agree with the
opinion of the House of Hillel, I.[21]

E. They separate wheat as heave-offering for bread;

F. but not bread [as heave-offering] for wheat, except
according to a calculation [of how much wheat the bread con-
tains].

G. They separate figs as heave-offering for dried figs
according to number;[22]

H. and dried figs [as heave-offering] for figs according to volume.

I.   But [they do] not [separate] figs [as heave-offering
for dried figs according to volume;

J.   nor dried figs [as heave-offering] for figs according to number.

K.   Rabban Simeon b. Gamaliel says, "Baskets of figs
and baskets of dried figs are all [of] equal [status].

L.   "They separate heave-offering and remove tithes
from one for the other [without regard to differences in size
and number]."

T. 4:1b (y. Ter. 2:4; G: b. Men.
54b)

M.   Said R. Ishmael b. R. Yose, "Father would take ten
dried figs from the drying place (mwqsh) [as heave-offering
and tithes] for ninety figs which were in the basket [ready
for consumption]."

T. 4:2 (y. Ter. 2:4, b. Men. 54b)

T. is informed by M. 2:4's statement that heave-offering may
be separated from produce of one type for produce of another type,
as long as all of the produce is of a single species. At issue
here is the method by which a householder who separates heave-
offering in this way assures that the priest will receive the
proper percentage of the produce. Both bread and wheat (E-F) are
a single kind and, therefore, heave-offering may be separated from
one for the other. Yet since bread contains less wheat per volume
than unbaked wheat, a householder who separates bread as heave-
offering for wheat must do so in accordance with the actual quantity of wheat contained in the bread. We do not take into account
the higher value of the bread, or the amount of work the householder invested in its preparation.[23] The problem at H-J is
equivalent. When figs are dried they shrivel and become smaller
than figs which have not been dried. If a householder separates
by count dried figs as heave-offering for other figs (J), the
priest will receive a much smaller volume of produce than would
otherwise be his share. For this reason, a householder who wishes
to separate dried figs as heave-offering for other figs must do so
by giving a percentage of the volume of all of the produce (H).
Conversely, figs which are not dried are separated by number as
heave-offering for dried figs (G), thereby providing the priest
with an enhanced volume of produce. If, in such a case, heave-
offering were separated by volume (I), the priest would receive
fewer pieces of fruit than he would otherwise receive. Simeon,

K-L, rejects the notion that heave-offering must be separated in such fashion that the priest receive the greatest possible amount of produce both in volume and number (HY). Since figs and dried figs are regarded as a single kind, the householder may separate heave-offering from one for the other by whatever method of calculation he prefers.

According to Ishmael, M, his father would separate heave-offering and tithes from dried figs for other figs by counting the produce. This places Yose in opposition to the rule stated at H, and in agreement with Simeon, K-L (HY, MB).

I.   A.   They separate hard olives (*qwlpsyn*) as heave-offering for olives for oil (*zyty šmn*);

      B.   but not olives for oil [as heave-offering] for hard olives.

      C.   R. Judah says, "[They] even [separate] olives for oil [as heave-offering] for hard olives."

II.   D.   They separate wine which has been clarified (*yyn šlwl*) as heave-offering for [wine] which has not been clarified;

      E.   but not [wine] which has not been clarified [as heave-offering] for [wine] which has been clarified.

      F.   R. Judah says, "[He] even [separates wine] which has not been clarified [as heave-offering] for [wine] which has been clarified,

      G.   "provided that he separates [the heave-offering] from that which is the choicest."

                          T. 4:3

III. H.   *They separate wine which has not been boiled as heave-offering for that which has been boiled;*

      I.   *but not that which has been boiled [as heave-offering] for that which has not been boiled* [= M. 2:6/O-P].

      J.   Rabban Simeon b. Gamaliel says, "[They] even [separate wine] which has been boiled [as heave-offering] for that which has not been boiled."

      K.   And so would Rabban Simeon b. Gamaliel say, "Also, (E, ed. princ. lack: *also*),[24] the laws of uncovered [liquids] [see M. 8:4] and of wine used for libations are not applicable in the case of wine which has been boiled (*yyn mbwšl 'yn bw mšwm glwy w'yn bw mšwm yyn nsk*)."

                          T. 4:4 (K: see y. Ter. 8:5,
                          b. A.Z. 3a)

A-B+C and D-E+F-G provide two further disputes illustrating
the positions of Judah, M. 2:4H, and the anonymous opinion of
M. 2:4G. Wine which has been purified of all natural elements and
hard olives keep longer than wine which has not been clarified and
olives which are used to make oil. The anonymous opinion of A-B
and D-E holds that in a case in which heave-offering the householder is going to separate will not be given to a priest for some
time, he should separate it from that produce which keeps, in this
case, from hard olives and wine which has been clarified. Judah
rejects this ruling. His principle is as stated at G. The householder must separate heave-offering from the best of his produce,
regardless of the amount of time that will pass before the heave-
offering will be turned over to a priest.[25]

The case of H-I+J is formally parallel to the two cases just
reviewed, giving us a triplet. Simeon, J, rejects the rule of
M. 2:6/O-P, cited at H-I. He holds that heave-offering may be
separated from produce of lower quality--wine which has been
boiled--for produce which is of better quality--wine which has not
been boiled. Alternatively, we may follow HD and Lieberman, who
interpret Simeon's position in light of K, which is, however,
formally autonomous. According to this view, Simeon holds that
since wine which has been boiled cannot be rendered inedible by
being left uncovered or by coming into contact with a gentile, it
is choicer than wine which has not been boiled and is subject to
these stringencies.[26] This being the case, the householder may
use wine which has been boiled as heave-offering for wine which
has not been boiled.

> A. A [type of] vegetable which normally keeps for one
> day (*šdrkw lhštmr ywm 'ḥd*) [from the time it is picked]--
>   they use it as heave-offering [for other produce]
> (*twrmyn ᶜlyw*)[27] for one day.
>
> B. A [type of] vegetable which normally keeps for two
> days--
>   they use it as heave-offering [for other produce] for
> two days.
>
> C. A [type of] vegetable which normally keeps for three
> days--
>   they use it as heave-offering [for other produce] for
> three days.
>
> D. Chate-melons (*hqšw'yn*),[28] musk-melons (*hdlwᶜyn*),[29]
> endives (*trwqsymwn*)[30] and spinach (*htrdyn*), which normally
> keep for one day--

they use them as heave-offering [for other produce] for
one day.

E. Lettuce (*hhᵃryn*),[31] vetches (*hqršyn*),[32] turnips
(*hlpt*)[33] and cauliflower (*hkrwb*), which normally keep for
two days--

they use them as heave-offering [for other produce] for
two days.

F. Leeks (*hqplwtwt*)[34] and cucumbers (*hmlppwnwt*),[35]
which normally keep for three days--

they use them as heave-offering [for other produce] for
three days.

G. This is the general principle:

H. [in the case of] anything which keeps [for a set
length of time]--

they use it as heave-offering [for other produce for
that same length of time].

I. R. Nehemiah says, "He may not separate heave-offering from strawberries (*twtym*) which he picked in the morning
for strawberries which he picked in the evening."

T. 4:5a

T. continues to supplement M. with rules on the separation
of heave-offering from one batch of produce for another.[36] According to T. produce may be separated as heave-offering for
other produce only during that period of time in which it is at
its freshest and, therefore, best quality. Nehemiah (H) treats
strawberries as a special case. Since they spoil quickly, strawberries picked in the morning may not be used as heave-offering
for strawberries picked in the afternoon, even of that same day.

TERUMOT CHAPTER THREE

The chapter carries forward several topics already familiar
from the tractate's first two chapters. M. 3:1-2 take up the
issue introduced by M. 1:5 and 2:1. M. 3:3-4 similarly develop
M. 1:1D-G. Only at M. 3:5-9 do we have fresh problems, which, together with M. 4:1-5, bring to a close the issues of M.'s first
large thematic unit. While topically diverse, the chapter is
formally unitary. M. 3:1, 5, 6 and 8 all commence h + singular
participle. Only M. 3:3 and 3:9 differ slightly, beginning h +
noun.

M has been clear up to this point that produce may be separated from one batch as heave-offering for produce of a different
batch. M. 1:5 and M. 2:1, however, have stated that such means of
separating heave-offering may not be employed in cases in which
the batches are comprised of produce of different kinds, or, for
instance, if one of the batches is not liable to the separation of
heave-offering. M. 3:1-2 now asks how we adjudicate cases in
which there is a doubt whether or not a separation of heave-
offering from one batch of produce on behalf of another batch
meets these requirements. M. 3:1 rules that in such cases of
doubt, that which has been separated as heave-offering must be
considered valid heave-offering. Since, however, there is a possibility that this heave-offering does not comprise the priestly
share required of the produce at hand, the householder must separate heave-offering a second time. This done, we take into account the fact that both of the quantities of heave-offering which
were separated cannot be the true heave-offering required of the
produce. Therefore neither of these quantities of heave-offering
alone is subject to the stringencies normally accorded heave-
offering (M. 3:1J-3:2/O). If either by itself falls into a batch
of unconsecrated produce, for instance, it does not impose the
status of heave-offering on that produce. This occurs only if
both quantities of heave-offering together fall into unconsecrated
produce.

The chapter's second substantive unit depends on the rule of
M. 1:1D-G, which states that only the owner of a batch of produce
may separate heave-offering from that produce. M. 3:3-4 questions
the implications of this rule for cases of joint ownership of produce. Specifically, Aqiba and sages dispute whether each partner

is to be considered a part-owner in all of the produce--such that
he may separate the heave-offering required of all of the produce
--or whether he has full ownership of a determinate share of the
produce. According to this latter view, each of the partners may
separate the heave-offering required of his share of the produce
alone. Yose (M. 3:4D-E) glosses, bringing into play the consideration of the proper percentage of the produce which should be
separated as heave-offering (see M. 4:3). A redactional gloss at
M. 3:4 introduces the consideration of agency, and with it the
rule that in cases in which their work requires it, laborers may
separate heave-offering on behalf of their employer (M. 3:4N-P).

       M. 3:5 introduces a new topic of discussion, the oral desig-
nation by which a householder localizes within his produce the
agricultural gift--heave-offering, or tithes--which he wishes to
separate. Simeon, sages, Eleazar Hisma' and Eliezer b. Jacob dispute whether in his designation the householder must declare a
specific portion of the batch to be the offering or, alternatively, whether he need simply state that the offering is located
within the produce, as opposed to within some different batch.
Simeon, Eleazar Hisma' and Eliezer b. Jacob are in agreement
against sages that the latter is the case. Thus they hold that
only in the physical separation of the heave-offering from the
batch of produce does a specific portion of the batch take on the
status of a priestly gift. M. 3:6-7 carries forward the issue of
the oral designation. The issue here is the order in which first
fruits, heave-offering, first tithe and second tithe should be
designated and separated. M. 3:8 concludes the unit with special
problems, specifically, cases in which a householder wishes to
separate one offering--e.g., heave-offering--but, in his designation, states that he wishes to separate a different offering--
e.g., first tithe. The point is that unless the householder both
has proper intention and correctly announces that intention, his
actions in separating agricultural offerings are not effective.

       M. 3:9 concludes the chapter, asking who has the ability to
designate and separate agricultural offerings. All parties agree
that non-Israelites have the right to separate from their produce
heave-offering and tithes and to give these things to Levite or
priest. Simeon, however, claims that heave-offering separated by
a gentile does not have the status of a sanctified priestly gift.

       Attributions are for the most part to Ushans. They are as
follows: Aqiba and Yose in M. 3:3; Simeon, Eleazar Hisma and
Eliezer b. Jacob at M. 3:5; Judah and Simeon in M. 3:9. T.

supports the conclusion that the issues before us are still
salient at Usha. Specifically, we have Yose, T. 4:5J, and Ishmael
b. R. Yose, T. 4:6E (both supplement M. 3:1).   T. 4:7 assigns
M. 3:1E-I to Rabbi.   T. 4:9 cites Rabbi and Simeon b. Gamaliel in
dispute over the issue of M. 3:5.   T. 4:11 assigns to Yose a
secondary gloss of the issue of M. 3:8. The issues of M. 3:9 are
disputed at T. 4:12-14 by Simeon b. Gamaliel, Rabbi and Simeon b.
Eleazar.

3:1-2

A.   One who separates a chate-melon[1] as heave-offering
[for other chate-melons] and it is found to be bitter,

B.   [or who separates] a watermelon[2] [as heave-offering
for other watermelons] and it is found to be rotten (srwḥ)--

C.   [that which he has separated is valid] heave-
offering.

D.   But he must separate heave-offering again.

E.   One who separates a keg of wine as heave-offering
[for other wine] and it is found to be vinegar--

F.   if it was known before he separated it as heave-
offering [for the other wine] that it was vinegar,

[that which he has separated is] not [valid] heave-
offering.

G.   (O[1], B, Ca, L, M, O[2], S, P, Z add: But) if it
turned into vinegar after he separated it as heave-offering,

lo, this is [valid] heave-offering.

H.   (O[1], B, Ca, L, O[2], S, Z add: And) if there is a
doubt [as to whether it was vinegar when it was separated as
heave-offering],

[that which he has separated is valid] heave-offering.

I.   But he must separate heave-offering again.

J.   The first [produce separated as heave-offering at
A-D and E+H-I] does not impose the status of heave-offering
[on other unconsecrated produce with which it is mixed] by
itself [i.e., if it alone is mixed with other such produce].

K.   And [non-priests who unintentionally eat it] are not
required to pay back [its value and] the [added] fifth.

L.   And so [is the case regarding] the second [produce
separated as heave-offering].

M. 3:1 (A-C: b. Yeb. 89a, b. Qid.
46b)

M.   [If] one of them [i.e., one of the quantities of

produce separated as heave-offering at A-D or E+H-I] fell
into unconsecrated produce--

it does not impose the status of heave-offering [upon
the mixture].

N.   [If] the second [produce separated as heave-offer-
ing] fell elsewhere [i.e., into a different batch of unconsecrated produce]--

it does not impose the status of heave-offering [upon
the mixture].

O.   [But if] the two [quantities of produce separated as
heave-offering] fell into the same place [i.e., into the same
batch of unconsecrated produce]--

they impose the status of heave-offering [on that pro-
duce] in accordance with [the bulk of] the smaller of the
two [quantities of produce separated as heave-offering].

M. 3:2

M. turns to the disposition of cases of doubt concerning the
validity of a designation of heave-offering. It is uncertain,
A-D and E+H-I, whether or not at the time produce was separated
as heave-offering it was fit to be used as such. The produce is
found to be inedible, A-D, and so not liable to the separation of
heave-offering (see M. 1:5F). In a parallel case, E-I, what was
thought to be wine turns out to be vinegar, which may not be used
as heave-offering for wine (T. 4:7G). The problem is to determine
the validity of such separations of heave-offering in cases in
which it is not known whether the produce actually was ineligible
for use as heave-offering at the time it was so designated. According to C-D and H-I, we take into account both the possibility
that the designation was valid and that it was invalid. The wine
may have turned to vinegar, or the produce become inedible, only
after it was designated heave-offering. The original separation
of heave-offering therefore is deemed to have been valid. The
fact that the produce later will have spoiled does not affect this.
We must however take into account the possibility that the produce
or wine was spoiled from the start, such that the first separation
of heave-offering was not valid. In light of this possibility,
the householder is required to separate heave-offering a second
time (D, I), thereby assuring that his produce is properly prepared for consumption.[3]

In the case of wine, E-I, there is a further possibility.
The householder, or some other individual, may have known the

condition of the wine at the time it was designated heave-offering
on behalf of other wine. If it is known that the wine already had
become vinegar at the time it was designated heave-offering (F),
there is no element of doubt, and the designation is not valid.
If, however, it is clear that it was wine which was separated as
heave-offering for wine, the designation is declared valid, and
there is no need for the householder to separate heave-offering a
second time. The householder has fulfilled his obligation. It is
not his concern that the produce he separated as heave-offering
spoiled.[4]

J-L and M-O (which simply restates J-L) draw out the implications of the fact that neither of the quantities of produce
separated as heave-offering at C-D and H-I may be considered true
heave-offering. As I noted, the status of the first produce
separated as heave-offering is in doubt. Yet since it is possible
that the first heave-offering is valid, the status of the second
produce separated as heave-offering is likewise in doubt. This
being the case, neither of these batches of heave-offering is
subject to the stringencies applicable to a true priestly gift.
If either alone is mixed with unconsecrated produce, it does not
impose the status of heave-offering upon that produce (J, M-N).
We simply assume that it was not true heave-offering in the mixture.[5] Likewise, a non-priest who unintentionally eats either of
these quantities of produce is not required to pay back the added
fifth, normally paid by a commoner who eats a holy thing (Lev.
22:10-14; see M. 1:8-9). The situation is different if both of
the quantities of heave-offering are mixed into a single batch of
unconsecrated produce (O). In such a case it is certain that true
heave-offering has been mixed with unconsecrated produce. Still,
only one of the quantities of produce in fact is true heave-offering, and it is not known which. At issue therefore is the method
by which the householder determines whether or not the mixture
contains sufficient heave-offering to impose a status of sanctity
upon all of the produce (see M. 4:7). According to O, we assume
that the smaller of the quantities of designated produce comprised
the true heave-offering.[6] This rule is lenient, making it likely
that the mixture will contain more than the one hundred parts unconsecrated produce to one part heave-offering needed to neutralize the heave-offering (M. 4:7). Notably, as A-D has made clear,
this same leniency does not apply in cases of doubt about the
actual separation of heave-offering. The central concern here,
then, is that the required heave-offering be removed from the

householder's produce. The ultimate disposition of the priestly
gift is secondary, and therefore subject to less stringent rules.
This is essentially the position of Judah, M. 2:4H.

> J.   And so would R. Yose say,[7] "You find nothing bitter
> in a chate-melon except its inner part (*'yn lk mr bqšwt 'l'*
> *pnymy šbw* [see M. 3:1A].
>
> K.   "Lo this one [i.e., a householder who separated a
> bitter chate-melon as heave-offering for other chate melons]
> adds [other produce] to its outer part [to compensate for the
> bitter inner part] and separates [this additional produce as
> heave-offering for the chate-melons]."

> T. 4:5b (y. Ter. 3:1; b. B.B. 143a)

Yose disagrees with M. 3:1A+C-D, holding that a householder
who has separated a bitter chate-melon as heave-offering for other
chate-melons need not separate heave-offering a second time.
Since only the inner part of the bitter chate-melon is not edible
(A), even a bitter chate-melon has the status of food and may be
considered valid heave-offering for other chate-melons. In order
to make up for the loss the priest will incur by receiving with
his portion produce which is inedible, Yose holds that the householder simply declares an additional quantity of produce to be
heave-offering.[8] In this, Yose is consistent with views cited in
his name at T. 4:2 and, as we shall see, at T. 4:6. In those
pericopae he likewise is concerned that the priest be given his
full share of heave-offering.

> A.   One who separates a keg of wine as heave-offering
> [for other wine] (E, y. Ter. 3:1, Maimonides, *Heave-offering*,
> 5:22: *htwrm hbyt šlyyn*; V: *htwrm 't hbwr*) and it is found
> to have been left uncovered [and is therefore not fit for
> consumption (M. 8:4)],
>
> B.   [or who separates] a watermelon [as heave-offering
> for other watermelons] and it is found to be punctured [with
> the teeth marks of a snake, and is therefore unfit for con-
> sumption (M. 8:6)]--
>
> C.   that which he has separated is [valid] heave-
> offering.
>
> D.   [But] he must separate heave-offering again [cf.,
> M. 3:1A-D].
>
> E.   R. Ishmael b. R. Yose says in the name of his father,
> "They separate wine as heave-offering for vinegar, but they

do not separate vinegar as heave-offering for wine [see
M. 3:lE-I],

F. "(E, ed. princ. lack: *'pylw twrmyn 'yn twrmyn*)[9]

G. "except according to a calculation [of the relative
values of the two types of produce]."

T. 4:6 (A-D: y. Ter. 3:1; E:

y. Kil. 1:1)

The case at A-D is formally and substantively parallel to
that at M. 3:lA-D. Here, as there, it is unclear whether at the
time produce was separated as heave-offering for other produce it
was fit to be used as such. Since the separation may have been
proper, the produce separated as heave-offering is considered
valid heave-offering (C). Yet since the original separation may
not have been valid, the householder is required to separate
heave-offering a second time (D).

According to Ishmael, E-G, his father rejects M. 3:1's
assumption that wine and vinegar are distinct kinds such that
heave-offering may not be separated from one for the other. He
holds that they are a single kind, but that wine is of better
quality. *De jure* wine may therefore be separated as heave-offering for vinegar, but not vinegar for wine (E). At G, Yose departs
from this expected paradigm for the separation of heave-offering
from one batch of produce for another. He holds that even *de jure*
the householder may separate vinegar as heave-offering for wine,
providing that in doing so he is careful to give the priest enough
vinegar to compensate for its low value. As in the preceding
pericope, then, Yose considers the most basic element of the
proper separation of heave-offering to be that the priest receive
a sufficient percentage of the householder's produce.

A. *"One who separates a keg of wine as heave-offering*
[*for other wine*] *and it is found to be vinegar--*

B. *"if it was known before he separated it as heave-
offering that it was vinegar,*

*"[that which he has separated is] not [valid] heave-
offering.*

C. *"But if it turned into vinegar after he separated it
as heave-offering,*

"lo, this is [valid] heave-offering.

*"[And if] there is a doubt [as to whether it was
already vinegar when it was separated as heave-offering],*

"[that which he has separated is valid] heave-offering.

E.   *"But he must separate heave-offering again* [= M. 3:1E-I]*"*--

F.   the words of Rabbi.

G.   For Rabbi says, "Wine and vinegar are two [distinct] kinds."

H.   But sages say, "[They are] one kind."

T. 4:7 (G: y. Ter. 2:5, b. B.B. 84b)

T. attributes M. 3:1E-I to Rabbi, and, at F, offers his reason for holding that a separation of vinegar as heave-offering for wine is not valid. Sages, H, disagree. Like Yose, T. 4:6E-G, they claim that wine and vinegar are a single kind, such that heave-offering may be separated from one for the other. Sages therefore reject the rule of M. 3:1E-I.[10]

A.   [If] it was his intention (*hyh blbw*) to separate wine as heave-offering for wine--

B.   [if] that which [comes up] in his hand is vinegar, that which he has separated is not [valid] heave-offering.

C.   [But if] that which [comes up] in his hand is wine, the heave-offering of the wine has been separated (*hyyn twrm*).[11]

D.   And he must separate heave-offering again for the vinegar.[12]

E.   [If it was his intention to separate vinegar as heave-offering for vinegar][13]--

F.   [if] that which [comes up] in his hand is vinegar, the heave-offering of the vinegar has been separated.

G.   And he must separate heave-offering again for the wine.[14]

H.   [If] he was checking a keg of wine [from time to time] in order to use it as heave-offering for other wine [which came into his possession] and it was found to be vinegar--

I.   for the preceding three days it is certain [that it had already become vinegar];

J.   from this time and back, there is a doubt [as to whether or not the wine had already become vinegar].

K.   But [in the case of] wine from his tank--

L.   they use it as heave-offering [for other produce] for a full forty days [without checking it], on the assumption that it still is wine.

                    T. 4:8 (H-J: y. B.B. 6:1; b. Qid.
                    79a, b. B.B. 96a; K-L: y. Git.
                    3:8; see also M. Git. 3:8)

T.'s rules depend on M. 3:1E-I's understanding that wine and
vinegar are distinct kinds, such that heave-offering may not be
separated from one for the other (=Rabbi, T. 4:7G). In the cases
at A-D and E-G the individual has an assortment of kegs and does
not know which contain wine and which contain vinegar. If he
decides to separate heave-offering for the wine (A), his separation is valid only in the case that he actually selects as
heave-offering a keg of wine (C). If he accidentally picks vinegar instead, his separation is not valid. The vinegar may not be
considered heave-offering for the wine. Further, since his
original intention was to separate heave-offering for wine, we do
not regard the vinegar he separated to comprise the heave-offering
required of the kegs of vinegar. E-G reverses the case. Now the
individual intends to separate heave-offering for vinegar. If he
actually takes vinegar as heave-offering, his separation is valid
(F). He must of course perform an additional separation of heave-
offering for the wine (G).

The individual at H-L has set aside a keg of wine, the contents of which he designates heave-offering for other wine which
comes into his possession. When all of the wine in the keg will
have been designated heave-offering, he will give the whole keg to
a priest. In the meantime he must occasionally examine the wine
in the keg to make sure that it has not turned into vinegar and
become unfit for use as heave-offering for wine. At issue is the
status of separations of heave-offering performed between the time
at which there certainly was wine in the keg and the point at
which the householder finds that the wine has turned to vinegar.
According to I, we assume that for three days prior to the final
examination, the wine already has become vinegar.[15] Produce for
which wine in the keg was used as heave-offering during this time
will have the status of produce from which heave-offering never
has been separated (cf. M. 3:1F). Prior to these three days,
until the point at which it is known that there was wine in the
keg, separations of heave-offering which were performed relying
on the wine in the keg are in a status of doubt (cf. M. 3:1H).
The householder must separate heave-offering a second time to
assure that heave-offering is properly removed from this produce.

Yet since it is possible that the original separation of heave-
offering was valid, that portion of vinegar in the jug which was
declared heave-offering during this time is regarded as valid
heave-offering. L distinguishes between wine which already has
been transferred into kegs and that which is still in the tank.
Since wine in the tank is newer and not likely to spoil (MB), the
householder may assume that it did not turn to vinegar for a full
forty days from the last time he examined it.

3:3-4

A.   Partners who separated heave-offering [from the same
commonly owned produce] one after the other--

B.   R. Aqiba says, "That which was separated by both of
them is [valid] heave-offering."

C.   But sages say, "[Only] that which was separated by
the first is [valid] heave-offering."

D.   R. Yose says, "If the first [partner] separated the
required measure [of heave-offering] ($k\check{s}y^{c}r$) [see M. 4:3],
that which was separated by the second [partner] is not
[valid] heave-offering.

E.   "But if the first [partner] did not separate the
required measure [of heave-offering], that which was separated
by the second [partner] is [also valid] heave-offering."

M. 3:3 (see b. Tem. 13a, y. Ter.
1:1, y. Git. 5:4)

F.   In what [case] does the opinion [of Aqiba, A (Bert,
TYY, Sens, MR)] apply (*bmh dbrym 'mwrym*)?

G.   [To the case] in which neither [of the partners] con-
ferred (*dbr*) [with the other].

H.   But:

I.   [In a case in which one] gave permission to a member
of his household, to his slave, or to his maid-servant to
separate heave-offering--

J.   that which that individual separates is [valid]
heave-offering.

K.   [If he] retracted [the permission]--

L.   if he retracted [it] before [the other individual]
separated heave-offering--
that which [that individual] has separated is not [valid]
heave-offering.

M.   But if he retracted [it] after [the other individual]
separated heave-offering--

that which [that individual] has separated is [valid] heave-offering.

    N. Workers do not [automatically] have permission to separate heave-offering [from the produce with which they are working],

    O. except for those who tread [the grapes or olives in the tank] (*hdrwkwt*),

    P. for they at once impart to the tank [susceptability to] uncleanness [so Albeck].

M. 3:4 (K-M: y. Ter. 1:1; K-L:
b. Qid 59a)

The issue expressed in the dispute between Aqiba and sages (A-B+C) is how the character of joint ownership affects the separation of heave-offering. Since heave-offering may be separated only once from a batch of produce, we cannot simply assume that each of the part-owners individually may separate heave-offering. Yet as we recall from M. 1:1D, only the owner of a batch of produce may separate heave-offering from that batch. It therefore is not clear that one of the joint owners of a batch of produce may alone effect the separation of the heave-offering required of the collectively owned batch. In light of these considerations, the problem is to establish the rights and responsibilities of individual owners of a crop.[16] There are two ways in which logically to view the problem. On the one hand, we may hold that each partner--autonomous of the others--owns a specific portion of the produce. In this case each partner individually must separate heave-offering from his portion. On the other hand, ownership may be understood to be collective, such that any one of the partners may separate heave-offering for all of the produce. If this is the case, once one of the partners has separated heave-offering, the produce no longer will be liable. Heave-offering separated later by any of the other partners will not be valid heave-offering.

    Aqiba, B, takes the position that each of the individuals owns a determinate share of the produce. By his actions the first partner exempts from liability to the separation of heave-offering only that portion of the produce which he owns. The separation performed by the second partner--who now separates heave-offering from his own portion of the produce--likewise is valid.[17] Sages, C, take the opposite point of view, holding that the partners collectively own all the produce. By his actions either of these

individuals exempts the entire batch from further liability to the
separation of heave-offering. Once the first partner separates
heave-offering, that which the second partner separates cannot have
the status of a sanctified priestly gift.

On formal grounds Yose's opinion (D), like the statements at
B and C, may respond directly to A. It is clear on substantive
grounds, however, that in its present redactional setting, Yose's
view responds to and qualifies the position of sages, C.[18] Yose
agrees with sages' view that either of the partners can, by his
actions, exempt all of the produce from further liability to the
separation of heave-offering (as at D). He takes seriously, however, M.'s notion that a set percentage of each batch of produce
should be separated as heave-offering (M. 4:3). According to
Yose, only if the first partner actually separates the required
amount of heave-offering does he exempt the produce from further
liability to the separation of heave-offering. In this case
heave-offering separated by the second partner is not valid. If,
on the other hand, the first partner separates less than the required quantity of heave-offering (E), Yose holds that the produce
remains subject to the separation of heave-offering.[19] Produce
separated as heave-offering by the second partner will in this
case also have the status of valid heave-offering.[20]

F-H+I-J+K-M qualifies the opinion of Aqiba, B, making use of
the standard *bmh dbrym 'mwrym* formulation. Since I-J+K-M is
clearly autonomous of F-H and its present redactional context,[21]
let us begin by examining its meaning as an independent unit of
law. When viewed thus, I-J makes a rather simple point. This is
that a householder may assign an agent to separate heave-offering
for him. We know as much from M. 1:1D-E. While K-M is somewhat
more interesting, its point likewise is hardly surprising. It
holds that a householder who has authorized another individual to
separate heave-offering for him may nullify the permission he has
granted. This is the case until such time as that other individual
actually has separated heave-offering. Once the agent has separated heave-offering, the produce retains its consecrated status
regardless of the householder's change of mind. The process by
which produce is designated heave-offering is not reversible.

When viewed through the eyes of the redactor who joined I-J
to F-H, the point of I-J is somewhat more subtle. F-G, first,
claims that Aqiba's view--that each of the partners separates
heave-offering for his own portion--is operative only in a case in
which the joint owners did not previously discuss the way in which

they would separate heave-offering. I-J now indicates the ruling
for the opposite case. What if the partners did confer, and
decided that one of them would separate heave-offering for both?
According to I-J, in such a case the separation of heave-offering
performed by the one partner exempts from liability both his portion and that of his co-owner, just as in a case in which a householder assigns an agent to separate heave-offering for him. If
the second partner later separates heave-offering, that which he
separates cannot be considered valid heave-offering.

While formally autonomous, N-P is related to I-J in substance, offering a further problem in the separation of heave-
offering by an agent. Workers whose task does not require it may
not separate heave-offering from the produce with which they are
working. If, however, the completion of their work presupposes
their separating heave-offering, we assume that the householder
considers these workers his agents, and they may separate heave-
offering for him. This is the rule, O-P states, in the case of
workers who tread grapes or olives. Once the treading has begun
it is impossible to protect the liquid in the vat in a state of
cleanness. It therefore is standard procedure immediately to
separate heave-offering, thereby assuring that the priest will receive as his portion produce which he may eat. In light of this
consideration, while the workers have not explicitly received permission to separate heave-offering, this is considered part of
their task, and they are permitted to do so.

I.   A.   A sharecropper who separated heave-offering [both
from his share and from the portion of the produce which
belongs to the householder], and the householder came and
intervened--

      B.   if he intervened before [the sharecropper] separated
heave-offering, that which he has separated is not [valid]
heave-offering.

      C.   But if he intervened after he separated heave-
offering, that which he has separated is [valid] heave-
offering.

      D.   But [the sharecropper] is not permitted to set aside
(*lhwsy*) tithes, except for his own share.

II.   E.   A worker who separated the heave-offering of the
threshing floor--

           that which he has separated is not [valid] heave-
offering.

F. But if the householder had said to him, "Gather in
(*knws*) the threshing floor for me," that which he has separated is [valid] heave-offering,

G. for the threshing floor may not be gathered in unless heave-offering is separated from it.

T. 1:7

III. H. Workers who separated the heave-offering of the tank
[of wine or oil]--

that which they have separated is not [valid] heave-
offering.

I. But if it was a small tank and others also used
it[22]--

that which they have separated is [valid] heave-
offering.

T. 1:8 (y. Ter. 3:4)

T. supplements M. 3:4. In their redactional context within
the first chapter of T., these materials form part of a larger
unit of materials dealing with a householder's implicit authori-
zation of another individual to separate heave-offering for him.
This develops M. 1:1D-E's statement that, unless permission has
been granted, heave-offering may be separated only by the owner
of the produce. By placing T. 1:7-8 within that unit, T. indicates that M. 3:4's several rules are to be read in light of
M. 1:1D-E, as I have done.

A-C+D reads the concerns of M. 3:4K-M into a case such as
that of M. 3:4N-P. Like the workers who tread the grapes or
olives in the vat (M. 3:4/O-P), a sharecropper--who must complete
the processing of all of the produce--is viewed as an agent of
the householder. He therefore may separate heave-offering. As
in the case of any agent, the sharecropper's right, however, may
be rescinded, so long as the householder does this before heave-
offering has been separated (B-C). I assume that the sharecropper
may not remove tithes for the householder (D) because these gifts
need not be maintained in cultic cleanness. This being the case
there is no reason for the sharecropper to separate them for the
householder before the wine or oil is rendered unclean.[23]

E-G and H-I simply repeat the point of M. 3:4N-P. Workers
may not normally separate heave-offering from produce belonging
to their employer. If the task to which they have been assigned
requires their doing so, they are considered agents and heave-
offering they separate is valid.

3:5

I.   A. One who says, "The heave-offering of this heap is within it," or "Its tithes are within it," [or] "Its heave-offering of the tithe is within it"--

       B. R. Simeon says, "He has [validly] designated [these agricultural gifts]."

       C. But sages say, "[He has not validly designated these things] unless he will say, '[They are] in its [i.e., the heap's] northern portion,' or '[They are] in its southern portion.'"

II.   D. R. Eleazar Hisma' says, "One who says, 'The heave-offering of this heap [is separated] from it, for it,' has [validly] designated [the heave-offering]."

III. E. R. Eliezer b. Jacob says, "One who says, 'A tenth of this [first] tithe is made heave-offering of the tithe for it [i.e., for all of the first tithe],' has [validly] designated it."

M. 3:5 (A-B: b. Erub. 37b; A-C:

see T. M. S. 3:17)

In order to separate agricultural gifts, the householder must perform two distinct procedures. He first must make an oral declaration of his intention to separate a particular offering from some batch of produce. Through his declaration the householder localizes within the produce the gift which he desires to separate. Only after the offering has been so designated may he actually separate it from the batch of produce and give it to its proper recipient, priest or Levite.[24] Under debate in M. 3:5 is the proper procedure for the designation of heave-offering, first tithe and heave-offering of the tithe. The pericope is formulated as a triplet, giving us three different formulas for the designation of agricultural gifts, A+B (disputed by sages, C), D and E. While A-C refers to heave-offering, tithe and heave-offering of the tithe, D speaks specifically only of heave-offering, and E, only of heave-offering of the tithe. Still, that the pericope is unitary in nature is evidenced by the fact that each of its sections exhibits parallel formulation, viz., $h'wmr$ + statement of designation + qr' $\check{s}m$. Thus while we cannot claim that the several statements of law found here have a common source, it is clear that their final linguistic formulation was for use as a unit.

Simeon, B, states that to designate an agricultural gift, the householder need only indicate in what produce the gift is located.

Simeon's notion is that the designation of agricultural offerings
is intended only to demarcate one particular batch of produce
from other batches. The purpose of the designation is not to impart the status of an agricultural gift to any specific produce
within the batch. By his designation, rather, the householder
simply restricts himself to separating the offering from a particular batch of produce and not from a different one (Maimonides,
Commentary and *Heave-offering* 3:8). If the householder does not
at this point impose the status of an agricultural gift upon any
specific portion of the produce, we must ask when, according to
Simeon, does he do this. It appears that in Simeon's view, this
is in the householder's actual separation of the offering from the
produce. Only at this point does the particular produce which he
separates take on a consecrated status. For Simeon, thus, even
after the householder has designated the offering within the batch
of produce, he still may choose which produce, and how much of it,
he actually will separate as the offering.

Sages, C, have a fundamentally different understanding of the
purpose of the designation of agricultural gifts. They hold that
the designation must indicate which specific portion of the householder's produce is to be considered the offering. In order for
the designation to accomplish this, it must include a statement of
the exact place within the produce from which the householder intends to separate the priest's or Levite's share, e.g., the north
or south side of the batch. The householder thereby differenti-
ates between that which is to be considered the offering and the
rest of the produce (y. Ter. 3:5).

Eleazar Hisma' and Eliezer b. Jacob both agree with the
method and purpose of the designation suggested by Simeon.[25]
Eleazar Hisma' holds that to designate heave-offering, the householder simply states that he intends to separate the offering from
a particular batch of produce for that same batch. Eliezer b.
Jacob (E) repeats the same statement in reference to heave-offering of the tithe. Like Simeon, each of these authorities must
hold that it is in the actual separation of the offering that a
specific quantity of produce takes on the status of the desired
gift. This conception is quite different from that held by sages.

    A. "One who says, 'The heave-offering of this heap [of
produce] is in its northern portion [see M. 3:5C]--

B.   "the half of it [i.e., of the heap] facing north is [in the status of] a mixture of heave-offering and unconsecrated produce ($mdwm^{c}$)"--the words of Rabbi.

C.   But sages say, "He marks it [i.e., the heap] out ($^{c}w\acute{s}y$ 'wtw) in the form of [the Greek letter] Chi."

D.   Rabban Simeon b. Gamaliel says, "He takes the heave-offering from its [i.e., the heap's] most northern part ($spwn$ $spwnw$)."

T. 4:9 (y. Ter. 3:5)

T. develops the statement of sages, M. 3:5C, that a house-holder designates heave-offering or other agricultural gifts by indicating in which portion of the produce he deems the gift to be located. At issue now is the actual effect of a householder's statement that the heave-offering required of a batch of produce is located in the batch's northern part (A). According to Rabbi, B, such a statement is sufficiently ambiguous as to require that we deem the heave-offering to be dispersed throughout the northern half of the heap of produce. The householder therefore must treat as a mixture of heave-offering and unconsecrated produce a full half of the batch. All of the produce in this mixture goes to the priest, as if it were heave-offering.[26] Rabbi's statement thus is striking. According to it, the method of designation suggested by sages, M. 3:5C, will impose the status of heave-offering upon fifty percent of the produce. Sages, C, disagree with Rabbi. They state that in a case such as is described at A, the householder does, in fact, localize the heave-offering in a specific portion of the produce, such that the status of dm^{c} does not apply to any portion of the heap. We simply imagine a cross drawn over the batch, and consider the produce which is in the quadrant facing north to be heave-offering. While this statement is less radical than Rabbi's, it still is notable, requiring that the householder separate as heave-offering a full quarter of his produce. It therefore is not likely that T.'s sages are the same as those cited at M. 3:5C. Simeon b. Gamaliel, D, states that only that produce which is in the most northern portion of the heap, a small percentage of the whole, need be considered heave-offering.[27] According to Simeon, then, by his statement the householder will have designated the proper quantity of heave-offering. While it appears that all three of T.'s authorities would agree that sages, M. 3:5C, have the correct notion of the purpose of the designation of agricultural gifts, Simeon b. Gamaliel alone considers the

specific language they offer to be a practical means of effecting
the designation.

3:6-7

A. One who separates (1) heave-offering before first
fruits (*hmqdym trwmh lbkwrym*),

(2) first tithe before heave-offering,

(3) or second tithe before first [tithe],

B. even though he transgresses a negative commandment
(*l' t^{c}šh*),

C. that which he has done is done [and valid];

D. as it is written, *You shall not delay to offer from
the fulness of your harvest and from the outflow of your
presses* (Ex. 22:29).

> M. 3:6 (Mekhilta D'Rabbi Ishmael,
> Mishpatim #17, Horovitz, p. 318
> l. 9 - p. 319 l. 4; cf. Mekhilta
> D'Rabbi Simeon b. Yohai 22:28,
> Epstein, p. 213 ls. 8-11, b. Tem.
> 4a, 5b)

E. And from where [do we know] that first fruits should
be separated before heave-offering,

F. for this [i.e., heave-offering] is called heave-
offering (*trwmh*) [Num. 18:11] and first (*r'šyt*) [Num. 18:12],

G. and this [i.e., first fruits] is called heave-
offering (*trwmh*) [Dt. 12:6][28] and first (*r'šyt*) [Ex. 23:19].

H. Still ('*l'*) first fruits should be separated first,
since they are the first fruits of all [produce].

I. And [they should separate] heave-offering before
first [tithe],

J. since it [i.e., heave-offering] is [called] "first."

K. And [they should separate] first tithe before second
[tithe],

L. since it has in it [an offering called] "first"
[i.e., heave-offering of the tithe (Albeck)].

> M. 3:7 (H: y. Pe. 1:5)

Having discussed the proper formula for the designation of
the various agricultural gifts, we turn to the order in which
these gifts are separated, a logical progression of ideas. The
main point is made at A+C, which assumes the proper order for the
separation of agricultural offerings to be first fruits, heave-
offering, first tithe, second tithe. As T. 4:10 will observe, it

is important for the householder to remove the offerings in this
order. If instead he separates first tithe before heave-offering,
for instance, the produce he designates first tithe still will be
liable to the separation of heave-offering, and, therefore, not
yet fit for consumption by a Levite. What if the householder disregards the correct order? According to C, his offerings are in
all events valid. Despite the difficulty raised by T, such validity depends upon the proper separation of each individual gift,
not on the order in which they are separated.

On formal grounds we would expect D to provide biblical support for the rule of C. Substantively, however, it can refer only
to B, specifying the 'negative commandment'--that is, the biblical
prohibition--which an individual who changes the order of the
offerings trangresses (Maimonides, *Commentary* and *Heave-offering*
3:23). The prohibition is *You shall not delay to offer* (Ex.
22:29). In the present context, this means that the householder
should not "delay" offering the various agricultural gifts in
their appointed order (Albeck).

E-L now supplements A, providing the reasoning which stands
behind the order of the offerings assumed there. Let us begin by
recalling those verses which are understood to refer to heave-
offering (F) and first fruits (G). M.'s understanding of the
terms *trwmh* and *r'šyt* at Num. 18:11-12 as referring to heave-
offering already has been explained (above, p. 2). As regards
first fruits, Dt. 12:6 includes the phrase *trwmt ydkm* (*the offering of your hand*) among a list of offerings which are brought to
"the place which the Lord your God will choose" (Dt. 12:5), that
is, the temple in Jerusalem. These offerings are to be eaten
there by the individual who brings them. Since M.'s first fruits
are also brought to the temple in Jerusalem and eaten there by the
householder, the term *trwmt ydkm* (= *trwmh*) in this context is
taken to refer to first fruits and not to heave-offering, which,
for M., is eaten anywhere, by priests. The term *r'šyt* understood
by M. to indicate first fruits is at Ex. 23:19. This verse reads,
The first of the first fruits of your ground (*r'šyt bkwry 'dmtk*)
you shall bring into the house of the Lord, your God. The juxtaposition of the term *r'syt* to the term *bkwrym*, M.'s standard name
for first fruits, indicates that the term *r'šyt* itself is a designation for first fruits.

As F-G states, then, the terms *trwmh* and *r'šyt* are used both
in contexts in which they can be understood to refer to heave-
offering, and in contexts in which they may refer to first fruits.

From these usages we thus cannot deduce which of these offerings
takes precedence and should be separated first. According to H,
it is only in light of the term *bkwrym* itself that we may infer the
correct order for these two offerings. *Bkwrym*, the first ripe produce of the householder's field, must be separated before heave-
offering and the rest of the agricultural gifts.

This much established I-L turns to the correct order for the
separation of heave-offering, first tithe and second tithe. Heave-
offering, it notes, may be distinguished from the other two offerings in that, as we have seen, it has the title "first." It therefore must be separated before first tithe, M.'s parlance for the
Levitical tithe of Num. 18:21 (*To the Levites I have given every
tithe in Israel for an inheritance*...).[29] This Levitical tithe is
nowhere referred to as "first." What of the order for the separation of first tithe and second tithe? M. derives its notion of the
latter offering from Dt. 14:22-29, which refers both to a tithe
eaten by each Israelite in Jerusalem, and to a tithe which is separated at the end of every three year period and given to the poor
of the community of Israel.[30] As regards the Levitical tithe,
Scripture states that the Levite himself must separate from it *a
tithe of the tithe* (Num. 18:26), referred to one verse later as *an
offering to the Lord from all of your tithes* (*trwmt yhwh mkl
m^c śrwtykm*). Described by the term *trwmh*, this offering, M.'s heave-
offering of the tithe, is the agricultural gift called 'first'
which is contained in M.'s first tithe. No such tithe of the tithe
is prescribed for removal from the tithe mentioned at Dt. 14:22-29.
This offering, M.'s second tithe, therefore is separated only after
first tithe (1).

A. *One who separates (1) heave-offering before first
fruits, (2) first tithe before heave-offering, (3) or second
tithe before first [tithe]*

B. *even though he transgresses a negative commandment*

C. *that which he has done is done [and valid]* [=M.
3:6A-C].

D. The second [tithe] may not be eaten until he removes
from it first [tithe].

E. And the first [tithe] may not be eaten until he removes from it heave-offering.

F. For [the separation of] heave-offering does not
hinder [the offering of] first fruits.

G. In the same way:

H. One who makes dough from untithed produce,

I.   whether he separated dough-offering before heave-
offering, or separated heave-offering before dough-offering,

J.   that which he has done is done [and valid].

K.   The dough-offering may not be eaten until he will
separate from it heave-offering.

L.   And the heave-offering may not be eaten until he
will remove from it dough-offering.

> T. 4:10 (F: y. Ter. 3:5; H-L:
> y. Dem. 5:1)

T. provides the consideration which is basic to M.'s concern
for the correct order of the separation of agricultural gifts.
The designation of produce as one of the agricultural offerings
does not exempt that produce from liability to other gifts which
should already have been separated from it. If produce from which
first tithe has not been taken is designated second tithe, it retains liability to the removal of first tithe. It may not be
eaten until such time as first tithe is removed from it (D). The
same is the case as regards produce which is designated first
tithe before heave-offering is separated from it (E). A Levite
may not eat such first tithe unless heave-offering first is separated from it. F is formally out of phase with D-E, referring
back to A1 and explaining why a householder may validly separate
heave-offering before first fruits (HY). Since the separation of
heave-offering does not prevent the subsequent separation of first
fruits, by separating heave-offering first, the householder will
not have escaped his responsibility to separate all of the required offerings. We declare the separation of heave-offering
valid and require him afterwards to offer first fruits.

G+H-L exemplifies the same point. Heave-offering normally
is separated from flour before that flour is made into dough,
which is subject to the removal of dough-offering. If dough is
made from untithed produce it is liable at the same time to the
separation of heave-offering and dough-offering. The householder
must be careful to separate both of these gifts from all of the
produce, even from that which already has been designated as one
or the other of the offerings (K-L).

3:8

A.   (1) One who [in designating agricultural gifts]
intends to say, "Heave-offering," but says, "Tithe," "Tithe,"
but says "Heave-offering,"

    B.   (2) [or who, in designating a sacrifice, intends to
say,] "Burnt-offering," but says, "Peace-offering," "Peace-
offering," but says, "Burnt-offering;"

    C.   (3) [or who, in making a vow, intends to say],
"That I will not enter this house," but says, "That house,"
"That I will not derive benefit from this one," but says,
"From that one"

    D.   has not said anything,

    E.   until his mouth and heart agree.

                         M. 3:8 (A-B: y. Naz. 5:1; A+C:
                         b. Pes. 63a)

    The point is at D+E. In cases in which an oral declaration
is required, neither unexpressed intention nor an unwitting designation alone is of legal weight. As each of the three parallel
examples shows, the individual must both have proper intention
and correctly state that intention if he is to impose a special
status upon produce (A), an animal (B), or restrict himself to a
vow (C).[31]

    I.   A.   [If] he was going to separate heave-offering

          B.   [but] at the time of his separation said, "Lo, this
    is first tithe,

          C.   [Lieberman supplies, following E and ed. princ.:]
          lo, it is first tithe.

    II.   D.   [If] he was going to separate first tithe,

          E.   [but] at the time of his separation said, "Lo, this
    is second tithe,"

          F.   lo, it is second tithe.

    III. G.   [If] he was going to separate second tithe,

          H.   [but] at the time of his separation said, "Lo, this
    is poor man's tithe,"

          I.   lo, it is poor man's tithe.

    I.   J.   [If] he intended to say, "Second tithe," but said,
    "Poor man's tithe," "Second tithe," but said, "First tithe"--

          K.   he did not say anything.

    II.   L.   [If he intended to say] "Poor man's tithe,"[32] but
    said, "Second tithe"--

          M.   his words are valid.[33]

    III. N.   R. Yose says, "If he intended [to separate] poor
    man's tithe [but said, 'Second tithe'], he did not say any-
    thing.

O.   "[But] if he intended [to separate] the tithe [which
is] second to first [tithe in that year, i.e., poor man's
tithe, but said 'Second tithe'], his words are valid."

T. 4:11

T. is formed of two formally autonomous units, A-I and
J-M+N-O, each of which supplements M.'s discussion of the requirements of intention and oral declaration for the valid designation of agricultural offerings (M. 3:8A).   A-E, first, contradicts M. 3:8.   It holds that if a householder intends to separate
one agricultural gift, but designates the produce as a different
gift, the designation is valid.   Unlike M., T. thus claims that we
rule on the basis of what the individual says, not what he
thinks.[34]

J-O reverts to M.'s conception of the matter.   The householder desires to designate second tithe, but says first tithe or
poor man's tithe.   His designation is not valid (K).   L-M suggests a slight twist.   The individual says second tithe instead of
poor man's tithe.   Since in the third and sixth years of the
sabbatical cycle poor man's tithe takes the place of second tithe,
we need not assume that the individual has said anything other
than what he intended.   We therefore declare his designation as
poor man's tithe valid (Lieberman, TK, I, p. 348).   Yose, N-O,
rejects the contention that the individual's reference to second
tithe automatically may be taken to represent the intention to
separate poor man's tithe.   This is the case, he states, only in
the circumstance described at O.   Like M. 3:8 Yose thus wants to
be sure that the individual has said exactly what he means.

3:9

A.   A gentile[35] and a Samaritan--

B.   (1) that which they separate is [valid] heave-
offering,

(2) and that which they take as tithes is [valid] tithes,

(3) and that which they dedicate [to the Temple] is
[validly] dedicated.

C.   R. Judah says, "A gentile's vineyard is not subject
to ('yn lnkry) [the restrictions] of the fourth year (Lev.
19:24)."

D.   But sages say, "It is (yš lw)."

E.   Heave-offering separated by a gentile imposes the
status of heave-offering [upon unconsecrated produce with
which it is mixed] and [non-priests who unintentionally eat

it] are liable on its account to [pay back its value and]
the [added] fifth (Lev. 22:10-14).

    F.   But R. Simeon exempts [heave-offering separated by
a gentile from these stringencies].

                    M. 3:9 (A-B(1): b. Git. 23b,
                    b. Qid. 41b; C-D: y. Pe. 7:5,
                    y. M.S. 5:2; E-F: b. Qid. 41b)

The pericope is in three formally autonomous parts, A-B, and
the disputes at C-D and E-F.[36] Their redaction as a unit is,
however, on solid substantive grounds. A single question prevails
throughout the pericope, that of the status of a non-Israelite as
regards the agricultural laws. According to A, both a gentile and
a Samaritan may validly separate agricultural offerings and, in
like manner, may dedicate that which they wish to the Temple.
This rule, then, holds that non-Israelites have the same power to
impose a status of sanctity on portions of their produce and on
other objects as do Israelites, a striking claim. At E-F Simeon
disputes this notion. E states that heave-offering separated by
a gentile is just like that separated by an Israelite. It is
subject to all of the stringencies accorded a holy thing. It is
subject to the law of the added fifth, which requires that a non-
priest who unintentionally eats a holy thing pay back its value
plus an additional fifth (M. 6:1). If mixed with unconsecrated
produce in a ratio of more than one part to one hundred, it imparts the status of heave-offering to the mixture (M. 4:7).
Simeon, F, rejects E's notion that a gentile is equivalent to an
Israelite as regards the agricultural laws. He holds that, while
heave-offering separated by a gentile may be given to a priest,
for which reason it has the name heave-offering, it does not have
the status of a holy thing. It is not subject to the law of the
added fifth and does not impart the status of heave-offering to
unconsecrated produce with which it is mixed.[37] It is notable
that the status which Simeon accords to heave-offering separated
by a gentile is that of produce about which there is doubt whether
or not it was properly separated as heave-offering (see M. 3:1-2).
In a case in which a householder has separated heave-offering in
such a status, he must separate heave-offering a second time, in
order to assure that heave-offering is properly removed from his
produce. We can only assume that Simeon, in like manner, would
require that an Israelite who wishes to eat produce which has been
tithed by a gentile, himself separate heave-offering from that

produce. It thus is clear that according to Simeon, a gentile who
separates heave-offering does nothing more than give a gift of
produce to a priest. A gentile does not have the ability to remove the true heave-offering required of produce grown in the Land
of Israel. This can be accomplished by Israelites alone.

C-D refers to the distinct question of whether or not produce
grown on land owned by a gentile in the Land of Israel is subject
to the restrictions of the fourth year of growth (Lev. 19:24).
According to Scripture the crop of an orchard or vineyard in its
fourth year of growth is consecrated as a thanksgiving to the
Lord (*hlwlym lyhwh*; RSV: *an offering of praise to the Lord*).
M. M.S. 5:1-4 states that, like second tithe, the produce must be
brought to Jerusalem and eaten there in cultic cleanness. According to Judah, these restrictions do not apply to produce grown
in a gentile-owned field in the Land of Israel. Judah holds that
the stringency of the fourth year falls only upon Israelites, who
received the Land of Israel from God. Land owned by a gentile is
not subsumed under the category of land given by God to the people
of Israel and therefore is not subject to the law of the fourth
year (see y. Dem. 5:9). Sages, D, disagree, holding that like the
other agricultural laws, the law of the fourth year applies to
produce grown by a gentile in the Land of Israel. That is, they
hold that even though a gentile presently owns the land, as part
of the original inheritance given by God to the Israelites, that
land still is subject to all of the agricultural stringencies,
including the restrictions of the fourth year.

K. Truly (*'bl*) [the laws of] ^c*orlah* and mixed seeds in
a vineyard (*kl'y hkrm*) are the same for [the field of] a
gentile in the Land of Israel, in Syria and outside of the
Land [of Israel].

L. But (*'l' š*) R. Judah says, *"A gentile's vineyard in
Syria is not subject (yn lnkry) to [the laws] of the fourth
year."*

M. [E and ed. princ. add:] *But sages say, "It is
(yš lw)"* [= M. 3:9C-D].

N. Said R. Judah, *"M^cśh b:* Segabion (E: *sgbywn;* V:
sbwn), the head of the synagogue (reading with E, ed. princ.:
byt hknst; V reads *knst*) at Achziv purchased a vineyard in
its fourth year [of growth] from a gentile in Syria, and gave
him payment. Then he came and asked Rabban Gamaliel, who was
passing from place to place [whether the produce of that field

is liable to the restriction of the fourth year and should
not have been purchased]. (*w*) [Gamaliel] said to him, "Wait
until we can dwell upon (*nḥḥ*) the law."

[Since the story does not conclude with Gamaliel's
passing judgment, Judah assumes that the field was not held
liable to the law of the fourth year (Lieberman).]

O. They said to him [i.e., to Judah], "Is that evidence? [Gamaliel] also sent a messenger to him [i.e., to
Segabion] secretly (*bydy šlyḥ ḥrš*; see Lieberman, TK, I,
p. 318) [so as not to embarrass him, and said,] "That which
you have done is done, but do not do it again."

[From this it is obvious that Gamaliel held the field
to be liable to the restrictions of the fourth year.]

T. 2:13b (L-M: y. Pe. 7:6,

y. M.S. 5:3)

K introduces a citation, at L-M, of M. 3:9C-D's dispute between Judah and sages. This is followed by the debate at N-O.
The pericope, therefore, clearly is supplementary to M. 3:9. Its
redaction in the second chapter of T. is, however, on solid substantive grounds. It appears there within a group of rules dealing with the liability of produce grown in Syria (mentioned here
at K, L and N) to the separation of heave-offering and tithes.
T. thus has its own theory of the context in which M.'s materials
are best explored.

We recall from T. 2:12 that while produce grown by a gentile
in the Land of Israel is liable to the separation of heave-offering and tithes, that grown by the gentile in Syria is not. K now
states that this is not the case as regards the laws of *orlah*
(which prohibit consumption of the fruit of an orchard or vineyard
in its first three years of growth; Lev. 19:23), and of mixed
seeds (Lev. 19:19, Dt. 22:9-11). It states that these laws apply
equally to fields owned by gentiles within and outside of the Land
of Israel. According to K, then, as regards these laws, the produce of a gentile is like that of an Israelite, and liable wherever
it is grown. The practical result is that even outside of the
Land of Israel, an Israelite may not without reservation eat produce grown in a gentile-owned orchard or vineyard.

As redacted in T., Judah's statement, L, qualifies K. T. has
made this statement pertinent to its present context by adding the
words *in Syria*, lacking in M.[38] Thus Judah is made to state that
unlike the laws of *orlah* and mixed seeds, the stringencies of the

fourth year to not apply to the field of a gentile in Syria.
Sages' claim (N) is that just as the laws of ^{c}*orlah* and mixed
seeds in a vineyard apply to the field of a gentile in Syria, so
those of the fourth year apply. The position of each party in
the debate is clear on the basis of Lieberman's explanation, which
I have interpolated.

A. A gentile who separated heave-offering--
that which he has separated is [valid] heave-offering
[cf. M. 3:9A-B].

B. In what case does this statement apply?

C. [It applies if the gentile separated heave-offering]
on the threshing floor.

D. [If he] separated heave-offering [on the threshing
floor] and [immediately] gave it to a priest, [or if he re-
moved] first tithe and [immediately] gave it to a Levite,
[or if he removed] poor man's tithe and [immediately] gave
it to a poor person--
his [i.e., the gentile's] produce has been set right
[and may be eaten by an Israelite].

E. [If he] brought (E: *hknys*) his produce into his
house, it has been spoiled (*prwtyw mqwlqlym*) [and no longer
may be consumed by an Israelite who does not himself tithe it
(Lieberman)].

F. An Israelite who is suspect [as regards his observance of tithing laws who tithed his produce as at D and]
who [then] brought his produce into his house--
his produce has been set right [reading with E; V reads
mqwlqlym).

G. "A Samaritan is [treated] like a gentile"--the words
of Rabbi.

H. Rabban Simeon b. Gamaliel says, "A Samaritan is
[treated] like an Israelite."

T. 4:12 (G-H: y. Ber. 7:1 and
parallels, see T. Pes. 1:15)

A-F cites and qualifies the rule of M. 3:9A-B1. The point is
that only if a gentile publicly separates agricultural gifts and
immediately gives them to their proper recipient may the gifts be
assumed properly to have been separated. E states that even after
the gentile properly separates the various offerings, if he takes
the produce out of public view, it is forbidden for consumption by
an Israelite. We assume that the gentile will mix untithed

produce with that which he already has already prepared for consumption. According to F, this is not the case for an Israelite
who is suspect as regards his observance of the agricultural laws.
While we require that such an individual publicly separate heave-
offering and tithes, if he later brings his produce out of the
public eye, we do not assume that he will mix it with untithed
produce.

When interpreted within their present redactional context,
the opinions of Rabbi and Simeon b. Gamaliel, at G-H, hardly require comment. Rabbi holds that like a gentile, a Samaritan
(M. 3:9A) may not be trusted at all as regards the proper tithing
of his produce. Simeon disagrees. He holds that like an Israelite, once a Samaritan tithes his produce, it is deemed fit for
consumption, even if the Samaritan brings it into his home and
out of public view.

> A. A gentile who set apart the (1) first-born [of a
> clean animal (Lieberman, TK, I, p. 349)], (2) the first-born
> of an ass (*pṭr ḥmwr*), (3) or dough-offering--
>
> B. they notify him that he is not obligated [to offer
> these things];
>
> C. they put it [i.e., the animal the gentile set aside]
> to work and shear it [in order to show that the animal does
> not have the status of a first-born];
>
> D. but then they accept from him [the animal, or the
> dough-offering].
>
> E. And the dough-offering may be eaten by commoners.
>
> I.   F. "[If the gentile] took heave-offering from within
> his house--
>
> G. "they treat it like untithed produce [mixed] with
> heave-offering"--the words of Rabbi.
>
> H. Rabban Simeon b. Gamaliel says, "They treat it like
> great heave-offering alone."
>
> II. I. "[If the gentile] took first tithe from within his
> house--
>
> J. "they treat it like untithed produce [mixed] with
> first tithe"--the words of Rabbi.
>
> K. Rabban Simeon b. Gamaliel says, "They treat it like
> first tithe alone."
>
> III. L. "[If] he took second tithe from within his house--
> "[if] he said, 'It has been redeemed [by coins, and
> therefore no longer is consecrated as second tithe],'

"he has not said anything.

M. "[But if he said,] 'Redeem it for yourselves,'

N. "they treat it like untithed produce [mixed with] second tithe"--the words of Rabbi.

O. Rabban Simeon b. Gamaliel says, "They treat it like second tithe alone."

T. 4:13 (A-E: b. Men. 67a, see

T. Hal. 2:6; F-K: y. Ter. 3:8)

P. An Israelite who is suspect [as regards his observance of the tithing laws] who took second tithe from within his house and said, "It has been redeemed (reading with E: *pdwy hw'*)"--

he has not said anything.

Q. [But if he said,] "Redeem it for me," [or] "Redeem it for yourselves"--

his words are valid.

R. "And a Samaritan is [treated] like a gentile"--the words of Rabbi.

S. Rabban Simeon b. Gamaliel says, "A Samaritan is [treated] like an Israelite."

T. A Samaritan who separated heave-offering and gave it to a [Samaritan-] priest [so Lieberman, TK, I, p. 351]--

that which he has separated is [valid] heave-offering.

U. R. Simeon b. Eleazar says, "[It is] heave-offering, but he must separate heave-offering again."

V. They [i.e., sages of T] said to him, "How is this case [i.e., that of the Samaritan] different from [that of] a priest who separated heave-offering [from unclean produce] and placed it [i.e., the heave-offering] before his cattle?"

W. He said to them, "The difference is this: that [i.e., the heave-offering separated by the priest] was separated in sanctity, and this [i.e., the heave-offering separated by the Samaritan] was [add with E, ed. princ.: not] separated in sanctity."

T. 4:14 (R-S: T. Ter. 4:12G-H)

T. concludes its discussion of the status of the gentile as regards the agricultural laws and the cult. T. 4:13, first, is in two parts, A-E and the triplet at F-O. A-E is in agreement with Simeon, M. 3:9F. It holds that offerings set apart by gentiles do not have the consecrated status of offerings given by Israelites, but that the priest in all events accepts them. A-E

thus states that the restrictions which Num. 18:15-18 places on
the first born of clean and unclean animals are not applicable to
animals owned by gentiles. Likewise, dough made by a gentile is
not subject to the separation of dough-offering, referred to at
Num. 15:17-21. If a gentile anyway attempts to present the first
born of one of his animals at the Temple, he is notified that he
is not liable to this offering (B). In order graphically to illustrate that his offering does not have the status of a first-
born, the priest uses the beast in such a way as to derive
secular benefit from it (C). This is forbidden in the case of
sanctified animals. Still, as D states, the animal ultimately is
accepted by the priest. This same paradox is emphasized at E,
for the case of dough-offering. While the dough is accepted by
the priest, it may be eaten by commoners, which is forbidden of
true dough offerings. The gentile thus does not have the same
status under the law as does an Israelite. A gentile who wishes
to take part in Israelite cult activities, however, is not excluded from doing so.

F-H, I-K and L-O return to T. 4:12's question of the extent
to which a gentile may be trusted to take proper care of produce
which he has designated heave-offering or tithes. The gentile
here separates agricultural offerings in his home, unobserved.
All parties agree with M. 3:9A-B, that the gentile's separation of
the offerings is valid. Rabbi (G, J and N), however, holds
that we do not trust the gentile to keep the gifts he has separated from becoming mixed with produce which has not yet been
tithed. Heave-offering, first or second tithe he takes from his
house therefore is deemed to be a mixture of the offering and untithed produce. Not knowing the quantities of the constituent
elements of the mixture, we cannot judge whether or not the offering actually has the status of heave-offering or tithe (see M.
4:7). Unlike Rabbi and T. 4:12, Simeon b. Gamaliel holds that we
trust the gentile both properly to tithe his produce and not to
mix with untithed produce heave-offering or tithes he separates
(H, K, O).

L+M-O makes the additional point that according to Rabbi we
in no case believe a gentile who claims to have redeemed second
tithe which he separated. As before, however, if he claims to
have produce in the status of second tithe, Rabbi states that we
assume it is a mixture of second tithe and untithed produce.
Again Simeon b. Gamaliel disagrees, holding that what the gentile
claims to be second tithe may in fact be regarded as such.

T. 4:14 continues T. 4:13's discussion, referring to Israelites who are not trusted to observe the agricultural laws. P-Q
introduces R-S and T-U+V-W, which itself follows upon the issue of
R-S. According to P-Q, like a gentile, an Israelite who is not
trusted as regards his observance of the agricultural restrictions
may not be trusted properly to have redeemed second tithe. If,
however, he claims to have separated second tithe and simply re-
quests that others redeem it for him, that which he has separated
is held to have the status of second tithe. This is the same
view Simeon b. Gamaliel, O, took as regards the gentile. R-S
repeats T. 4:12G-H. T-U+V-W, which is formally autonomous of R-S,
follows, disputing the status of heave-offering separated by a
Samaritan. Like M. 3:9A-B, both the anonymous rule at T and
Simeon b. Eleazar, U, hold that what is separated by a Samaritan
is valid heave-offering. At issue is whether or not giving the
heave-offering to a priest who is a Samaritan fulfills the requirement to give heave-offering to a priest (Lieberman, TK, I,
p. 352). According to T, it does. Simeon b. Eleazar holds that
this is not the case. He states that the Samaritan must separate
heave-offering a second time, in order to give an Israelite priest
his share. In the debate which follows, sages of T agree with
Simeon that one who gives heave-offering to a Samaritan priest
does not give it to its proper recipient. They argue however that
this is not grounds on which to rule that heave-offering must be
separated a second time. They adduce the case of a priest who
separates heave-offering from unclean produce, planning to give
the heave-offering, which he himself cannot eat, to his cattle.
While in such a case the heave-offering is not given to a priest--
but, rather, to cattle--we do not require that heave-offering be
separated a second time. Why then, V asks, should we require the
Samaritan to separate heave-offering a second time? Simeon b.
Eleazar states that the case of the priest is not comparable to
that of the Samitan. It is not, first of all, forbidden for the
priest to give unclean heave-offering to his cattle (M. 11:9).
Further, as a priest, he has the right to keep for himself heave-
offering which he separates. We cannot rule that his separation
did not fulfill the requirement that heave-offering be given to a
priest. This is not the case, Simeon holds, for the Samaritan
who, by intending to give the heave-offering to a Samaritan priest,
did not fulfill the requirements of the valid separation of heave-
offering. For this reason, that individual must separate heave-
offering a second time.

TERUMOT CHAPTER FOUR

The chapter is in two parts, M. 4:1-6, which concludes M.'s first thematic unit, and M. 4:7-13, which opens the long shank of the tractate. The first part of the chapter concerns the percentage of his produce an individual should separate as heave-offering (M. 4:3-5), and cases in which he separates only a portion of this required amount (M. 4:1-2, M. 4:3S-T). The main point is that the quantity of heave-offering contained in a batch of produce depends on the owner of the produce. The more generous the owner, the greater the quantity of heave-offering he should separate. There is, however, a minimum acceptable percentage of the batch, one sixtieth, which even the most miserly individual must separate and give to the priest. M. 4:6 is a singleton which concludes this section of the chapter. The householder should separate heave-offering at three set times during the harvest months. This prevents him from separating produce of low quality from the beginning and end of the harvest as heave-offering for the high quality produce picked in the middle of the summer (cf., M. 2:4-6).

The second part of the chapter discusses mixtures of heave-offering and unconsecrated produce. This topic will occupy M. through Chapter Five. The basic principle is that when heave-offering is mixed with unconsecrated produce such that it constitutes a minute proportion of the mixture (approximately one percent or less), it loses its integrity within the other produce and therefore becomes permitted for consumption by a non-priest (M. 4:7). M. 4:8-13 develop this principle. Joshua and Eliezer (M. 4:8-11) dispute whether or not heave-offering which can be distinguished from the unconsecrated produce with which it is mixed simply should be recovered and given to a priest. While formally independent of each other, M. 4:12 and 13 relate to a single problem, doubts involving mixtures of heave-offering and unconsecrated produce. They rule that if it is not known into which of several batches of unconsecrated produce heave-offering has fallen, all of the produce is deemed to join together as a single batch to neutralize the heave-offering.

The main issues of both parts of the chapter are attributed to Yavnean authorities, and, in the case of the question of the percentage of a batch of produce which should be separated as

heave-offering, to the Houses. Secondary discussion of that same
issue is attributed to Ishmael and Simeon Shezuri (T. 5:6b). The
quantity of produce needed to neutralize heave-offering is disputed by Eliezer, Ishmael, Tarfon and Aqiba (M. 4:7); Joshua and
Eliezer (M. 4:8-11) dispute other questions related to neutralization, as does Yose (M. 4:13). Ushans appear in discussion of
derivative issues. Specifically, we have Meir, M. 4:1-2, and
Judah, M. 4:3M. Ushans cited in T. are as follows: Rabbi,
T. 5:1; Rabbi and Judah, T. 5:6a; Judah and Simeon b. Judah,
T. 5:10a; Meir and Judah, T. 5:10b-11.

4:1-2

A. One who separates (*hmpryš*) part of the heave-offering and tithes [required of a batch of produce]

B. [subsequently] removes [more] heave-offering from
that [same] batch for that [same] batch.

C. But [he may] not [separate heave-offering] from that
batch [from which he already has separated some heave-offering and tithes] for a different batch.

D. R. Meir says, "Also: he removes heave-offering and
tithes [from that batch from which he already has removed
some heave-offering and tithes] for a different batch."

M. 4:1

E. "One whose produce was in a store-room and gave a
se'ah [of produce] to a Levite [as first tithe] and a *se'ah*
[of produce] to a poor person [as poor man's tithe]

F. "takes another eight *se'ahs* [of produce] and eats
them [without further tithing]"--the words of R. Meir.

G. But sages say, "He does not take produce [to eat]
except in accordance with a calculation [of the percentage of
tithes which remain to be separated from the batch as a
whole]."

M. 4:2 (y. Ma. 3:1)

While these two pericope are formally autonomous of each
other, the recurrence in each of Meir in dispute with anonymous
authorities indicates that they are to be read as a unit. Together, as we shall see, the pericopae illustrate a single legal
problem. This is the effect upon a batch of produce of the separation of a portion of the heave-offering and tithes required
from that same batch. There are two possible positions, one taken
by sages, A-C and G, and the other by Meir, D and E-F. According
to sages, a batch of produce is not divisible. Any agricultural

offerings separated from the batch apply to that batch as a whole. This means that if a householder separates less than the tenth of the batch required in the case of tithes, or fortieth required for heave-offering (M. 4:3), all of the produce in the batch is left partially exempt from the separation of these offerings. Since the batch is partially exempt, the individual may not later use it as a source of heave-offering or tithes for other, fully liable, produce (A-C). Further, if the householder wishes to eat some of the produce, he must set that food apart from the rest of the batch and separate from it the remainder of the heave-offering and tithes for which it is liable (G).[1] Meir's view is that the batch is divisible. Heave-offering or tithes separated from it release for consumption a commensurate quantity of produce, while leaving the rest of the batch fully untithed (E-F). The householder therefore may take produce from the partially tithed batch as heave-offering or tithes for a wholly untithed batch. He simply declares that the produce he is separating is yet untithed. He likewise may eat without further tithing the quantity of produce for which he already has separated sufficient heave-offering and tithes (E-F).[2]

A. [If] one had a pile [of produce] which had been evened over (*mwrḥt*)[3] [and therefore is liable to the separation of heave-offering and tithes]--

B. [if] he wished to declare it heave-offering for a different batch,

he does so.

C. [If] its [i.e., the pile's] heave-offering was removed--

D. [if] he wished to designate it [i.e., the pile] first tithe for a different batch,

he does so.

E. [If] its [i.e., the pile's] first tithe was removed--

F. [if] he wished to designate it [i.e., the pilᵉ] second tithe for a different batch,

he does so.

G. (G-H are lacking in E) [If] its [i.e., the pile's] second tithe was removed--

H. [if] he wished to designate it [i.e., the pile] poor man's tithe for a different batch,

he does so.

T. 4:15a

T. supplements the view of sages, M. 4:1A-C, that once heave-
offering is separated from a batch of produce, that batch no longer
may be used as a source of heave-offering for other produce. T.
adds that even so, as long as first tithe, for instance, has not
been separated from the batch, the householder may declare the
produce to be the first tithe required of other produce. The
point is that the separation of the various offerings is carried
out in fully independent processes. The demarcation of a batch
for the purposes of the separation of heave-offering does not require that tithes also be separated within that same batch.
Notably, since M. 4:1A refers to both heave-offering and tithes,
it is likely that T. here offers a fine clarification of M.'s
point, and is not simply reading into M. its own views.

G-H is difficult, since second tithe and poor man's tithe
are separated in different years of the sabbatical cycle, and
therefore never are separated from the same batch of produce.
This being the case E's reading, which omits G-H, is preferable.

A. "One who picks (reading with E: *ḥlwqt*) a chate-
melon [in order to keep it] for designation as heave-offering
[for other produce] (*lhywt mpryš ʿlyh whwlk*),

B. "makes a mark [on the melon itself] (E: *rwšm*) and
says, 'Up to this point it [i.e., the chate-melon] has the
status of heave-offering,' [or,] 'Up to this point it has
the status of heave-offering'"--the words of Rabbi.

C. Rabban Simeon b. Gamaliel says, "He separates heave-
offering and calculates the quantity he is used to separating
[without actually making a mark on the chate-melon or designating a specific portion of the chate-melon to be heave-
offering]."

D. "[If] he needed to raise up ten or fifteen (E:
kʿśr 'w khmš ʿśrh) kegs of wine [as heave-offering for a vat
of wine],

E. "he raises the first [keg he fills] and says, 'Lo,
this is heave-offering,' and [raises] the second [and] says,
'Lo, this is heave-offering' [and so on with all of the
kegs]"--the words of Rabbi [reading with E; V and ed. princ.
read: Rabban Simeon b. Gamaliel).

F. Rabban Simeon b. Gamaliel (reading with E; V and ed.
princ. read: Rabbi) says, "He [fills and] raises all of them
to the edge of the tank and [then] says, 'Lo, this is heave-
offering.'"

T. 5:1 (y. Hal. 3:5)

T.'s two disputes bring together the issues of M. 3:5 and
M. 4:1-2 by asking how heave-offering is designated in a case in
which the householder separates only a portion of the priestly
gift required of his produce. In both cases Rabbi holds that each
separation of heave-offering must be accompanied by an oral designation. Simeon b. Gamaliel prefers to have the individual wait
until all of the required heave-offering has been separated before
he designates it.

At A the householder sets aside a piece of produce, portions
of which he deems heave-offering for other produce he wishes to
eat. Only when all of the piece of produce has been designated
as heave-offering will he give it to a priest. Rabbi (B) claims
that at each separation of heave-offering, the householder marks
off the portion of the chate-melon which he deems to be heave-
offering and orally designates it as such. By specifying exactly
which part of the chate-melon has the status of heave-offering,
the householder prevents the whole of the piece of produce from
taking on the status of a mixture of heave-offering and untithed
produce. This is Rabbi's same concern above, T. 4:9B.[4] Simeon
b. Gamaliel, C, does not share this concern. He holds that without actually making a mark on the produce or designating a specific portion as heave-offering, the individual keeps track of
the percentage of the chate-melon which has been used as heave-
offering. Only later, when all of the chate-melon is heave-
offering, does he actually designate the produce to be a priestly
gift and give it to a priest. It appears that Simeon b. Gamaliel's
position is close to that of Simeon, M. 3:5B, who allows the householder to declare the heave-offering required of a batch of produce to be contained within that produce, without stating its
exact location within the batch. Thus neither he nor Simeon b.
Gamaliel is concerned that produce take on the status of a mixture
of heave-offering and untithed produce.

For reasons of logistics, D-F, a householder has no choice
but to separate heave-offering a small quantity at a time. In
order to separate heave-offering from a large vat of wine, he must
fill, one at a time, a number of kegs. As before, Rabbi wants him
to designate each keg as he fills it (cf., HD). Neither Meir nor
the anonymous authority of M. 4:1-2 should object to the individual's subsequent separation of heave-offering from the partially
tithed batch on behalf of that same batch. Like Rabbi, Simeon b.
Gamaliel has the same position he holds above. He states that the
householder should wait until he can designate at once all of the
required heave-offering.

A. *"One whose produce is in a store-room gives a se'ah
to a Levite [as first tithe] and a se'ah to a poor person
[as poor man's tithe], [and] takes another eight se'ahs [of
produce] and eats them [without further tithing]* [= M. 4:2D-E,
with slight changes].

B. "Whether or not that *se'ah* [which he gave to the
Levite or poor person] still exists [i.e., whether or not it
has been eaten],

C. "he takes [other produce] through its agency and
eats [that other produce, without further tithing]"--the
words of R. Meir.

D. But sages say, "If that same *se'ah* [which he separated as first tithe or poor man's tithe] still exists, he
takes other produce through its agency [and eats that other
produce, without further tithing] (*mpryš ᶜlyh whwlk*) [see
M. 4:2E].

E. "But if not, *he does not take produce [to eat] except in accordance with a calculation [of the percentage of
tithes which remain to be separated from the batch as a
whole]* [= M. 4:2F]."

T. 5:2 (y. Ter. 4:1)

T. restates the dispute between Meir and sages, M. 4:2,
interpolating, at B-D, a concern unknown to M. This is whether or
not at the time the householder decides to consume produce from
which a percentage of the required offerings has been separated,
those offerings have been eaten by their recipients. Meir's
position is the same as at M. 4:2A-B.[5] Whether or not the offerings he has separated have been consumed, the householder may eat
a commensurate quantity of produce.[6] Sages, however, distinguish
between cases in which the offerings already have been eaten, and
those in which they have not. According to T., the position sages
hold in M. applies only in a case in which the agricultural offerings separated from the larger batch of produce have not been
eaten by the time that the householder decides to consume a portion of that same batch (E).[7] If, however, the offerings have
not yet been eaten, D, sages concur with Meir that the householder
may deem them to comprise the full quantity of agricultural gifts
required of a portion of the larger batch. Sages' reasoning is
apparent in light of the larger issue salient here. This issue
is the householder's power to deem agricultural offerings to
apply to a specific portion of a batch. Sages' view is that the

householder has the power to do this if the offerings have not yet
been eaten by Levite or poor person. In such cases the offerings
still are available as objects of his intention, such that he may
designate them to be what he wishes. Once they have been consumed,
their disposition is set. They must be considered agricultural
offerings for the whole batch of produce from which they were
separated.

M. 4:3

A.   [This is] the [required] measure of heave-offering:

B.   [If a man is] generous (^{c}yn yph), [he separates]
one-fortieth [of his produce].

C.   The House of Shammai say, "One-thirtieth."

D.   And [if he is] average ($hbynwynt$), [he separates]
one-fiftieth [of his produce].

E.   And [if he is] miserly ($hr^{c}h$), [he separates] one-
sixtieth [of his produce].

F.   [If] he separated heave-offering and there came up
in his hand one-sixtieth [of the produce]--

[that which he has separated is valid] heave-offering,

G.   and he need not separate heave-offering again.

H.   If he [anyway separated] more [heave-offering]
(hzr $whwsyp$),

[the additional produce separated as heave-offering] is
liable to the separation of tithes [i.e., it is not true
heave-offering].

I.   [If he separated heave-offering and] there came up
in his hand one sixty-first [of the produce]--

[that which he has separated is valid] heave-offering,

J.   but he must separate heave-offering again,

K.   [in order to derive] the quantity [of heave-offering
he is used [to separating].

L.   [And he may separate the additional heave-offering]
by measure [of volume], by weight, or by a count [of the
number of pieces of produce being separated as heave-
offering].

M.   R. Judah says, "Also: [he may separate the additional quantity of heave-offering] from [produce] which is
not nearby ($šl'$ mn $hmqp$) [i.e., from a different batch]."

M. 4:3 (B+E: see b. Hul. 137b)

We turn to the question of the percentage of his produce a
householder is expected to separate as heave-offering. The

pericope is in two parts, A-E (in which C disputes B) and F-M.
According to A-E, the quantity of produce an individual should
separate as heave-offering depends on his particular disposition.
The more generous the person by nature, the larger the percentage
of his produce he is expected to separate as heave-offering. A
more miserly person separates less.[8] In all, then, the amount of
heave-offering contained in a batch of produce is determined by
the householder himself. By his actions in designating and separating heave-offering, he sets aside either a large or small
portion of his produce to be holy. The fixed percentages established here serve as guidelines for the separation of heave-
offering. This seems to be a function of M.'s concern for the
observance of the tithing laws by the community as a whole.[9]

F-H+L-M clearly knows A-E, making use of the figure given
there as the smallest quantity of heave-offering separated by any
householder. It holds that without regard to the disposition of
the householder, a separation of this amount fulfills the requirement to separate heave-offering from a batch of produce. Thus, if
a householder separates one-sixtieth of his produce, he need not
separate heave-offering a second time, even if in general he is a
generous person. While he may, if he so desires, give to the
priest an extra quantity of produce, since the produce from which
this share is separated no longer is liable to the separation of
heave-offering, the extra share does not have the status of a
priestly gift (H). The householder therefore must separate from
it tithes, as he does from all untithed, unconsecrated produce.[10]
What if the individual separates less than the required one-
sixtieth? I-K's point is that the produce still is liable to the
separation of heave-offering, such that the householder may separate as much additional heave-offering as he wishes.[11] That is,
we do not rule that he may make up only the minimum required
amount (one-sixtieth). Rather, we allow him to separate the
quantity which is usual for him. While the householder need
separate only one-sixtieth of his produce, as long as this percentage has not been separated, the produce is liable and the
householder may separate as much heave-offering as he desires.

Let us now turn to the glosses of J-K at L and M. L holds
that the householder may separate by measure any additional
heave-offering he needs to designate. This method of separating
heave-offering is expressly forbidden by M. 1:7. Here it is permitted, in order to allow the householder accurately to separate
the small quantity of heave-offering he needs to give to the

priest. Judah, M, refers to the issue of M. 4:1. Like sages,
M. 4:1C, he assumes that normally, if some heave-offering has been
separated from a batch of produce, additional heave-offering must
be taken from that batch for that same batch. In the present
case, Judah waives this restriction. As T. 5:6L will make clear,
Judah's point is that here the first separation of heave-offering
left the batch fully exempt from the further separation of that
offering. The additional produce which the householder designates
is not true heave-offering, and, therefore is not subject to the
restrictions which usually apply to that gift.[12]

> I. But if (E lacks *w*; HD deletes *w'm*) he said, "Lo, I
> am going to separate heave-offering and [afterwards] calcu-
> late [the percentage of my produce which I separated]. If
> there will arise in my hand one-sixtieth [of the produce],
> that which I separate shall be [valid] heave-offering
> [following Lieberman's emendation: *trwmty trwmh*), but if
> not, that which I separate shall not be [valid] heave-
> offering,"
>
> J. [if] he separated heave-offering and there arose in
> his hand one-sixtieth [of the produce], that which he has
> separated is [valid] heave-offering,
>
> K. although he has separated heave-offering by a [fixed]
> measure.

T. 4:15b

T. supplements M. 4:3 with a case in which a householder
stipulates that his separation of heave-offering will be valid
only if he separates one-sixtieth of his produce. This is the
percentage set by M. 4:3 as the minimum acceptable measure for
the priest's share. J-K rules that although the householder who
separates heave-offering in such a manner in effect separates
heave-offering by a fixed measure (forbidden by M. 1:7) the separation is valid. This is because in the actual separation of the
heave-offering, the householder in no way measured out the heave-
offering.[13]

Despite the disjunctive *but if*, at A, the pericope has no
commonality of issue with T. 4:15a (above, p. 133). HD's deletion
of these words, supported by the reading of E, is therefore on
solid substantive grounds. I find no redactional grounds for the
juxtaposition of the two pericopae.[14]

> A. [*This is*] *the* [*required*] *measure of heave-offering*
> [= M. 4:3A]:

B.   The House of Shammai say, "[If a man is] generous
[he separates] one-thirtieth [of his produce] [see M. 4:3C].

"And [if he is] average [he separates] one-fortieth [of
his produce].

"And [if he is] miserly [he separates] one-fiftieth [of
his produce]."

C.   The House of Hillel say, "[*If a man is*] *generous,*
[*he separates*] *one-fortieth* [*of his produce*] [= M. 4:3B].

"*And* [*if he is*] *average* [*he separates*] *one-fiftieth* [*of
his produce*] [= M. 4:3D].

"*And* [*if he is*] *miserly* [*he separates*] *one-sixtieth* [*of
his produce*] [= M. 4:3E]."

T. 5:3a

According to C, the opinion cited anonymously at M. 4:3A-E
is that of the House of Hillel. B cites the opinion of the House
of Shammai, M. 4:3C, and supplies the Shammaites' view on the
quantity of produce average and miserly individuals should separate as heave-offering. While the balanced numerical progression
formed by the opinions of the two Houses (thirty, forty, fifty :
forty, fifty, sixty) is notable, I see no particular importance to
the figures given.

A.   [If] he intended to separate as heave-offering one-
tenth [of his produce] and there came up in his hand (1) one-
twentieth, (2) one-thirtieth, (3) one-fortieth, (4) one-
fiftieth, (5) one sixtieth [of the produce]--

that which he has separated is [valid] heave-offering.

T. 5:5

B.   [If] he intended to separate as heave-offering one-
sixtieth [of his produce] and there came up in his hand (1)
one-fiftieth, (2) one-fortieth, (3) one-thirtieth, (4) one-
twentieth, (5) one-tenth--

that which he has separated is not [valid] heave-
offering.

C.   But if he said, "Lo, I will separate heave-offering"
[and did not specify how much he wished to separate],

D.   he separates heave-offering and [afterwards] calculates [what percentage of the produce he actually separated
as heave-offering].[15]

E.   *If* [in a case like that of C-D] *he separated heave-
offering and there came up in his hand one-sixtieth* [*of the
produce*]--

that which he has separated is [valid] heave-offering,
and he need not add to it [other produce separated as heave-
offering] [= M. 4:3F-G].

F.   *[If he separated heave-offering and there came up in*
his hand] one sixty-first *[of the produce]*--

G.   *he must add [to that which he already has separated*
other produce separated as heave-offering] [= M. 4:3I-J, with
slight variations].

H.   Rabbi says, "The greater part of a *se'ah* is like a
se'ah itself."

I.   How much may he add [to produce already separated
as heave-offering]?

J.   Even one to one [i.e., as much again as he already
has separated].

K.   Rabban Simeon b. Gamaliel says, "*[As much as to*
derive] the amount which he is used to separating" [= M.
4:3K].

L.   R. Judah says, "The additional heave-offering is (1)
taken from clean [produce] for unclean [produce], and (2)
does not impart the status of heave-offering [to unconsecrated food with which it is mixed], and (3) [non-priests
who accidentally eat it] are not liable on its account to
pay back the [added] fifth."

M.   To which case does this apply?

N.   [To the case] in which he intended to separate one-
sixtieth and there came up in his hand one sixty-first.

O.   But if he said, "Lo, I will separate heave-offering
and [afterwards] calculate [whether or not I have separated
the required one-sixtieth of the produce]"--

this [i.e., additional heave-offering he later sepa-
rates] is true heave-offering.

T. 5:6a (see y. Ter. 4:3)

T. comments on and qualifies M. 4:3, asking how the
householder's intention to separate a specific amount of heave-
offering affects the validity of his actions when he separates
other than this amount. Do we rule that the separation is valid,
or, alternatively, that since the householder has not carried out
his intention, that his actions are of no weight? According to
A-B we distinguish between cases in which the householder separates more than he intended and cases in which he separates less.
If he separates less, the separation is valid (A). All of the

produce which was separated as heave-offering was intended as
such.[16]   If, on the other hand, he separates more heave-offering
than he stated that he would, the separation is not valid (B).   In
such a case the householder has taken as heave-offering produce
which was not intended to be heave-offering.   We rule that the
separation was performed in error and require that the householder
begin again.

I follow Lieberman (TK, I, p. 358) in reading C-D+E-F as a
unit.[17]   The point is that the minimum acceptable percentage, one-
sixtieth, is applied in cases, unlike those of A-B, in which the
householder does not state beforehand that he intends to separate
some other quantity.   This hardly seems to be the point M. 4:3
wished to make, although it is in line with the general theory of
the offering we have seen so far.   H glosses G.   Rabbi's point is
that we may round off to a full *se'ah* the amount of heave-offering
the householder separates.   This is to the advantage of the householder, who thus may be relieved of the obligation to separate
heave-offering a second time.   I-J+K turns to M. 4:3's question of
how much additional heave-offering the householder may separate
in a case in which he needs to do so.   J claims that he may separate only as much as he already has separated.   If he separates
more than this, the householder is viewed not simply to be taking
additional heave-offering, but, to be performing a second, autonomous, separation of that offering.   We already know that heave-
offering may not be separated twice from the same batch of produce.
K assigns M. 4:3K to Simeon b. Gamaliel.   His point is clear, as I
have explained it in M.

L supplements Judah's statement, M. 4:3M, making explicit
that in Judah's view, heave-offering separated in a householder's
additional separation does not have the status of a true priestly
gift.   For this reason it does not impose the status of heave-
offering upon unconsecrated produce with which it is mixed, and
non-priests who accidentally eat it are not required to pay back
both its values and the additional fifth, required in the case of
holy things.   For Judah, then, the quantity of heave-offering contained in a batch of produce depends solely on the householder and
is established in that individual's first separation of the offering, no matter how much he separates.   Any additional heave-offering he separates does not have the status of a priestly gift.
Judah thus rejects M. 4:3F-K's view of the nature of the obligation to separate heave-offering.   The meaning of M+N-O, which
glosses Judah's statement, is clear on the basis of the language

I have interpolated into the translation (following HY and Lieberman, TK, I, p. 358). If the householder makes explicit from the
start that he intends to separate as heave-offering a full one-
sixtieth of his produce (O), he may continue to separate valid
heave-offering until he attains this quantity. Otherwise (N) his
first separation of heave-offering leaves the produce exempt from
the further separation of heave-offering, and any additional
heave-offering the householder separates (in order to give the
priest his proper share) does not have the status of a true
priestly gift.

     P.   R. Ishmael and R. Simeon Shezuri (reading with E;
V reads R. Ishmael Shezuri and R. Simeon; see Lieberman, TK,
I, p. 359) say, "All heave-offering [which is separated from
a type of produce] which priests are not careful [to keep in
a state of cleanness],

     Q.   "such as the heave-offering of pods (*klysyn*; Jastrow,
p. 643, s.v., *klys*; Lieberman, *loc. cit.*: *prosopis
stephaniana*) and carobs,

     R.   "is taken [in a ratio of] one [part heave-offering]
to sixty [parts produce].

     S.   "And the heave-offering of unclean produce is taken
[in a ratio of] one [part heave-offering] to sixty [parts
produce]."

T. 5:6b (y. Bik. 3:1)

     A.   These are taken (*ntlyn*) [as heave-offering] in [a
ratio of] one [part heave-offering] to sixty [parts produce]:

     B.   (1) that which grows from [the seeds of produce
which is] heave-offering, (2) mixtures of heave-offering [and
unconsecrated produce], (3) heave-offering [separated from
produce] which became unclean either accidentally or intentionally, (4) heave-offering [separated from produce] which
was [already liable to the separation of heave-offering and
was] dedicated [to the Temple], and (5) heave-offering
[separated from produce grown] outside of the Land [of
Israel],

     C.   (6) black cumin (*qsh*) , (7) pods (*klysyn*), (8) carobs,
(9) fruits ripened through caprification (*hgmzywt*; Jastrow,
p. 252), (10) lupines (*trmwsyn*), and (6) Idumean barley,

     D.   and (11) the heave-offering of produce grown in an
earthen vessel and (13) heave-offering separated by executors
[of the estate of orphans].

T. 5:7

T. accepts M. 4:3F-K's notion that one-sixtieth of a batch is
the minimum acceptable percentage to be separated as heave-offering. It lists various types of produce from which *only* this percentage need be separated, even by a householder who normally
separates a greater amount. While M. 5:6b and 5:7 are formally
autonomous of each other, they are juxtaposed because they share
this common theme.

Ishmael and Simeon Shezuri's point, T. 5:6P-S, is that in the
case of produce which will not be eaten by the priest (unclean
produce; undesirable types of produce), the householder need
separate only the minimum amount.[18] This is so because that which
the householder separates in all events will go to waste. T. 5:7
continues by listing various categories of produce from which
heave-offering is separated in a ratio of one part heave-offering
to sixty parts produce. The reasons for the specific entries are
as follows. Produce which grows from seeds in the status of
heave-offering (T. 5:7B1) is itself considered heave-offering.
Unlike a true priestly gift, however, heave-offering and tithes
must be separated from it (M. 9:3), and the remainder of the produce is sold to the priest. Since the market value of heave-
offering is low,[19] the householder is permitted actually to give
to the priest a minimal quantity of the offering, thereby reducing
his loss. The case of mixtures of heave-offering and unconsecrated
produce (B2) is the same. Although such mixtures have the status
of heave-offering (M. 4:7), the priest's share must be separated
from them and given to a priest. The remainder of the mixture is
sold to that same individual. Since all of the produce will become the property of the priest, we allow the householder to separate the minimum percentage of heave-offering. Unclean heave-
offering, B3 (mentioned also at T. 5:6S), may not be consumed by
a priest but, rather, is left to rot. Since all that he separates goes to waste, we allow the householder to separate the
minimum amount. B4 refers to produce which already is liable to
the separation of agricultural gifts at the time it is dedicated
to the Temple. While the required offerings must be separated,
only the minimum percentage of heave-offering is taken for a particular priest. This is because all of the produce already is
the property of the cult. I do not understand the reference at
B5 to heave-offering separated from produce grown outside of the
Land of Israel, nor that of D11 to the separation of heave-offering
from produce grown in a vessel (which is not punctured to allow
the growth of a single root in the ground). M. elsewhere states

explicitly that neither of these sorts of produce is liable to the
separation of heave-offering.[20] If T. here simply does not share
that view, its point is that such produce has an ambiguous status
under the law. While not comparable to produce grown in the soil
of the Land of Israel, produce grown outside of the Land or in a
vessel still is subject to the separation of heave-offering. In
light of this ambiguous status, we separate the smallest acceptable quantity of the offering. The items at C all are types of
produce which generally are not kept for consumption (see T. 5:6Q).
Only the minimum percentage need be separated from these things.
Executors of the estates of orphans likewise separate only the
minimum quantity (D13). This is in the best interests of the
orphans.

> A. Said R. Yose, "How [do we know] that heave-offering
> is separated [in a ratio of] one [part heave-offering] to
> fifty (reading with ed. princ.; V. reads: sixty) [parts
> produce]?
>
> B. "As it is written, *And from the people of Israel's*
> *half you shall take one drawn out of every fifty [of the*
> *persons, of the oxen, of the asses, and of the flocks, of all*
> *the cattle, and give them to the Levites who have charge of*
> *the tabernacle of the Lord]* (Num. 31:30).
>
> C. "The same percentage which I took in a different
> context (*mqwm 'ḥr*), lo, such is the proper percentage here.
>
> D. "Just as the percentage stated there [i.e., in Num.
> 31:30] is one-fiftieth, so the percentage here is one-
> fiftieth.
>
> E. "How do we know that if he separated heave-offering
> and there arose in his hand one-sixtieth [of the produce]
> that that which he has separated is [in all events valid]
> heave-offering?
>
> F. "As it is written, *This is the offering which you*
> *shall make: one-sixth of a ephah from each homer of wheat*
> *and one-sixth of a ephah from each homer of barley* (Ez.
> 45:13)."
>
> G. R. Ishmael b. R. Yose says, "[We know it from an
> analogy to] the cities of the Levites."
>
>   T. 5:8a (y. Ter. 4:3)

Yose offers scriptural basis for the percentages set in
M. 4:3 for the separation of heave-offering. A-D, first, proves
that one-fiftieth of a batch is the proper percentage for the

average separation of heave-offering. After the war against the
Midianites (Num. 31), God told Moses that one half of the booty
was to be given to the warriors who actually participated in the
battle, and the other half was to be divided among the people of
Israel. As stated in Num. 31:30, the people of Israel gave from
their share two percent (one in fifty) to the Levites in charge of
the tabernacle. Yose's claim is that this same percentage is the
proper one for the separation of heave-offering. At E Yose offers
scriptural proof that a separation of one-sixtieth of the produce
is in all events sufficient. Ez. 45:13 states that the people of
Israel are to give as an offering to God one-sixth of an *ephah*
out of each *homer* of wheat and barley. Since, as Ez. 45:11 states,
there are ten *ephahs* in a *homer*, this offering equals one-sixtieth
of the produce. Ishmael b. R. Yose suggests a different method of
deriving the figure one-sixtieth. "Cites of the Levites" refers
to Dt. 4:43, which describes Moses' designation of three cities
of refuge beyond the Jordan. One of the three, Golan in Bashan,
is set apart for the Manassites. The same place name, Bashan,
appears in Dt. 3:4's description of the sixty cities taken by the
Israelites from Og in Bashan (*And we took all his cities at that
time...sixty cities, the whole region of Argob, the kingdom of
Og in Bashan*). Ishmael, then, understands the setting apart of
the single city to have been equal to an offering of one in sixty,
a solid basis for the claim that heave-offering is separated in
this same percentage (so HD, cited by HY and Lieberman, TK, I,
p. 362).

     T. 5:8b is found after M. 5:1

                         4:4

     A.   One who says to his agent, "Go and separate heave-
offering [for me]"--

     B.   [the agent] separates heave-offering in accordance
with the disposition ($d^c t$) of the householder.

     C.   [And] if he does not know the disposition of the
householder,

     D.   he separates the average amount,

     E.   one-fiftieth.

     F.   [If the agent at A-B or C-D unintentionally] sepa-
rated one-tenth less or more [than the percentage he needed
to separate]--

     that which he separates [still] is [valid] heave-
offering.

G. [Six MSS. add: But) if he purposely added even
one-hundredth--

that which he has separated is not [valid] heave-
offering.

M. 4:4 (A-F: b. Ket. 99b, 100a,
b. Qid. 41a, b. Bik. 61a)

M. 4:4 advances M. 4:3's theme of the percentage of a batch
which should be taken as heave-offering. The point of the
unitary pericope is that it is the responsibility of an agent to
separate as heave-offering that percentage of the produce which
would be separated by the owner of the batch himself (A-B).[21]
Since the agent acts on behalf of the householder, this notion is
hardly surprising. What if the agent does not know what percentage
of the produce the householder normally separates? He simply
separates one-fiftieth of the batch (D-E), the percentage which
M. 4:3 holds is separated by the average person. We assume that
if the householder has not stated otherwise, he falls into this
category. What is interesting here follows at F and G, which relate to the case in which the agent separates some quantity other
than that required by the terms of his agency.[22] According to F,
as long as the agent's intention is to carry out the will of the
householder, his mis-estimation in the physical separation of the
heave-offering is not of concern. The separation was performed
with proper intention and is considered valid. If, however, the
agent purposely separates as heave-offering more than he should,
G, his separation is not valid. By purposely taking as heave-
offering produce which the householder did not wish to be such, he
has voided his appointment as agent. His separation of heave-
offering from produce which belongs to someone else therefore is
invalid (M. 1:1D3).[23]

A. *One who says to his agent, "Go and separate heave-
offering [for me]" [= M. 4:4A]--*

B. *[the agent] separates the average amount, one-
fiftieth [= M. 4:4D-E].*

C. [If he said to his agent], "Go and separate [for me]
one-fiftieth [of my produce]"--

D. *[if the agent] added or deducted one-tenth, that
which he has separated is [valid heave-offering] [= M. 4:4F].*

E. *But if he purposely added even one-[hundreth]--that
which he has separated is not [valid] heave-offering*
[= M. 4:4G].

T. 5:4

By interpolating C, T. provides the ruling for a case not referred to by M. An agent specifically is told what percentage of
the householder's produce he should separate as heave-offering.
As in a case in which the agent has not been told the percentage
of the produce to take as heave-offering, the validity of the
separation depends on his intention in performing it. If the
agent wished to separate the required percentage of the produce,
whether or not he actually removes that amount, the separation is
valid. If he purposely separates more heave-offering than the
householder desires, his separation is not valid.

4:5

A. One who separates much heave-offering (*hmrbh btrwmh*):

B. R. Eliezer says, "[He may separate as much as] one-
tenth,

C. "[an amount] equal to [that separated as] heave-
offering of the tithe.

D. "[If he wishes to separate] more than this, let him
designate it [i.e., the surplus] heave-offering of the
tithe[24] for a different batch."[25]

E. R. Ishmael says, "[He may separate so much as to
render] half [of the batch] unconsecrated produce and half
[of the batch] heave-offering."

F. R. Tarfon and R. Aqiba say, "[He may separate as
much heave-offering as he wishes] provided that he leaves
there [some] unconsecrated produce."

M. 4:5 (F: Sifré Bammidbar #5,
Horovitz, p. 8, ll. 6-9)

At issue is what percentage of a batch of produce has the
potential, upon the designation of the householder, of taking on
the status of heave-offering. The issue is treated in a tripartite dispute composed of the superscription at A, followed by
the opinions at B (glossed by C-D), E and F. Eliezer (B) claims
that only one-tenth of a batch of produce may be designated a
priestly gift. This is the same as the percentage of first tithe
which the Levite gives to a priest, as heave-offering of the tithe
(C). Eliezer thus claims that the two different types of heave-
offering are analogous. Just as heave-offering of the tithe, the
biblical tithe of the tithe (Num. 18:25), is one-tenth of the
Levite's share, so only one-tenth of the householder's produce
potentially is heave-offering. This analogy is sound in light of
the fact that Scripture offers no paradigm for the rabbinic

heave-offering, but only for heave-offering of the tithe. The
gloss at D makes further use of this analogy. A householder who
wishes to separate as heave-offering more than the allowed one-
tenth may designate an additional quantity of produce to be heave-
offering of the tithe for a different batch.[26] Although the first
batch no longer is liable to the separation of heave-offering, it
still may be used as a source for this other offering. The householder thus succeeds in giving to a priest as much produce as he
wishes, and all in the sanctified status of a priestly gift.

Both Ishmael, E, and Tarfon and Aqiba, F, hold that a much
greater portion of a batch of produce potentially is heave-offering. Ishmael, first, says that up to one half of the batch validly may be designated as a priestly gift. He simply requires that
at least half of the product of man's labors remains fully in the
possession of man, as unconsecrated food. Aqiba and Tarfon go
still further than does Ishmael. They state that the householder
validly may designate to be heave-offering all but a small portion
of his produce. Basic to their understanding is a conception of
heave-offering fundamentally different from that of Ishmael and
Eliezer. They claim that heave-offering is comparable to that
which a householder dedicates for the use of a priest (*hrm kwhnym*;
see, e.g., M. Ar. 8:6). Through such a dedication a householder
may sanctify for a priest anything he wishes. In the case of
heave-offering there is only a slight qualification. Tarfon and
Aqiba state that the householder must leave aside some small quantity of unconsecrated produce. By doing this the householder
actually separates the offering from his own food and thereby
distinguishes the offering as holy.

D. *R. Ishmael says, "[He may separate so much as to*
render] half [of the batch] unconsecrated produce and half
[of the batch] heave-offering [= M. 4:5E],

E. "provided that the unconsecrated produce is greater
in quantity than the heave-offering."

T. 5:3b

T. glosses Ishmael's opinion. Man must take for himself the
greater part of the produce he grows.[27]

4:6

A. At three times [in the year] do they calculate [the
quantity of untithed produce in] the [storage] basket [in
order to allow the separation of the proper quantity of heave-
offering]:

B.   (1) at [the time of] the first ripe fruits, (2) [at
the time of] the late summer fruits, and (3) in the middle
of the summer.

C.   (1) One who counts [the produce] is praiseworthy,
and (2) one who measures [the volume of the produce] is more
praiseworthy than he; but (3) one who weighs [the produce]
is the most praiseworthy of the three.

M. 4:6

The pericope is in two parts, A-B and the gloss at C.   The
point is a simple one.   At three set times in the harvest months
the householder should calculate the quantity of produce he has on
hand and separate heave-offering from that produce.   In this way
he is sure not to separate low quality produce such as is picked
at the beginning and end of the harvest as heave-offering for the
high quality produce picked in the middle of the summer (see
M. 2:6S).[28]   C's point already has been made at M. 1:7.   While the
householder may not measure out as heave-offering a set quantity
of produce, he may calculate the quantity of produce he has, in
order to facilitate the accurate estimation of the amount of
heave-offering he needs to separate.   It is preferred that the
householder weigh the produce.   This is more accurate than counting or calculating volume, methods which do not take into account
differences in size and weight among individual pieces of fruit.
The concern here thus is the same as that of A-B.   The householder
should not separate heave-offering in a way which provides the
priest with produce of poor quality or with less than the proper
share.

4:7

A.   R. Eliezer says, "Heave-offering is neutralized
[i.e., takes on the status of unconsecrated produce] (^{c}wlh)
[when one part of heave-offering is mixed] in [a total of] a
hundred and one [parts of produce]."

B.   R. Joshua says, "[It is neutralized when there is
one part of heave-offering] in a hundred [parts of produce]
plus [a bit] more.

C.   "And this *more* has no [fixed] measure."

D.   R. Yose b. Meshullam says, "[This *more* is] an additional *qab* per hundred *se'ahs*,

E.   "[which equals] one-sixth of [the quantity of]
heave-offering in the mixture (*štwt lmdm^{c}*)."

M. 4:7 (y. Or. 2:1; see M. Hal.
1:9, M. Or. 2:1, Sifré Bammidbar
#121, Horovitz, p. 149, 11. 3-4)

M. 4:7 introduces the notion that, under certain circumstances, heave-offering mixed with unconsecrated produce loses its
sanctified status and may be eaten as unconsecrated food by the
householder himself. This process, designated by the Hebrew root
^{C}LH, occurs when the heave-offering constitutes less than approximately one percent of a mixture with unconsecrated produce. When
this happens, the householder simply takes from the mixture and
gives to a priest a quantity of produce equal to that of the heave-
offering which was lost (M. Or. 2:1; see also M. 5:2-3, 5, 7-8 and
T. 5:9). The priest thus does not lose his share. If the heave-
offering is more than approximately one percent of the mixture,
all of that mixture must be treated as heave-offering and given to
a priest. M. 4:7 itself is a dispute over what appears to be a
matter of minutiae. This is the exact proportions in which heave-
offering mixed with unconsecrated produce is neutralized. I find
no particular significance to the specific figures cited.

Eliezer, A, holds that heave-offering is neutralized when one
part of that offering is mixed with a hundred parts of unconsecrated produce. Joshua and Yose b. Meshullam deem heave-offering
to be neutralized in a slightly smaller quantity of unconsecrated
food. Joshua says that heave-offering is neutralized if there is
in a mixture as a whole slightly more than a hundred parts of
produce, i.e., one part heave-offering and a bit over ninety nine
parts unconsecrated produce. Yose b. Meshullam states that this
extra bit of unconsecrated produce must be a *qab* in quantity.
Since there are six *qabs* in a *se'ah*, his statement that this extra
qab is equal to one-sixth of the quantity of heave-offering in
the mixture (E) applies only in a case in which there is in the
mixture a *se'ah* of heave-offering and a hundred *se'ahs* plus an
additional *qab* of unconsecrated produce. In such a case the extra
qab of unconsecrated produce indeed is equal in quantity to one
sixth of the *se'ah* of heave-offering in the mixture.

A. ^{C}*Orlah* and [produce grown in] a vineyard in which
were grown diverse kinds of seeds are neutralized [when one
part of either of these is mixed] in [a total of] two hundred
and one [parts of produce].

B. R. Simeon says, "[They are neutralized when there is
one part of these in] two hundred [parts of produce]."

C. One does not need to remove (*lhwsy'*, following the
emendation of GRA and HD; see Lieberman, TK, I, p. 356) [the
forbidden produce from the mixture].

D. And so would R. Simeon say, "Any heave-offering
[separated from a kind of produce] that priests are not careful [to keep in a state of cleanness which is neutralized in
unconsecrated produce]--

E. "(V lacks this stich; I follow E and ed. princ., as
emended by GRA and HD; see Lieberman, *loc. cit.*:) one does
not need to remove it [from the mixture]."

F. (Deleting *kgwn* with E and ed. princ.) Heave-offering, ^{c}*orlah* (reading with E and ed. princ.; V reads: *trwmt*
^{c}*wrlh*) or [produce grown in] a vineyard in which were grown
diverse kinds of seeds, [which became mixed with unconsecrated produce]--

G. [in cases of] doubts concerning their status, they
are [deemed to be] permitted [for consumption] (*spqn mwtr*).

H. [If there is] a doubt (1) [whether or not] they were
eaten by a non-priest, a doubt (2) [whether or not] they were
stolen, a doubt (3) [whether or not] they were lost, [or] a
doubt (4) [whether or not] they fell into unconsecrated
produce--

[in such cases of] doubt concerning their status, they
are [deemed to be] permitted [for consumption].

T. 5:9 (A: see M. Or. 2:1)

A-C+D-E supplements M., applying the concept of neutralization to the cases of ^{c}*orlah* and produce grown in a vineyard or
orchard in which were grown diverse kinds of seeds. F-H likewise
supplements M. 4:7, giving the rule for cases of doubt involving
mixtures.

The term ^{c}*orlah* refers to the crop of the first three years
of growth of a vineyard or orchard. Such produce may not be consumed (Lev. 19:23). Produce from a vineyard in which were grown
seeds of diverse kinds likewise may not be eaten (Dt. 22:9).
According to A produce in either of these categories becomes permitted for consumption when mixed with two hundred parts of permitted produce.[29] Simeon, B, permits a slightly greater proportion of forbidden produce, specifically, one part to a hundred
and ninety-nine parts of unconsecrated produce (such that there
are in the mixture as a whole two hundred parts).[30] I already
have stated (above, p. 151) that when heave-offering is

neutralized, the householder takes from the mixture for the priest
a quantity of produce equal to that of the heave-offering which
was lost. C states that in the case in which $^{c}orlah$ or produce
grown in a field in which were grown diverse kinds of seeds is
neutralized, the householder may consume all of the produce in the
mixture, without separating from it a quantity of produce equal to
the forbidden produce which fell in. Since, unlike heave-offering, that which was neutralized in the mixture is not an offering
which is the property of a particular individual (priest, Levite
or poor person), there is no reason for the householder to recover it from the mixture (HD). Simeon, D, states that the same
is the case when heave-offering of an undesirable kind of produce
is neutralized. Since the priest is not expected to eat such
produce, the householder need not give it to him. It is clear
then that unconsecrated produce in which heave-offering is neutralized has the status of fully unconsecrated produce. It may be
eaten without the further separation of heave-offering.

F-G+H refers to cases in which it is not clear whether or not
$^{c}orlah$, produce grown in a field in which were grown diverse kinds
of seeds, or heave-offering have been mixed with a quantity of
unconsecrated produce sufficient to neutralize them. In cases in
which produce from such mixtures *may* have been used in an improper manner, we assume that the original mixture contained
enough permitted produce to neutralize the forbidden food.[31] The
individual involved incurs none of the penalties associated with
the improper use of such types of produce.[32]

> A.   R. Judah says, "Sweet pomegranates [in the status of
> heave-offering] are forbidden [for consumption as unconse-
> crated produce] whatever [the ratio in which they are mixed
> with other pomegranates; i.e., they never are neutralized].
> B.   "How so?
> C.   "[If] one of them [i.e., a sweet pomegranate which
> is heave-offering] fell into ten thousand [pomegranates]--
> "all of them [i.e., all of the pomegranates] are for-
> bidden [i.e., they all take on the status of heave-offering].
> D.   "[If a pomegranate] fell from [this] ten thousand
> into a (E, ed. princ. add: different) ten thousand
> [pomegranates]--
> "all of them are forbidden."
> E.   R. Simeon b. Judah says in the name of R. Simeon,
> "[If] one of them [i.e., a sweet pomegranate which is heave-
> offering] fell into ten thousand [pomegranates]--

"all of them are forbidden.

F.   "[If, afterwards, a pomegranate] fell from [this] ten thousand into a third [batch],

G.   "[and] from this third [batch] into a different batch--

H.   "[in cases of] doubts [concerning the status of the pomegranates in the final batch], they are [deemed] permitted (reading with E; V reads: *forbidden*) [for consumption as unconsecrated produce],

I.   "since there is a doubt [whether or not] there is [in this case] a mixture of heave-offering and unconsecrated produce."

J.   Said R. Judah b. Baba', "I am one of those who is fit to instruct.

K.   "For if there come before me shoots of beets (*hylpy trdyn*) [which are heave-offering], I say that they are neutralized [in a mixture of one part heave-offering in a total of] a hundred and one [parts of produce].

L.   "And not only this, but a court should rule that every [kind of produce which is heave-offering] is neutralized [in a mixture of one part heave-offering in a total of] a hundred and one [parts of produce]."

M.   [*If*] *(1) nuts ('gzyn) [which are ᶜorlah] are split open, (2) pomegranates [which are ᶜorlah] are cut open, (3) jugs [containing wine which is ᶜorlah] are opened, (4) cucumbers [which are ᶜorlah] are cut into, or (5) loaves [of pressed figs which are ᶜorlah] are broken into pieces*

they are neutralized [when mixed with unconsecrated produce of this same type to create a total of] two hundred and one [parts of produce] [= M. Or. 3:8].

N.   "[If jugs containing wine which is ᶜorlah] fell [among jugs of permitted wine] and [afterwards] were opened,

O.   "whether [they were opened] intentionally or unintentionally--

P.   "lo, they are not neutralized"--the words of R. Meir.

Q.   But R. Judah and R. Simeon say, "Whether [they were opened] intentionally or unintentionally, they are neutralized."

R.   R. Yose says, "[If they were opened] unintentionally, they are neutralized.

"[But if they were opened] intentionally, they are not neutralized."

S.   And so would R. Yose say, "(1) A sealed [jug of wine
in the status of] heave-offering which became mixed among
open [jugs of unconsecrated wine] and [then] was [itself]
opened,

"[or] (2) a sealed [jug containing wine in the status of
heave-offering which was mixed] among sealed [jugs of unconsecrated wine] which [then] were opened,

"or (3) an open [jug of wine in the status of heave-
offering which became mixed] among open [jugs of unconsecrated wine] which [later] were sealed (following Lieberman,
TK, I, p. 367)--

"lo, these are neutralized.

T.   "For they did not deem [a mixture to remain] forbidden [for consumption as unconsecrated food] except [in a
case in which] a sealed [container of heave-offering is
mixed] among sealed [containers of unconsecrated produce]."

> T. 5:10a (A-H: b. Zeb. 74a, see
> M. Kel. 17:5; J-M: see M. Or.
> 3:7-8)

T. continues to provide rules on the neutralization of heave-
offering and other forbidden produce, supplementing M. 4:7.   The
pericope is in two parts, A-D+E-I, glossed by J-L, and M, a
verbatim citation of M. Or. 3:8, glossed by N-P+Q-R, a dispute
which is itself augmented at S-T.

I can interpret A only by assuming that sweet pomegranates
are a highly desirable and valuable type of produce.[33]   Judah
states for this reason that if sweet pomegranates in the status of
heave-offering are mixed with other, less valuable, pomegranates,
the heave-offering is not neutralized.   In this way a householder
cannot purposely cause the priest to lose his share of such
desirable produce.   Judah's view is exemplified at C-D.   A single
sweet pomegranate imparts the status of heave-offering to ten
thousand unconsecrated pomegranates with which it is mixed (C).
As D states, further, pomegranates from the batch in which this
first mixture occurred have the same status as the original sweet
pomegranates which were heave-offering.   They impart the status
of heave-offering to any quantity of pomegranates with which they
are mixed.   Simeon b. Judah, E-H, rejects the notion that derivative batches have the same ability to impart the status of heave-
offering as had the original sweet pomegranates.   It is not, after
all, known whether there actually is in one of these batches a

sweet pomegranate in the status of heave-offering. Thus he states
that at two removes from the original heave-offering, we rule
leniently regarding the status of the mixture. This is the same
as in other cases of neutralization in which there are two
elements of doubt (cf., T. 5:9F-H).[34] Judah b. Baba', J-L, rejects the notion that, because of their value, certain types of
produce are not neutralized. He states that all heave-offering
is neutralized when mixed with a hundred parts of unconsecrated
produce, in accordance with the position of Eliezer, M. 4:7A.[35]

M+N-R cites and glosses M. Or. 3:8. Except for its interest
in the rules governing neutralization, it therefore is out of
place in the present context. M. Or. 3:7 holds that if any of the
five kinds of produce listed at M. are $^{c}orlah$, they are not
neutralized, no matter how large the quantity of permitted produce
with which they are mixed. As is the case with sweet pomegranates,
this prevents the householder purposely from mixing these particularly valuable types of produce with other food in order to
recover them for his own use. M. Or. 3:8, cited here at M, states
that if the produce is in some way damaged or loses its value, it
is neutralized when mixed with two hundred parts permitted produce,
as is the case for all produce in the status of $^{c}orlah$ (T. 3:8A).
N-R glosses, referring to jars containing wine made from grapes in
the status of $^{c}orlah$. If closed jars are mixed in any proportion
among other jars, all of the wine takes on the status of $^{c}orlah$
and may not be consumed. What if after such a mixture occurs, the
jar containing the wine which is $^{c}orlah$ is opened? Meir, P, states
that, since all of the wine already had taken on the status of
$^{c}orlah$, it remains forbidden. The rule of M3 is not invoked.
Judah and Simeon, Q, disagree, holding that even if the householder intentionally opens the jars of wine, the rule of M3 is
applied, and the $^{c}orlah$ is neutralized. Yose, R, offers a
mediating position. If the householder purposely opens the jars,
his actions are of no effect, and all of the wine retains the
status of $^{c}orlah$. If, however, the jars unintentionally are
opened, the $^{c}orlah$ is neutralized in the usual two hundred parts
of permitted produce.

S-W carries out an exercise like that of N-R, now for the
case of heave-offering. The claim is that, as in the case of
$^{c}orlah$, if a closed jug of wine in the status of heave-offering is
misplaced among other jars containing unconsecrated wine, the
heave-offering is not neutralized. Since the jugs are sealed, we
deem there to have been no mixing of heave-offering and

unconsecrated produce. Yose states that whether or not the heave-
offering is neutralized depends on the ultimate condition of the
jars, sealed or opened. If any of the jars finally are left open,
there is deemed to be a mixing of heave-offering and the other
produce, and the heave-offering is neutralized. Although attributed to Yose, S-T, thus appears to agree with the position of Judah
and Simeon, Q, who likewise are concerned only with the final
condition of the jars. This surely should not be agreeable to
Yose, who, at R, is concerned with the intention of the householder who opened or sealed the vessels.

4:8-11

A. R. Joshua says, "Black figs neutralize white ones,
and white ones neutralize black ones.

B. "[And in the case of] cakes of pressed figs--

(1) "large ones neutralize small ones, and small ones
neutralize large ones;

(2) "round ones neutralize square ones, and square ones
neutralize round ones."

C. R. Eliezer deems [heave-offering mixed with such
different types of its same genus of produce to remain] forbidden [for consumption as common produce].

D. And R. Aqiba says, "When it is known which [type of
produce in the status of heave-offering] fell [into the unconsecrated produce, the two different types] do not neutralize one another.

E. "But when it is not known which [type of produce in
the status of heave-offering] fell [into the unconsecrated
produce, the two different types of produce] neutralize one
another."

M. 4:8 (A-B: M. Or. 3:1)

F. "How so?

G. "[If there were] fifty [unconsecrated] white figs
and fifty [unconsecrated] black figs [together in a basket]--

H. "[if] a black fig [which was heave-offering] fell
into the basket, the black figs are forbidden [for consumption as unconsecrated produce], and the white figs are
permitted [for consumption as unconsecrated produce].

I. "[If] a white fig [which was heave-offering] fell
[into the basket], the white figs are forbidden [for consumption as unconsecrated produce], and the black figs are
permitted [for consumption as unconsecrated produce].

J. "But if he does not know what [color fig] fell [into
the basket, white and black figs] neutralize one another [and
all of the figs in the basket are permitted for consumption
as unconsecrated produce]."

K. And in this [i.e., the rules of A-C], R. Eliezer is
stringent and R. Joshua is lenient.

M. 4:9

L. But in this [case] R. Eliezer is lenient and R.
Joshua is stringent:

M. In [a case in which] one stuffed a *litra* of dried
figs [in the status of heave-offering] into the mouth of a
jar [filled] with [a hundred *litras* of] unconsecrated [dried
figs], but does not know which [jar]--

N. R. Eliezer says, "They regard them as if they were
loose figs, and the bottom ones neutralize the top ones."

O. R. Joshua says, "[The heave-offering] will not be
neutralized unless a hundred jars are there."

M. 4:10

P. A *se'ah* of heave-offering which fell into the mouth
of a store-jar,

Q. and one skimmed it off--

R. R. Eliezer says, "If in the layer removed were a
hundred *se'ahs*,

S. "[the heave-offering] is neutralized in a hundred
and one [parts of produce]."

T. But R. Joshua says, "[The heave-offering] is not
neutralized."

U. A *se'ah* of heave-offering which fell into the mouth
of a store-jar--

he should skim it off.

V. But if so, why did they say heave-offering is
neutralized in a hundred and one [parts of unconsecrated
produce]?

[That is the case only] if one does not know whether or
not it [i.e., the produce which is heave-offering] is mixed
up [with the unconsecrated produce] or where [in the unconsecrated produce] it fell.

M. 4:11 (y. Ter. 4:8)

At issue again is under what circumstances heave-offering
mixed with unconsecrated produce is neutralized. Three Eliezer-
Joshua disputes (M. 4:8A-C, M. 4:10 and M. 4:11P-T) illustrate

two distinct theories of neutralization. Aqiba's statement,
M. 4:8D-E, along with the long explanation following it, M. 4:9F-J,
intervene with essentially secondary material. This separates K
from its referent at M. 4:8A-C.[36] Joshua's position of M. 4:11T
is carried forward by the anonymous case at M. 4:11U-V.

According to Joshua, A, distinguishing features such as color
and size of produce are irrelevant in determining whether or not
heave-offering is neutralized.[37] This is in keeping with the law
of M. 2:6S, which states in regard to the initial separation of
heave-offering that different types of the same genus of produce
are homogeneous.[38] Eliezer disagrees. He holds, for example,
that white figs in the status of heave-offering are not neutralized by black figs. In such a mixture the heave-offering can be
distinguished and may, therefore, be recovered. This being the
case there is no reason to deem the heave-offering to be neutralized. Joshua and Eliezer thus have very different understand-
ings of the mechanics of neutralization. For Joshua neutralization
may occur whenever heave-offering and unconsecrated produce are
combined. Eliezer, on the other hand, holds that heave-offering
is neutralized only if it actually is lost within the unconsecrated
produce, such that the status of each individual piece of produce
in the mixture is in doubt. Aqiba's position, D-E, is most easily
explained on the basis of the example given at G-K. A householder
has a basket containing both black and white figs. If it is known
what color figs in the status of heave-offering fall into the
basket, only figs of that same color are deemed to be part of the
mixture. If, on the other hand, it is not known whether black or
white figs in the status of heave-offering fell into the basket,
each black and white fig in the basket is in a status of doubt
whether or not it is heave-offering. All the figs therefore join
together to neutralize the heave-offering with which they were
mixed. Aqiba's view thus is in essential agreement with Eliezer.[39]
This view holds that if heave-offering can be recovered, leaving
no doubt as to the status of the produce with which it had been
mixed, the heave-offering is not neutralized.

At L+M-O the positions of Joshua and Eliezer are reversed.[40]
Eliezer claims that even though the figs in the status of heave-
offering can be recovered from the mouth of the jar, they are
neutralized by the other produce in the vessel. Joshua says that
since the heave-offering in the mouth of the jar remains distinct
from the unconsecrated produce under it, it is not neutralized.
Only if the jar containing the heave-offering is mixed among a

hundred other jars of figs, such that the heave-offering may be
considered lost among the unconsecrated produce in the mouths of
the other jars, is that heave-offering neutralized.[41]

M. 4:11P-T provides a further case in which Eliezer and
Joshua dispute the status of heave-offering which has been placed
on the surface of a batch of unconsecrated produce. Neusner already has shown at some length that the superscription, at Q, and
Eliezer's position, R, have been contaminated by the words *he
should skim it off*, at U.[42] Accepting Neusner's conclusion and
omitting Q and the words cited in Eliezer's name at R, the dispute here simply is a replay of M. 4:10. Eliezer states that even
though the heave-offering may be recovered from the surface of
the store-jar, it is deemed mixed with the unconsecrated produce.
If sufficient unconsecrated produce is present it is neutralized.
Joshua, T, as at O, disagrees. As long as the heave-offering is
not actually mixed with the unconsecrated produce, it is not
neutralized. U-V, then, explains and supports Joshua's position.
If the heave-offering is not actually lost within the unconsecrated produce, it is recovered and retains the status of a
priestly gift. The rules of neutralization apply only in a case
in which heave-offering actually is lost in a mixture with unconsecrated produce.

U. "When you reason, [you can] state a general rule
(*kŝtmṣ' 'wmr kll*; see Lieberman, TK, I, p. 368):

V. "that R. Eliezer says, 'If it is known [what type of
heave-offering] fell [into unconsecrated produce, the heave-
offering] is not neutralized, and if it is not known, it is
neutralized;'

W. "R. Joshua says, 'Whether or not it is known [what
type of heave-offering] fell [into unconsecrated produce] it
is not (V lacks: *not*; it is supplied by Lieberman on the
basis of E and ed. princ.) neutralized'"--the words of R.
Meir (*dbry r m'yr* is supplied by Lieberman, following E and
ed. princ.).

X. R. Judah says, "R. Eliezer says, 'Whether or not it
is known [what type of heave-offering] fell [into the unconsecrated produce], it is not neutralized.'

Y. "R. Joshua says, 'Whether or not it is known [what
type of heave-offering] fell [into the unconsecrated produce],
it is (Lieberman omits *not*, following E and ed. princ.)
neutralized.'

Z.   "R. Aqiba says, 'If it is known [what type of heave-
offering] fell [into the unconsecrated produce], it is not
neutralized,

"But if it is not known [what type of heave-offering]
fell [into the unconsecrated produce], it is neutralized'"
[X-Z: see M. 4:8].

T. 5:10b (y. Ter. 4:9)

Meir attributes to Eliezer, V, the position held by Aqiba at
M. 4:8D-E. In light of what we have seen, this is quite logical,
making explicit the fundamental agreement between the views of
the two authorities. At W Meir cites in Joshua's name the opposite of the opinion that authority holds in M. This is a confused state of affairs, for which I can offer no solution.[43]
Judah, X-Z, simply repeats the substance of the opinions of each
of M. 4:8's authorities.

A.   "(1) *A litra of dried figs [in the status of heave-
offering] which one stuffed into the mouth of a jar [filled
with dried figs], but does not know into which [jar] he
stuffed them* [= M. 4:10M, with slight variation],

"(2) [or which one stuffed] into a bee hive [filled with
dried figs], but does not know into which bee hive he stuffed
them,

"(3) [or which] one pressed on a circle of pressed figs,
but does not know on which circle of pressed figs he pressed
them--

B.   "R. Eliezer says, 'They regard the [figs on] top [of
the jar, bee hive, or pressed figs] as if they are loose [and
therefore are mixed with the rest of the produce].

"'If there are there [in the jar, etc.] a hundred and
one *litras* [of produce, the heave-offering] is neutralized,
[see M. 4:10N].

"'But if not, it is not neutralized.'

C.   "R. Joshua says, 'If there are a hundred mouths [of
jars, etc., the heave-offering] is neutralized [see M. 4:10/O].

"'And if not, [produce in] the mouths [of the jars, etc.]
is forbidden and [produce in] the bottoms [of the jars, etc.]
is permitted [i.e., retains the status of unconsecrated food]'"
--the words of R. Meir.

D.   R. Judah says, "R. Eliezer says, 'If there are there
a hundred mouths [of jars, etc., the heave-offering] is
neutralized.

"'And if not, [produce in] the mouths [of the jars, etc.]
is forbidden and [produce in] the bottoms [of the jars, etc.]
is permitted.'

E. "R. Joshua says, 'Even if there are there three
hundred mouths [of jars, etc., the heave-offering] is not
neutralized.'

F. "If he pressed it [i.e., a *litra* of dried figs in
the status of heave-offering] upon a circle of pressed figs,
but does not know where [on the circle] he pressed it, all
agree that it is neutralized."

T. 5:11 (b. Bes. 3b, b. Zeb. 73a)

A-C gives Meir's greatly expanded version of M. 4:10's dispute between Eliezer and Joshua. The two additional examples,
given at A2-3, do not change matters. Although expanded in
language, the opinions of Eliezer (B) and Joshua (C) likewise remain exactly the same as they were in M. Judah, D-H, offers a
different version of the dispute. He attributes to Eliezer (D)
the opinion, in M., held by Joshua. At E Judah has Joshua reject
the notion that heave-offering in the mouth of one jar can be
neutralized by unconsecrated produce in the mouths of other jars.
Judah's Joshua, then, should hold the opinion given in M. to
Eliezer, viz., that only if there is sufficient produce in the jar
containing the heave-offering is the priestly gift neutralized.[44]
At F Judah states that Eliezer and Joshua agree that if heave-
offering is lost in a batch of unconsecrated produce, such that it
cannot be recovered, it is neutralized. Judah thus offers credence
to my understanding of the basic issue which Joshua and Eliezer
debate, specifically, whether or not heave-offering is deemed to be
neutralized in cases (such as those of A1-3) in which it is not
mixed with or actually lost in the unconsecrated produce into which
it falls.

A. *A se'ah of heave-offering which fell into the mouth
of a store-jar* [= M. 4:11T]--

B. they regard it as if it [i.e., the heave-offering]
were wheat on top of barley.

C. *One should skim it off* [= M. 4:11T].

D. Rabban Simeon b. Gamaliel says, "[If] a bit of
heave-offering remained [with the produce in the store-jar],
it is neutralized in a hundred and one parts."

E. "Heave-offering of the tithe [separated] from doubtfully tithed produce (*dmyy*), which fell back into (*ḥzrh*) the

batch [from which it was separated] imparts the status of
heave-offering [to that batch].

"But if it fell into a different batch, it does not impose the status of heave-offering [upon the produce]"--the
words of R. Eliezer

F. But sages say, "Whether it fell back into its same
batch or into a different batch, it imposes the status of
heave-offering [upon the produce into which it falls]."

G. R. Simeon says, "Whether it fell back into its same
batch or into a different batch, it does not impose the
status of heave-offering [upon the produce with which it is
mixed]."

T. 5:12 (y. Dem. 4:1)

The pericope is in two parts, A-D and E-G. A-C cites M. 4:11T,
adding the gloss at B, in order to clarify M.'s point. This is,
as I have stated, that when heave-offering can be distinguished
from the unconsecrated produce with which it is mixed, it is not
neutralized. Simeon b. Gamaliel, D, glosses. If in skimming the
heave-offering from the unconsecrated produce the householder
leaves behind some heave-offering, this small quantity is deemed
neutralized in the other produce.

E-G is autonomous of M. Heave-offering of the tithe separated from *demai* is in a status of doubt as to whether or not it
is a sanctified priestly gift. Eliezer, E, says that such heave-
offering of the tithe is deemed true heave-offering only in conjunction with the produce from which it actually was separated.[45]
This is so becuase it is this offering which in fact freed that
produce for consumption. Thus if it is mixed with that produce in
a ratio of more than one part of heave-offering to a hundred parts
of unconsecrated produce, it imposes the status of heave-offering
upon that produce.[46] If this heave-offering of the tithe falls
into other produce, we assume that it is not a true priestly gift.
It does not impose the status of heave-offering on that other
produce. Sages, F, state that heave-offering of the tithe separated from *demai* is treated in all respects like a true priestly
gift and, therefore, imposes the status of heave-offering on any
produce with which it is mixed in sufficient quantity. Simeon
takes the opposite view. Since the heave-offering of the tithe
might not be a sanctified priestly gift, he holds that it is in no
event treated as one. This view is closest to that of T. 5:9F-H,
which holds that in cases of doubt concerning mixtures of

heave-offering and unconsecrated produce, the mixtures are deemed
permitted for consumption as unconsecrated produce.[47]

    A. "Flour (*hqmhyn*) and fine flour (*hswltwt*) neutralize
[heave-offering] in conjunction with one another"--the words
of R. Nehemiah.

    B. But sages say, "They do not neutralize [heave-
offering in conjunction with one another]."

T. 6:6

    C. (Lieberman supplies C-E from ed. princ.) "A *log* of
water which fell into ninety-nine [*logs*] of wine, and afterwards a *log* of wine [which was heave-offering] fell [into the
mixture]--

    D. "[the water and the wine] neutralize [the wine which
is heave-offering] in conjunction with one another"--the
words of R. Nehemiah.

    E. But sages say, "They do not neutralize [the heave-
offering] in conjunction with one another.

T. 6:7

The two formally balanced disputes supplement M. 4:8-11's
rules for the neutralization of different kinds of a single genus
of produce.[48] Fine flour, A-B, can be distinguished from other
flour with which it is mixed. Nehemiah takes the position of
Joshua, M. 4:8A-B, that the distinguishing features are irrelevant.
The two types of flour work together to neutralize heave-offering.
Sages have the position of Eliezer, M. 4:8C, that heave-offering
is not neutralized by a different type of its same genus of
produce.

The problem at C-E is slightly different. This is whether
wine which is heave-offering is neutralized by water. Nehemiah
states that the water indeed increases the volume of the wine so
that the heave-offering is neutralized. Sages, on the other hand,
states that the water, which itself is not produce, does not have
the power to neutralize heave-offering.

4:12

    A. (1) Two bins [the combined content of which is a
hundred *se'ahs* of unconsecrated produce],

    or (2) two store-jars [the combined content of which is
a hundred *se'ahs* of unconsecrated produce]

    B. into one of which fell a *se'ah* of heave-offering,

    C. and it is not known into which of them it fell--

D.   [the bins or store-jars] neutralize [the heave-
offering] in conjunction with one another ($m^c lwt$ zw $'t$ zw)
[i.e., we deem the heave-offering to have fallen into a
single batch of a hundred *se'ahs* of produce].

E.   R. Simeon says, "Even if they [i.e., the two baskets
or store-jars] are in two [different] cities--

"they neutralize [the heave-offering] in conjunction with
one another."

M. 4:12

M. 4:12 advances the theme of M. 4:8-11, offering a case of
doubt concerning a mixture of heave-offering and unconsecrated
produce. A-D is glossed by Simeon, E.   A *se'ah* of heave-offering
falls into one of two bins (A1) or store-jars (A2), but it is not
known which.   Individually the containers do not hold enough unconsecrated produce to neutralize the heave-offering; together
they do.   Yet, since there are a hundred *se'ahs* of produce which,
by one *se'ah* of heave-offering, have been rendered suspect as
regards their status, D rules that the heave-offering is neutralized.   This position is closely parallel to that of Eliezer,
M. 4:8N, which holds that we deem heave-offering to be neutralized
by produce with which it is not actually mixed.   Simeon, E, adds
little.   Even if the containers are in two different cities, for
the reason stated above, the rule of D applies.

4:13

A.   Said R. Yose, "A case ($m^c \acute{s}h$) came before R. Aqiba
concerning fifty bundles of vegetables, among which had fallen
a similar bundle, half of which was heave-offering.

B.   "And I said before him, '[The heave-offering] is
neutralized.'

C.   "Not that heave-offering is neutralized in [a mixture of one part of heave-offering in a total of] fifty one
[parts of produce, but,] rather, because there were there a
hundred and two half [*se'ahs*, only one of which was heave-
offering]."

M. 4:13 (y. Ter. 4:13)

The case is exactly the same as that at M. 4:12.   Among fifty-
one bundles of unconsecrated vegetables is a bunch composed half
of heave-offering, half of unconsecrated produce.   It is not known
which bundle contains the heave-offering.   Since the status of all
of the unconsecrated produce is in doubt, Yose rules that it all
joins together to neutralize the heave-offering.   The point is

made clear at C. Of the hundred and two half *se'ahs* of produce
in the mixture, only one half *se'ah*, less than one percent of the
mixture, has the status of heave-offering.[49]

TERUMOT CHAPTER FIVE

The chapter carries forward M. 4:7-13's discussion of the
neutralization of heave-offering. It is in two parts. M. 5:1-4
present cases in which either the heave-offering or the unconsecrated produce with which it is mixed is unclean. M. 5:5-8+9 are
on whether or not produce taken to replace heave-offering which
is neutralized is true heave-offering. Both parts of the chapter
flow from a single set of disputant opinions, Eliezer's, M. 5:2C,
and that of sages, expressed first at M. 5:2D. Eliezer's view is
that if heave-offering is neutralized in unconsecrated produce,
the produce which the householder takes to replace it is the same
produce which originally fell into the batch. This produce therefore is true heave-offering, and, further, has the same status of
cleanness as the heave-offering which was lost. The batch from
which it was taken, likewise, is composed solely of unconsecrated
produce, just as it was before the mixture occurred (M. 5:6-7).
Sages disagree. They hold that the replacement heave-offering
contains only that proportion of true heave-offering which is contained in the mixture from which it is separated. According to
this view, if the original heave-offering, or the unconsecrated
produce with which it was mixed, is unclean, the replacement
heave-offering is a mixture of clean and unclean produce. While
the priest may consume this produce, he must do so in such a way
as to prevent the unclean produce in the batch from imparting uncleanness either to the clean heave-offering or to himself. It
also follows from this view that the batch in which the heave-
offering was neutralized still contains some heave-offering. This
being the case, sages cannot agree to the anonymous rule of M. 5:7.

Only M. 5:1 and M. 5:9 stand outside the framework of the
dispute between Eliezer and sages. M. 5:1 introduces the problem
of mixtures in which either the heave-offering or the unconsecrated produce is unclean, the topic of M. 5:2-4. Clean heave-
offering is mixed with unclean unconsecrated produce and imparts
its own status to that produce. M. 5:1I-J rules that since the
original heave-offering is clean, the batch must be given to a
priest, who cooks and eats the produce in such a way that the
unclean unconsecrated produce does not impart uncleanness either
to the clean heave-offering or to himself. If, however, the
heave-offering in the mixture is unclean (M. 5:1A-C), the batch

is left to rot. The priest could not eat the origiinal heave-
offering and therefore may not benefit from the mixture. M. 5:9
is autonomous of the specific issues of the preceding pericopae,
concluding M.'s discussion of the neutralization of heave-offering. In each of its three cases a mixture of heave-offering and
unconsecrated produce changes in quantity. Unless it is certain
that the ratio of heave-offering to unconsecrated produce has
changed, the mixture retains its same status of consecration.

As usual T. restates and expands M.'s rules, adding significant statements of its own only at T. 5:15 (on the neutralization
of *ᶜorlah* and other forbidden produce), and at T. 6:11a (on the
neutralization of heave-offering of one kind in a different kind
of unconsecrated produce). As in Chapter Four, important attributions here are to Yavneans, most notably, to Eliezer. The
Houses are cited pseudepigraphically,[1] M. 5:4. Simeon appears at
M. 5:8. In T. we have Yose (T. 5:13), Judah (T. 5:14), Eleazar
b. ᶜArakh and Simeon (T. 5:15).

5:1

I.   A.   A *se'ah* of unclean heave-offering which fell into
less than a hundred [*se'ahs*] of unconsecrated produce,

B.   or [which fell] into first tithe, or second tithe
or [produce] dedicated [to the Temple],

C.   whether these things are clean or unclean--

D.   let [all of the produce in the mixture] rot.

II.   E.   (Eight MSS. add: But) if that *se'ah* [of heave-
offering which fell into the other produce] was clean--

let [all of the produce in the mixture] be sold to
priests, at the [low] value of heave-offering,

F.   less the value of that same *se'ah* [of heave-offering
which fell into the unconsecrated produce].

G.   And if it fell into first tithe--

let him designate [the mixture] heave-offering of the
tithe.

H.   And if it fell into second tithe or [produce] dedicated [to the Temple]--

lo, these may be redeemed.

III. I.   (Five MSS. lack: And) if the unconsecrated produce
[into which the heave-offering fell] was unclean--

let [all of the produce in the mixture] be eaten[2] in
small bits, or roasted, or kneaded with fruit juice, or
divided into [little] lumps [of dough],

J. such that there will not be in a single place an
egg's bulk [of produce].

M. 5:1 (A+D-F: b. Ned. 59a)

In these three cases heave-offering imparts its own status
to produce with which it is mixed. The problem, A-D and I-J, is
that either the heave-offering or the produce into which it falls
is unclean. May the resultant mixture be eaten by a priest, as is
clean heave-offering, or must it be left to rot, as is unclean
heave-offering? The point, as we shall see, is that we rule according to the status of the heave-offering which originally fell
into the other produce. If it was clean, the mixture is consumed
by a priest. If it was unclean, the mixture is left to rot.
Before turning to the specifics of the cases before us, we may
note that the pericope is formally unitary. Each of its cases
(A-D, E-H and I-J) depends on A for sense. Only B and G-H, which
introduce the problem of mixtures of heave-offering and first
tithe, second tithe, or produce dedicated to the Temple, are
secondary to the concern of the pericope.

Unclean heave-offering, A, imparts the status of heave-offering to unconsecrated produce or, B, to other agricultural offerings or sanctified produce. Since the original heave-offering is
unclean and may not be eaten by a priest, all of the produce in
the mixture is deemed to have this same status and must be left
to rot (D). At E-F clean heave-offering falls into clean unconsecrated produce. The mixture, composed entirely of clean produce
in the status of heave-offering, is sold to a priest at the low
market value of that offering.[3] Since the *se'ah* of heave-offering
which originally fell into the unconsecrated produce already is
the property of a priest, however, that quantity of produce is
given without remuneration to that individual (F). G-H refers to
the circumstances adduced at B. If heave-offering is mixed with
first tithe, the householder gives all of the produce to a Levite,
who then designates it heave-offering of the tithe for other first
tithe which he owns. In this way the Levite receives the tithe
which rightfully is his, yet the produce ultimately is eaten by a
priest, as it must be. If heave-offering is mixed with second
tithe or with produce dedicated to the Temple, H, the householder
redeems with coins the consecrated produce in the mixture. The
coins take on the sanctified status previously held by the second
tithe or dedicated produce. The mixture now may be sold to a
priest, as at E-F.[4] The householder, of course, must dispose of

the consecrated coins as appropriate, using them to purchase produce in Jerusalem, in the case of second tithe, or turning them
over to the Temple treasury, in the case of produce dedicated to
the Temple.

At I-J, finally, clean heave-offering imparts its own status
to unclean unconsecrated produce. Since here the original heave-
offering is clean and should be consumed by a priest, the mixture
may not simply be left to rot, as at A-D. The problem is to prepare the produce for consumption in such a way that the unclean
produce in the mixture does not convey uncleanness to the clean
heave-offering, or to the priest who eats it. For this reason
the mixture is prepared dry, or with fruit juice, so that the
heave-offering is not made susceptible to uncleanness. It is
eaten by the priest in quantities of less than an egg's bulk,
which do not convey uncleanness.

5:2-4

I.   A.   A *se'ah* of unclean heave-offering which fell into[5]
a hundred [*se'ahs*] of clean [unconsecrated] produce [and so
is neutralized]--

      B.   R. Eliezer says, "Let it be lifted out (*trwm*) and
burned.[6]

      C.   "For I say, 'The *se'ah* which fell [into the unconse-
crated produce] is the [same] *se'ah* that is raised up.'"

      D.   But sages say, "[The heave-offering] is raised up
(*t^{c}lh*) [out of the mixture] and is eaten dry, roasted,
kneaded with fruit juice, or divided into lumps [of dough],

      E.   "so that there is not in a single place as much as
an egg's bulk [of produce]."

M. 5:2 (b. Bek. 22a-b; see Sifré
Bammidbar #121, Horovitz, p. 149,
ll. 3-6)[7]

II.   F.   A *se'ah* of clean heave-offering which fell into a
hundred [*se'ahs*] of unclean unconsecrated produce--

      G.   let it be raised up and eaten dry, roasted, kneaded
with fruit juice, or divided into lumps [of dough],

      H.   such that there is not in a single place as much as
an egg's bulk [of produce].

M. 5:3

III. I.   A *se'ah* of unclean heave-offering which fell into a
hundred [*se'ahs*] of clean heave-offering--

J. the House of Shammai declare [the mixture] forbidden [for consumption by a priest].

K. But the House of Hillel permit.

L. Said the House of Hillel to the House of Shammai, "Since clean [heave-offering] is forbidden to non-priests, and unclean [heave-offering] is forbidden to priests, if clean [heave-offering] can be neutralized, so unclean [heave-offering] can be neutralized."

M. Said to them the House of Shammai, "No! If unconsecrated produce, to which leniency applies and which is permitted to non-priests, neutralizes clean [heave-offering], should heave-offering, to which stringency applies and which is forbidden to non-priests, [have that same power and] neutralize unclean [heave-offering]?"

N. After they had agreed:

O. R. Eliezer says, "Let it be raised up and burned."

P. But sages say, "It has been lost through its scantiness."

M. 5:4

M.'s concern, as at M. 5:1, is the adjudication of problems of cleanness in mixtures of heave-offering and unconsecrated produce. M. 5:2-4's three cases have heave-offering neutralized in other produce. At issue, thus, is the status of the produce taken from the mixture to replace the lost heave-offering (see p. 151 and M. Or. 2:1). A-E's case is like that of M. 5:1A-D, with unclean heave-offering mixed with clean unconsecrated produce. F-H's case parallels that of M. 5:1I-J, clean heave-offering mixed with unclean unconsecrated produce. The final case, I-K+L-M+N-P, has no equivalent at M. 5:1.

At A-E unclean heave-offering is mixed with a hundred times its quantity in clean unconsecrated produce. Eliezer (B) states that the householder takes a *se'ah* of produce from the mixture and deems it to be the same as that which fell in. Since it is unclean, it is burned. Sages, on the other hand, hold that since it is neutralized, the heave-offering is diffused in the clean produce. Produce taken to replace the lost priestly gift therefore is a mixture of clean and unclean produce. The priest eats it in such a way as to prevent the unclean produce in the mixture from imparting uncleanness either to the clean produce or to himself, just as at M. 5:1I-J.

M. 5:3 carries forward sages' view. Clean heave-offering is

neutralized in unclean unconsecrated produce. The produce which
subsequently is separated from the mixture for a priest is treated
as a mixture of clean and unclean produce, exactly as at D-E.
Eliezer, who holds that the householder deems the *se'ah* of produce
which is separated from the mixture to be the same as that which
fell in (B), can hardly agree. In his view the produce taken from
the mixture is clean, and may be eaten as such.

Unclean heave-offering, as we know, may not be eaten by a
priest. M. 5:4 asks whether such heave-offering becomes permitted
for consumption when it is mixed with a great quantity of clean
heave-offering, just as heave-offering mixed with unconsecrated
produce is neutralized and may be eaten by a non-priest. The
House of Shammai state that it does not, and so prohibit I's mixture from consumption by a priest. The Hillelites, on the other
hand, state that the small quantity of unclean heave-offering may
be disregarded, just as we ignore a small quantity of heave-
offering which is mixed with unconsecrated produce. They therefore permit the mixture to the priest. The debate which follows
at L-M is problematic. Instead of having the Houses argue the
issue in terms such as I have explained it, and which the language
of J-K (forbids/permits) requires, it has the Houses debate whether
unclean heave-offering is *neutralized* in clean heave-offering.
The debate therefore refers to a dispute such as the following:

A.   A *se'ah* of unclean heave-offering which fell into
a hundred [*se'ahs*] of clean heave-offering--

B.   The House of Shammai say, "[The unclean heave-
offering] is neutralized."

C.   But the House of Hillel say, "It is not neutralized."

This, however, is nonsensical, for it is meaningless to speak of
heave-offering's being neutralized in heave-offering. None of the
produce in question loses the status of a priestly gift. It thus
seems likely that the debate, which directly reflects the language
and concerns of M. 5:2-3, was formulated at the time at which the
dispute was set in its present redactional framework. It does not
go back to the historical Houses. Still, we can make sense of
each of the House's positions. The Hillelites argue that both clean
heave-offering and unclean heave-offering are forbidden to some
individuals. Since the two categories of heave-offering are
equivalent in this respect, they likewise are equivalent as regards neutralization. The Shammaites reply that while unconsecrated produce does in fact neutralize heave-offering,

heave-offering, to which greater stringency applies, cannot serve
to neutralize other heave-offering. While the Shammaites are given
the last word, their argument, which remains within the conceptual
framework established by the Hillelites, is hardly more logical
than the Hillelite one.

N is joining language, linking the opinions of Eliezer and
sages to the foregoing. While later rabbinic tradition will
assume that it is the House of Shammai which conceded to the
position of the Hillelites, this is not stated or assumed here.
What is important for our purposes is that the positions of Eliezer
and sages revert to the formulation of the Houses' dispute found
at J-K. These authorities do not use the terminology of the
debate at L-M. Eliezer is consistent with his position at
M. 5:2B-C. The householder (or priest) may take a *se'ah* of heave-
offering from the mixture and claim that it is the same *se'ah* that
originally fell in. Like all heave-offering which undoubtedly
has a status of uncleanness, this *se'ah* is burned (M. Tem. 7:5).
The rest of the heave-offering is clean and may be eaten by a
priest. This position is essentially the same as that of the
House of Shammai who, at J, state that we may not disregard the
unclean heave-offering in the mixture. Eliezer simply adds that
the unclean priestly gift can be removed from the clean heave-
offering. Like Eliezer, sages do not make reference to the concept of neutralization. They simply state that the unclean heave-
offering is *lost* in the clean, that is, comprises so insignificant
a proportion of the mixture that it is disregarded. This is the
position of the Hillelites, K. It seems likely, then, that the
Houses' dispute at I-K is pseudepigraphic, modelled on the Eliezer/
sages tradition at O-P. T. will offer further evidence for this
view.

A. Just as heave-offering is neutralized in unconsecrated produce [in a mixture of one part of heave-offering
in a total of] a hundred and one [parts of produce],

B. whether or not [the heave-offering] is mixed up [in
the unconsecrated produce],

C. so unclean [heave-offering] should be neutralized in
clean [heave-offering] in [a mixture of] a hundred and one
[parts] [see M. 5:4I+K-L],

D. whether or not [the unclean heave-offering] is mixed
up [in the clean heave-offering].

E. R. Yose says, "If it is mixed up--
"it is neutralized.

F. "But if it is not mixed up--
"it is not neutralized."

G. [If] it fell into unclean unconsecrated produce, all
agree that it is neutralized.

T. 5:13

The anonymous rule at A+C restates the Hillelite position in
the debate, M. 5:4L-M, that unclean heave-offering is neutralized
when mixed with a large quantity of clean heave-offering. B-D is
interpolated, allowing for Yose's position, E-F. This is that the
unclean heave-offering is neutralized only in a case in which it
cannot be recovered from the clean heave-offering with which it is
mixed. This puts Yose in essential agreement with Eliezer,
M. 5:4/O, who states that the unclean heave-offering should be removed from the clean. Notably, the attestation here to Yose of an
issue debated by the Houses sheds further doubt on the authenticity
of the attribution of those materials to the Houses. G states
that all parties agree that unclean heave-offering is neutralized
in unclean unconsecrated produce. The rules of M. 5:1-3 have not
led us to expect otherwise.

A. An [unclean; see Lieberman, TK, I, p. 373 and y. Ter.
4:13] chate-melon in the status of heave-offering, which was
mixed with a hundred unconsecrated chate-melons,

B. and so an [unclean] piece of bread (*prwsh*; ed. princ.
reads: *lhm hpnym*) in the status of heave-offering which was
mixed with a hundred pieces of unconsecrated bread--

C. lo, these are neutralized [see M. 5:2].

D. R. Judah says, "They are not neutralized."

E. (Lieberman supplies from E and ed. princ.:) If the
slices touched each other, they have made each other unclean.

F. But if the food [i.e., the heave-offering] was invalid, having been made invalid through contact with one who
had immersed on the selfsame day,

all agree that it is neutralized.

T. 5:14 (y. Ter. 4:13)

A-C repeats the rule of M. 5:2D.[8] Unclean heave-offering is
neutralized in clean unconsecrated produce. The important position
here is that of Judah, D, who rejects this rule and states that
the unclean heave-offering is not neutralized. It is possible
that this view is the same as that of Eliezer, M. 5:2B, who holds
that we simply remove the unclean heave-offering from the mixture.
This however is not made explicit.[9] E likewise is enigmatic. If

produce is prepared with water, as bread is, it is susceptible to
uncleanness and is made unclean by contact with the unclean heave-
offering. This however does not seem to shed light on Judah's
position. Nor does F help matters. Heave-offering is rendered
'invalid' through contact with a person who was unclean and who
immersed on the day of contact. While such heave-offering may not
be consumed, it does not impart a status of uncleanness or invalidity to other produce with which it comes into contact
(M. Par. 4:11). Concerning the imparting of uncleanness to other
produce, then, invalid heave-offering is just like clean heave-
offering. It follows that Judah will allow its neutralization,
just as he deems clean heave-offering to be neutralized. I do
not, however, see that this elucidates Judah's position at D.[10]

A. Untithed produce (*tbl*) which is mixed with unconsecrated [i.e., tithed] produce--

lo, this [i.e., the untithed produce] renders forbidden
[the produce with which it is mixed] (*'wsr*) in any amount
[i.e., no matter how small a quantity of untithed produce is
mixed with tithed produce, the tithed produce may not be
eaten].

B. If he [i.e., the householder] has in a different
place produce which needs to be tithed (*prnsh*; MB), he takes
[this produce as tithes for the untithed produce mixed with
unconsecrated produce] in accordance with a calculation [of
the percentage of the mixture which is untithed].

C. But if not [i.e., if the householder has no produce
which needs to be tithed]--

D. R. Eliezer and R. Eleazar b. ᶜArak say, "He designates the (Lieberman, TK, I, p. 374, adds: heave-offering
and) heave-offering of the tithe which is in it [i.e., in the
untithed produce],

E. "and it [i.e., these offerings] are neutralized in
a hundred and one parts [of produce]."

F. And so [is the case as regards] first tithe.

G. First tithe from which heave-offering of the tithe
has not been separated (*mᶜśr tbl*) which is mixed with unconsecrated produce--

lo, this [i.e., the first tithe] renders forbidden [the
produce with which it is mixed] in any amount.

H.   If he [i.e., the Levite] has in another place first
tithe from which heave-offering of the tithe has not been re-
moved--

he takes [this produce as heave-offering of the tithe
for the first tithe in the mixture] in accordance with a
calculation [of the quantity of first tithe in the mixture].

I.   But if not [i.e., if he has no first tithe from
which heave-offering of the tithe has not been separated]--

J.   [R. Eliezer and] R. Eleazar b. ᶜArak say, "He
designates the heave-offering of the tithe which is in it
[i.e., in the first tithe mixed with the unconsecrated produce,] and it is neutralized in a hundred and one parts [of
produce]."

K.   (GRA, MB, HY omit:) But if it was untithed produce
and first tithe or second tithe [which were mixed together]--
lo, this [mixture] is forbidden.

L.   For they did not deem produce with which consecrated
produce may have been mixed (*spq mdwm*ᶜ) permitted, except in
the case of produce which can be rendered permitted [through
some action of the householder] (*dbr šyš lw mtyryn*).

M.   R. Simeon says, "Any produce (*dbr*) which can become
permitted (*šyš lw mtyryn*) [for consumption as unconsecrated
food],

N.   "such as untithed produce, second tithe, produce
dedicated [to the Temple] or new produce [i.e., produce for
which the ᶜ*omer* is not yet separated (Rashi, b. Ned. 57b])--

O.   "(omit 'and' with E and ed. princ.) sages did not
establish [for such produce] a measure [in which it is
neutralized].

P.   "(Lieberman supplies from the margin of V:) And any
type of produce which cannot become permitted,

Q.   "such as ᶜ*orlah* and mixed seeds in a vineyard--

R.   "sages established [for such produce] a measure [in
which it is neutralized]."

S.   They said to him, "But is it not the case that [pro-
duce of] the seventh year cannot become permitted? Yet sages
did not establish [for such produce] a measure [in which it
would be neutralized if mixed with permitted produce]."

T.   [Simeon] said to them, "[Produce grown in] the seventh
year does not render forbidden [produce with which it is mixed]
in any quantity, except as regards the obligation to remove from
one's possession all produce grown in the seventh year (*by*ᶜ*wr*).

"But as regards eating, [produce of the seventh year]
does not render other produce forbidden except if it imparts
flavor [to that other produce. If it does not, it is deemed
neutralized]."

> T. 5:15 (A: see M. Hal. 3:10; G:
> y. Dem. 7:8, y. Hal. 3:1; K: T. Ter.
> 6:17; M-S: y. Sheb. 6:3, y. Ned.
> 6:8, b. Ned. 57b; S: see M. Sheb.
> 7:7)

T. gives rules for the neutralization of untithed produce and
first tithe which are mixed with tithed, unconsecrated produce.
Two formally and substantively parallel units, A-E and G-J, are
linked by F. The expected third rule occurs at K-L, and itself
introduces the general principle stated by Simeon, N-O+P-R,
followed by the debate at S-T.

Untithed produce in any amount imposes the status of forbidden
food on tithed produce with which it is mixed (A). If the householder has other produce which needs to be tithed, however, he
simply designates that produce to be the tithe required of the
untithed produce in the mixture. The untithed produce is rendered
permitted for consumption, and, with it, the rest of the produce
in the mixture (B). What if the householder has no produce which
he can designate to be required tithes (C)? In this case he
simply designates the needed offerings to be within the mixture
itself. These offerings now are mixed with a quantity of unconsecrated produce sufficient to neutralize them (D-E). As before
the mixture becomes permitted for consumption. According to G-J,
the same is the case if first tithe from which heave-offering of
the tithe has not been removed is mixed with unconsecrated produce.
The Levite renders the first tithe permitted for consumption either
by designating the required heave-offering of the tithe in a different batch of first tithe, or in the mixture itself. In either
case, the first tithe, along with the unconsecrated produce with
which it is mixed, may then be eaten by the Levite.

K appears again at T. 6:17, and is comprehensible only in
that context. For this reason GRA and HD, followed by HY, delete
the lemma from the present pericope. Without questioning the
primacy of K to T. 5:15, I reserve its interpretation for T. 6:17.

Simeon, M-R, offers the general principle covering the rules
of A-E and G-J. His statement repeats the sense of L. The point
is that neutralization does not apply to produce which can be

rendered permitted for consumption by some simple action of the
householder, e.g., the removal of tithes, in the case of untithed
produce, or deconsecration, in the case of second tithe. The
reason, of course, is that the householder himself can rectify the
situation, without incurring any loss or causing a loss of agricultural offerings or holy things. Neutralization applies, Simeon
states, only in the case of produce which the householder cannot
through other means render permitted for consumption. Sages, S,
offer an apparent contradiction to Simeon's principle. Produce of
the seventh year, they state, is not subject to the rules of neutralization, yet cannot be rendered permitted for consumption
through some action of the householder. Simeon replies that produce of the seventh year is, in fact, subject to the rules of
neutralization. If it is mixed with unconsecrated produce in such
a small quantity that it cannot be tasted, the produce of the
seventh year does not impose a forbidden status on that other
produce.

A. *A se'ah of unclean heave-offering which fell into a
hundred se'ahs of clean heave-offering--*

B. *The House of Shammai declare [the mixture] forbidden [for consumption by a priest].*

C. *But the House of Hillel permit.*

D. *Said the House of Hillel to the House of Shammai,
"Clean [heave-offering] is forbidden to non-priests (zrym),
and unclean [heave-offering] is forbidden to priests. Just
as clean [heave-offering] is neutralized, so unclean [heave-
offering] can be neutralized" [= M. 5:4I-L].*

E. Said to them the House of Shammai, "No! If you say
[this] as regards clean [heave-offering], which is neutralized
in unconsecrated produce [and then is] eaten by (Lieberman
corrects to read:) priests [i.e., the produce taken from the
mixture to replace the lost heave-offering is eaten by
priests], will you say [that this is the case] for unclean
[heave-offering], which is not neutralized in unconsecrated
produce [and then] eaten by priests [= the position of
Eliezer, M. 5:2A+B]?"

F. Said to them the House of Hillel, "Lo, unclean
[heave-offering] which fell into unconsecrated produce will
prove [the case], for it is not neutralized in unconsecrated
produce [and then] eaten by non-priests, but, lo [even so],
it is neutralized."

G. Said to them the House of Shammai, "No! If you say
[this] as regards unconsecrated produce to which applies
great leniency (*shtyrn hytr mrwbh*), will you say [it] for
heave-offering, to which [only] slight leniency applies [in
that it may be eaten by priests]?"

H. Said to them the House of Hillel, "But in what case
was Torah stringent, in [the case of] non-priests who eat
heave-offering (*'wkly trwmh lzrym*) or [in the case of]
priests who eat heave-offering? In [the case of] non-
priests who eat heave-offering, [whether it is] a clean [non-
priest] who ate clean [heave-offering], or a clean [non-
priest] who ate unclean [heave-offering], or an unclean [non-
priest] who ate unclean [heave-offering]--

"they all are liable to death.

I. "But in [the case of] priests who eat heave-
offering--

"[If it is] a clean priest who ate clean [heave-
offering]--

"this is as he is commanded (*kmswtw*).

"[If it is] a clean [priest] who ate unclean [heave-
offering]--

"[he has transgressed] a positive commandment.

"And [if it is] an unclean [priest] who ate clean
[heave-offering], or an unclean [priest] who ate unclean
[heave-offering]--

"[he has transgressed] a negative commandment.

J. "And is it not an argument *a minori ad majus*
(*ql whwmr*)? If in a case in which Torah was stringent, that
of non-priests who eat heave-offering, lo, [the heave-offer-
ing] is neutralized in unconsecrated produce [and then] eaten
by non-priests, in a case in which Torah is lenient, that of
priests who eat heave-offering, is it not logical that [the
heave-offering] is neutralized in (correct to read:) heave-
offering [and then] is eaten by priests?"

K. *After they had agreed:*

L. *R. Eliezer says, "Let it be raised up and burned."*

M. *But sages say, "It has been lost through its scantiness"* [= M. 5:4N-P].

T. 6:4

T. cites all of M. 5:4, providing, at E-J, an expanded
version of the Houses' debate, M. 5:4L-M. The Hillelites now are

left in the winning position. The fact that the Shammaites, E,
argue on the basis of a rule attributed to Eliezer, M. 5:2B, is
further evidence of the pseudepigraphic nature of the debate.

5:5-6

A.   A *se'ah* of heave-offering which fell into a hundred
[*se'ahs* of unconsecrated produce, and was thereby neutra-
lized],

B.   and one lifted it out [i.e., took a new *se'ah* of
heave-offering for the priest], and [the replacement heave-
offering] fell into a different batch [of unconsecrated
produce]--

C.   R. Eliezer says, "[That which falls into the second
batch] imparts the status of heave-offering [to the produce
with which it is mixed] as does true heave-offering
(*ktrwmt wd'y*)."

D.   But sages say, "It does not impart the status of
heave-offering except in accordance with a calculation [of
the percentage of the produce which is true heave-offering]."

M. 5:5

E.   A *se'ah* of heave-offering which fell into less than
a hundred [*se'ahs* of unconsecrated produce], and [that produce thereby] took on the status of heave-offering (*wndm^cw*),

F.   and [produce] fell from the mixture (*hmdwm^c*) into a
different batch--

G.   R. Eliezer says, "[That portion of the mixture which
falls into the second batch] imparts the status of heave-
offering [to the produce with which it is mixed] as does true
heave-offering."

H.   But sages say, "A mixture of heave-offering and unconsecrated produce (*hmdwm^c*) does not impart the status of
heave-offering [to produce with which it is mixed] except in
accordance with a calculation [of the quantity of true heave-
offering contained in the mixture].

I.   "And that which has been leavened [with heave-
offering (Albeck)] does not impart the status of heave-offering
to that which it leavens except in accordance with a calculation [of the quantity of true heave-offering in the mixture].

J.   "And [water from an immersion pool which was made
unfit by being mixed with] drawn water does not impart a
status of invalidity to [other] immersion pools except in

accordance with a calculation [of the percentage of drawn
water it contains]."

M. 5:6 (E-H: b. Shab. 142a, b. Tem.

12a; H-J: M. Tem. 1:4)

M. 5:5-6 carries forward the theme of the foregoing through
two disputes between Eliezer and sages, A-C+D and E-G+H. These
differ only in their superscriptions, A and E. M. 5:5 has a
se'ah of heave-offering neutralized in unconsecrated produce. The
se'ah of produce taken to replace the heave-offering then falls
into other unconsecrated produce. Eliezer is consistent with his
view of M. 5:2C, that the *se'ah* of heave-offering which was lifted
out of the mixture is the same as that which originally fell in.
It therefore has the effect of true heave-offering in imparting
its own status to the produce with which it subsequently is mixed.
Sages likewise are consistent with their view, M. 5:2D. The
original heave-offering was neutralized, and so the replacement
heave-offering contains only slightly less than one percent of
true heave-offering. Only this true heave-offering imparts the
status of heave-offering to unconsecrated produce with which the
replacement heave-offering later is mixed.

At M. 5:6 the heave-offering falls into less than a hundred
times its quantity in unconsecrated produce. The whole mixture
is given the status of heave-offering. What if some of this produce falls elsewhere? Eliezer again is consistent with his
position of M. 5:2C. He rules that the heave-offering which dis-
appears into the unconsecrated produce is the same as that which
later falls out. Sages, H, persist in stating that the heave-
offering has been diffused in the unconsecrated produce. That
which falls out of the mixture contains only that proportion of
true heave-offering which is contained in the larger batch as a
whole. As at M. 5:5D, only the true heave-offering in the mixture
imparts the status of heave-offering to the unconsecrated produce
with which it is mixed.[11] I-J extends sages view to the cases of
unconsecrated dough which has been leavened with heave-offering,
and to immersion pools which have been mixed with drawn water and
so made unfit. The principle is the same in either case. In
subsequent mixtures, we take into account only the percentage of
the dough, or water, which originally had a forbidden status.

A.   *A se'ah of heave-offering*[12] *which fell into less*
than a hundred [se'ahs of unconsecrated produce] [= M. 5:6E]--

B.   lo, it [i.e., all of the produce] takes on the
status of heave-offering.

C.   [One who eats it unintentionally] is not [however]
liable to repay its value and the added fifth [see M. 6:1].

D.   And they do not use it to repay the value and added
fifth for (reading $^c l$; Lieberman, TK, I, p. 378) another
batch [of heave-offering which accidentally was eaten by a
non-priest], except in accordance with a calculation [of the
quantity of unconsecrated produce in the mixture].

E.   *A se'ah of heave-offering which fell into a hundred*
[se'ahs of produce and was neutralized], and one lifted it
out [of the mixture, for a priest] [= M. 5:5A-B]--

F.   if [the produce into which the heave-offering fell]
was untithed,

they designate it (following Lieberman, *loc. cit.*, and
reading *'wth* for *'wtn*) [i.e., the *se'ah* which is lifted out]
heave-offering (Lieberman, *loc. cit.*, deletes: and tithes)
for another batch [of untithed produce],

G.   or he designates the heave-offering [and tithe]
(E; V reads: heave-offering of the tithe; see Lieberman,
loc. cit.) which is in it.

H.   If [the produce into which the heave-offering fell]
was first tithe from which heave-offering of the tithe had
not been removed ($m^c \dot{s}r$ *tbl*)--

he designates it [i.e., the *se'ah* which is lifted out]
(emend to read:) heave-offering of the tithe for a different
batch,

I.   or designates the heave-offering of the tithe which
is in it.

J.   If [the produce into which the heave-offering fell]
was second tithe--

one deconsecrates it with coins at the value of heave-
offering,

K.   less the value of the [true] heave-offering which is
in it.

L.   If it was new produce [i.e., produce for which the
$^c omer$ had not been offered] [into which the heave-offering
fell]--

let him wait until Passover and [only then] give it to
a priest.

T. 6:1

M. *A se'ah of heave-offering which fell into less than
a hundred [se'ahs] of produce [and   that produce thereby] took
on the status of heave-offering* [= M. 5:6E]--

N. if [the produce] was untithed,

he designates it heave-offering and tithes for a different batch,

O. or he designates the heave-offering and tithes (E;
V reads: heave-offering of the tithe) which are in it.

P. If [the produce] was first tithe from which heave-
offering of the tithe had not been removed ($m^{c}\acute{s}r$ tbl)--

he designates it heave-offering and tithes for a different batch,

Q. or he designates the heave-offering of the tithe
which is in it.

R. If [the produce into which the heave-offering fell]
was second tithe--

he deconsecrates it with coins at the value of heave-
offering, less the value of the [true] heave-offering which
is in it.

S. If [the produce into which the heave-offering fell]
was new [i.e., produce for which the $^{c}omer$ had not yet been
offered]--

let him wait until Passover and [only then] give it to
a priest.

T. 6:2

T. A *se'ah* of heave-offering which fell into a hundred
[*se'ahs* of produce which was grown in the] seventh year--

U. lo, this (reading *zh* for *'ylw*, see Lieberman, *loc.
cit.*) [i.e., the heave-offering] is neutralized.

V. [If the heave-offering falls into] less than this
[amount of prohibited produce]--

let [all of the produce] rot.

T. 6:3 (b. Shab. 26a)

T. is in three parts, A-D, E-L+M-S and T-V. A-D, first,
cites and supplements M. 5:6. While mixtures of heave-offering
and unconsecrated produce are treated like heave-offering, they
are not subject to all of the stringencies accorded a true priestly
gift. A non-priest who eats such a mixture need not repay the
value and added fifth required in the case of true heave-offering
(M. 6:1). Both Eliezer and sages can agree to this. D is clear
as stated. The true heave-offering in the mixture already is the

property of the priest, and therefore may not be given to that
individual as repayment for other heave-offering which accidentally was eaten.

E-L cites M. 5:5A-B and offers four variants of its case.
Heave-offering is neutralized in produce which has not yet been
tithed, or which itself has a sanctified status. Produce taken
to replace the lost heave-offering must be properly tithed or removed from its prior sanctified status before it can be given to
a priest. In cases in which the heave-offering has been mixed
with untithed produce or first tithe from which heave-offering of
the tithe has not been removed (F-I), the householder may designate the required heave-offering or heave-offering of the tithe
within the replacement offering itself. Alternatively he can
designate the replacement offering to be the heave-offering or
heave-offering of the tithe required of other produce. Once
properly tithed, or designated a priestly gift, the replacement
offering may be eaten by the priest. J has the heave-offering
neutralized in second tithe. The householder deconsecrates the
replacement offering with coins. This produce now may be eaten
by a priest. If the produce with which the heave-offering is
mixed has not yet had the ^{c}omer offered for it, the householder
simply waits until Passover, when the produce becomes permitted.
He then gives the priest his share.[13]

T. 6:2 cites M. 5:6E and offers cases in which heave-offering
imparts its own status to untithed produce, first tithe from which
heave-offering of the tithe has not been separated, second tithe,
or produce which still is subject to the ^{c}omer. These cases thus
are exactly the same as those given at T. 5:15. Only T. 6:3
offers a problem not referred to there. Heave-offering is mixed
with produce forbidden by the laws of the seventh year. If there
is a sufficient quantity of this other produce, U, the heave-
offering is neutralized. If not, since there is no way to render
the produce of the seventh year permitted for consumption (see
T. 5:15S-T), the mixture must be left to rot.

5:7-8

A.   A *se'ah* of heave-offering which fell into a hundred
[*se'ahs* of unconsecrated produce, and so was neutralized]--

B.   if one lifted it out [of the mixture to give to a
priest] and a different [*se'ah* of heave-offering] fell [into
the same produce],

C.   lifted out of that [*se'ah*], and a different [*se'ah*
of heave-offering] fell [into the same produce]--

D. lo, this [i.e., the batch in which the mixtures occurred] is permitted [for consumption as unconsecrated produce],

E. until there [will have fallen into the batch] a greater quantity of heave-offering than there [originally was] unconsecrated produce.

M. 5:7

F. A *se'ah* of heave-offering which fell into a hundred [*se'ahs* of unconsecrated produce, and so was neutralized], and which one had not lifted out [of the mixture] before a different [*se'ah* of heave-offering] fell [into that same produce]--

G. lo, this [i.e., the batch of produce] is forbidden [for consumption by non-priests].

H. But R. Simeon permits.

M. 5:8 (b. Shab. 132a)

Two parallel cases, A-E and F-H, advance M. 5:2-6's discussion of the neutralization and replacement of heave-offering. M. 5:7 carries forward Eliezer's view, that produce the householder takes to replace heave-offering which was neutralized comprises the original heave-offering (M. 5:2C, M. 5:5C, M. 5:6G). Here, after this replacement offering is taken, more heave-offering falls into the same unconsecrated produce. Since according to Eliezer, the householder already has removed from the mixture the heave-offering which originally fell in, the second heave-offering likewise is neutralized. Sages, M. 5:5D, who hold that the householder removed only a percentage of the heave-offering which originally fell into the batch, should hardly agree.[14] E qualifies Eliezer's position, stating that D's rule applies only so long as less than a hundred *se'ahs* of heave-offering have fallen, a *se'ah* at a time, into the unconsecrated produce. It seems that after this point, even according to Eliezer, we must assume that enough heave-offering has been left in the batch to impart to it the status of heave-offering.

M. 5:8 again has heave-offering neutralized in unconsecrated produce. In this case, however, additional heave-offering falls into the mixture before a replacement offering is taken. The batch now contains two *se'ahs* of heave-offering and only a hundred *se'ahs* of unconsecrated produce. Even Eliezer, therefore, must agree to the rule of G, that the batch takes on the status of heave-offering. Simeon, H, disagrees, holding that the mixture

does not take on the status of heave-offering. He thus evidences
a conception of neutralization different from that of both Eliezer
and sages. As we have seen, these authorities hold that while
heave-offering which is neutralized may be eaten by non-priests,
it retains the essential qualities of a priestly gift. As at
M. 5:5-6, it still imparts the status of heave-offering to unconsecrated produce with which it is mixed. Simeon, however, holds
that once heave-offering is neutralized, it is in all respects the
same as unconsecrated produce. In the present case, therefore, he
rules that the second *se'ah* of heave-offering falls into a hundred
and one *se'ahs* of unconsecrated produce, and therefore, like the
first *se'ah* of heave-offering, is neutralized.

> A.   *A se'ah of heave-offering which fell into a hundred*
> [*se'ahs of unconsecrated produce, and so was neutralized*]
> *and which one had not lifted out before there fell* [*into*
> *that same produce*] *another* [*se'ah of heave-offering*]--
>
> B.   *lo, this* [*batch of produce*] *is forbidden* [*for con-*
> *sumption by non-priests*].
>
> C.   *But R. Simeon permits* [= M. 5:8F-H].
>
> D.   Said R. Eleazar b. R. Simeon, "In what case does
> this [i.e., the rule of B] apply?
>
> E.   "In the case in which he did not know about it [i.e.,
> about the first heave-offering that fell into the unconse-
> crated produce], and then [more heave-offering] fell [into
> that same produce].
>
> F.   "But if he knew about it [i.e., about the first
> heave-offering that fell into the unconsecrated produce] and
> then [more heave-offering] fell [into that same produce]--
> "lo, this [batch of produce] is permitted [for con-
> sumption as unconsecrated food],
>
> G.   "since it [i.e., the first heave-offering] already
> was neutralized."

T. 6:5

Eleazar b. R. Simeon claims that the rule of M. 5:8F-G
agrees in conception with the position of his father, M. 5:8H. He
states that, unlike his father, the anonymous rule simply refers
to a case in which the householder is not aware that heave-offering already has been mixed with his produce. Such a case is judged
as if the two *se'ahs* of heave-offering had fallen at one time into
the unconsecrated produce, and so imparted their own status to the
batch. In Eleazar's view, thus, the householder must know about

the first mixture if it is to be treated separately from the
second one. Needless to say, M. does not know the distinction
Eleazar makes between the case to which M. 5:8F-G refers, and that
on which his father, M. 5:8H, rules. Nor does the language of M.
support such a distinction.

> A.   A *se'ah* of *Corlah* which fell into two hundred [*se'ahs*
> of permitted produce]--
>
> B.   [if] he knew about it, and afterwards a different
> [*se'ah* of *Corlah*] fell [into the same produce]--
>
> C.   lo, this [batch of produce] is permitted [for con-
> sumption; see M. 5:8],
>
> D.   (E adds:) until there will be more forbidden produce
> [in the batch] than there is permitted produce [see M. 5:7C].
>
> E.   [But if it fell] into less than this [quantity of
> permitted produce], lo, this is forbidden [for consumption].
>
> > T. 6:8
>
> F.   (Lieberman supplies F-H from E) A *se'ah* of *Corlah*
> which fell into two hundred [*se'ahs* of permitted produce]--
>
> G.   [if] he knew about it, and afterwards a different
> [*se'ah* of *Corlah*] fell [into the same produce]--
>
> H.   lo, this [batch of produce] is permitted [for con-
> sumption; see M. 5:8],
>
> I.   until there will be more forbidden produce [in the
> batch] than there is permitted produce [see M. 5:7E].
>
> > T. 6:9

T. 6:8-9 present two versions of the same pericope, different
only in the inclusion of the gloss at T. 6:8E. The pericopae repeat the rule of M. 5:8F-G, as it applies to *Corlah*, that is,
produce from the first three years of growth of an orchard or
vineyard (Lev. 19:23). As we recall, such produce is neutralized
in two hundred parts of permitted produce. B and G indicate that
the pericopae follow the understanding of Eleazar b. R. Simeon,
T. 6:5.

> A.   A *se'ah* of heave-offering which fell into a hundred[15]
> [*se'ahs* of unconsecrated produce] (E adds:) and one lifted it
> out [to replace the lost heave-offering],
>
> B.   and afterwards unconsecrated produce in any amount
> fell [into the replacement offering; Lieberman, TK, I, p. 386,
> following HD]--
>
> C.   lo, this [replacement offering] is permitted [for
> consumption by a non-priest].

D.   A *se'ah* of heave-offering which fell into a hundred
[*se'ahs* of unconsecrated produce, and one lifted it out]--

E.   they do not remove the darnel (*zwnyn*)[16] which is in
it [i.e., in the replacement offering; Lieberman, TK, I,
p. 386].

F.   [If the heave-offering fell into] less than this
[quantity of unconsecrated produce, and so imparted its own
status to all of the produce in the batch]--

they may remove the darnel which is in it [i.e., which
is in the batch of produce].

G.   A *log* of wine [in the status of heave-offering] which
had been clarified (*slwl*) which fell into a hundred *logs* of
[unconsecrated] wine which had not been clarified (*ᶜkwryn*)--

they do not remove the lees (*šmrym*) which are in it
[i.e., in the *log* of wine taken to replace the lost heave-
offering].

H.   (Ed. princ. adds:) [If it fell into] less than this--
they remove the lees which are in it [i.e., in the mixture of heave-offering and unconsecrated wine].

I.   A *log* of wine [in the status of heave-offering] which
had not been clarified, which fell into a hundred *logs* of
[unconsecrated] wine which had been clarified--

they do not remove the lees which are in it [i.e., in the
log of wine taken to replace the lost heave-offering].

J.   (E adds:) [If it fell into] less than this--
they remove the lees which are in it [i.e., in the mixture of heave-offering and unconsecrated wine].

T. 6:10 (G: y. Ter. 5:9)

T. explores two distinct problems, A-C and D-J, both of which
advance in a general way the discussion of the rules for the neutralization and replacement of heave-offering. At A-C a small
quantity of unconsecrated produce is mixed with produce taken to
replace heave-offering which was neutralized. We rule that the
replacement offering itself loses its consecrated status, and may
be consumed by a non-priest. This is the case because the replacement offering is deemed to contain only a small quantity of true
heave-offering. The rule, then, follows the view of sages, M. 5:5D,
who hold that replacement heave-offering contains the same proportion of true heave-offering as does the batch of produce from which
it was taken. Eliezer, M. 5:5C, who holds that the replacement
offering is in all respects true heave-offering, cannot agree.

D-F+G-H+I-J makes a single point three times. The householder's separation of a replacement offering constitutes a designation of that produce to be heave-offering. For this reason the
householder may not take from that which he separates darnel (E)
or lees (G, I), even though these things are not edible and so are
not normally made agricultural offerings. F, H and J have the
heave-offering impart its own status to the unconsecrated produce
with which it is mixed. In this case, there has been no designation of the produce in the batch to be heave-offering. For this
reason, the inedible produce in the batch is not deemed to have
the status of heave-offering and may, accordingly, be taken by the
householder for his own use. I am not able to explain why this
should be the case at J, where it is known that the inedible portion of the produce, the lees, had the status of heave-offering
from the beginning.[17]

5:9

I.   A.   A *se'ah* of [wheat in the status of] heave-offering
which fell into a hundred [*se'ahs* of unconsecrated wheat, and
thereby was neutralized], and one ground it [i.e., all of the
wheat in the mixture], and it diminished [in quantity]--

B.   just as the unconsecrated [wheat in the mixture]
diminished [in quantity], so the heave-offering diminished
[in quantity].

C.   (11 MSS. lack: and) [The mixture therefore remains]
permitted [for consumption by non-priests].

II.   D.   A *se'ah* of [wheat in the status of] heave-offering
which fell into less than a hundred [*se'ahs* of unconsecrated
wheat, and thereby imparted its own status to the whole
batch], and one ground it [i.e., all of the wheat in the
batch], and it increased [in quantity]--

E.   just as the unconsecrated [wheat] increased [in
quantity], so the [wheat in the status of] heave-offering
increased [in quantity].

F.   (6 MSS. lack: and) [The mixture therefore remains]
forbidden [for consumption by a non-priest].

G.   If it is known that the unconsecrated wheat is of
better quality than the [wheat in the status of] heave-
offering--

H.   [the mixture becomes] permitted [for consumption by
a non-priest].

III. I. A *se'ah* of heave-offering which fell into less than
a hundred [*se'ahs* of unconsecrated produce], and afterwards
[more] unconsecrated [produce] fell there [i.e., into the
same batch]--

    J. if [this happened] unintentionally,
[the mixture becomes] permitted;

    K. but if [it happened] intentionally,
[the mixture remains] forbidden.

M. 5:9 (A-C: y. Or. 1:4; see
T. B.M. 3:11)

The formally identical cases at A-C and D-F (glossed at G-H)
make a single point. Produce in which heave-offering has been
mixed is ground and as a result either increases or diminishes
in quantity. We assume that the heave-offering and the unconsecrated produce were equally affected by the processing, and so the
proportion of forbidden produce to permitted produce in the mixture does not change.[18] At G-H it is known that the unconsecrated
produce is of high quality. When it is ground it will increase
in quantity. In this case, since we are assured that processing
has caused the proportion of heave-offering in the mixture to drop,
that offering is deemed to have been neutralized. I-K develops
D-H. Now unconsecrated produce actually is added to a batch upon
which heave-offering previously had imposed its own status. Do
we rule that the heave-offering is neutralized, as at G-H, or that
the batch retains its forbidden status? According to J-K, this
depends on whether or not the householder purposely added the unconsecrated produce to the mixture. If his intention was to recover the produce for his own use, his actions are void. The
batch retains its sanctified status. If, however, the unconsecrated produce was mixed unintentionally with the other produce,
the new proportion of heave-offering to unconsecrated produce is
taken into account. If there now is sufficient unconsecrated
produce in the mixture, the heave-offering is neutralized.[19]

I. A. Leaven [in the status of heave-offering] which was
mixed (*bllw*) with other leaven [which was not heave-offer-
ing], and one leavened dough with it [i.e., with the mixture]--

    B. if there is not [a sufficient quantity] of forbidden
[leaven] to impart taste [to the dough]--

    [the dough] is permitted [for consumption by non-
priests].

II.   C.   [In the case of] grain [in the status of heave-
offering which is mixed] with [unconsecrated] barley--
      let him pick [the grain in the status of heave-offering
from the mixture].
      D.   If he ground them [i.e., the grain and barley in the
mixture] [see M. 5:9]--
      [the mixture is forbidden from consumption by non-priests
if there is in it a sufficient quantity of heave-offering] to
impart flavor [to the batch as a whole].
III. E.   [In the case of] beans [in the status of heave-
offering which are mixed] with [unconsecrated] lentils--
      let him pick [the beans in the status of heave-offering
from the mixture].
      F.   If he boiled them--
      [the mixture is forbidden for consumption by non-priests
if there is in it a sufficient quantity of heave-offering] to
impart flavor [to the batch as a whole].
      G.   R. Yose say, "Fava-beans (*grys šl pwl*)[20] and chick
peas (*grys šl twph*),[21] lo, these are a single species."

                    T. 6:11a (A-B: see M. Or. 2:11;
                    E: see M. Or. 2:7)

      T. is autonomous of M. Its only point of contact with M. 5:9
is the reference, at D, to the grinding of a batch in which heave-
offering and unconsecrated produce have been mixed.
      In each of T.'s three cases heave-offering of one species of
produce is mixed with unconsecrated produce of a different species.
Since the heave-offering can be distinguished by taste from the
other produce, the usual rule, that heave-offering is neutralized
in a hundred parts of unconsecrated produce, is not invoked. We
hold, rather, that without regard to its quantity, if the heave-
offering imparts taste to the mixture, the mixture takes on the
status of heave-offering.[22] If the heave-offering cannot be
tasted, it is deemed insignificant, and therefore is neutralized.
If possible, however, the householder simply removes the forbidden
produce from the mixture (C, E). In context, Yose's point, G, is
that since the two types of beans are a single species, their
neutralization in conjunction with one another is determined on the
basis of quantity of heave-offering, and not on the basis of taste.
      T. 6:11b-6:19 are found after M. 7:5-6, to which they are
supplementary.

TERUMOT CHAPTER SIX

M. 6:1A announces a new topic of discussion, cases in which
a non-priest unintentionally eats heave-offering. The issue is
the non-priest's responsibility to replace the priestly gift which
he wrongly ate. The answer comes directly from Scripture. Lev.
22:14 states that if a non-priest unintentionally eats a holy
thing, in this case, heave-offering, he pays to the priest the
value of the holy thing, plus an added fifth. Through the payment
of the value (the principal, as designated by M.) the non-priest
compensates the priest for his lost share. The additional fifth
is a fine, through which the non-priest makes atonement for mis-
appropriating sanctified produce. With this as its generative
principle, M.'s task is to delineate 1) exactly who is liable to
pay the principal and added fifth, and 2) what produce may be used
as payment. It is on the basis of these two questions that the
chapter's discrete pericopae are organized. M. 6:1-4 gives rules
which establish the non-priest's responsibility to pay restitution
for heave-offering he unintentionally eats. M. 6:5-6 outlines
what produce may be used to pay the principal and added fifth.
Only this latter unit yields an interesting issue of law. This is
whether the holy thing which was eaten actually is replaced, or
whether the priest simply is compensated for the value of that holy
thing.

T. adds little of interest. Its only substantive contribution is at T. 7:3-4a, which describe in detail the circumstances
under which a non-priest incurs liability to pay the principal and
added fifth. Attributions are as follows: Meir, M. 6:3; Aqiba,
T. 7:10a; Eliezer and Aqiba, M. 6:6, T. 7:9; Simeon, T. 7:1; Yose
and Simeon, T. 5:8b; Abba Saul, T. 7:2.

6:1

A. [A non-priest] who unintentionally eats heave-
offering pays back the principal (qrn) and an [added] fifth.

B. The same [rule applies to] ($'hd$) (1) one who
[unintentionally] eats [produce in the status of heave-
offering], to (2) one who [unintentionally] drinks [liquids
in the status of heave-offering], and to (3) one who [unin-
tentionally] anoints [himself with oil in the status of
heave-offering].

C. The same [rule applies to] (4) [one who unintentionally misappropriates] clean heave-offering, and to (5) [one who
unintentionally misappropriates] unclean heave-offering.

D. He pays back [the principal and added] fifth, and
[if he should eat the added fifth (Bert)], a fifth of the
[added] fifth.

E. He does not pay restitution ($m\check{s}lm$) with heave-
offering; rather [he pays it with] unconsecrated produce
($hwlyn\ mtwqnym$), and this takes on the status of heave-
offering ($n^c\acute{s}yn\ trwmh$).

F. And [since] the restitution is heave-offering,[1]
[even] if the priest wishes, he may not refuse [it]
($'ynw\ mwhl$).

                         M. 6:1 (b. Pes. 31b-32a, b. B.M.
                         54b, y. Ket. 3:1)

Lev. 22:14 states, "And if a man eats of a holy thing unwittingly ($b\check{s}ggh$), he shall add the fifth of its value to it, and
give the holy things to the priest." The present pericope, and
those which follow at M. 6:2-6, depend on this rule, stated at A
in M.'s own language. They delineate the rules for the payment of
restitution and the added fifth for heave-offering which unintentionally is consumed by a non-priest. The rule of A is expanded
at B-C, D and E+F.

A non-priest who unintentionally[2] eats heave-offering compensates the priest by replacing the heave-offering with other
produce. He also gives the priest an additional fifth of the
heave-offering's value. This, it must be assumed, is a fine, in
atonement for the offense of eating a holy thing.[3] As may be
expected, the same restitution--principal and added fifth--is
required (B) no matter how the non-priest uses the heave-offering.
Whether he eats, drinks or anoints himself with it, he has misappropriated a holy thing. The point at C is a close corollary to
that of B. Unclean heave-offering, we know, may not be eaten by
a priest, but is burned. Even so, if it is consumed by a non-
priest, that individual is liable to repay the principal and added
fifth, for he has misused a holy thing. It is of no regard that
the priest could not have eaten the heave-offering. D-F describes
the manner of repayment of the principal and added fifth. Payment
is made with unconsecrated produce. It may not be made with
produce in the status of heave-offering, which already is the
property of the priest. Nor may it be made with untithed produce,

portions of which belong to priest and Levite (E). Once given as
restitution, the unconsecrated produce acquires the status of
heave-offering, in place of the misappropriated priestly gift. It
therefore is subject to the stringencies which normally apply to
that offering. In the event that the restitution or added fifth
unintentionally is eaten by a non-priest, the usual compensation
must be paid to the priest (D). The fact that the produce given
as the principal and added fifth has the status of true heave-
offering is further emphasized at F. Since these things are true
heave-offering, the priest has no choice but to accept them.

H. R. Yose says, "Restitution for heave-offering [which
a non-priest unintentionally ate], its [added] fifth, and the
fifth of its [added] fifth [see M. 6:1A, D]--

I. "lo, these are like [true] heave-offering in that
they obligate [one who intentionally eats them] to the death
penalty (myth), [and in the case of one who unintentionally
eats them] to the principal and [added] fifth,

J. "in that they render forbidden [for consumption by
non-priests] less than a hundred parts [of unconsecrated
produce with which they are mixed],

K. "[and] in that they are neutralized in a mixture
containing a hundred and one [parts of produce, of which the
restitution/heave-offering is one part]" [see M. 4:7A].

L. R. Simeon says, "[That heave-offering is neutralized]
in a hundred [parts of produce, and not a hundred and one, is
proven] from an argument a minori ad majus (ql whwmr).

M. "Just as we find in the case of heave-offering of
the tithe, that it is one [part] in (read with E:) a hundred
[i.e., one tenth of first tithe, which itself is one tenth of
unconsecrated produce], lo, [the proportion here] also is one
in (E reads:) a hundred [parts of unconsecrated produce]."

N. They said to him, "No. If you say [that the proportion one to a hundred applies] to heave-offering of the
tithe, which is taken as consecrated produce from consecrated
produce [i.e., first tithe],[4] but [which previous to its
separation] did not have the designation of a forbidden thing,
will you say that it applies to this [i.e., to heave-offering
mixed with unconsecrated produce], which is taken as consecrated [produce] from that which is unconsecrated, and which
[already] was designated as forbidden?"

T. 5:8b (H-I: T. Toh. 1:7; L-M:
see y. Or. 2:1)

Yose, H-K, repeats and expands upon the rule of M. 6:1D-F.
The point, again, is that produce paid as restitution for heave-
offering which accidentally is eaten by a non-priest has the
status of true heave-offering. A non-priest who intentionally
eats the restitution or added fifth therefore is liable to death
(I). One who eats it unintentionally is liable to the payment of
the principal and added fifth. Yose's statement, K, that, like
all heave-offering, the restitution and added fifth are neutralized in a hundred and one parts of unconsecrated produce introduces L-N. Simeon there claims that heave-offering is neutralized
when it comprises one part in only a hundred parts of unconsecrated
produce, the same proportion of a batch as is separated as heave-
offering of the tithe.[5] He is answered, N, that the case of the
neutralization of heave-offering is not analogous to the separation of heave-offering of the tithe. Unlike heave-offering
which is mixed with unconsecrated produce, heave-offering of the
tithe does not have the status of a holy thing until the time of
its separation, when it is designated a consecrated priestly gift.

I.   A.   R. Simeon says, "One who unintentionally anoints himself with oil (reading with E, ed. princ.; V reads: wine)
in the status of heave-offering pays the principal, but does
not pay the [added] fifth.

II. B.   "One who [unintentionally] eats produce in the status
of heave-offering which has on it puncture marks [from snakes],

     C.   "or one who [unintentionally] drinks wine [in the
status of heave-offering] which has been left uncovered [and
may contain venom from snakes; see M. 8:4]

     D.   "pays the principal and the [added] fifth.

III. E.   "A *nazir* who unintentionally drank wine in the status
of heave-offering pays the principal (read with E:) and the
[added] fifth (V reads: but does not pay the added fifth).

IV. F.   "[If] one [unintentionally] ate heave-offering on
the Day of Atonement, he pays the principal and the [added]
fifth.

V.   G.   "[If he unintentionally drank] wine [in the status
of heave-offering mixed] with vinegar [in the status of heave-
offering], he pays the principal and the [added] fifth (so V,
ed. princ.; E reads: [If he drank] wine [in the status of
heave-offering mixed] with oil [in the status of heave-offer-
ing], he pays the principal, but does not pay the [added]
fifth.)."

                         T. 7:1

T. supplements M. 6:1 with five cases in which a non-priest
unintentionally consumes heave-offering. At A Simeon rejects
M. 6:1B(3)'s rule that using oil in the status of heave-offering
as a lotion obligates the offender to repay the value of the heave-
offering and the added fifth. Simeon claims that while the priest
must be compensated for his loss, the non-priest need not pay the
added fifth. Simeon's reasoning, it seems, is that the non-priest
does not receive the same benefit from anointing himself with
heave-offering as he does from eating the offering.[6] At B-D the
non-priest eats produce in the status of heave-offering which has
on it puncture marks from snakes, or drinks liquids which have
been left uncovered. Lest they contain venom, these things are
forbidden for consumption, and thus would not have been eaten by
the priest. The case is comparable to that in which the non-priest
eats unclean heave-offering (M. 6:1C), and we rule that in all
events the non-priest must pay both the principal and the added
fifth. A *nazir* is a person who has taken a vow neither to cut his
hair nor to drink wine (Num. 16:1-21). If he breaks his vow by
drinking wine, he is liable to a sin offering. If the wine is
heave-offering (E), he must also pay the added fifth. The consumption of heave-offering is a separate transgression, which requires its own atonement. The point at F is the same. If a person
eats heave-offering on the Day of Atonement when all consumption
of food and drink is prohibited (M. Yom. 1:1), he still is liable
to the added fifth. According to G, even if heave-offering is
consumed in an unusual fashion, the restitution and added fifth
must be paid. We should expect no different.

> A. One who [unintentionally] eats unclean heave-offer-
> ing pays to the priest [the heave-offerings's] value as if it
> were wood.
>
> B. Abba Saul says, "Any [heave-offering] which is worth
> a *perutah* requires restitution."
>
> C. They said to him, "They did not mention 'the value
> of a *perutah*' except [for the case of] something dedicated
> [to the Temple which was put to secular use]."
>
> > T. 7:2 (b. Pes. 32b; C: see Sifra
> > *Hobah, pereq* 20:7, Sifra, *'Emor,*
> > *pereq* 6:3)

A rejects M. 6:1C's rule that consumption of unclean heave-
offering obligates a non-priest to the same restitution as does
the eating of clean heave-offering. According to A, since unclean

heave-offering is burned, a non-priest who eats it repays only
the value the produce would have were it wood.

The dispute at B-C is separate, comprehensible only in light
of the rule of T. 7:3G (below), that restitution need be made only
by a person who eats more than an olive's bulk of heave-offering.
Abba Saul rejects that rule, stating that, regardless of its
quantity, if the heave-offering is worth a *perutah* or more, the
principal and added fifth must be paid to the priest.[7] C disagrees, for the stated reason.[8]

A. *The same [rule applies to] (1) one who [unintention-*
ally] eats [produce in the status of heave-offering], to (2)
one who [unintentionally] drinks [liquids in the status of
heave-offering], and to (3) one who [unintentionally] anoints
[himself with oil in the status of heave-offering] [= M.
6:1B].

B. [If] one ate [heave-offering and then] ate heave-
offering again--

C. if there is from the beginning of the first act of
eating (*'kylh*) to the end of the last act of eating [no more
time than is needed to eat] a half-loaf of bread (*prs*)--

[the several acts of eating] join together [to create
the quantity of heave-offering which obligates payment of the
added fifth, *viz.*, an olive's bulk (see H, M. 7:3C-D)].

D. But if not--

[the acts of eating] do not join together [and the added
fifth is not paid].

E. [If] one drank [liquids in the status of heave-
offering,] drank [liquids in the status of heave-offering]
again, [and then] drank [liquids in the status of heave-
offering] again--

F. if there is from the beginning of the first act of
drinking (*štyyh*) to the end of the last act of drinking [no
more time than is needed to drink] a quarter-*log*--

[the several acts of drinking] join together.

G. But if not--

they do not join together.

H. Just as [the quantity of heave-offering which obligates payment of the added fifth in the case of] eating is an
olive's bulk, so [the quantity in the case of] drinking is an
olive's bulk.

I.   [But] eating and drinking do not join together.

> T. 7:3 (T. Ker. 2:2-3, T. Pes. 1:12,
> T. Yom. 4:3, T. Miq. 7:5; B-C: see
> M. Ker. 3:3; G: see Sifra, *'Emor*,
> *pereq* 6:3)

J.   [If] one [unintentionally] ate an olive's bulk of
heave-offering], even if it was [comprised] of each of five
[different] kinds [of produce][9]--

> lo, these join together.

K.   [If] he [unintentionally] ate a half-olive's bulk,
and was informed [of what he had done],

L.   and [then] went and ate another half-olive's bulk of
the same kind (read with HD: *mmyn 'hd*; V reads: *myn 'hr*)[10]--

> lo, these do not join together.

> T. 7:4a (T. Ker. 2:3)

T. cites and complements M. 6:1. The point is that a non-
priest incurs liability to pay the added fifth only if he eats at
least an olive's bulk of heave-offering within a circumscribed
period of time (B-C). Less than an olive's bulk is considered
insignificant. While such a small quantity of heave-offering
must be replaced, atonement is not required (see M. 7:3C-D). By
the same token, if even a larger quantity of heave-offering is
consumed, but over a long period of time, the individual bites of
heave-offering are deemed to be distinct one from the other.
Again, liability to the added fifth is not incurred. E-H makes
the same point for the case of liquids in the status of heave-
offering.

I-K offers circumstances in which the requisite quantity of
heave-offering is consumed without necessitating payment of the
added fifth. Eating and drinking, first, are deemed separate
acts of consumption (I). If an individual eats half an olive's
bulk of heave-offering and then drinks the same quantity, he is
not culpable. At K-L the individual consumes some heave-offering,
is informed of his actions, and afterwards eats more heave-offering. Since the consumption of an olive's bulk occurred in separate spells of inadvertence, the individual acts of eating do not
join together, and liability to the added fifth is not incurred.
The case at J is different. In a single spell of inadvertence
the individual eats more than one kind of heave-offering. Since
only eating is involved, within the requisitie amount of time,
and in a single spell of inadvertence, the quantities of produce
join together and both the principal and added fifth must be paid.

L. Just as they give heave-offering only to a priest
who is a *haber* [*viz.*, one who is scrupulous about Levitical
cleanness; see T. Dem. 2:3], so they pay restitution [for
heave-offering unintentionally consumed by a non-priest] and
the [added] fifth only to a priest who is a *haber*.

                    T. 7:4b (T. Dem 3:1; see b. Hul.
                    130b)

M. One who [unintentionally] eats the heave-offering of
a [priest who is an] *[c]am ha'ares*[11] [*viz.*, one who is not
careful about cleanness] pays restitution and the [added]
fifth to a priest who is a *haber*.

N. And the [priest who is a] *haber* takes the monetary
equivalent [of the heave-offering] (*dmym*) and compensates
the [priest who is an] *[c]am ha'ares*.

                    T. 7:5 (T. Dem. 3:2)

O. The heave-offering of a [priest who is a] *haber* and
the heave-offering of [a priest who is] an *[c]am ha'ares* which
were mixed up together--

P. they compel the [priest who is an] *[c]am ha'ares* to
sell his portion to [the priest who is] a *haber*.

                    T. 7:6 (T. Dem 3:3)[12]

The point, as at M. 6:1D-F, is that the restitution and added
fifth are in all ways true priestly gifts. They therefore must be
given to a priest who is sure to eat them in cleanness, as is required of other heave-offering (L).[13] According to M-N this holds
even if the heave-offering which was eaten belonged to a priest
who is not careful about cleanness. Restitution is made to a
priest who is a *haber*, and he compensates the other priest for his
loss. O-P is cognate to A-N, though not related to M. 6:1.
Heave-offering which belongs to an *[c]am ha'ares* is mixed with that
of a *haber*. The batch may not simply be divided between the two
priests, since this would entail giving heave-offering to an *[c]am
ha'ares*. The *[c]am ha'ares* therefore is forced to accept monetary
compensation in place of his own heave-offering.

A. One who [unintentionally] eats clean heave-offering
pays restitution with clean unconsecrated produce [see M.
6:1E].

B. [If] he [anyway] paid restitution with unclean unconsecrated produce, what is the law (*mhw*)?

C. Sumkos says, "[If he did it] unintentionally, the
restitution is valid [i.e., takes on the status of heave-
offering].

D. "[But if it was [intentional, his restitution is not
valid, [and the offender must give clean produce to the
priest]."

E. But sages say, "Whether [he gave the priest unclean
produce] intentionally or unintentionally, the restitution is
valid [and so has the status of heave-offering].

F. "But [if it was of unclean produce,] he must pay
restitution again, with clean [unconsecrated produce]."

G. An Israelite to whom they gave heave-offering from
the estate of the father of his mother [who was a priest],
and he ate it,

H. and so a creditor [who received heave-offering in
repayment] of a debt, [and ate it,]

I. and so a wife [who received heave-offering as payment for her marriage settlement, [and ate it],

J. pays the principal and the [added] fifth to a priest
who is a *haber*,

K. and the [priest who is a] *haber* (reading with ed.
princ.:) gives them its [i.e., the heave-offering's] monetary
value.[14]

T. 7:7 (A-F: b. Yeb. 90a, b. Git.

54a)

The pericope is in two parts, A-F and G-K. While autonomous
of each other, both are supplementary to M. 6:1. A non-priest who
unintentionally ate clean heave-offering, A, pays the principal
and added fifth with clean unconsecrated produce. He thus compensates the priest with produce which that individual may eat.
What if the non-priest gives the priest unclean produce? Sumkos,
C-D, states that the validity of the non-priest's actions depends
on the intention with which they are carried out. If the payment
of the principal and added fifth is made with proper intention to
give the priest his share, it is valid. The unclean produce takes
on the status of heave-offering in place of the clean heave-offering which was eaten. If, however, the non-priest intentionally
gives the priest produce which he cannot eat, that produce does
not take on the status of heave-offering. Other produce must be
given to replace the priest's share. According to Sumkos, then,
the payment of the principal and added fifth requires the same

proper intention as is needed in the initial designation of heave-
offering (see above, pp. 2-3). Sages disagree. They hold that
whether or not the householder knows that the produce is unclean,
that which he gives as restitution takes on the status of heave-
offering. If it was unclean the non-priest simply provides the
priest with more, clean, produce. Unlike Sumkos, sages thus are
concerned that the priest ultimately receive produce which he may
eat.

G-K presents three cases in which heave-offering becomes the
legal possession of a non-priest. Instead of selling the heave-
offering to a priest, as he should do, the non-priest eats the
offering himself. Proper restitution must be made, to replace the
misused holy thing. Since the original heave-offering was the
property of the person who ate it, however, the priest who receives the restitution subsequently pays that individual for the
heave-offering he receives.

6:2

A. The daughter of an Israelite who [unintentionally]
ate heave-offering and afterwards was married to a priest--

B. if she ate heave-offering of which a priest had not
yet effected acquisition,

she pays the principal and [added] fifth to herself.

C. But if she ate heave-offering of which a priest
[already] had effected acquisition,

she pays the principal to [its] owner [i.e., to the
priest whose heave-offering it was] and the [added] fifth to
herself.

D. For they have said,

E. "One who unintentionally eats heave-offering pays
the principal to [its] owner and the [added] fifth to whom-
ever[15] he wishes."

M. 6:2

The pericope carries forward the theme of M. 6:1, rules for
the repayment of heave-offering unintentionally eaten by a non-
priest. A-C is glossed by D+E, which repeats in general terms C's
rule. Through marriage to a priest, an Israelite-woman gains the
right to eat heave-offering.[16] Even after she has this right, she
must pay restitution for heave-offering she unintentionally ate
when she had non-priestly status. She thereby replaces the im-
properly-consumed consecrated produce and pays a fine for her
offense. To whom, however, does she pay the principal and added

fifth? If the heave-offering which she ate had not yet been given
to a priest, the woman may keep the restitution and added fifth for
herself (B). She now has the same right to these things as has any
priest or person with priestly status.[17] If, however, the heave-
offering already was in the hands of a priest, that individual
must be compensated for his loss (C). The principal therefore is
paid to him. Since the added fifth belongs to no particular
priest, E, the woman may keep that for herself.

6:3

    A. "One who [unintentionally] gives his workers or
guests heave-offering to eat:

    B. "he pays the principal, and they pay the [added]
fifth"--the words of R. Meir.

    C. But sages say, "They pay [both] the principal and
the [added] fifth,

    D. "and he pays them the cost of their meal."

M. 6:3

At issue is whether the principal, like the added fifth is
paid only by those who eat heave-offering, or whether it also is
paid by people who in other ways benefit from sanctified produce.
This is disputed by Meir, A-B and sages, C. The facts of the
case are as follows. A non-priest gives another non-priest heave-
offering to eat, such that two individuals together are responsible for the misuse of a priestly gift. It is clear both to Meir
and sages that the person who actually eats the heave-offering
pays the added fifth. According both to Lev. 22:14 and M., this
is a fine paid for the unintentional consumption of a priestly
gift. The question is which of the individuals is responsible for
replacing the heave-offering, the one who initially misappropriated it, or the one who ate it. Meir, A-D, takes the position
that any person who receives benefit from heave-offering must pay
the principal. Since the householder here used heave-offering in
place of his own produce, he is liable for replacing it.[18] Sages,
C-F, hold that liability to the principal, as to the added fifth,
is incurred only by a non-priest who actually makes use of heave-
offering. In the present case the principal is owed by the workers
or guests, who ate the priestly gift. The householder (D) is held
to his initial responsibility, the cost of the meal the others ate.
Notably, the practical results of Meir's sages' views are the same.
The workers or guests pay the added fifth, and the householder
pays the value of the produce they ate.

6:4

I.   A.   One who steals heave-offering, but does not eat it,
pays as restitution twice the monetary equivalent of the
heave-offering.

II. B.   [If] he [unintentionally] ate it--
     he pays twice the principal and an [added] fifth [of
one of the principals]:

     C.   [one] principal and the [added] fifth [he pays] out
of unconsecrated produce,

     D.   and [the other] principal [he pays] in the monetary
equivalent of the heave-offering.

III. E.   [If] he stole heave-offering which was dedicated
[to the Temple] and [unintentionally] ate it--

     F.   he pays two [added] fifths and the principal,

     G.   for [the requirement of] the payment of two-fold
restitution is not applicable in [the case of] items dedicated [to the Temple].

                         M. 6:4 (A: T. B.M. 7:21; A-D:
                         b. B.M. 54a; E-G: y. Ter. 1:1;
                         G: M. B.M. 4:9)

     The pericope is unitary, in three parts, A, B-D and F-G. At
issue is what restitution is paid by a non-priest who first steals
and then unintentionally eats heave-offering. We already know
that for eating sanctified produce, he pays a principal and added
fifth (M. 6:1). Stealing, A indicates, likewise carries with it
a fine. A thief who is caught is required to pay double the value
of that which he stole (Ex. 22:7).[19] The individual at A therefore pays the priest twice the value of the heave-offering which
he took, just as if it were unconsecrated produce. At B a single
individual owes fines both for stealing and for unintentionally
eating heave-offering. At issue is how he is at one time to pay
both of the fines. There are two alternatives. We may rule that
he needs to pay each of the fines individually. This would mean
payment both of twice the value of the heave-offering, for stealing, and of a principal and added fifth, for eating the priestly
gift. The second possibility is that the principal paid for eating the heave-offering also is counted towards the payment of the
two-fold monetary restitution required for stealing. This is the
view taken at B-D. For eating heave-offering, the offender pays
a principal in unconsecrated food and an added fifth of that
principal. He further pays once the monetary value of the

heave-offering, which, along with the principal already paid, is
deemed to constitute the fine for stealing.

E builds on the foregoing and offers a further complication.
The heave-offering which was stolen had still earlier been dedicated to the Temple.[20] Now there are three transgressions with
which to contend, a non-priest's eating heave-offering, his eating
produce dedicated to the Temple, and stealing. The description of
what restitution must be paid, F-G, offers no surprises. We simply
take account of two facts. The first is that a non-priest who
eats produce dedicated to the Temple, like one who eats heave-
offering, pays an added fifth.[21] The second fact is stated at G.
This is that two-fold restitution does not apply in the case of
the theft of items dedicated to the Temple.[22] We rule, therefore,
that the non-priest must pay one principal, which replaces the
sanctified produce which he ate, and two added fifths, one each
for the transgressions of eating heave-offering and eating produce dedicated to the Temple.

A. One who steals heave-offering which is dedicated
[to the Temple,] but does not eat it, pays the principal, but
does not pay the [added] fifth.

B. And two-fold [restitution] is not required [see
M. 6:4G],

C. as it is written, *He shall pay double to his
neighbor* (Ex. 22:9).

D. [He pays double to his neighbor,] but not for that
which is consecrated.

E. [*If*] he [*unintentionally*] ate it [= M. 6:4E],

F. *he pays two added fifths* [and the principal (HY)]
[= M. 6:4F]:

G. a principal and [added] fifth with unconsecrated
produce, and they become holy like heave-offering (E; V
reads: *qdš btrwmh*).

H. The principal he gives to the treasurer [of the
Temple], but the [added] fifth [remains with] the owner [i.e.,
the non-priest who separates it; he may give it to whichever
priest he wishes (HY)].

I. (Omit: That; so ed. princ.)[23] The principal is
liable to the law of sacrilege [since it replaces produce
which was dedicated to the Temple].

J. [But] that [added] fifth is not liable to the law of
sacrilege, [for it is not dedicated to the Temple, but simply
has the status of heave-offering].

K.   [As for] the second [added] fifth--

L.   heave-offering or the monetary equivalent of heave-
offering (follow GRA, HY and Lieberman in reading *dmy* for
dmyy) he gives to the treasurer [of the Temple].

M.   (Follow E which lacks: And the [added] fifth [re-
mains] with [its] owners.)[24]

T. 7:8a

A-D proves from Scripture the law of M. 6:4G, that two-fold
restitution is not required of an individual who steals items
dedicated to the Temple. E-L cites and explains M. 6:4E-F's rule,
that a non-priest who steals and eats heave-offering dedicated to
the Temple pays the principal and two added fifths. The fifth
which is paid for the consumption of heave-offering, H-J, may be
given to whichever priest the offender wishes, as is always the
case for the added fifth paid for heave-offering unintentionally
consumed by a non-priest (M. 6:2E). This fifth is not liable to
the laws of sacrilege, which apply only to things dedicated or
belonging to the Temple.[25] The principal, on the other hand, replaces dedicated produce. It is paid to the Temple and is subject
to the laws of sacrilege. The same is so for the second added
fifth, paid for the sin of eating produce dedicated to the Temple.
Since this added fifth does not take on the status of heave-offering, but simply of an object dedicated to the Temple (MB), it may
be paid with funds, instead of with unconsecrated produce (L). It
is unclear to me why this added fifth may be paid with heave-
offering which, of course, already is the property of the
priesthood.[26]

T. 7:8b is below, after M. 7:7.

6:5

A.   "They do not pay restitution with (1) gleanings, (2)
forgotten sheaves, (3) [produce grown in] the corners [of a
field, which is left for the poor] or (4) ownerless property,

B.   "and not with (5) first tithe from which heave-
offering of the tithe has (Ve, N. Sa, T[3] add: not) been removed,

C.   "and not with (6) second tithe or [produce] dedicated [to the Temple] which have (N, Sa, T[3] add: not)[27] been
redeemed,

D.   "for a consecrated thing does not serve for the redemption of a consecrated thing"--the words of R. Meir.

E.   But sages permit [in the case of] these [i.e., all
of the items listed at A-C].

M. 6:5 (Cf., M. 1:5; Sifra, 'Emor,

pereq 6:5)[28]

Meir and sages dispute whether or not the payment of produce
as the principal and added fifth is subject to the stringencies
which normally apply to the designation of produce to be heave-
offering. The deeper issue--as we will see even more clearly at
M. 6:6--is whether the produce given as restitution is intended
to take on the sanctified status of the heave-offering which was
eaten, or whether it simply provides the priest with unconsecrated
produce in the quantity of that heave-offering. Meir, A-C, holds
that the payment of produce as the principal and added fifth does
in fact constitute a designation of that produce to be heave-
offering. It follows, according to Meir, that produce paid as
restitution must stand within a category of produce which is
liable to the separation of heave-offering (see M. 1:5F).[29]
This criterion excludes all of the items listed at A-C. A's
items, as we have seen (above, pp. 50-52), are left to the poor
(A1-3), or have no owner (A4). They therefore are exempt from
tithes.[30] First tithe itself is an agricultural offering and
cannot be designated to be a different offering. Whether or not
heave-offering of the tithe has been removed from it seems to me
to be irrelevant to this.[31] Second tithe or produce dedicated to
the Temple which has been redeemed may be consumed as unconsecrated produce by non-priests. Even so, since these things, like
those at A, never were liable to the separation of heave-offering
and tithes,[32] they may not be used to pay the principal and added
fifth. This being the case, D, which claims that Meir's reasoning
is that these categories of produce retain a sanctified status,
is not to the point and, moreover, does not seem to correspond to
the facts. I am not able to explain it.

Sages, E, reject the notion that produce paid as the principal and added fifth must fulfill the requirements of produce
designated to be heave-offering.[33] In their view, then, the produce paid as restitution simply compensates the priest for his
lost share, but does not take on the status of heave-offering in
place of the original priestly gift. It is, self-evidently,
Meir's view, and not that of sages, which stands behind M. 6:1.
That rule states that the unconsecrated produce paid as restitution takes on the status of heave-offering.

6:6

A. R. Eliezer says, "They pay restitution [for heave-
offering unintentionally eaten by a non-priest] with [produce
of] one kind on behalf of [produce] which is not of its same
kind,

B. "with the stipulation that he must pay restitution
with choicer [produce] for less choice [produce]" [see M.
2:4-6].

C. But R. Aqiba says, "They pay restitution only with
[produce of] one kind on behalf of [produce] which is of its
same kind.

D.[34] "Therefore:

E. "if he ate cucumbers [in the status of heave-offering grown on] the eve of the Sabbatical year, he waits for
cucumbers [grown in] the year after the Sabbatical year
(mws'y šbyᶜyt) and pays restitution with them."

F. On the basis of the same verse (mqwm) in accordance
with which R. Eliezer rules leniently, R. Aqiba rules
stringently.

G. For it says, [*If a man eats of a holy thing unwittingly, he shall add the fifth of its value to it,*] *and
give the holy thing to the priest* (Lev. 22:14).

H. "[He may give the priest] anything which is fit to
be holy"--the words of R. Eliezer.

I. But R. Aqiba says, "*And give the holy thing to the
priest.* [He must give the priest] that holy thing which he
ate."

M. 6:6 (Sifra, '*Emor*, *pereq* 6:6)

M. 6:6 carries forward the issue of M. 6:5, now with a dispute between Eliezer, A-B, and Aqiba, C. Aqiba's view is instantiated at D+E. F-H provides a scriptural basis for the views of
each of the disputing authorities.

We recall from M. 2:4-6 that produce of one genus may not be
designated heave-offering on behalf of produce of a different
species. Eliezer, A, states that this rule does not apply to the
payment of the principal and added fifth. His view, like that of
M. 6:5's sages, is that the produce paid as restitution does not
take the place of the heave-offering which was eaten. Rather, it
simply provides the priest with his due share of produce. B
elucidates Eliezer's fundamental concern, which is that the priest
receive his share from desirable produce. A non-priest who

compensates the priest with a kind of produce different from that
which was eaten must therefore give the priest produce of better
quality than that which was misappropriated.

Aqiba, C, rejects Eliezer's perspective, holding that the
same requirements which apply to the designation of heave-offering
apply to the payment of the principal and added fifth. He thus
has the same opinion as Meir, M. 6:5, and the anonymous rule of
M. 6:1. The consequences of the view that restitution must be
paid with produce of the same kind as was eaten are outlined at
D+E. A non-priest eats cucumbers in the status of heave-offering
which were picked at the end of the sixth year. We assume that
other cucumbers of the sixth year are not available for use in
compensating the priest (Bert, TYY). Since, according to Aqiba,
a different species of produce may not be used as restitution, and
since produce of the seventh year--which is not liable to the
separation of heave-offering--may not be used, the non-priest must
wait and pay the principal and added fifth with cucumbers picked
in the first year of the seven year cycle.

F-I is secondary, claiming Lev. 22:14 as the basis of the
opinions both of Eliezer and Aqiba. It is noteworthy only in that
it explains Eliezer's position in terms which should be quite
acceptable to Aqiba and to the anonymous rule of M. 6:1, but which
are not, as we have seen, intrinsic to Eliezer's view at A-B.[35]

> A. *R. Eliezer says, "They pay restitution [for heave-*
> *offering unintentionally eaten by a non-priest] with [produce*
> *of] one kind on behalf of [produce] which is not of its same*
> *kind, with the stipulation that he must pay restitution with*
> *choicer [produce] for less choice [produce]* [= M. 6:6A-B].
>
> B. "How so?
>
> C. "If he eats barley [in the status of heave-offering]
> and pays restitution with wheat [V; E reverses the words
> barley and wheat),
>
> D. "[or if he eats] dried figs and pays restitution
> with dates,
>
> E. "let a blessing be upon him."
>
> F. *R. Aqiba says, "They pay restitution only with*
> *[produce of] one kind on behalf of [produce] which is of its*
> *same kind"* [= M. 6:6C].
>
> G. R. Eliezer says, "Just as they pay restitution with
> the new [i.e., produce of the present year] for the old [i.e.,

produce of the previous year], so they pay restitution with
[produce of] one kind for [produce of] a different kind" [see
M. 6:6E].

T. 7:9 (b. Erub. 29b)

Eliezer's position, M. 6:6A-B, is cited and explained, A-E.
A non-priest who pays restitution with produce of a better kind
than that which he ate is worthy of a blessing, since he has gone
out of his way to improve the priest's lot. F cites Aqiba,
M. 6:6C, and introduces Eliezer, G, who reacts to the gloss of
Aqiba's statement, M. 6:6E (not cited in T.). We recall that
Aqiba there offers a case in which a non-priest has no recourse
but to pay restitution with produce of a different year from that
of the heave-offering he ate. Eliezer argues on the basis of the
rule of M. 1:5I-J, which states that produce of one year of the
sabbatical cycle may not be designated heave-offering for produce
of a different year. Eliezer states that if, as Aqiba holds, this
rule does not pertain to the payment of restitution, it follows
that the rule forbidding designation of produce of one kind as
heave-offering for produce of another kind likewise should not
pertain.

A.   "One who eats untithed produce ($htbl$)[36] pays restitution [for the tithes and heave-offering required of that
produce] with (1) gleanings, (2) forgotten sheaves, (3)
[produce grown in] the corners [of a field] or (4) produce
($tbw'h$) which has not reached a third [of its growth]"--
(E lacks:) the words of R. Eliezer.

B.   R. Aqiba says, "They do not pay restitution with
these things,

C.   "for they do not pay restitution with a thing that
does not become liable to tithes ($\check{s}l'$ b' $l^c wnt$ $hm^c \check{s}rwt$)."

T. 7:10a (see T. M.S. 3:11, b.
Hul. 130b)

T. 7:10a cites the substance of the case of M. 6:5 in the
names of the authorities of M. 6:6, quite correctly reading the
two pericopae as a unit on a single issue of law. The fact that
the superscription, A, refers to untithed produce, and not to
heave-offering, does not change matters.[37] The issue, in all
events, is the compensation paid by a non-priest for misapprop-
riating heave-offering and, here, tithes.

Eliezer, A, holds that the non-priest may compensate the
priest and Levite for offerings owed from untithed produce by

paying over produce of such categories as are not liable to the
separation of agricultural gifts.   Just as at M. 6:6A, then, he
holds that the restitution does not take on the status of the
tithe it replaces, but simply provides the priest or Levite with
his due share (= sages, M. 6:5E).   Aqiba, B-C, has the same view
that he holds at M. 6:6C (= Meir, M. 6:5A-D).   The restitution
takes on the status of the offerings which the non-priest ate.
Therefore it must be paid with produce which is liable to the
separation of agricultural offerings.

TERUMOT CHAPTER SEVEN

The chapter is in two parts, M. 7:1-4 and M. 7:5-7. Both
continue Chapter Six's essay on the penalty paid by non-priests
who eat heave-offering. The main point at M. 7:1-4 is that even
in a case in which the non-priest is not liable to the added fifth,
e.g., if he purposely ate heave-offering (M. 7:1), or if he is a
minor and not culpable (M. 7:3), he still must pay the principal.
In this way the priest is compensated for his loss in produce.
Within the framework of this discussion, of particular interest is
M. 7:2's dispute between Meir and sages', over the status of the
daughter of a priest who marries an Israelite and afterwards eats
heave-offering. At issue is whether the woman is treated like a
person of priestly status, such that she is not liable to the
added fifth, or as a non-priest, such that she is liable. M. 7:4
offers a general principle which summarizes the rules of M. 6:1-6
and M. 7:1-3.

M. 7:5-7 is a long and repetitive unit on a single problem,
the adjudication of cases of doubt concerning the misuse of heave-
offering. The point is familiar from elsewhere in Mishnah,[1] that
we attribute an impairment in status to that which already is impaired. Thus if it is not clear whether a *se'ah* of heave-offering
fell into a bin of heave-offering or a bin of unconsecrated produce, we assume that it fell into the heave-offering, leaving the
other produce free for consumption as unconsecrated food. The
substance of this elaborate formal construction is related to what
precedes only in that it provides a case in which a non-priest
eats the doubtful heave-offering. In principle, however, it is
separate from the unit in which it is redacted.

T. consists almost entirely of a long unit of materials,
T. 6:11b-19, which coordinates the rules of M. 4:12, on cases of
doubt concerning the neutralization of heave-offering, and
M. 7:5-7, which also concerns problems of doubt. The material is
important as an example of T.'s acting as a redactional commentary
to M. Through its sequence of comments on M., T. offers an
alternative, and in this case, completely logical, ordering of the
issues discussed in M.

M. 7:1-4 bear attributions only in M. 7:2's dispute between
Meir and sages. The only attributions at M. 7:5-7 likewise are to

Ushans, specifically, Meir and Yose.   The issue of M. 7:5-7 further
is attested by Judah and Simeon, T. 6:12.

                              7:1

    A.   [A non-priest] who intentionally eats heave-offering
pays back the principal, but does not pay the [added] fifth.

    B.   (Eleven MSS. add: "And") that which is paid as res-
titution [retains the status of] unconsecrated produce.

    C.   (Six MSS. add: "And") [therefore] if the priest
wished to refuse [it], he may refuse [it].

                         M. 7:1

What has changed from M. 6:1 is that here the non-priest intentionally eats heave-offering.   This is a sin for which he is
punishable by death (T. Ker. 1:5).   Since he is liable for that
punishment, he is not required to pay the fine of the added fifth
and to designate heave-offering to replace that which he ate.
This would constitute double punishment for a single crime.   The
non-priest simply compensates the priest from whom he took the
heave-offering.   He does this by giving that priest a quantity of
produce equal to that which was taken.   This produce does not take
on the status of the heave-offering which was eaten, and, therefore, the priest may refuse to accept it (C), as he can any other
gift of unconsecrated produce.[2]

                              7:2

    A.   "The daughter of a priest who married an Israelite
and afterwards [unintentionally] ate heave-offering pays the
principal, but does not pay the [added] fifth.

    B.   "And [if she commits adultery] her death is by
burning.

    C.   "[If] she married any person who is ineligible [for
marriage to priestly stock, e.g., a bastard (M. Yeb. 6:2), and
then unintentionally ate heave-offering],

    D.   "she pays the principal and the [added] fifth.

    E.   "And [if she commits adultery] her death is by
strangling"--the words of R. Meir.

    F.   But sages say, "Both of these [women] pay the prin-
cipal, but do not pay the [added] fifth,

    G.   "and [if they commit adultery] their death is by
burning."

                    M. 7:2 (Sifra, 'Emor, pereq 6:4)

The concern here is the anomolous status of the daughter of

a priest who marries an Israelite. While such a woman is of
priestly lineage, because of the marriage she becomes an outcaste
and loses the right she had while living in her father's house to
eat holy things. The problem is whether such a woman still is
treated as a person of priestly status, or whether she is treated
as an ordinary Israelite. The issue is disputed by Meir, A-E, and
sages, F-G.

The key to the exegesis of the pericope is in what on the
surface appears to be a secondary dispute at B+E vs. G. Meir
distinguishes between a priest's daughter who marries an Israelite
of unimpaired stock, and one who marries an Israelite who is not
fit for marriage to priests. His point is made through the contrast between B and E. Upon divorce or widowhood the woman at B
returns to her father's house and regains her previously held
priestly rights. It follows for Meir that she is treated like a
person of priestly status. If she commits adultery, she is
executed by burning, as are all women of priestly caste who commit
adultery (Lev. 21:9, M. San. 9:1). This is not the case at E,
where the woman has married an Israelite of impaired lineage.
Such a woman never may return to her father's house. Meir holds,
therefore, that she is treated under the law as an Israelite. If
she is unfaithful, her death is by strangulation, as it is for all
Israelite women who are unfaithful (M. San. 11:1). On this basis
we readily can interpret Meir's view regarding the restitution
these women pay if they unintentionally eat heave-offering (A, C).
The priest's daughter who marries an Israelite of unimpaired stock
is treated like a person of priestly status. If she eats heave-
offering she does not pay the added fifth, which is paid only by
non-priests. Since she had no right to eat the heave-offering,
however, she must replace it, as would any priest who ate heave-
offering belonging to some other priest. For this reason she pays
the principal. This is not the case at D. Since here the woman
is treated like an Israelite, if she eats heave-offering, she must
pay both the principal and the added fifth.

Sages reject Meir's distinction. By birth the woman is of
priestly stock. This is not changed by her marriage to a non-
priest, even one of impaired lineage. After her marriage she does
not have the right to eat heave-offering. If she does so anyway,
since she is of priestly stock, she need not pay the added fifth
required of non-priests. If she commits adultery, her death is by
burning, as it is in the case of all unfaithful priestly women.[3]

7:3-4

A.   (1) One who gives his minor children or his slaves, whether they are grown or minor, [heave-offering] to eat,

B.   (2) one who eats heave-offering [separated from produce grown] outside of the Land [of Israel],

C.   (3) and one who eats less than an olive's bulk of heave-offering

D.   pays the principal but does not pay the [added] fifth.

E.   [That which is given as] restitution [retains the status of] unconsecrated produce.

F.   [Therefore] if the priest wished to refuse [it], he may refuse [it].

M. 7:3

G.   This is the general rule (*kll*):

H.   Anyone who pays the principal and the [added] fifth--
[that which is given as] restitution [takes on the status of] heave-offering, and, [therefore, even] if the priest wished to refuse [it], he may not refuse [it].

I.   [And] anyone who pays the principal but does not pay the [added] fifth--
[that which is given as] restitution [retains the status of] unconsecrated produce, [and, therefore,] if the priest wished to refuse [it], he may refuse [it].

M. 7:4

M. 7:3 follows substantively from M. 7:1-2, offering three instances of non-priests who eat heave-offering and pay the principal but not the added fifth. M. 7:4 concludes the unit of materials begun at M. 6:1, offering a general principle which co-ordinates and contrasts the rules of M. 6:1-6 and M. 7:1-3.

M. 7:3 refers to three cases in which a non-priest eats heave-offering in such a manner that he does not incur liability for eating a holy thing. The non-priest is a minor or slave (A), and so is not responsible for his actions (M. B.Q. 8:4); or the heave-offering was separated from produce grown outside of the Land of Israel (B), and therefore does not have the sanctified status of true heave-offering (see above, p. 52); or the non-priest ate less than the quantity of heave-offering the eating of which constitutes a transgression (C; see T. 7:3H). The point is that while in such cases the non-priest need not pay the added fifth, for no liability for the misuse of sancrified produce has

been incurred, he must in all events compensate the priest for his
loss of produce. Since the individual was not in the first place
liable for eating heave-offering, the produce paid as the principal
does not take on the sanctified status of that offering. For this
reason, as I explained at M. 7:1, the priest need not accept the
compensation.

7:5-7

A. Two bins, one [filled] with heave-offering, and the
other [filled] with [less than a hundred *se'ahs* of] unconsecrated produce,

B. into one of which fell a *se'ah* of heave-offering,

C. but it is not known into which of them it fell--

D. lo, I say, "Into the [bin filled with] heave-offering it fell" [and so there has been no mixing of heave-
offering and unconsecrated produce].

E. [If] it is not known which [of the bins] is [filled]
with heave-offering and which is [filled] with unconsecrated
produce--

I.   F. [if] he ate [the produce in] one of them,

he is exempt [from payment of the principal and added
fifth, i.e., we assume that he ate unconsecrated produce].

G. And [as for] the second [bin]--

he [thereafter] treats it as heave-offering.

H. "But [dough made from] it is subject to [the separation of] dough offering [since it might be unconsecrated
produce]"--the words of R. Meir.

I. R. Yose exempts [it from the separation of dough
offering].

J. [If] a different person ate [the produce in] the
second [bin],

he is exempt [from payment of the principal and added
fifth, i.e., we assume that he ate unconsecrated produce].

K. [If] a different person ate [the produce in] both
[of the bins],

he pays restitution in accordance with [the quantity of
produce in] the smaller of the two.

M. 7:5

II.   L. [If the produce in] one of them [i.e., of the bins]
fell into unconsecrated produce,

it does not impart the status of heave-offering [to that
produce].

M.   And [as for] the second [bin]--
he [thereafter] treats it like heave-offering.

N.   "But   [dough made from] it is subject to [the separation of] dough offering"--the words of R. Meir.

O.   R. Yose exempts [it from the separation of dough
offering].

P.   [If the produce in the] second [bin] fell into a
different batch [of unconsecrated produce],
    it does not impart the status of heave-offering [to that
produce].

Q.   [If the produce in] both [of the bins] fell into a
single batch [of unconsecrated produce],
    they impart the status of heave-offering [to the pro-
duce] in accordance with [the quantity of produce in] the
smaller of the two [bins].

M. 7:6

III. R.   [If] he sowed [as seed the produce in] one of them
[i.e., of the bins, the crop which results] is exempt [from
the laws of heave-offering, i.e., it is not treated as heave-
offering (see M. 9:6)].

S.   And [as for] the second [bin]--
he [thereafter] treats it as heave-offering.

T.   "But [dough made from] it is subject [to the separation of] dough offering"--the words of R. Meir.

U.   But R. Yose exempts [it from the separation of dough
offering].

V.   [If] a different person sowed the second [bin], [the
resultant crop] is exempt [from the laws of heave-offering].

W.   [If] one person sowed both [bins]--

X.   in the case of a kind [of produce] the seed of which
disintegrates, [the crop] is permitted [for consumption as
unconsecrated produce (M. 9:5-6)].

Y.   But in the case of a kind [of produce] the seed of
which does not disintegrate, [the crop] is forbidden [for
consumption as unconsecrated produce, i.e., it is treated as
heave-offering].

M. 7:7

The long and formally unitary pericope makes a single point.
In a case in which we need not assume that heave-offering was eaten
by a non-priest or in some other way misused (specifically, mixed
with unconsecrated produce or used as seed), we do not make such

an assumption. The point has its simplest expression at A-D, with
E then acting as superscription to the three parallel cases at
F-K, L-Q and R-Y, any one of which alone would have been sufficient
to make the point that they all make together.

We know that if heave-offering is mixed with less than a
hundred times its quantity in unconsecrated produce, it imparts
the status of heave-offering to the produce. At A-D it is not
certain whether heave-offering was mixed with unconsecrated produce or with other heave-offering. We assume that it was mixed
with the heave-offering such that the unconsecrated produce retains its unconsecrated status. This same principle is applied
in each of the cases which follow. Now one of two bins contains
heave-offering, but it is not known which. If one of the bins is
eaten (F), mixed with unconsecrated produce (L), or used as seed
(R), the individual involved can declare that he used the bin containing unconsecrated produce. He therefore is not liable for
the misuse of a holy thing. For obvious reasons, however, he subsequently must treat the remaining bin of produce as if it contains heave-offering (G, M, S). Meir (H, N, T) holds that since
the status of the second bin is in doubt, dough offering must be
separated from the produce it contains, as if it were unconsecrated produce. Yose (I, O, U) is consistent in holding that the
second bin is treated as heave-offering. For this reason he claims
that the produce in this bin is not liable to the separation of
dough offering. J, P and V have a different non-priest make use
of the second bin. Is he liable for the misappropriation of
sanctified produce? We rule that he is not, for like the first
person, he may declare that the bin which he used did not contain
the heave-offering. Only if the same person makes use of the produce in both of the bins is it certain that he has misappropriated
heave-offering (K, Q, W). If he ate the produce, he must make
proper restitution. If it was mixed with unconsecrated produce,
the rule for mixtures applies. If the heave-offering was used as
seed, the resultant crop, as we shall see in a moment, may be in
the status of heave-offering. Assuming that the two bins contained
different quantities of produce, however, the issue is how to
determine the quantity of heave-offering which was misused. Did
the larger or smaller bin contain heave-offering? The answer is
fully in line with what has preceded. The individual may declare
that the bin containing the lesser quantity of produce was the one
which contained heave-offering. If he ate the offering, he needs
to compensate the priest with a commensurately smaller quantity

of produce (K). If the heave-offering was mixed with unconsecrated
produce, there is a greater chance that it will have been neutralized (Q). Only the case in which the individual surely has planted
heave-offering has a variation in ruling, signaled at W-Y by a
shift in formal patterning and in choice of language (*ptwr* at R
and V; *mwtr/'swr* at W and Y). The reason for the shift is that
not all seed in the status of heave-offering produces a crop which
likewise is deemed to be heave-offering (see below, M. 9:4-6). If
the seed is of a type which disintegrates in the soil, it is not
deemed integral to the plant which grows from it. The produce
yielded by that plant therefore does not have the status of heave-
offering. If, on the other hand, the seed remains intact in the
soil, the produce yielded by it is deemed to have the status of
heave-offering.

O. *R. Meir declares the second bin subject to [the
separation of] dough offering.*

P. *R. Yose exempts it* [= M. 7:5H-I, M. 7:6N-O,
M. 7:7T-U].

Q. But sages say, "Unconsecrated produce which [surely]
has been mixed with heave-offering (*mdwm^c*) [and, therefore,
has the status of heave-offering] is exempt from the separation of dough offering.

R. "That about which there is a doubt whether or not it
was mixed with heave-offering (*spq mdwm^c*) is eaten as heave-
offering, but [anyway] is liable to [the separation of] dough
offering."

T. 7:8b (T. Hal. 15:, y. Ter. 7:6)

Sages, R, agree with Meir. At M. 7:5-7 it is not certain
whether or not the produce in the second bin was mixed with
heave-offering. While it is treated as heave-offering, dough
offering still must be separated from it, as Meir says. According
to Q, Yose's opinion applies only in a case in which it is certain
that heave-offering was mixed with unconsecrated produce. The
resultant mixture surely has the status of heave-offering, and so
is not liable to the separation of dough offering.

T. 6:11b-19, which follow, are presented outside of their redactional context within T., and so require introduction. They
treat together the formally and substantively related materials of
M. 4:12 and M. 7:5-7, a fine example of T.'s improving upon M.'s
ordering of materials through its own sequence of comments on M.'s
pericopae. Thus while T. 6:11b-19 occur in T. along with that

document's materials on the neutralization of heave-offering (the
topic of M. Chapter Four), I have reserved them for the present
context. This allows them to be read with both M. 4:12 and
M. 7:5-6 in mind. At this time we need only recall the point of
M. 4:12. This is that if heave-offering falls into one of two
containers, neither of which holds a hundred *se'ahs* of unconsecrated produce, the containers are deemed to join together to
create the quantity of produce required to neutralize the heave-
offering.

H.   And so would (Lieberman supplies with ed. princ.:
R. Yose say), *"Two bins, one [filled] with [less than a*
hundred se'ahs of] unconsecrated produce, and the other
[filled] with heave-offering,

I.   *"and a se'ah of heave-offering fell into one of*
them, but it is not known into which of them it fell
[= M. 7:5A-C, with minor variations],

J.   "both of them are permitted."

T. 6:11b

I can make no sense of J. No matter into which of the two
bins we assume that the *se'ah* of heave-offering falls, the bin
which originally contained heave-offering does not become permitted for consumption as unconsecrated produce.

Lieberman, TK, I, p. 389, refers to M.'s version of this rule
and states that the point here is the same. He claims that
T. 6:11J refers only to the status of the bin which originally
contained unconsecrated produce. This simply is not what J says.
MB, HD and HY build an interpretation on the claim that the bin of
heave-offering mentioned here contains heave-offering separated by
mandate of the rabbis, but not required by biblical law. Since
neither this pericope nor M. recognizes any such distinction,
this interpretation is not viable.

A.   [If there were] (1) two bins [each containing less
than a hundred *se'ahs* of unconsecrated produce] in two store-
rooms,

(2) two (following Lieberman, TK, I, p. 389:) bins in
two attics,

(3) two bins in one attic,

B.   lo, these [join together to create the quantity of
unconsecrated produce needed to] neutralize [a *se'ah* of
heave-offering which falls into one of them] [see M. 4:12A-B].

C. R. Judah says, "They do not [join together to] neutralize [heave-offering]."

D. *R. Simeon says, "Even if they are in two different cities, they neutralize [heave-offering] in conjunction with one another"* [= M. 4:12E].

E. [If] this one [of the bins] contains a hundred [*se'ahs* of unconsecrated produce], and that one (Lieberman supplies from E and ed. princ.: does not) contain a hundred [*se'ahs* of unconsecrated produce, and a *se'ah* of heave-offering falls into one of them, but it is not known which,]

F. lo, I say, "Into [the bin which contains] a hundred [*se'ahs* of unconsecrated produce] it fell [and, therefore, was neutralized]."

G. [If] one [of the bins contained] a mixture of heave-offering and unconsecrated produce, and the other did not contain a mixture of heave-offering and unconsecrated produce,

H. lo, I say, "Into the mixture of heave-offering and unconsecrated produce it fell."

T. 6:12

T. coordinates the principle of M. 4:12 (given here at A-D) with that of M. 7:5-7 (stated at E-H). If neither of the suspect bins alone contains enough unconsecrated produce to neutralize the heave-offering, they are deemed to join together in order to do so (A-B). If, on the other hand, one of the bins contains enough produce to neutralize the heave-offering and the other does not, the householder simply declares the heave-offering to have fallen into the larger of the bins, and to have been neutralized (E-F). The same rule is applied if the produce in one of the doubtful bins already has an impaired status (G-H). The net result in either case is the same as at A-D.

A. Two bins, in this one are forty *se'ahs* [of unconsecrated produce] and in that one are (follow E in deleting: not) forty *se'ahs* [of unconsecrated produce]--

B. [if] a *se'ah* of heave-offering fell into one of them, and it is known into which of them it fell,

C. and afterwards a second [*se'ah* of heave-offering] fell [into one of them,] but it is not known into which place it fell,

D. lo, I can attribute [the impairment] (*ltlwt*) and say, "Into the place into which the first [*se'ah* of heave-offering] fell, there did the second fall [as well]."

E. [If] a *se'ah* of heave-offering fell into one of them [i.e., one of the original two bins,] but it is not known into which of them it fell,

F. and afterwards a second [*se'ah* of heave-offering] fell [into one of them] (Lieberman follows E in deleting seven words from text of V), and it is known into which of them it fell,

he may not attribute [the impairment] and say, "Into the place into which the second [*se'ah* of heave-offering] fell, there the first fell [as well]."

T. 6:13 (y. Ter. 4:12, 7:4; see
M. Miq. 2:3, T. Miq. 2:3-4)

T.'s two parts, A-D and E-F, once again illustrate the principle that if possible, we attribute an impairment in status to what already is impaired.[4] At A-E we know which of the bins has been mixed with heave-offering and so is in the status of a priestly gift. When a second *se'ah* of heave-offering falls into one of the bins, but it is not known into which (C), we declare that it fell into the one which already had been mixed with heave-offering (D). This is not the case at E-F. Now it is not known into which of the two bins the first *se'ah* of heave-offering falls. Since the status of neither of the bins already is impaired, there are no grounds on which to declare that the heave-offering fell into one of the bins and not the other. We must deem both of the bins to be in a status of doubt as to having been mixed with heave-offering. The fact that we know into which of the bins a second *se'ah* of heave-offering falls does not change matters (F). The bin into which that heave-offering falls, now surely has the status of heave-offering. The other retains its previous status of doubt.

A. [If] before him were two bins, one of [unconsecrated] wheat and one of [unconsecrated] barley,

B. (Supply from E:) and before them were two *se'ahs* [of produce in separate containers], one of [unconsecrated] wheat and one of barley [in the status of heave-offering]--

C. [if] one of them [i.e., of the *se'ahs* of produce] fell [into the produce in the bins], (Lieberman supplies following ed. princ.: and one of them was lost),

D. but it is not known which of them fell and which of them was lost,

E.   both of them [i.e., both of the bins] are permitted
[for consumption as unconsecrated produce, for they retain
their original status].

T. 6:14

The case is more complicated, but the principle is the same
as before. The householder declares that the *se'ah* of unconsecrated produce was mixed with the unconsecrated produce in the
bins, and that the heave-offering is lost. The produce in both of
the bins therefore retains its unconsecrated status.[5]

I.   A.   Two bins, one of unclean heave-offering and one of
clean heave-offering--
        B.   [if] a *se'ah* of [unclean] heave-offering fell into
one of them, but it is not known into which of them it fell,
        C.   lo, I say, "Into the clean [heave-offering] it fell."
        D.   But the clean heave-offering cannot be eaten in
cleanness until it will be ascertained that there is not in
each lump of dough so much as an egg's bulk.

T. 6:15

II.   E.   Two bins, one of unclean heave-offering and one of
[a hundred *se'ahs* (MB) of] clean unconsecrated produce--
        F.   [if] a *se'ah* of [unclean] heave-offering fell into
one of them, but it is not known into which of them it fell,
        G.   lo, I say, "Into the unclean heave-offering it fell."
        H.   But the clean unconsecrated produce may not be eaten
in cleanness until they will ascertain that there is not in
each lump of dough as much as an egg's bulk.

T. 6:16

III.   I.   [If] one bin [contained] clean heave-offering and
one [contained] clean unconsecrated produce,
        J.   [if] a *se'ah* of [unclean] heave-offering fell into
one of them, but it is not known into which of them it fell,
        K.   both are forbidden [for whichever way we were to
attribute the impairment, one of the bins would have to be
deemed forbidden].
        L.   If there is in them [sufficient produce] to neutra-
lize [the heave-offering] in conjunction with one another,
        they neutralize [the heave-offering] in conjunction with
one another.
        M.   But they may not be eaten in cleanness until they

will ascertain that there is not in each lump of dough so
much as an egg's bulk.

T. 6:17

T. 6:15-17 introduce problems of doubts concerning mixtures
of clean and unclean produce. The point, however, remains the
same as before. Wherever possible, we attribute an impairment in
status to what already is impaired. Unclean heave-offering, therefore, is deemed to have fallen into other unclean heave-offering,
and not into clean heave-offering or clean unconsecrated produce
(A-C, E-G).[6] Since in either of these cases there is a doubt
whether unclean produce actually was mixed with clean, the clean
produce is eaten in small amounts, such that, if it is unclean,
it does not impart uncleanness to the person who eats it.

The case at I-K is different. It is not known whether
unclean heave-offering falls into clean heave-offering or into
clean unconsecrated produce. In this case, the heave-offering
will render forbidden for consumption whichever bin it falls into.
If it falls into the heave-offering, it imparts to it uncleanness.
If it falls into the unconsecrated produce, it imparts to it both
the status of heave-offering and uncleanness. The householder may
not himself declare either of the bins to have been ruined. He
therefore must treat both bins as if they have been mixed with unclean heave-offering (K). L-M is difficult, for I do not understand how heave-offering and unconsecrated produce can neutralize
heave-offering in conjunction with one another. Lieberman, TK, I,
393, states that the meaning is that if either the bin of heave-
offering or the bin of unconsecrated produce contains a hundred
se'ahs of produce, we deem the unclean heave-offering to fall
there. If it is into the clean heave-offering that it falls,
that produce will be sufficient to neutralize the unclean heave-
offering (in accordance with the position of the House of Hillel,
M. 5:4), and the bin will remain permitted for consumption by a
priest. If it is deemed to fall into the unconsecrated produce,
both the status of sanctification of the heave-offering, and its
uncleanness will be neutralized. In either case, the possibility
that unclean produce has been mixed with the clean must be taken
into account (M). While Lieberman's interpretation makes sense,
it obscures the usual meaning of "neutralize in conjunction with
one another" at L (see, e.g., M. 4:12). I therefore offer his
exegesis as provisional.

A.   [If] there were before him two bins, one of heave-
offering and one of unconsecrated produce,

B.   and before them were two *se'ahs* [of produce in
separate containers], one of heave-offering and one of unconsecrated produce,

C.   and [the produce] fell from each of them [i.e., of
the small containers], but it is not known whether it fell
from this one into that one, or from that one into this one
[i.e., it is not known which produce was mixed with which]--

D.   lo, I say, "Heave-offering fell into heave-offering;
unconsecrated produce fell into unconsecrated produce."

E.   But if it was untithed produce, first tithe or second
tithe [in one of the bins, and not heave-offering]--
this [i.e., the bin of unconsecrated produce] is forbidden [for consumption].

F.   For they did not declare permitted [for consumption]
unconsecrated produce about which there is a doubt whether or
not it was mixed with heave-offering, except in a case in
which one may attribute the impairment such that the produce
in both of the bins is permitted (*dbr šyš lw mtyryn*).

                    T. 6:18 (A-D: b. Pes. 9b, b. Naz.
                    36b; E-F: see T. 5:15, T. 8:19)

A-D is no different from what has come before. Only E-F is
of interest, offering a case like that of T. 6:17. Into whichever
bin we deem the heave-offering to have fallen, that bin must be
considered forbidden for consumption. This being the case, neither
of the bins may be saved by the declaration that the heave-offering
fell into the other. The reason is clear as stated at F, and as I
have explained it at T. 6:17.

A.   [If] he separated heave-offering, first tithe and
second tithe, but does not know which of the offerings is
which--

B.   lo, this one measures [the quantity of] heave-
offering, first tithe, and second [tithe] (read *šny* with E;
V reads *šnyyh*) [in order to establish on the basis of quantity
which of the offerings is which].[7]

                    T. 6:19

The pericope is related to the foregoing only in that it
offers a case in which containers of produce have been confused.
It concludes T.'s material on this topic.

TERUMOT CHAPTER EIGHT

The chapter is formed of two long constructions of disputes
between Eliezer and Joshua, M. 8:1-3 and M. 8:8-12. These are
distinct from one another both in form and in the substance of
their particular cases. These units have been redacted together
because in both of them, problems regarding the improper consumption and disposition of heave-offering are employed to illustrate
a single encompassing legal issue. This issue is whether or not
in certain circumstances an individual may do what normally is
prohibited to him, and yet not be deemed to have transgressed.[1]
Eliezer's view throughout is that there are no such circumstances,
but that an individual who does what he normally should not always
is culpable. Joshua, on the other hand, takes into account extenuating circumstances. He holds that if the individual has no way
of knowing that what he is doing is improper, or if his actions
only hasten what anyway is inevitable, he has done no wrong. Unlike Eliezer, Joshua thus holds that culpability is relative to
the circumstances under which an action is performed.

These two units of disputes between Eliezer and Joshua are
separated by M. 8:4-7, which offer rules regarding liquids and
foods which are suspected of containing snake venom. The material
is relevant to this tractate only at M. 8:4A, which states that
heave-offering which is suspected of containing venom must be
destroyed. It seems that this rule is redacted in its present
location because it signals the specific interest of the cases
which follow at M. 8:8-12. This, as I said, is the proper treatment of heave-offering. M. 8:4B-7 are then included because
topically they belong with M. 8:7A. They are however autonomous
of the laws of heave-offering.

M. 8:1-3 and M. 8:8-12's attributions to the Yavneans Eliezer
and Joshua are paralleled by references to other Yavneans, Gamaliel
(M. 8:8F) and Nathan (T. 7:10bE). The discussion of foods which
are suspected of containing snake venom takes place at Usha.
Attributions are to Simeon (T. 7:12), Nehemia (M. 8:1, T. 7:13,
T. 7:14), Ishmael b. R. Johanan b. Beroqah (T. 7:14), Judah b.
Baba' (T. 7:15) and Simeon b. Menasia (T. 7:16).

8:1-3

I.   A.   (1) The wife [of a priest] who was eating heave-
offering,

B. [and] they came and told her, "Your husband has died," or "[Your husband] has divorced you" [such that the woman no longer has the right to eat heave-offering];

C. (2) and so [in the case of] a slave [of a priest] who was eating heave-offering,

D. and they came and told him, "Your master has died," "He sold you to an Israelite," "He gave you [to an Israelite] as a gift," or, "He has made you a freeman" [in any of which case, the slave no longer may eat heave-offering];

E. (3) and so [in the case of] a priest who was eating heave-offering,

F. and it became known that he is the son of a divorcee, or of a *ḥaluṣah* [and therefore may not eat heave-offering]--

G. R. Eliezer declares [all of these individuals] liable to payment of the principal and [added] fifth [of the heave-offering they unintentionally had eaten as non-priests].

H. But R. Joshua exempts.

II. I. [If a priest] was standing and offering sacrifices at the altar, and it became known that he is the son of a divorcee or of a *ḥaluṣah*--

J. R. Eliezer says, "All of the sacrifices which he had [ever] offered on the altar are invalid."

K. But R. Joshua declares them valid.

L. If it became known that he is blemished-- his service [retroactively] is invalid.

> M. 8:1 (E-H: b. Yeb. 34b; E-K:
> b. Pes. 72b; I-K: b. Mak. 11b;
> I-L: see b. Qid. 66b, T. Miq. 1:18)

III. M. And [in] all of these [cases] (*wkwlm*), if they had heave-offering in their mouths [at the time they were notified that they were not fit to eat heave-offering]--

N. R. Eliezer says, "Let them swallow [it] (*yblʿw*)."

O. But R. Joshua says, "Let them spit [it] out (*ypltw*)."

II. P. [If] they told him [i.e., anyone with heave-offering in his mouth], "You have become unclean," or "The heave-offering has become unclean"--

Q. R. Eliezer says, "Let him swallow [it]."

R. But R. Joshua says, "Let him spit [it] out."

S. [If they told him,] "You were unclean [at the time you began to eat the heave-offering]," or, "The heave-offering was unclean,"

T.   or [if] it became known that it [i.e., what he
thought was heave-offering] is untithed produce, first tithe
from which heave-offering [of the tithe] had not been taken
or second tithe or produce dedicated [to the Temple] which
had not been redeemed,

U.   or if he tasted a bed-bug (pšpš) in his mouth--

V.   lo, this one should spit it out.

                         M. 8:2 (U-V: b. Nid. 58b)

V.   W.   [If] he was eating a cluster of grapes [as a chance
meal, free from liability to tithe] and entered from the
garden into the courtyard [at which point the grapes are
subject to the separation of tithes (M. Ma. 3:5-6)--

X.   R. Eliezer says, "Let him finish [eating the
cluster]."

Y.   R. Joshua says, "He may not finish it [before he
separates tithes]."

VI. Z.   [If he was eating a cluster of grapes as a chance
meal and] dusk fell on the eve of the Sabbath [at which point
the produce he is eating is subject to the separation of
tithes (M. Ma. 4:2)]--

AA. R. Eliezer says, "Let him finish [eating the cluster]."

BB. R. Joshua says, "He may not finish it."

                         M. 8:3 (W-Y: y. Ma. 3:4; W-BB:
                         b. Bes. 35a)

The three pericopae are formally unitary, each comprised of
a pair of disputes between Eliezer and Joshua (M. 8:1A-H, I-K+L;
M. 8:2M-O, P-R+S-T; M. 8:3W-Y, Z-BB). The juxtaposition of these
disputes is justified by the fact that they each refer to the
same situation: an individual is carrying out an action under the
assumption that he is permitted to do so, when it is discovered
that he is not so permitted.[2] This situation yields two different
questions of law. At M. 8:1 the issue is whether or not an individual is held liable for performing an act which he had every
right to assume that he was permitted to perform. At M. 8:2-3
the problem shifts to whether or not the individual may complete
without permission an action which he was permitted to begin to
perform. On the basis of this substantive analysis, it is clear
that two related, though distinct, issues of law have been brought
together for reason of the common situation addressed and authorities cited. As we presently shall see, the joining of these
issues also is on solid substantive grounds, for, at least in the

case of Joshua, through their joining, a consistent approach to
the law is illustrated. Let us begin with M. 8:1 and then move to
the rule covered in M. 8:2-3.

The key to the exegesis of M. 8:1 is at I-L, which gives both
a case in which Eliezer and Joshua disagree and one in which they
agree. A priest is discovered to be of impaired lineage, and so
not to be fit to offer sacrifices (Lev. 21:7). Eliezer declares
that since the man never was fit to offer sacrifices, all sacrifices which he ever did offer are invalid. Joshua's position is
that the individual's past offerings are valid. This means that
Joshua regards the individual to have been a legitimate priest,
at least up until the time that his real status became known.[3]
Put simply, therefore, Joshua's position is that self-perception
determines actual status. Although in reality the priest never
was fit to serve, as long as he perceived himself as fit, Joshua
claims that his service was valid. That this is Joshua's view is
further evidenced from L. There Joshua agrees with Eliezer that
if the man is found to be blemished, his previous sacrifices are
retroactively invalid. In such a case the priest, aware of his
own physical defect, would have known all along that he is not
fit to serve (Lev. 21:17). Since such a person never could have
perceived himself as fit, Joshua has no grounds on which to declare his past service valid.[4] The same positions which Joshua
and Eliezer hold at I-L are operative at A-H. Eliezer holds that
the fact that the individuals believed that they had the right to
eat heave-offering is irrelevant.[5] They objectively no longer had
that right,[6] and so must pay the principal and added fifth, as
would any non-priest. As at K, Joshua holds that it is self-
perception which counts. The individuals were acting under the
assumption that they had the right to eat heave-offering. Even
when it turns out that they did not have that right, they are not
liable for a transgression.

At M. 8:2-3, as I said, the question shifts to whether or not
an individual may complete without permission an action which to
begin with was permitted.[7] Joshua's view remains consistent with
what has preceded. He states that as soon as the individual knows
that his actions are not permitted, he must stop doing them.
Eliezer's view, on the other hand, is that since the individual
was permitted to begin the act, he may complete it.[8] That this is
Eliezer's position is proven by his agreement with Joshua at S-V.
There it becomes clear that the individual should not even have
begun to eat the produce, since, from the start, it was unclean or

otherwise forbidden. In such a case, Eliezer has no basis on which
to rule that the person may continue to eat. I can, however, find
no way to correlate Eliezer's position here with his view at M. 8:1.
Here, as there, the individual objectively does not have the right
to continue eating the produce. We therefore would expect Eliezer
to rule, as he does at M. 8:1, that the person is liable for his
actions and may not go on eating.[9] It is evident from this that
the issues of M. 8:1 and M. 8:2-3 have been juxtaposed with
Joshua's view in mind. He is shown to have a consistent, and in-
novative, perspective on the law. Through the combination of the
two issues, Eliezer is shown simply to contradict himself.[10]

> E. Said R. Nathan, "R. Eliezer would say, 'Let him wait
> until the end of the Sabbath, or (w) let him leave the court-
> yard, and [then] finish eating'" [see M. 8:3W-BB].

T. 7:10b

Nathan removes the contradiction in Eliezer's position by
having Eliezer state that the individual may continue to eat without tithing only if he does so under the conditions under which
he initially was permitted to eat, i.e., outside of the courtyard
or after the Sabbath.[11]

> A. R. Joshua says, "Blood which is on a loaf [of
> bread]--
> "he scrapes its [i.e., the blood's] place [to remove the
> blood] and eats the rest.
> B. "[If] it is discovered [already] between his teeth--
> "he brushes it off (E reads: he eats it) and need not
> scruple [lest he has eaten blood]."
> I. C. One who eats a grain worm (Jastrow, p. 305, for *dyrh*),
> or an ant, or a louse which is [found] in produce is culpable
> [for having eaten a forbidden thing (cf., M. Par. 9:2)].
> II. D. [If he ate] a mite which is [found] in lentils,
> gnats that are [found] in pods, or worms that are [found] in
> dates and dried figs, he is exempt.
> III. E. [If any of these insects] separated [themselves from
> the produce] and returned [to it]--
> [the one who eats it is] culpable.
> IV. F. [If one ate] worms which are [found] in the roots of
> trees, or the leech which is [found] in vegetables,
> he is culpable.

V.   G.   [And as to] gnats (Jastrow, p. 560, for *ybhwšyn*)
which are [found] in wine and vinegar,
        lo, these are permitted.
VI.   H.   [If] he strained them [out of the wine or vinegar],
        lo, these are forbidden.
      I.   R. Judah says, "One who strains (read *hmsmm* with E;
V reads *hmpnyn*) wine and vinegar,
      J.   "and one who says a blessing over the sun--
      K.   "lo, this is a different path (*drk 'hrt*)."[12]

                    T. 7:11 (A-B: b. Ket. 60a, b. Ker.
                    21b, 22a; C-D: b. Hul. 67b, see
                    Sifra, *Shemini, pereq* 12:1; G-H:
                    see b. Hul. 67a; J-K: T. Ber. 7:6)

        The pericope is in three parts, A-B, C-H and I-K, each with
its own point, and all autonomous of M. Joshua, A-B, states that
the individual need not worry that the blood, which is forbidden
for consumption, was spread throughout the food. He simply scrapes
off all that is visible and eats the rest. I see no correlation
between this statement and Joshua's opinions on heave-offering and
the rules for tithing, M. 8:1-3.[13] C-H apparently has been redacted here in light of M. 8:2U's reference to an individual's
tasting a bed-bug in his mouth (so Lieberman, TK, I, p. 406).[14]
It lists several other types of insects which are either permitted
or forbidden as food. The belief in parthenogenesis generates
these rules. An individual is not held culpable for eating an
insect which, according to T., is generated by, and therefore is
an intrinsic part of, the produce in which it is found (Lieberman,
HY, MB). Such an insect is not considered an autonomous creature,
but part of the fruit. That this is the point is proven by E and
H. If insects which normally may be eaten without liability are
known to have left the produce in which they grew and to have re-
turned, or if the householder himself detaches them, he is liable
for subsequently eating them. At this point the insects are considered autonomous creatures, and forbidden as food. H's references to straining wine introduces the quite separate concern of
Judah, I-K. Judah's statement is enigmatic.[15]

                            8:4
        A.   Wine in the status of heave-offering which is left
uncovered-
        let it be poured out [lest a snake drank from it and
deposited in it venom].

B.   And there is no need to state [that this is the law
in the case] of unconsecrated [wine which is left uncovered].

C.   Three [kinds of] liquids are forbidden [for con-
sumption] on account of being left uncovered:

D.   (1) water, (2) wine and (3) milk.

E.   But all other liquids are permitted [for consumption,
even if they are left uncovered].

F.   Remaining [uncovered for] how long renders them
[i.e., the liquids listed at D] forbidden?

G.   Long enough for a snake to leave a nearby [hiding-]
place and drink [from them].

M. 8:4 (C-D + F-G: b. Hul. 10a)

M. 8:4 introduces a series of pericopae (M. 8:4-7) on the
rules governing liquids which have been left uncovered and foods
which have on them the marks of snake bites.   The issue is taken
up here as a facet of the question of the proper treatment of
heave-offering which may have become unfit for consumption, the
topic of M. 8:8-12.   What this pericope adds to that discussion
is at A.   Wine in the status of heave-offering in which a snake
may have deposited venom must be destroyed, lest it poison the
person who drinks it.   A's rule, however, is autonomous of the
statement of the rules of uncovered liquids at C-G, and, in fact,
of the rest of M.'s discussion of this topic.   These latter
materials have been given a place in this tractate at the redactional level, through the employment of the transitional
element at B.

A.   (1) Brine (*syr*), (2) vinegar, (3) fish-brine
(*hmwryys*), (4) oil, and (5) honey are permitted on account of
[the law of] uncovered liquids [i.e., these things are not
subject to that law].

B.   But R. Simeon prohibits.

C.   Said R. Simeon, (read with E, ed. princ.:) "In Sidon
I saw a snake drink brine."

D.   They said to him, "There is no evidence [to be drawn]
from [the actions of] insane creatures (*hšwtyn*)."

T. 7:12 (b. Hul. 49b; D: b. Shab.
104b, b. Nid. 30b)

Simeon offers evidence that snakes drink liquids other than
the three mentioned in M. 8:4C-D.   The snake which he saw is
declared exceptional, D, and so Simeon's view is rejected.

8:5

A.   [This is] the quantity of uncovered water [which is
permitted for consumption]:

B.   [any amount] such that the venom [of a snake] will
be diluted ('*BD*) in it [and not poison the water].

C.   R. Yose says, "[Water] in [uncovered] vessels [be-
comes forbidden] in any quantity [i.e., no matter how large
the vessel, water left uncovered in it is prohibited];

D.   "and [as for water in pools in] the ground--
      "[if there is more than] forty *se'ahs* [it is permitted]."

M. 8:5

Despite its present formulation, the pericope is not a dispute, for Yose, at C, does not respond to the superscription, A.
A asks for a quantity of water which is not liable to the law of
uncovered liquids.[16] Yose gives a quantity which is liable. This
discontinuity is indicative of the fact that the disputant parties
have entirely different notions about liability to the law of
uncovered liquids. B's view is that the rule of uncovered liquids
does not apply when there is sufficient liquid to dilute the venom.
In such a case the liquid presents no danger to life. Yose has a
different theory. He equates venom with uncleanness, and reasons
by analogy to immersion-pools. These render cultically clean
objects which are rinsed in them. Such pools are dug in the
ground and contain forty *se'ahs* of rain-water. When they meet
these requirements they are not invalidated by drawn water which
falls into them. Yose claims that if these same specifications
are met, uncovered water counteracts the effect of venom which is
deposited in it. The water thus must be contained in the ground,
not in a vessel (C), and must be forty *se'ahs* in quantity (D).
Under such conditions, the water neutralizes venom which is
deposited in it, just as an immersion pool counteracts uncleanness
of drawn water which is placed in it.[17]

A.   Water which has been left uncovered--

B.   (1) one may not spill it out in the public way, (2)
may not mix plaster with it, (3) and may not give it to a
gentile, or to cattle owned by others, to drink.

C.   But he may water his own cattle [with it].

D.   Water which has been left uncovered--

E.   (1) one may not sprinkle his house with it [in order
to lay down the dust], (2) and may not wash his face, hands
or legs with it.

F. Others say, "They did not say [that E2 is the case] except if he has a cut."

G. And how much [uncovered water is permitted; cf., M. 8:5A]?

H. [*In the case of water in a pool in the ground, forty se'ahs* [= Yose, M. 8:5D].

I. Others say, "Two *se'ahs*,

J. "whether [the water is] deep (*mkwnsyn*) or shallow (*mpwzryn*)."

K. R. Nehemia says, "[There must be enough water] for a keg made in Shihin (read with E and y. 8:6; V reads $šw^c yn$; see Lieberman, TK, I, p. 415) to be filled from it."

L. [As for] a spring--

M. as long as it is running (*mwšk*), it is not liable to [the law of] uncovered liquids.

N. Said R. Ishmael b. R. Johanan b. Beroqah "$M^c šh$ *š*: R. Johanan b. Beroqah went to [the home of] R. Johanan b. Nuri in Beth Shearim and found a pond (*gby*; alternatively: cistern) which did not have in it three *logs* of water. And he bent over and drank from it."

O. [As for] wine--

P. whether it is in the ground or in a vessel, it is forbidden [on account of the law of uncovered liquids; see M. 8:5E-D].

> T. 7:14 (y. Ter. 8:6; A-C: b. B.Q. 115b)

A-F augments M. with a list of uses, other than drinking, which may not be made of uncovered water. An individual may not use uncovered water in a way which endangers his own life, the life of others, or the property of others (A-B, E). He may, how- ever, endanger his own property (C; see M. B.Q. 8:6). F holds that if there is little likelihood that venom will enter his bloodstream, an individual even may wash himself with water which has been left uncovered. H-K offers its own dispute on the quan- tity of uncovered water which is not subject to the law of un- covered liquids. I and K, Nehemiah, suggest much smaller quan- tities than did Yose, M. 8:5D (cited anonymously at H). No reason is indicated. L-M and N continue the discussion. A spring is not subject to the law because the water in it constantly is changing. It is likely that the $ma^c aśeh$ at N is intended to illustrate this rule. Since a pond, like a spring, has its own

source of water, Johanan b. Beroqah did not hold it subject to the
law.[18] In terms of lexical items ("spring" at L; "pond" at N),
however, the unit surely is independent, and thus simply makes the
point that Johanan did not hold ponds subject to the law.   O-P
carries forward Yose's analogy between the ability of an immersion
pool to purify unclean things and water's ability to neutralize
venom which is deposited in it. Wine may not be used in an immersion pool. According to O-P, it likewise does not neutralize
venom which is deposited in it.

8:6

A.   (1) Figs, (2) grapes, (3) cucumbers, (4) gourds,
(5) watermelons, and (6) chate-melons which have on them
teeth marks [of snakes] (*nqwry*),

B.   even if they are in a jug (follow Albeck in reading
bkd; 7 MSS. read *kkd*; printed editions read *kkr*),

C.   it is all the same ('*hd*) whether they are large, or
small,

D.   it is all the same whether they are picked or unpicked,

E.   any [of them] which has moisture in it

F.   is forbidden.

G.   And [a beast which has been] bitten by a snake is
forbidden [for slaughter as food],

H.   as a danger to life.

M. 8:6 (G-H: see M. Hul. 3:5,
T. Hul. 3:19)

The pericope is in two formally autonomous parts, A-F and
G-H. These state for produce and meat the same law that M. 8:4
gave for liquids. Produce or meat which shows signs that it contains venom may not be consumed, for fear that the one who eats
it will be poisoned. The point at A+E-F is that only fresh produce is forbidden in this way. The moisture in such produce may
be venom, which also is a liquid.[19] Dry produce, self-evidently,
does not contain venom, and so is not forbidden for consumption,
even if it has on it marks of snake bites. B and C-D make a
single point. No matter how unlikely it is that a snake has
deposited venom in the produce, that produce still may not be
eaten. This applies if the produce is in a jug, such that it is
unlikely that a snake could have deposited venom in the pieces of
produce on the bottom,[20] and if the piece of produce is large, so
that only part of it may contain venom. I assume that the point

at D is that even if the produce still is on the vine, where the snake does not have easy access to it, it is forbidden.[21]

8:7

A. [A container of wine covered with] a wine-strainer (*mӗmrt šlyyn*) is forbidden on account of [the laws of] uncovered [liquids].

B. R. Nehemiah permits.

M. 8:7[22]

A claims that a wine-strainer does not prevent a snake from depositing venom in the jug or vat which it covers. Nehemiah, B, disagrees.[23]

A. [*A container of wine covered with a wine-*] *strainer is forbidden on account* [*the law of*] *uncovered* [*liquids*] [= M. 8:7A].

B. R. Nehemiah says, "If the bottom [vat; i.e., the one into which the wine is being strained] was covered [by the strainer], even though the top [of the strainer, where the wine being strained is poured] was uncovered--

"lo, this [i.e., the wine which has been strained] is permitted [see M. 8:7B],

C. "for the venom of a snake is like a sponge, and stays in its own place [i.e., it does not pass through the strainer into the lower vat]."

D. Dough which one kneaded in water which had been left uncovered,

E. even though it is [dough] of heave-offering,

F. must be burned.

G. And there is no need to state [that this is the rule] as regards unconsecrated [dough; see M. 8:4A-B].

H. R. Nehemiah says, "[If] one baked it, lo, this is permitted,

I. "since the venom of a snake burns up (*klh*) in fire."

I. J. (1) Water used in pickling [vegetables], (2) water used in boiling [food], and (3) water used in soaking lupines [Lieberman, TK, I, p. 412 for *my trmwsyn*] is not liable to [the law of] uncovered [liquids].

II. K. Water in which one soaked pickled [vegetables], foods which had been boiled (*šlqwt*) or lupines--

L. if [the vegetables] were of sufficient [quantity] to impart taste [to the water, the water] is permitted [i.e., not subject to the law of uncovered liquids].

M. But if not, it is forbidden [i.e., is subject to
the law].

III. N. Water in which one rinsed quince (Jastrow, p. 1047,
for $^{c}wbtyn$; see also Lieberman, TK, I, p. 413), or Damascene
plums (Jastrow, p. 324, for $drmsqnywt$) for a sick person,

O. (read with E, y. and Maimonides, cited by Lieberman,
TK, I, p. 414:) is forbidden [i.e., is subject to the law].

IV. P.[24] Water which was left uncovered and which one
[subsequently] heated is forbidden on account of [the law of]
uncovered [liquids].

V.   Q. [And as for] hot water [in an uncovered pot]--

R. as long as it releases steam, it is not subject to
[the law of] uncovered [liquids].

T. 7:13 (A-I: y. Ter. 8:5; A-C:

Suk. 50a, b. B.Q. 115b)

The pericope is in three parts, A-C, D-I, and the five related rules at J-R. A-C cites M. 8:7 and, at B-C, offers an
expanded version of Nehemiah's view, that venom does not pass
through a strainer. D-F+G gives the logical rule that foods which
are made from forbidden water themselves may not be eaten. The
basis for Nehemiah's qualification of this rule, H, is clear, as
given at I. J-N depends on M. 8:4C-E's rule that only water, wine
and milk are subject to the law of uncovered liquids, and that
other liquids which have been left uncovered remain permitted for
consumption. The question here is under what conditions water
which has been used in the preparation of food is deemed no longer
to be water and therefore not to fall under the law. The criterion
is clearly stated at K-M. If the taste of the water has been
changed, it no longer is considered water, and so may be left uncovered without becoming forbidden for consumption. While K-M
thus gives the point of the whole construction in which it is
found, it must be noted that it is formally autonomous of that
construction. It uses the apodosis "prohibited/forbidden," while
the other cases at J-R use "liable to the law/not liable to the
law." It therefore is not surprising that the substance of J3 is
repeated at K. Only P and Q-R require further comment. P holds
that water which is left uncovered and then is heated does not
become permitted, but remains subject to the law. Unlike in the
preceding cases, this liquid still is deemed to be water.
Nehemiah, however, should not agree, for he holds (I) that heat

destroys venom. Q-R assumes that a snake will not drink from water which is boiling.

A. $M^c \acute{s}h$ w: A snake was found dead in a vat of wine.
(w) They came and asked R. Judah b. Baba' [to rule on whether or not the wine was forbidden] and he declared the vat permitted for them.

B. Wine which still is fermenting (yyn twss)--

C. as long as it is fermenting, it is not liable to [the law of] uncovered liquids.

D. And how long [after its manufacture is wine deemed still to be] fermenting?
Three days.

T. 7:15 (y. Ter. 8:6; B-D: b. Ta. 30a, b. San, 70a, b. A.Z. 30b)

Judah b. Baba, A, says we may assume the snake already was dead when it fell into the vat. It therefore could not deposit venom in the wine (see Lieberman, TK, I, p. 416). It is unclear, however, why the wine in the uncovered vat is not in all events forbidden.[25]

I. A. An [open] bottle (lgyn) [filled with liquid] which they placed in a chest, a strong box, or a cupboard (V: 'lpsnh; E: plsqr; y. Ter. 8:5: mgdl; see Lieberman, TK, I, p. 416, and Jastrow, p. 1183)--
lo, this is forbidden [on account of the law of uncovered liquids].

B. [If] he checked them [i.e., the storage places, to see that no snake was in them and then] placed (read with E: hnyh) [the bottle of liquid, in the storage place]--
lo, this is permitted.

II. C. A bottle in its case (E: tyqw)--

D. lo, it is forbidden.

E. [If] he inspected it [i.e., the case] and then placed it [i.e., the bottle, in it]--
lo, this is permitted.

III. E. [If] he placed it in a pit,

F. even if it is a hundred 'ammah deep--

G. lo, this is forbidden.

IV. H. [If] he placed it in a turret (mgdl)

I. even if it is a hundred 'ammah high--

J. lo, this is forbidden.

V.   K.   [If] he placed it in a store-room (*trqlyn*),

      L.   even if it is painted (*mpwyyḥ*),

      M.   even if it is whitewashed (*mswyyd*)--

      N.   lo, this is forbidden.

      O.   [If] they cover [the bottle], but do not seal [it],

      P.   (Read with y. Ter. 8:5 and Lieberman, TK, I, p.
417:)

           it is forbidden.

      Q.   But if the seal had an [open] space (V: *ḥs*; E: *ḥss*)
in it [cf., Lieberman, TK, I, p. 417]--

           lo, this is permitted.

      R.   How wide can the opening [in the seal, or in the
neck of the bottle] be [before the bottle is subject to the
law of uncovered liquids]?

      S.   Wide enough for the small finger of a child (*qṭn*) to
fit in.

      T.   Cooked food with teeth marks [of snakes] on it, and
stalks of cabbage and anything which has moisture in it [see
M. 8:6E] is forbidden [on account of the law of uncovered
liquids].

      U.   R. Simeon b. Manasia says, "He throws out the [part
with the] bites and eats the rest."

      V.   Mushrooms are forbidden as a danger to life.

      W.   [If there were] bite marks on a fig and it was made
into a dried fig,

      X.   on a date, and it was made into a dried [date]--

      Y.   both of these are permitted [for consumption].

                        T. 7:16 (C-E, O-Q: y. Ter. 8:5)

     The five cases at A-K make a single point. Unless we have
solid evidence to the contrary, we assume that a snake had access
to an uncovered bottle. This same point is made in the formally
autonomous continuation of the pericope, P-Q+R-S. A container
must be tightly sealed if it is not to be subject to the law of
uncovered liquids. A simple cover is not permissable, for we
assume that a snake can lift a corner of it and drink from the
liquid. An opening the size of a child's finger, R-S, does not
allow a snake to place its head in the bottle in order to drink.
     T-Z states in its own language the law of M. 8:6E. Food
which is moist is subject to the law. Simeon b. Menasia, U, disagrees, holding that the venom does not contaminate all of the
food, but only the area around the bite.[26] V is interpolated,

possibly because it shares with M. 8:6G the phrase "as a danger to
life." It has nothing to do with cases of snake bites, and so
does not belong.[27] When the produce at W-Y is dried, the venom
is removed with the rest of the moisture. The produce therefore
becomes permitted for consumption.

A. [If] one saw a bird peck at a fig, or a mouse ($^c kbr$)
gnaw at a watermelon--

B. both of these are forbidden [on account of the law
of food with snake bites on it (M. 8:6)].

C. For I say, "Lest they [already] had (Lieberman
supplies hyw with E and ed. princ.) snake bites on them."

D. [As for] a watermelon at which [the mouse] gnawed,
and ten men [later] ate from it [without being poisoned]--

E. the rest [of the watermelon], lo, this [still] is
forbidden.

F. And so [in the case of] a jug [of wine] which was
left uncovered, and [later] ten men drank from it [without
being poisoned]--

G. the rest [of the wine], lo, this is forbidden.

T. 7:17 (A-C: y. Ter. 8:5, b. Hul.

9a-b; D-G: y. Shab 1:4)

Food and liquids are forbidden on account of venom even if
there is some evidence that they are safe for consumption. The
marks on the fig or watermelon, A-B, seem to derive from a bird or
mouse, and not from a snake. We assume that these creatures
gnawed at a place on the produce at which a snake already had
bitten (C). Even though individuals who eat forbidden food or
liquid (D-E, F-G) are unaffected, the rest of the same food or
liquid remains forbidden, lest there is venom in the portion which
has not yet been consumed (y. Shab. 1:4).

8:8-12

A. A jug of [wine in the status of] heave-offering concerning which there arose a suspicion of uncleanness (spq
$twm'h$)--

B. R. Eliezer says, "If it was lying in an exposed
place, he should place it in a concealed place.

C. "And if it was uncovered, he should cover it."

D. R. Joshua says, "If it was lying in a concealed
place, he should place it in an exposed place.

E. "And if it was covered, he should uncover it."

F.   Rabban Gamaliel says, "Let him not do anything new
with it."

M. 8:8 (b. Bek. 33b, y. Shab. 1:8;

A-E: b. Pes. 15a 20b)

G.   [As to] a jug [of wine in the status of heave-
offering] which broke in the upper vat, and the lower [vat]
is unclean--

H.   R. Eliezer and R. Joshua agree (*mwdh*) that if he can
save from it a fourth in a state of cleanness, he should save
[it].

I.   But if not:

J.   R. Eliezer says, "Let it go down [into the lower
vat] and be made unclean.

K.   "But let him not make it unclean with his hand [i.e.,
through his own actions]."

M. 8:9 (b. Pes. 15a, 20b, b. Men.

48a-b)

L.   And so [in the case of] a jug of oil [in the status
of heave-offering] which was spilled--

M.   R. Eliezer and R. Joshua agree that if he can save
from it a fourth in a state of cleanness, he should save [it].

N.   But if not:

O.   R. Eliezer says, "Let it run down and be soaked up
[in the ground].

P.   "But let him not soak it up with his hands."

M. 8:10

Q.   But as regards both of these cases (lit.: But on
this and this):

R.   Said R. Joshua, "This is not heave-offering concerning which I am warned against rendering unclean.

S.   "Rather, [it is heave-offering which a priest is
warned] against eating."

T.   And "not to render it unclean." How so? [I.e., in
what case must the individual not render heave-offering unclean?]

U.   [If] one was walking from place to place, and loaves
[of bread] in the status of heave-offering were in his hand--

V.   [if] a gentile (all MSS.: *nkry*; printed edition:
^{c}wbd kwkbym)[28] said to him, "Give me one of them and I shall
make it unclean, and if not, lo, I shall make all of them
unclean"--

W. R. Eliezer says, "Let him make all of them unclean,
but let [the Israelite] not give him [i.e., the gentile] one
of them that he make it unclean."

X. R. Joshua says, "Let him place one of them before
him, on a rock."

M. 8:11

Y. And so [in the case of] women to whom gentiles said,
"Give [us] one of you that we may make her unclean, but if
not, lo, we will make all of you unclean"--

Z. let them make all of them unclean, but they should
not hand over a single Israelite.

M. 8:12

It is the obligation of the householder to protect heave-
offering in a state of cleanness, for only in such a state may the
offering be eaten by a priest. At issue here is the point at which
the householder may consider his responsibility discharged, such
that he no longer need concern himself with the cleanness of the
priestly gift. In normal circumstances the individual's responsibility ends either at the point at which he presents the clean
heave-offering to a priest or, alternatively, when the offering
perchance is made unclean. In either case, the householder no
longer has control over the cleanness of the offering, and so is
not expected to protect it. Mishnah characteristically states its
problem through a case of doubt. Heave-offering either is suspected of being unclean, or is in a situation in which the householder no longer can prevent it from being made unclean. In both
cases the heave-offering ultimately will not be eaten by a priest.
Since, however, it is not yet certainly unclean, and still is in
the control of the householder, we must ask whether that individual
is responsible to protect it. The larger issue to be addressed
is whether or not he is culpable if, through his own actions, he
hastens the priestly gift's becoming unclean.

When matters are stated in this way, it is clear that the
issue here is the same as at M. 8:1-3, specifically, the circumstances under which an individual is or is not blameworthy for
performing actions which normally are forbidden. Eliezer and
Joshua's positions are consistent with what has come before.
Eliezer, first, is concerned only with the objective facts of the
individual's original responsibility. If, as in the present case,
the householder is responsible for protecting heave-offering until
it is in the hands of a priest or is certainly unclean, then he is

culpable for any actions by which he renders the heave-offering
unclean before these conditions are met. The fact that the
heave-offering is suspected already of being unclean, or will in
all events become unclean, is of no concern to Eliezer. The
householder's responsibility remains what it originally was, to
protect the heave-offering in cleanness. Unlike Eliezer, Joshua
takes into account the actual impact of the actions of the householder. Joshua holds that the householder does no wrong if
through his own actions he does what is in all events inevitable.
In the present case, no matter what the householder does, the
heave-offering ultimately will not be eaten by a priest. Joshua
therefore declares that the householder is not culpable if he
himself renders the priestly gift unclean.

We turn now to the specifics of the pericopae before us.
M. 8:8A-E is a formally unitary and balanced dispute, setting out
the positions of Eliezer and Joshua. Even though heave-offering
which is suspected of being unclean may not be eaten by a priest,
Eliezer holds that the householder must continue to protect it
against being made certainly unclean. Joshua's view is that the
householder no longer is accountable for the heave-offering and
therefore may take actions to assure that it becomes certainly unclean. The heave-offering then may be destroyed, assuring that it
will not accidentally be consumed by a priest.[29] Gamaliel, F,
presents a mediating position, which shows no formal similarity to
the balanced views of Joshua and Eliezer and, indeed, does not
recur in these materials. Gamaliel holds that the individual must
leave the doubtfully unclean heave-offering as it is. He should
not protect from uncleanness what already may not be consumed by a
priest. He may not, however, take actions designed to render the
heave-offering certainly unclean.

M. 8:9 and M. 8:10 are formally and substantively parallel,
providing two examples of essentially the same case. Heave-
offering has been spilled and is about to become unclean (G) or to
be soaked up in the ground (L). The householder, however, cannot
save the priestly gift without himself rendering it unclean. As
we would expect, Eliezer, M. 8:9J-K and M. 8:10/O-P, states that
the householder must let the heave-offering become unclean or be
soaked into the ground by itself, but himself may do nothing improper with the offering.[30] Joshua's position is lacking from
both pericopae. Instead there is an agreement-clause at M. 8:9H
and M. 8:10M, and a general statement of Joshua's view at
M. 8:11R-S. The question is whether or not these materials in

fact reflect the opinion which Joshua holds at M. 8:11R-S. When
we turn to the agreement-clauses, we see that they do not reflect
his particular view. They tell us only what should be obvious to
all parties. If the householder can save the heave-offering in
cleanness, he should do so.[31] R-S, on the surface, does not help
matters. Joshua's statement there is not even formulated as a
response to Eliezer's view. When examined more closely, however,
R-S does, in fact, counter Eliezer's view, and is compatible with
Joshua's position at M. 8:8. Joshua states that the issue here is
the prevention of the consumption of the heave-offering. This
being the case, Joshua holds that what the householder does to the
heave-offering itself does not matter.[32]

In light of these considerations, we see that the problem
here is not the content of Joshua's statement, but the reason that
it has been formulated in the somewhat elliptical way that it is
before us. The reason for this formulation becomes clear when we
turn to the case at M. 8:11U-X. The case is complete in itself,
and formally separate from the preceding. Yet it is attached to
Joshua's opinion with T, which cites Joshua's statement at R. It
appears, therefore, that R-S+T has been formulated in such a way
as to tie to the preceding construction a further set of cases.
The artificial nature of the link is clear, when we see that U-X
does not continue Joshua's statement. While T leads us to expect
an example in which Joshua holds that the householder must protect
the cleanness of heave-offering, this is not what U-X presents.
U-X, rather, is a replay of the disputes which have gone before,
with the positions of both Eliezer and Joshua remaining exactly
the same. Eliezer's view is that the householder may not bear
responsibility for the gentile's making unclean a loaf of bread in
the status of heave-offering. Should the gentile make all of the
loaves unclean, that is not the householder's fault. Joshua, likewise, is consistent with his previous position. Since the loaves
are sure to be made unclean, the householder is no longer responsible for them. He may place a loaf on a rock, where assuredly the
gentile will make it unclean. This is comparable to M. 8:8, where
Joshua has the householder place the heave-offering in an open
place, where it will be rendered certainly unclean.

Although stated anonymously, M. 8:12 gives another example of
Eliezer's view. Despite the extenuating circumstances, the women
may not take responsibility for the rape of one of their number.
They must, rather, allow each one of themselves to be raped.[33]

G. R. Eleazar says, "[As to] an individual who was coming along the road and had in his hand figs, grapes or cucumbers [in the status of heave-offering] which could not reach
the city [before spoiling]--
     "he should throw them into the ravine or into thorn
bushes.

H. "[If] he was passing among gentiles or Samaritans
and had with him foods (dbrym) [in the status of heave-
offering] which could not reach the city [before spoiling],
     "he should place them on a rock" [see M. 8:11].

I. R. Yose says, "He should place them in his sack until
they stink [and only then may he leave them for others to
find]."

T. 1:14b[34]

T. supplements M. 8:11's dispute on the householder's responsibility to protect heave-offering from being made unclean.
Eleazar,[35] G, has the position Eliezer holds at M. 8:11W. While
the householder may abandon heave-offering which is going to spoil,
he must ensure that it will not be eaten or made unclean by another person. He therefore hides the priestly gift in a ravine
or thorn bush. H is problematic, for it assigns to Eleazar the
position held in M. by Joshua, and contradicts the statment at G.
Now Eleazar states that the householder may leave the heave-
offering on a rock, where it will be taken by a gentile or Samaritan.[36] Yose, I, rejects both G and H. He holds that the heave-
offering must be protected until it actually is spoiled and no
longer is fit for use as food.

A. They do not mix with one another [batches of heave-
offering] of suspended status of uncleanness (tlwywt).

B. But they do mix heave-offering which was rendered
unclean by an offspring of uncleanness with heave-offering
which was rendered unclean by a Father of uncleanness,

C. even though they [thereby] add uncleanness to its
[i.e., the heave-offering rendered unclean by an offspring's]
uncleanness.

D. If he declared ('mr) of [heave-offering of] suspended
status of cleanness, "It is clean," lo, this is [deemed to be]
clean.

E. If he said, "Lo, I am going to leave it [i.e., the
heave-offering of doubtful status] until I can ask of its
status," lo, this is unclean.

F. [If] a suspicion of uncleanness was born concerning
a loaf [of bread] and [this happened while] it was in his hand
[see Lieberman, TZ, p. 148],

G. or [if] a suspicion of uncleanness [was born to it
while it was] on top (read with E: $^c l$; V reads $\check{s}^c l$) of a
table--

H. he takes it [i.e., the loaf] and places it in a concealed place [see M. 8:8B].

T. 7:18 (See M. Pes. 1:6-7, T. Pes.
1:5; E: see T. Toh 8:14)

The pericope is in three parts, A-B+C, D-E and F-H, all supplementary to M. 8:8-12's discussion of the proper treatment of
heave-offering which either is unclean or is suspected of being
unclean. Heave-offering which is suspected of being unclean, we
know, may not be consumed. Even so, according to A, several
batches of such heave-offering may not be mixed together. This is
because one of the batches may in fact contain clean heave-offering. In mixing it with the other batches the householder himself
would render unclean this clean heave-offering. This clearly is
Eliezer's view. Joshua, M. 8:8D-E and M. 8:11R, who holds that
the householder need not continue to protect from uncleanness
heave-offering which already may be unclean, will hardly agree.[37]
At B, since the heave-offering surely is unclean and must be
destroyed, it is of no concern that the householder raise its
level of uncleanness. Eliezer, as well as Joshua, can agree to
this.

The point at D-E is made through the contrast between the two
cases described. The decisive factor in the ultimate status of
cleanness of the suspect heave-offering is the householder's
attitude towards that heave-offering. If he declares it to be
clean and therefore protects it as such, the heave-offering indeed
is deemed to be clean. If, however, the householder leaves the
heave-offering unprotected and goes to ask of its status, it immediately must be considered unclean.[38] F-H states anonymously
the view of Eliezer, M. 8:8B.

A. [As to] a jug [of wine in the status of heave-offer-
ing] which broke in the upper vat, and in the lower vat is
unclean [wine] [= M. 8:9G, with slight variations]--

B. all agree that it should go down [into the lower vat]
and impart to [all of the wine] the status of heave-offering.

C. *But he should not make it unclean* (read *ytm'ynh* with
E; V, ed. princ. read *ydm^{c}nh*) *with his hands* [= Eliezer,
M. 8:9K].

T. 7:19

T. cites the opinion of Eliezer, M. 8:9K, and claims that
Joshua agrees. This clearly is not the case, as M. 8:11Q-S
explicitly states.[39]

A. [As to] a group of men to whom gentiles said, "Give
us one of your number that we may kill him, and if not, lo,
we will kill all of you"--

B. let them kill all of them, but let them not give over
to them a single Israelite [see M. 8:12].

C. But if they singled one out,

D. such as they singled out Sheba the son of Bichri
[2 Sam. 20]--

E. let them give him to them, that they not all be
killed.

F. Said R. Judah, "To what case does [the rule of A-B]
apply?

G. "To the case in which he [i.e., the one who would
be handed over] is inside and they [i.e., the killers] are
outside.

H. "But if he is inside and they are inside, since he
is [in all events] going to be killed, and they [i.e., the
other Israelites] are going to be killed, let them give him
over to them so that they all not be killed."

I. And so it says [in Scripture], *Then the woman went
to all the people in her wisdom* (2 Sam. 20:22).

J. She said to them, "Since he is going to be killed,
and you are going to be killed, give him to them that you all
not be killed."

K. R. Simeon says, "Thus she said to them, 'Anyone who
is a rebel against the kingship of the House of David is
liable to execution.'"

T. 7:20 (A-E+K: y. Ter. 8:10)

A-B's case and ruling are parallel to those found at M.
8:12.[40] C-E, F-H and I-J+K all clarify that rule. If the gentiles
single out for death a particular Israelite, the other Israelites
may hand him over, and are not held responsible for his murder.
Judah's statement, which follows, is out of place, for it ignores
C-E and refers directly to A-B.[41] Judah's point, however, is the

same as that of C-E. If it is certain that a particular one of
the Israelites is going to be killed, he may be handed over, and
the others saved. I-J is clear, giving the principle which stands
behind C-E. Simeon, K, rejects the case of Sheba the son of Bichri
(2 Sam. 20) as evidence for the proposition of C-E. Simeon claims
that Sheba was killed because he was a traitor and deserving of
death, not because he was singled out.

TERUMOT CHAPTER NINE

The theme of the chapter is the status of a crop grown from seed of heave-offering, tithes, or other produce subject to special restrictions. At issue is whether or not such a crop shares the status of the seed from which it was grown. If, for instance, seed of heave-offering is planted, we must determine whether or not the crop which results likewise has the status of heave-offering. If so, it may be eaten only by a priest. A like case is that in which produce which has been made liable to the separation of tithes, but which has not been tithed, is planted. We must specify whether such a crop is subject to tithes from the beginning of its growth, or whether, like crops grown from tithed seed, it incurs this liability only at the time of its harvest and processing. The chapter offers two independent, and contradictory, notions of the conditions under which a crop is deemed to have the status of the seed from which it was grown. The first is at M. 9:1-4, the second, at M. 9:5-7.

According to M. 9:1-4, what grows from heave-offering has the status of heave-offering and may be eaten only by a priest. What grows from other agricultural offerings, or from produce subject to special restrictions (e.g., produce which is liable to the separation of tithes), however, does not share the status of the original seed. Ths reason for this distinction between heave-offering and other types of produce is clear when we specify the main difference between heave-offering and these other types of produce. The difference is that while heave-offering is consecrated, other agricultural offerings and categories of produce are not. An individual who plants heave-offering thus misuses what is holy and intrinsically cannot be eaten by him. This consideration does not apply to other categories of produce, which, while restricted to consumption by specific persons or in special circumstances, are not holy. Since any produce may be used for the same purpose, the householder may replace with other produce the seed which he planted. There is no reason now that he may not eat that seed or, indeed, the crop which grows from it.

The second theory of the chapter, stated at M. 9:5-7, is that whether or not the crop shares in the status of the seed from which it grew is determined on the basis of the nature of that seed, and not by the type of restriction to which it is subject. If the

seed constitutes part of the crop which grows from it (as in the
case of onions, M. 9:6F), the crop has the same status as was held
by the seed.[1] According to M. 9:5-7, this applies to heave-offering as well as to other produce subject to special restrictions.
If, however, the seed is not integral to the crop, but is destroyed in the growth process, then even in the case of heave-
offering, that crop does not have the status which originally was
held by the seed. The crop is deemed a separate entity, and distinct from that seed.

As is usual, the fact that M. contains two sets of divergent
materials on the same topic is indicated through the language and
redactional placement of the chapter's pericopae. Chapter Nine is
composed of two parallel constructions, each delineating one of
the theories just reviewed. In each unit, M. begins with the
rules for heave-offering (M. 9:1+2-3; M. 9:5) and continues with
the law as applied to other types of produce (M. 9:4; M. 9:6H-J).
M. 9:7K-N concludes the whole with a special case regarding heave-
offering. Each of the chapter's units likewise has it own particular language for indicating the status of the crop in question.
M. 9:1-4 uses *heave-offering/common food,* while M. 9:5-7 has *permitted [for consumption as common food]/forbidden.* A clear perspective on the formulation and redaction of M.'s materials thus
is fundamental to a proper understanding of the substance of the
law.

The central principles of the chapter are stated anonymously.
We do, however, have an important attribution to Tarfon (M. 9:2) of
an issue clearly dependent upon the principle of M. 9:1-4. In T.
Judah and Meir (T. 8:1) and Simeon (T. 8:3) attest other secondary
considerations regarding that same theory. Discussion of the
theory of the second part of the chapter is attested only at Usha.
Attributions are to Judah (M. 9:6, 7), Simeon (alt.: Judah; T.
8:4) and Simeon b. Eleazar (T. 8:7).

9:1-3

A.   One who sows [as seed grain in the status of] heave-
offering--

B.   if [he does this] unintentionally, he should plough
up (*ywpk*) [the seed].

C.   But [if he does it] intentionally, he must leave [it]
to grow.

D.   (Eight MSS. add: And) if [the grain] reached a third
of its growth (*hby'h šlyš*)--

E.   whether [he sows it] unintentionally or intentionally, he must let [it] grow.

F.   But in [the case of] flax [in the status of heave-
offering]--

G.   [even if he sows it] intentionally, he must plough
[it] up.

H.   And [the field in which the heave-offering was sown]
is subject to [the laws of] (1) gleanings, (2) forgotten
sheaves and (3) [produce growing in] the corner of a field.[2]

M. 9:1

I.   And poor Israelites and poor priests glean [in such
a field].

J.   And the poor Israelites sell their portion to the
priests at the price of heave-offering;

K.   and the money [which they receive] is theirs [i.e.,
the poor Israelites'].

L.   R. Tarfon says, "Only poor priests should glean,

M.   "lest they [i.e., the poor Israelites] forget and
put [the produce they glean] in their mouths."

N.   Said to him R. Aqiba, "If so, only clean [priests]
should glean."

M. 9:2 (H-J: y. Ter. 6:1)

O.   And [the field] is subject to (4) tithes and (5)
poorman's tithe.

P.   And poor Israelites and poor priests take [the
poorman's tithe].

Q.   And the poor Israelites sell their [portion] to the
priests at the price of heave-offering;

R.   and the money [which they receive] is theirs [i.e.,
the poor Israelites'].

S.   He who threshes by hand [the produce grown in such a
field] is praiseworthy.

T.   But he who threshes [it] with cattle (hdš), How
should he do this [so that the cattle does not eat the grain
which has the status of heave-offering]?

U.   He hangs a feed bag from the neck of the beast and
places in it [unconsecrated produce of] the same kind [as is
being threshed].

V.   It turns out that he does not muzzle the animal, but
[also] does not feed it heave-offering.

M. 9:3 (T-U: T. B.M.   8:11, b.

B.M.   90a)

The three pericopae present an extended essay on the rules
for heave-offering which is planted as seed. The single principle which emerges is that the crop grown from such seed is
treated as heave-offering and must be eaten by a priest (see
M. 9:4A). The crop, however, still is subject to the agricultural
restrictions which normally apply to produce growing in a field.
The problem, then, is to establish procedures for handling produce
which is at the same time subject to two sets of restrictions,
those applied to sanctified produce, and those pertinent to all
produce which grows in a field. While M. 9:1-3 are not a formal
unity, they do deal in logical order with three questions which
arise in this situation. M. 9:1 opens with the question of the
rights and responsibilities of the householder who has planted
heave-offering. A formal doublet at M. 9:2+3/O-R next discusses
the problem of the liability of the field to the agricultural
obligations which apply at the time of the harvest, e.g., gleanings. The problem is that while such things as gleanings normally
are collected by all poor people, in the present case, they may be
eaten only by priests. M. 9:3S-V concludes with the next logical
step. Once the produce has been grown and harvested, it must be
processed. The processing of sanctified produce, we shall see,
has its own particular problems.

The rules at M. 9:1 depend on the notion that a crop grown
from seed in the status of heave-offering itself has the status of
a priestly gift.[3] The point here is made through the contrast between B and C. If the householder accidentally plants heave-
offering, he is allowed to uproot the crop. In this way he avoids
the considerable loss incurred in cultivating a crop which has the
low market value of heave-offering. If he planted the heave-
offering intentionally, the individual is not given the option of
correcting his wrong action (y. Ter 9:1). He must allow the crop
to grow. Later he will have to sell it to a priest, the only
person who may eat this food. D-E and F-G each augment the rule
of A-C, giving us three rules in all. At a third of its growth,
the crop is deemed food. At this point it has the status of heave-
offering. The farmer may not now plough it up, for he thereby
would destroy what already is sanctified and ready for consumption
by a priest. Flax, F-G, has its own rule because of the particular
characteristics of that plant.[4] Its seeds are a food, and therefore can take on the status of heave-offering. The more valuable
part of the plant, however, is used to make linen. This is not a
food and so even when grown from consecrated seed, remains

unconsecrated. Farmers who plant flax seed which has the status
of heave-offering therefore would be able to use the plant fibers
for their own benefit by making linen. In order to prevent this,
they are required to plough up the plants.

H-K and O-R are formally balanced units making a single point.
A crop grown from seed in the status of heave-offering is itself
deemed a priestly gift. Still, this crop is subject to the agricultural restrictions which normally apply to produce cultivated
by an Israelite in the Land of Israel. The non-priests who have
the right to collect that which is left for the poor (H), or is
designated as tithe (O), simply sell their portion to a priest.
The dispute between Tarfon and Aqiba, L-N, is clear, bearing an
exegetical gloss at M.[5] I cannot, however, account for the redactional placement of the dispute, for Tarfon's consideration
should apply to tithes, listed at O-R, as well as gifts to the
poor, H-K.

S-V depends on the rule of Dt. 25:4, which states that an ox
being used to tread grain must not be muzzled. This is a problem
here, for the animal likewise may not be allowed to eat the produce (M. 11:9). The solution to this problem is stated at V.

>   A.   "One who sows [as seed] flax in the status of heave-
> offering--
>   B.   "before it has reached a third of its growth, he
> should plough [it] up.
>   C.   "After it has reached a third of its growth, he must
> let [it] grow"--the words of R. Meir.[6]
>   D.   R. Judah says, "[If he planted it] unintentionally,
> before it has reached a third of its growth, he should plough
> [it] up.
>   "After it has reached a third of its growth, he must let
> [it] grow.
>   E.   "[And if he planted it] intentionally, in either
> case, he should plow [it] up" [see M. 9:1F-G].
>   T. 8:1

T. applies to the law of flax considerations of the stage of
growth of the crop, and the intention of the farmer who originally
planted it, thus filling out M.'s discussion. Meir's theory
(A-C) is that like all other crops, once the flax reaches the
stage at which its seeds are considered food, it is sanctified as
heave-offering and may not be destroyed. Judah disagrees, stating
that this applies only if the farmer unintentionally planted the

seed. If he intentionally planted the flax, he must in all events
plow it up, lest he make use of the non-edible fiber. While this
fiber itself does not have the status of heave-offering, by using
it, the individual derives benefit from the sanctified seed which
he wrongly planted.

A. *But he who threshes [produce grown from seed in the*
status of heave-offering] with cattle, How should he do this
[so that the cattle does not eat the grain, which has the
status of heave-offering]?

B. *He brings a feedbag and hangs it from the neck of the*
beast and places in it [unconsecrated produce] of the same kind
(read with E: *m'wtw hmyn;* v reads: *hwlyn;* ed. princ. reads:
hwlyn m'wtw hmyn) [as is being threshed] [= M. 9:3T-U].

C. R. Simeon says, "He places in it vetches,

D. "for they are of better quality than all [other produce fed to cattle]."

T. 8:3

Simeon, C-D, disputes the rule of M. 9:3T-U, cited at A-B.
He holds that the householder must provide the beast with produce
of better quality than the heave-offering which it is threshing.
This assures that the animal is not being mistreated through the
use of the feedbag.

9:4

I. A. That which grows from [seed in the status of] heave-
offering has the status of heave-offering.

II. B. And what grows from [the seed of produce] that grew
from [seed in the status of] heave-offering is unconsecrated.

III. C. But [as regards] (1) produce which is liable to
tithes, (2) first tithe, (3) after-growths (*spyhy*) of the
seventh year [of the sabbatical cycle], (4) heave-offering
[separated from produce grown] outside of the Land of Israel,
(5) mixtures of heave-offering and unconsecrated produce and
(6) first fruits--

that which grows from them is common food (*hwlyn*)[7]
[i.e., does not have the same status as the seed from which
it grew].

IV. D. That which grows from [seed] which is dedicated [to
the Temple] or second tithe is unconsecrated.

E. And he redeems (B, C, and N read: they redeem) them
[i.e., the seed] when they are sown.[8]

> M. 9:4 (y. Ned. 6:4; A-C: y. Bik.
> 2:2, y. Sheb. 6:3; A-B: b. Shab.
> 17b, b. Pes. 34a, b. Ned. 60a, see
> y. Ter. 6:1)

The pericope continues the topic of M. 9:1-3, exploring the
question of the status of consecration of crops grown from seed
of heave-offering, or from other seed of special status. The
principle here is that that which grows from sanctified seed
itself is sanctified (A). What grows from produce which, while
subject to certain restrictions, is not sanctified, or which can
be redeemed, however, does not share the status of that from which
it grew (B-D). The pericope is unitary, composed of four units
containing the same apodosis, *gdwly (hn)....trwmh/hwlyn*. These
units form three substantive sections. A-B, on heave-offering,
sets the stage for what follows, and accounts for the redaction of
this pericope in our tractate. C is on crops which grow from other
sorts of restricted produce, and D+E is on the status of produce
which grows from seed which, although consecrated, can be redeemed.

The point of the pericope is made by the contrast between A
and B. That which grows from heave-offering is consecrated and
must be eaten by a priest.[9] As M. 9:1-3 has stated, however, unlike true heave-offering, this crop likewise is subject to agricultural restrictions which apply to unconsecrated produce. The
crop, which thus does not have the same status as true heave-offering, itself does not produce a consecrated crop.[10] C applies this
same logic to types of produce which, although subject to a special
set of restrictions, are not consecrated. Like that which grows
from seed that grew from heave-offering, the crop which grows from
these things does not share the status of the seed from which it
grew. The reasons that the list's specific items are included
here are as follows. Untithed produce (C1) contains offerings
and therefore may not be consumed before it is tithed. Since the
offerings have not yet been designated, however, they are not
deemed sanctified. If untithed seed is sown, it therefore does
not produce a crop which must be tithed at once. Neither first
tithe (C2) nor after-growths of the seventh year (C3) have a
status of consecration,[11] and so do not produce crops which have
their same status. Heave-offering separated from produce grown
outside of the Land of Israel (C4) does not have the status of

true heave-offering (M. 1:5) and for that reason does not produce
a sanctified crop. Unconsecrated produce into which a sufficient
quantity of heave-offering falls (C5) must be eaten by a priest.
The batch, however, is not true heave-offering and therefore does
not produce a sanctified crop. First fruits (C6) do not have a
status of consecration and, therefore, if planted as seed, do not
produce a sanctified crop.

D gives the opposite of what we would expect, stating that
what grows from produce dedicated to the Temple, or from second
tithe, both of which are deemed holy, is unconsecrated. The rule
is corrected by, and makes sense only in light of, its gloss at
E. The farmer who plants either of these types of consecrated
produce simply redeems the seed, leaving it in an unconsecrated
status. As we would expect, the crop which results therefore is
unconsecrated.

A. One who sows the added quantity of heave-offering
[which he separates in a case in which his initial separation
was not of sufficient quantity (see M. 4:3)],

B. or [who sows] the *se'ah* [of heave-offering] taken up
[for a priest] from a hundred [*se'ahs* of unconsecrated produce
into which a *se'ah* of heave-offering fell (see M. 5:2-3)]--

C. that which grows from these things is unconsecrated.

D. *That which grows from* [*seed*] *which is dedicated* [*to
the Temple*] [= M. 9:4D]--

E. [non-priests who unintentionally eat it] are not
liable to the principal and [added] fifth.

F. And they do not pay out from this [produce] the
principal and [added] fifth owed for a different batch [of
produce dedicated to the Temple which was eaten by a non-
priest],

G. except according to a calculation [of the percentage
of original consecrated seed which is an integral part of the
produce].

H. And it is liable to [the separation of] dough
offering.

I. Hands [which have not been cleaned of their usual
second degree uncleanness] and one who has immersed on the
self-same day do not render [the produce] unfit [for con-
sumption],

J. just as they [do not] render unconsecrated produce
unfit [see T. Toh. 1:6].

T. 8:2

T. supplements M. 8:4's rules on the status of consecration
of crops which grew from seed subject to various restrictions.
The point is the same as that of M. If the seed is not sanctified,
that which grows from it has no special status, and as T. now adds
(D-J), is subject to the same rules that apply to unconsecrated
produce. The types of heave-offering listed at A and B do not
have the status of true heave-offering (see above, M. 4:3, and
M. 5:2-3).[12] D-J is self-evident on the basis of the rule of
M. 9:4D+E. What grows from the seed of produce dedicated to the
Temple does not have a consecrated status.

> A. [As regards a *litra'* of first tithe which was planted
> [as seed] and, lo, there is in [the grown crop] about ten
> *litra's* [of produce; see M. 9:4C2]--
> B. [the crop] is liable to [the separation of] heave-
> offering, first tithe and second tithe.
> C. And [as regards] the first tithe which is in it [i.e.,
> the first tithe which he separates from the grown crop], he
> [also] designates it heave-offering of the tithe (follow
> Lieberman in reading *trwmt m^{c}śr*; V and E read *trwmh wm^{c}śr*)
> for the first tithe which he [originally] planted.
> > T. 8:5 (see b. Ned. 58b)
> D. [As regards] a *litra'* of second tithe which was
> planted and, lo, there is in [the grown crop] about ten
> [*litra's* of produce]--
> E. [the crop] is liable to [the separation of] heave-
> offering, first tithe and second tithe.
> F. And he goes and redeems the second tithe which he
> [originally] planted [see M. 9:5D-E].
> > T. 8:6

T. supplements M. 9:5C-E's laws, which state that crops grown
from seed in the status of first tithe or second tithe do not have
the status of these offerings. T.'s point is that since the crop
has no special status, the usual agricultural offerings must be
separated from it. According to C, the householder also must
designate the heave-offering of the tithe required for the first
tithe which he originally planted. Thus, all of the required
offerings are paid. D-F clarifies the point of M. 9:4D-E. An
individual who sows seed in the status of second tithe redeems the
seed. The crop which grows from the redeemed seed is unconsecrated.[13]

9:5

A.   [If there are] a hundred garden-beds (*lgnh*) [planted]
with [seed in the status of] heave-offering and one [planted]
with unconsecrated [seed, but it is not known which contains
the unconsecrated seed],

B.   all are permitted [for consumption as unconsecrated
food] in the case of a kind [of produce] the seed of which
disintegrates.

C.   But in the case of a kind the seed of which does not
disintegrate,

D.   even if there are a hundred beds [sown] with unconsecrated seed and one [planted] with heave-offering,

E.   all of them are forbidden.

M. 9:5

According to the present pericope, the decisive factor for
determining the status of consecration of a crop grown from sanctified seed is the nature of the seed. If the seed is not an integral part of the produce which grows from it, then, according
to A-B, the produce does not have the consecrated status of the
seed. If, however, the seed is integral to the crop, as in the
case of onions (M. 9:6E), the crop is sanctified (C-E). This
principle clearly is not known to, and does not agree with, the
law as stated at M. 9:1-4, which holds that what grows from heave-
offering always is consecrated.[14]

The problem of the confusion of garden-beds containing consecrated and unconsecrated seed is irrelevant to the principle
just stated. It serves only to emphasize the fact that the status
of the crop depends solely on the nature of the seed from which it
grows, and not on the likelihood that any single garden-bed
actually contains heave-offering. Thus at A-B, even though the
majority of garden-beds contain consecrated seed, the crop of none
of them is deemed consecrated. At C-E, on the other hand, because
of the presence of a single bed planted with heave-offering, all
of the garden-beds are deemed to have a sanctified status.

A.   *[If there are] a hundred garden-beds [planted] with
[seed in the status of] heave-offering and one [planted] with
unconsecrated [seed, but it is not known which contains the
unconsecrated seed],*

B.   *all are permitted in the case of a kind [of produce]
the seed of which disintegrates.*

C. *But in the case of a kind the seed of which does not disintegrate* [= M. 9:5A-C]--

D. [the consecrated produce in the one garden-bed] is not neutralized.

E. For [produce in the status of heave-offering which still is in the] ground is not neutralized in a hundred and one parts [see M. 4:7].

F. If he picked [all of the produce]-- [the heave-offering] is neutralized,

G. providing that he did not purposely pick it [in order to have the heave-offering neutralized].

H. R. Simeon (E reads: Judah) says, "Also: if he purposely picks [the produce, the heave-offering] is neutralized in a hundred and one parts."

T. 8:4 (see M. Or. 1:6, b. Git. 54b)

T. cites M. 9:5 and offers a reason for its rule, an example of T. in its best capacity as commentator on M. M. 9:5C-E has one *se'ah* of heave-offering planted among a hundred *se'ahs* of unconsecrated produce. In such a case we might expect the law of neutralization (M. 4-7) to be invoked, such that the heave-offering loses its status of sanctification. T. states that the law of neutralization does not apply to produce growing in the ground, and therefore, as M. states, the produce in all of the garden-beds must be treated as heave-offering. F-H offers the next logical question, the status of the produce after it is picked. At this point the law of neutralization certainly will apply. G, like Yose at T. 5:10R, holds that if the individual purposely picks the produce in order to cause the heave-offering to be neutralized, his actions are of no effect. Simeon (alt: Judah) holds that neutralization is a mechanical process, which occurs no matter what the intentions of the householder. This same view is attributed both to Judah and Simeon at T. 5:10Q, above, p. 154.

9:6-7

A. Produce which is subject to the separation of tithes (*tbl*)--

B. that which grows from it is permitted [for consumption as a chance meal (Bert, TYY, Rashi to b. Ned 60a), in [the case of] a kind [of produce] the seed of which disintegrates.

C. But in [the case of] a kind the seed of which does not disintegrate--

D. [even] what grows from [the seed of a crop] which
grew from it is forbidden [for consumption as a chance meal,
for like the seed, it is deemed subject to tithes].

E. What is a kind [of produce] the seed of which does
not disintegrate?

F. [A kind] such as arum, garlic or onions.

G. R. Judah says, "Garlic is like barley [i.e., its
seed disintegrates]."

M. 9:6 (A-D: b. Pes. 34a, b. Ned.
60a)

H. One who weeds alongside a gentile (all MSS.: *nkry*)
[in a field of] leeks [grown from seed which has not been
tithed]--

I. even though his [i.e., the gentile's] produce has
the status of untithed produce,

J. [the Israelite] makes a chance meal of it [without
tithing].

K. Saplings [from seed] in the status of heave-offering
which became unclean--

L. if (G^2, C, M, O^2, S, Z: and) he planted them, they
no longer render unclean [that with which they come into
contact.

M. And [the fruit of the saplings] is forbidden for consumption [by non-priests (b. Pes. 34a, Sens, Albeck)] until
he [once] trims off that fruit (*h'kl*) [which has the status
of heave-offering].

N. R. Judah says, "Until he trims off [the fruit] and
does so a second time [i.e., also trims off the next crop
which grows]."

M. 9:7 (J-K: b. Pes. 34a)

The unit is in three parts. A-D+E-G and H-J are on problems
regarding a crop grown from seed of untithed produce. K-N then
returns us to the problem of heave-offering planted as seed,
thereby concluding M.'s redactional unit on that topic. A-J,
first, states for untithed produce the same principle which M. 9:5
gave for heave-offering. If the seed is integral to the crop, the
crop is deemed to have the same status as that seed. In this case,
that means that the crop may not be eaten as a chance meal. Even
before the harvest, it is held to be fully liable to the separation
of heave-offering and tithes.[15] If, however, the seed is not an
integral part of the crop which grows from it, the crop has no

special status, and may be consumed as a chance meal. Although
formally autonomous of A-G, the case at H-J follows from the facts
just stated. The produce of the gentile was grown from untithed
seed of a type which does not disintegrate. It therefore should
not be available for consumption as a chance meal. Since produce
grown by a gentile is not liable to the separation of tithes, however, the restrictions which apply to the original seed are abro-
gated, and the Israelite is allowed to eat the produce as a chance
meal without tithing.

K-L is obvious. Once the saplings are planted in the ground,
they lose their status of uncleanness, and no longer convey uncleanness to that which comes into contact with them. M-N's problem is more interesting. Since the saplings which grew from heave-
offering will continually bear fruit, we must establish the point
at which the fruit no longer is deemed to have the status of heave-
offering. According to M the first crop of the sapling is heave-
offering,[16] subsequent crops are not. This is comparable to
M. 9:4B's view that only the first generation of produce grown
from seed in the status of heave-offering has that same status.
Judah's position is that the second generation of produce likewise
has the status of heave-offering.[17]

> A. *One who weeds* [*a field of*] *leeks* [*grown from seed
> which had not been tithed*] *alongside a* Samaritan--
>
> B. even though his [i.e., the Samaritan's] *produce is
> untithed,*
>
> C. [the Israelite] (follow b. Ned. 58b in omitting *l'*)
> *makes a chance meal of it* [*without tithing*] [= M. 9:7G-I].
>
> D. R. Simeon b. Eleazar says, "In the year following
> the seventh year [of the sabbatical cycle] (*bmws'y šby^c yt*)
> [even if the other person is an] Israelite [who is suspected
> as regards his observance of the laws of the seventh year
> (b. Ned. 58b)],
>
> "it is permitted [to eat his produce; see M. 9:4C2]."
>
> T. 8:7 (b. Ned. 58b)

A-C states the rule of M. 9:7G-I for the case of a Samaritan.
The point, of course, is the same.[18] D is redacted here because
of the similarity between its case and that of A-C. It depends,
however, on the rule of M. 9:4C3, that what grows from seed of
produce of the sabbatical cycle does not have a forbidden status.
For this reason, the householder need not scruple that he is eating food which grew from produce of the seventh year.

C. R. Nathan b. R. Joseph says, "Onion sets (štly bšlym)
[which were grown from seed which was liable to the separation of tithes] are forbidden [for consumption as a chance
meal] for three years [of growth] [see M. 9:7:-M].

D. "From this point and on [that which grows from them]
is permitted [just as if it had been grown from a seed of
produce which had been tithed]."

T. 8:8b[19]

T. makes for the case of what grows from untithed produce the
same point that M. 9:7L-M made for the case of the crop of saplings
grown from seed in the status of heave-offering. As in M., since
the onion sets[20] continually will produce crops, we must determine
the point at which those crops cease to have the status of the
originally untithed seed. I am unable to determine why the crop
of the onion sets should be forbidden for three years, while, as
M. states, only the first crop of the saplings grown from heave-
offering has the status of that offering.

TERUMOT CHAPTER TEN

The chapter raises a fresh problem related to cases in which heave-offering is mishandled. Now the offering is cooked, or in some other way prepared with unconsecrated produce. At issue are the conditions under which the unconsecrated produce is deemed to take on the status of the heave-offering with which it is prepared. A single principle of law is introduced, M. 10:1, and applied to a series of diverse cases, M. 10:2, 3-4, 5-6, 7-10 and 11-12. This principle states that permitted food takes on a forbidden status if it is flavored by prohibited produce. If, for instance, produce in the status of heave-offering is cooked or otherwise prepared with unconsecrated food, and imparts its flavor to the dish as a whole, the unconsecrated food is deemed to take on the status of heave-offering. Even if the householder later removes the prohibited produce from the mixture, the other food remains forbidden, for in a concrete way it has benefitted from the heave-offering.

Once the chapter's central proposition has been stated at M. 10:1, it easily can be applied to cases involving various types of forbidden produce. Alongside heave-offering, we discuss problems involving unclean produce and produce subject to other agricultural restrictions. What is of greater interest to M., however, is the application of its principle to cases describing diverse methods of preparing food. That is to say, we want to know what happens when dough is raised with forbidden leaven (M. 10:2), when permitted food absorbs forbidden vapors (M. 10:3-4), when water is flavored with heave-offering (M. 10:5+6), and when permitted food is pickled (M. 10:7-10), boiled or cooked (M. 10:11-12), with forbidden produce. These discrete units do not develop the principle stated at the outset, but simply employ it. Nor do they build on one another. Judah alone transcends this otherwise uninteresting context. He supplies his usual position, that all matters of law are judged in light of the intention of the person involved, and that intention is determined on the basis of action. He thus holds that the status of unconsecrated produce cooked with heave-offering is not determined simply on the basis of whether or not the heave-offering has flavored that unconsecrated food. The further condition required by Judah is that the householder intended to use the heave-offering to flavor his food, and that this intention be indicated by the fact that the householder purposely added the

heave-offering to the unconsecrated dish for its flavor. This
view is instantiated at M. 10:1H, M. 10:3 and T. 8:9a.

Only one other view in the chapter is worthy of note. This
view is expressed anonymously at M. 10:1A-D (see my comment to
that pericope) and is clearly represented in the position of Aqiba,
M. 10:8E+F, explained at T. 9:4b. It disagrees with the chapter's
central notion that permitted food takes on a forbidden status
when it is flavored by that which is prohibited. This view holds,
rather, that unconsecrated food becomes forbidden when it is made
into a single, homogeneous dish with prohibited produce. This
occurs when the prohibited produce is cut up and then cooked with
the permitted produce. In this view, thus, what is determinative
is not the flavoring-power of the forbidden food, but the fact
that it is inextricably mixed with the other produce. Besides
this position, assigned to Aqiba, all of the attributions in this
chapter are to Ushans. It appears therefore that while the discussion of cases in which unconsecrated food is prepared with
heave-offering may have begun at Yavneh, whatever was there accomplished was rejected at Usha and replaced with conceptions distinctive to that age.

10:1

A.   [As regards] an onion [in the status of heave-offer-
ing] which one placed [i.e., cooked] among [unconsecrated]
lentils--

B.   if [the onion] is whole, it is permitted [to eat the
lentils as unconsecrated food].

C.   But (C, L, O^2, K lack: w) if one cut up [the onion
and then placed it among unconsecrated lentils]--

D.   [it is forbidden to eat the lentils as unconsecrated
food] if [the onion] imparts [to them its] flavor.

E.   And [as regards] all other cooked foods ($tb\check{s}yl$)--

F.   whether [the onion in the status of heave-offering]
is whole or cut up,

G.   [it renders forbidden the unconsecrated food with
which it is cooked] if it imparts [its] flavor [to that food].

H.   R. Judah permits [for the consumption of a non-
priest] a pickled-fish [which was cooked with an onion in the
status of heave-offering],

I.   for the purpose [of the onion] is only to absorb the
stench [of the fish, and not to flavor the brine].

M. 10:1 (I-J: y. M.S. 2:1)

Unconsecrated produce which is cooked with heave-offering,
like that which in other ways is mixed with a priestly gift
(M. 4:7-5:9), itself may become forbidden for consumption by a non-
priest. At issue here are the specific conditions under which this
takes place. The formal unity of the pericope belies the fact
that in it are juxtaposed two different theories of these conditions (A-D, E-G+H-I). The first, expressed at A-D, is that the
essential factor is whether or not the heave-offering has been cut
up into the other food, and so made an integral part of the dish
as a whole. The second conception, at E-G+H-I, is that the decisive
factor is whether or not the heave-offering has imparted its own
flavor to the unconsecrated produce. Matters are confused by the
fact that the juxtaposition at the redactional level of these two
distinct notions has led to a reformulation of D to read "if it
imparts flavor," instead of the simple "it is forbidden" which
B+C leads us to expect. Let us, then, examine the pericope in
order to understand the point made by each of its parts, and the
way in which these two parts have been read concurrently at the
redactional level.

The point of A-E is made through the contrast between B and
C, which distinguish between cases in which a piece of produce in
the status of heave-offering is cooked whole with unconsecrated
produce, and cases in which the heave-offering is cut up.[1] On the
basis of this distinction, we easily can determine what A-D deems
the decisive factor for the status of the unconsecrated food.
This is whether or not the heave-offering has been made an integral
part of the dish in which it is cooked. If the heave-offering is
placed whole into that dish, it remains separate from the unconsecrated food, and therefore, that food remains permitted to non-
priests (B). Both the unconsecrated food and the heave-offering
have retained their own integrity. If, on the other hand, the
householder cuts the heave-offering up into the unconsecrated
produce, he makes a single dish of the priestly gift and the other
food.[2] It should follow that even if he later attempts to remove
the heave-offering from the dish, his initial act is decisive, and
the unconsecrated food is forbidden for consumption by non-priests.
In light of this, D is problematic. It claims that if heave-
offering is cut up into unconsecrated food, the essential factor
in determining the status of that food is whether or not it has
been flavored by the priestly gift. This consideration is out of
phase with, and indeed contradicts, the principle of B-C. If, as
B-C claims, the issue is whether or not the heave-offering has been

cut up into the unconsecrated food, then taste should be of no
concern. Conversely, if, as D states, what is important is whether
or not the heave-offering imparts its flavor to the other food, it
should make no difference whether the heave-offering is whole or
cut up. It thus is clear that D introduces into A-C a second and
distinct legal conception. The source of this second conception
is obvious when we turn to E-G.

According to E-G, all that is important in determining the
status of food which is cooked with heave-offering is whether or
not the heave-offering has flavored that food.[3] If it has, then
even if the heave-offering is removed, the unconsecrated produce
may not be eaten by a non-priest, who, by eating it, would benefit
from the consecrated produce. If it is not, however, the heave-
offering may be removed, and the unconsecrated dish, upon which it
has had no effect, may be eaten by a non-priest. It is in light of
this conception that D was formulated as we presently have it. F,
likewise, is irrelevant to the case of E-I, and simply takes account of the consideration of A-D.

This brings us to Judah's qualification, H-I. Judah claims
that in a case in which the heave-offering is not intended to add
flavor to the unconsecrated food, it does not render that food
forbidden to non-priests. For Judah what is important is not the
actual effect the heave-offering has upon the unconsecrated dish,
but the intention of the householder who created the mixture. As
long as the householder did not intend to benefit from the heave-
offering as a food substance, we take no account of the fact that
it may in all events have flavored his unconsecrated dish.[4] As
we shall see, Judah holds this same position at M. 10:3.

10:2

A. [As regards] an apple [in the status of heave-offer-
ing] which one chopped up and placed in dough,

B. and [as a result the dough] was leavened--

C. lo, this [i.e., the dough] is forbidden [for consumption by a non-priest].

D. [As regards] barley [in the status of heave-offering]
which fell into a well of water--

E. even though the water [in the well] was tainted [by
the barley],

F. (Fourteen MSS. add: the water) is permitted [for
consumption by a non-priest].

M. 10:2 (y. Pes. 2:4; A-C: b. Men.

54a, y. Hal. 1:1, y. Shab. 3:3, see

M. Or. 2:4; C-E: y. Or. 2:4)

The pericope is composed of two autonomous cases, A-C and
D-F, illustrating the same issue as M. 10:1. A-C depends on the
rule of M. Or. 2:4, that unconsecrated produce which is leavened
by produce in the status of heave-offering is deemed to take on
that same status.[5] Here the dough, which has benefitted from the
leavening action of the apple in the status of heave-offering, is
deemed forbidden to non-priests.[6] At D-F the barley in the status
of heave-offering ruins the flavor of water. The water remains
permitted to a non-priest, since the individual who drinks it in
no way benefits from the heave-offering with which it is mixed.[7]
This radical interpretation of M. 10:1's theory is that of Judah,
10:1H-I and, as we shall see, M. 10:3C. It claims that heave-
offering imparts its own status to unconsecrated food it flavors
only if the householder desires that flavor.

> G. [*As regards*] *an apple* [*in the status of heave-*
> *offering*] *which one chopped up and placed in dough, and* [*as*
> *a result the dough*] *was leavened* [= M. 10:2A-B]--
>
> H. R. Yose says, "That which is leavened [by the apple]
> is not deemed [truly] leavened [and therefore the law of M.
> Or. 2:4 does not apply; the dough remains permitted to non-
> priests]."
>
> I. "It is all the same whether [heave-offering] imparts
> flavor [so as] to improve [the taste of food], or spoil [it].
>
> J. "In either case (E reads: Lo, this) [the food to
> which the heave-offering imparted flavor] is forbidden [for
> consumption by a non-priest]"--the words of R. Meir.
>
> K. R. Simeon says, "[If the heave-offering] improves
> [the taste of unconsecrated food, that food] is forbidden.
>
> L. "[But if the heave-offering] spoils [its taste], it
> [remains] permitted [for consumption by a non-priest],
>
> M. "as in the case of vinegar [in the status of heave-
> offering] which fell into [unconsecrated] beans."
>
> > T. 8:9b (y. Ter. 10:2; G-H: y. Hal.
> > 1:1, y. Shab. 3:3, y. Pes. 2:4; I-M:
> > y. Bik. 2:5, y. A.Z. 5:3, b. A.Z.
> > 67b; M: M. A.Z. 5:2)
>
> A. (1) Beans [in the status of heave-offering] which
> fell into a well of water,
>
> B. (2) [or] dates upon which fell wine [in the status
> of heave-offering],

C. (3) or dried figs upon which fell oil [in the status
of heave-offering],[8]

D. lo, this [i.e., the water, dates or dried figs] is
forbidden [for consumption by non-priests].

E. But R. Simeon permits.

T. 8:10

M. 8-9G-H cites M. 10:2A-B and adds Yose's disputing opinion.
Yose claims that the leavening action of the apple is not comparable to that of normal leaven, and therefore the rule of
M. Or. 2:4 does not apply. Although it does not directly refer
to M., I-M must be read as supplementary to the case of M. 10:2,
in which barley in the status of heave-offering imparts to water
a tainted flavor. M. has the position of Simeon, against Meir,
that if the heave-offering ruins the flavor of food, that food is
not deemed forbidden. T. 8:10[9] follows with a triplet of cases
exemplifying the positions of Meir and Simeon. The anonymous
view of A-D is that of Meir. He deems the unconsecrated produce
forbidden for consumption by non-priests, for it was flavored by
heave-offering. Simeon (E), we must assume, holds that the heave-
offering spoiled the taste of the unconsecrated produce. He therefore deems that produce still permissible for consumption by non-
priests (MB, HY).

I. A. [As regards one part of] leaven in the status of
heave-offering which fell into [more than a hundred parts of
unconsecrated] dough and one lifted it [i.e., the leaven] out
[of the mixture; see M. 5:2-3, 5, 7-8 and T. 5:9], but afterwards [the dough anyway] was leavened--

B. [the dough] is permitted [for consumption as unconsecrated food].

T. 8:11 (y. Or. 2:3)

II. C. [As regards one part of] leaven made from produce of
the seventh year [of the sabbatical cycle] which fell into
[more than a hundred parts of] dough [of any other year of
that cycle]--

D. [if] he knew about it [i.e., that forbidden leaven
had been mixed with permitted dough, such that the leaven is
neutralized; see T. 6:5, 8-9] and afterwards it [i.e., the
dough] was leavened--

E. [the dough] is forbidden [on account of the laws of
the seventh year].[10]

T. 8:12 (y. Or. 2:9)

III. F. [As regards] leaven in the status of heave-offering and leaven of the seventh year which [together] fell into dough,

G. neither of them [alone] sufficient in quantity to leaven [that dough] (*l' bzh ....wl' bzh*)--

H. if (*w*) they joined together and leavened [the dough]--

I. [the dough] is forbidden to non-priests [but permitted to priests; M. Or. 2:14].

J. R. Eleazar b. R. Simeon (y. Or. 2:9, followed by HD and Lieberman, reads: R. Simeon) declares it permitted to non-priests [and also to priests; M. Or. 2:14].

K. [If] each [alone] was of sufficient quantity to leaven [the dough],

L. but together they leavened [the dough]--

M. [the dough] is forbidden [even] to priests.

N. R. Eleazar b. R. Simeon declares [it] permitted to priests [but not to non-priests].

T. 8:13 (y. Or. 2:9; F-J: M. Or. 2:14)

T.'s triplet of cases supplements M. 10:2 with an extended essay on the leavening of unconsecrated dough by leaven in a forbidden status. Since T. 8:11-12 together make a single point, and T. 8:13 makes a separate one, I deal independently with these two parts of the pericope.

T. 8:11-12 coordinates the rule of M. 10:2 with the law of neutralization, given in M. Chapters Four and Five.[11] T. asks which rule takes precedence in a case in which leaven in the status of heave-offering or of the seventh year is neutralized in unconsecrated dough, yet leavens that dough. If the law of neutralization applies, the batch will be deemed permitted for consumption as unconsecrated food. If the law of M. 10:2 applies, the unconsecrated dough must in all events be deemed forbidden, for it was leavened by forbidden produce. The point made here is that the rule of M. 10:2 is operative. If the dough's being leavened can be attributed to the heave-offering or leaven of the seventh year, that dough is forbidden for consumption. This principle emerges in the contrast between the cases at T. 8:11 and 12, the details of which must now be explained. We recall that in the case in which heave-offering is neutralized, the householder is required to take from the batch for a priest the heave-offering

which originally fell in (just as here at T. 8:11A; see Eliezer,
M. 5:2). In this way the priest does not lose his share. In the
present case, the leaven in the status of heave-offering thus is
not present in the batch at the time the dough is leavened. The
leavening therefore need not be attributed to the heave-offering,
and the dough remains permitted for consumption by non-priests.
The facts for the neutralization of produce of the seventh year
are different and, it follows, so is the rule at T. 8:12. The
neutralization of produce of the seventh year is completed as
soon as the householder discovers that a mixture has been created
(just as here at T. 8:12D; see T. 6:8-9 and HD). Since the produce which is neutralized does not belong to any particular individual, the householder does not remove it from the batch in which
it was neutralized. In the present case, therefore, the forbidden
produce certainly accounts for the leavening of the dough and, for
this reason, that dough is deemed forbidden.

The problem at T. 8:13 is separate. Now two different categories of forbidden leaven are mixed with dough. The one category,
heave-offering, renders the dough forbidden for consumption by
non-priests, but not by priests. The other, leaven subject to the
restrictions of the seventh year, renders the dough forbidden to
non-priest and priest alike. We have two different cases, F-J,
which has neither of the categories of leaven alone sufficient to
leaven the dough, and K-N, where the two categories of leaven do
together what either could have done alone. In each case we must
determine which of the restrictions applies. According to I, if
neither of the types of leaven alone could have leavened the dough,
but together they do so, the dough can be eaten by priests, but
not by non-priests. This is because as regards non-priests, we
must take into account the restrictions pertinent to both categories of leaven. From the point of view of the non-priest, the
dough was leavened by forbidden leaven, and so is prohibited.
This is not the case for priests. Since the heave-offering does
not render the dough forbidden to them, we do not take account of
its leavening action. This leaves the leaven in the status of the
seventh year alone to be considered. Since this leaven alone was
not of sufficient quantity to leaven the dough, that dough is not
rendered forbidden. Eleazar B. Simeon's view, J, is that even as
regards non-priests, each of the prohibitions must be considered
separately. Since neither of the categories of leaven was sufficient to leaven the dough, that dough is liable neither to the
restrictions of the seventh year nor of heave-offering.

L-N has each of the categories of leaven sufficient to raise the dough. M holds that the dough therefore is prohibited both to priests and to non-priests, for it has the status of produce of the seventh year, as well as that of heave-offering. Eleazar again disagrees, declaring that the dough is permitted for the consumption of priests. His view is that we deem the leaven in the status of heave-offering alone to account for the dough's being leavened. Since the leaven of the seventh year thus is irrelevant to the dough's being leavened, the dough is not subject to the restrictions of the seventh year and is permitted to priests.

10:3-4

A. One who scrapes hot bread [from the side of an oven] and places it on top of a jug of wine in the status of heave-offering--

B. R. Meir deems [the bread] forbidden [for consumption by non-priests].

C. But R. Judah deems [it] permitted.

D. R. Yose deems [it] permitted in [the case of] bread made from wheat,

E. but deems [it] forbidden in [the case of] bread made from barley,

F. for barley absorbs [the wine vapor].

M. 10:3 (b. Pes. 76b, b. A.Z. 66b;
see M. Mak. 3:3)

G. [As regards] an oven which one fired with cumin in the status of heave-offering and baked (seventeen MSS. add: bread)[12] in it--

H. the bread is permitted [for consumption by a non-priest].

I. For the flavor of cumin is not [imparted to the bread,] but [only] the smell of cumin.

M. 10:4 (b. A.Z. 66b)

The two pericopae share a common issue, whether or not the bread is deemed to absorb the vapor of the wine or cumin, such that it is rendered forbidden for consumption by non-priests. They are, however, formally autonomous and, as we shall see, do not make the same point. We must, therefore, treat each separately.

On the surface the point of M. 10:3 is quite simple. As is clear from F, the issue is whether or not the bread absorbs the wine vapor.[13] Meir, B, holds that it does, and therefore declares the bread forbidden for consumption by non-priests. Judah, C,

holds that it does not, and so deems the bread permitted. Yose,
D-F, offers the expected mediating position. Matters are complicated, however, when we examine these three positions more closely.
We note that in his theory, Yose agrees with Meir alone. He states
that if the bread absorbs, it is forbidden. Judah's view clearly
is out of phase with the others, for as I have explained it,
Judah simply rejects the fact assumed by Meir, that the bread in
question absorbs. The alternative, and I believe more likely,
interpretation of Judah's view is that Judah accepts the fact that
the bread absorbs the vapor of the wine, but rejects the contention that this renders the bread forbidden for consumption by non-
priests.[14] Judah's view here thus is consistent with a position
which occurs throughout Judah's rulings in M. This is that matters are to be judged in accordance with the intention of the individual, and that intention is determined on the basis of deed.[15]
In the present case, if the man wished to put wine in the bread,
he would have done so in a more direct manner than by placing the
warm bread on top of a wine jug. Since he did nothing more than
this, we must assume that he did not want the wine in the bread.
We therefore deem the effect of the vapor upon the bread to be
null. This is to say that for Judah, what is decisive is not
whether or not some of the wine has entered the bread, but whether
or not the householder intentionally placed that wine in the bread.
On the basis of the deed of the householder, we must declare that
he did not, and therefore deem the bread to have retained its unconsecrated status. This is, of course, the same position which
Judah holds at M. 10:1H-I.

     M. 10:4 is separate from the foregoing. It rules that bread
baked in an oven fired with cumin in the status of heave-offering
is permitted for consumption by a non-priest. The point is as
stated at I. The burning cumin does not impart flavor to the
bread, but only gives it the aroma of cumin. This ruling is not
representative of any of the three position at M. 10:3.

                          10:5-6
     A. [As regards] fenugreek[16] which fell into a vat of
[unconsecrated] wine--[17]

     B. in [the case of fenugreek which is] heave-offering
(follow nine MSS. which add: or) second tithe,

     C. if the seed [without the stalk] is sufficient to
impart flavor [to the wine, that wine is subject to the law
of heave-offering or second tithe].

D. But not [if the seed is not sufficient to impart
flavor to the wine without] the stalk.

E. In [the case of fenugreek which is produce of] (1)
the seventh year [of the sabbatical cycle], (2) of a vineyard
in which were sown diverse kinds, or (3) [if it] is dedicated
[to the Temple]--

F. if the seed and stalk [together] are sufficient to
impart flavor [to the wine, that wine is subject to the law
of produce of the seventh year, diverse kinds, or that which
is dedicated to the Temple].

M. 10:5 (E-F: y. Sheb. 9:5)

G. One who had bundles of fenugreek grown in a vineyard
in which were sown diverse kinds--

let them be burned.

H. [If] he had bundles of fenugreek which were liable
to the separation of tithes (šl tbl)--

I. he crushes [some of the stalks] and determines the
quantity of seed which [all of the stalks together] contain

J. and separates [the tithes required] for [this quantity of] seed.

K. But he does not need to separate tithes for the
stalks.

L. (Seven MSS. add: And) if he separated tithes [for
the stalks],

M. he may not say, "I shall crush [all of the stalks]
and shall take [the stalks for myself] and give the seed [to
its proper recipients, priest and Levite]."

N. Rather, he must give [to priest and Levite] the
stalks along with the seed.

M. 10:6 (G: M. Or. 3:6; H-K:

b. Bes. 13a)

M. takes up the special case of fenugreek, a type of produce
the seed of which is a food, but the stalk of which, while edible,
generally is not eaten. The special nature of this plant is
problematic in cases in which the fenugreek is in the status of
heave-offering and is mixed with unconsecrated food (A-D),[18] is
subject to other agricultural restrictions (E-F+G), or is liable
to the separation of tithes (H-N). In each case we must determine whether the seed alone is subject to the pertinent restrictions, or whether these restrictions apply as well to the stalk,
which, as I just have said, may in certain circumstances be used

as a food. As we shall see, the status of the stalk is determined
on the basis of the nature of the restriction, on the one hand,
and by the express designation of the householder, on the other.
The stalks are not deemed to be liable to designation as, or to
have the status of, tithes. This is because the householder
normally does not eat them. Yet if he designates them to be
tithes, the designation is valid, for by doing this he expresses
his intent to use the stalks as food. The stalks, however,
automatically are subject to restrictions (e.g., that of diverse
kinds) which apply to a field as a whole. This is because the
householder may in no event benefit from such produce. Whether
or not he specifically designated the stalks to be food is irrelevant in this case.

The point of M. 10:5 is made through the contrast between
A-D and E-F. The former presents cases in which the fenugreek has
the status of heave-offering or second tithe, the latter, cases
in which the fenugreek is subject to restrictions which apply to a
field as a whole, or in which the fenugreek has been dedicated to
the Temple. In the former case, the stalks are not deemed to have
the status of the agricultural offering, for they are not considered food. In determining the status of unconsecrated food with
which the fenugreek has been mixed, we therefore do not take into
account the flavoring-power of the stalks. This is not the case
for the types of restrictions listed at E. Here the stalks are
deemed subject to the restrictions imposed upon the field as a
whole, or are consecrated, having been dedicated along with the
seed to the Temple. If this fenugreek is mixed with unconsecrated
food, we must take into account the flavoring capacity of the
stalks, which, like the seed, have a restricted status.

The same contrast which is operative at A-D+E-F is found at
G and H-K. G simply repeats in its own terms what we know from
E-F. The restriction pertinent to produce from a field in which
were grown diverse kinds of seed applies to the whole of the fenugreek plant. The stalks, as well as the seed, therefore must be
burned. As regards the separation of tithes, H-K, only the seed
is liable, for this is the part which the householder normally
eats. He therefore calculates the quantity of tithe to be separated from the seed alone, using the method outlined at I-J. L-N
makes the next logical point. If the householder himself designates tithes for both the seed and stalks, his designation is
valid. Having indicated that he deems the stalks to be food, he

must give to the proper recipients the required quantity of them, as well as of the seed.

> A. One who separates bundles of fenugreek as (follow E in adding: second) tithe (see Lieberman, TK, I, p. 429, HD and HY) [for other produce]--
> B. lo, this one must redeem both the stalks and the seed (E reads: the seed and the stalks) [see M. 10:H-N].
>
> T. 8:8a

T. clarifies the point of M. 10:5A-D in light of M. 10:6L-N. Stalks of fenugreek are not liable to the separation of second tithe, and therefore are not normally deemed to have a consecrated status (M. 10:5A-D). If, however, a householder purposely separates the stalks as second tithe, they are deemed to have that status and must be treated as sanctified offerings, just as M. 10:6L-N states.

> A. [As regards] fenugreek [in the status of heave-offering] which fell into a well of water [= M. 10:5A]--
> B. R. Meir deems [the water] forbidden [for consumption by non-priests].
> C. But R. Judah permits.
> D. Said R. Simeon, "To what case does [the opinion of R. Meir] apply?
> E. "To a case in which the fenugreek sank [into the water].
> F. "But if it did not sink, lo, this [i.e., the water] is permitted [for consumption by non-priests]."
>
> T. 8:9a

T. 8:9a applies to the case of M. 10:5 (cited at A) the principles of Meir and Judah, M. 10:3.[19] Meir, as we would expect from M. 10:3B, assumes the fenugreek to have flavored the water in the well. He therefore deems that water forbidden to non-priests. Just as at M. 10:3C, Judah holds the effect of the fenugreek upon the water to be null. On the one hand, the householder did not intentionally place the fenugreek in the water; on the other, he does not desire the water, which now has the flavor of fenugreek.[20] Simeon, D-F, seems to assume that if the fenugreek does not sink in the water, it does not impart flavor to the water.[21] This qualification of Meir's view does not mitigate the basic disagreement between Meir and Judah.

A.   (1) [As regards] wine in the status of heave-offering which fell upon pieces of [unconsecrated] fruit--

B.   let one wipe them off, and they are permitted [for
consumption as unconsecrated produce].

C.   (Lieberman follows ed. princ. in deleting four words
from the text of V.   See TK, I, p. 433, for other problems of
reading.)

D.   (2) And so [in the case of] oil in the status of
heave-offering which fell upon pieces of [unconsecrated]
fruit--

E.   let one wipe them off, and they are permitted.

F.   (3) And so [if the oil in the status of heave-
offering fell] into [unconsecrated] wine--

G.   let one skim it off, and the wine is permitted.

H.   (4) [If] it fell into brine--

I.   let one skim off [enough unconsecrated oil] to remove the flavor of oil which is in it [i.e., in the brine;
thereafter, that brine is permitted].

T. 8:14 (T. Miq. 1:4)

The pericope is not related specifically to M. 10:5-6, but
complements in a general way the discussion of the laws of Chapter
Ten.   The point of each of the four rules is the same.   The householder may rinse or skim the unwanted heave-offering off of his
unconsecrated food, and that heave-offering is not deemed to have
rendered the food forbidden.[22]   The householder did not cause the
heave-offering to fall on the food in the first place, and his
later actions in wiping off the heave-offering indicate he does
not wish to benefit from it.   This view, which takes no account of
whether or not the heave-offering actually imparted flavor to the
unconsecrated produce, self-evidently is that already offered by
Judah, M. 10:1H-I, M. 10:3C and T. 8:9C.

A.   [As regards leather] garments [such as sandals, MB,
HY] which one lubricated [first] with unclean [olive-]oil
and then with clean oil,

B.   or which one lubricated [first] with clean oil and
then with unclean oil--

C.   R. Eliezer says, "I rule [on the cleanness of the
garments] in accordance with [the status of cleanness of] the
first [oil which was used]."

D.   But sages say, "The last" [=M. Or. 2:13].

E. For Eliezer says, "Let a man lubricate his garments [first] with (read:) clean oil (all MSS.: unclean) and then with (read:) unclean oil (all MSS.: clean). (Supply with E: For) when they exude [oil from the other side of the leather], they will exude the first, [clean, oil]."

F. But sages say, "Let a man lubricate his garments [first] with (read:) unclean oil (all MSS.: clean) and then with (read:) clean oil (all MSS.: unclean). (Supply with E: For) when they exude [oil from the other side of the leather], they exude the latter, [clean, oil]."

G. [As regards] garments which one lubricated with unclean oil and then wiped off—

H. he uses them in [cases requiring preservation of] cleanness.

I. [If] liquids then exuded from them [i.e., the garments]—

[the garments] are unclean.

T. 8:15 (A-D: M. Or. 2:13)

The pericope belongs with M. Or. 2:13 and is unrelated to the present discussion. I cannot account for its placement in this context.[23] Its rule, however, is as follows. Olive-oil is used to soften leather. Presumably individuals prefer to use for this purpose unclean oil, which may not be eaten by people who wish to eat their food in cleanness (Lieberman, TK, I, p. 434). At issue between Eliezer and sages is how such unclean oil may be used, without its rendering unclean the person who later wears the garment. I have corrected the positions of each authority, at E and F, to be in line with the rulings at C and D. Eliezer, C, holds that the status of cleanness of the garment is determined on the basis of the first oil that is used. Thus one should use some clean oil first, and then apply the unclean. His view, as I have corrected E to read, is that what goes into the leather first is also that which comes out first. The clean oil thus coats the leather and prevents the unclean oil from rendering unclean the person who wears the garment. Sages, D, have the opposite view, that the cleanness of the garment is judged on the basis of the status of cleanness of the last oil that is used. As I have corrected F, their view is that this second oil permeates the leather and seeps out to the surface, where it, and not the first oil which was used, will come into contact with the person wearing the garment.

Contrary to my interpretation, Lieberman, TK, I, p. 434, upholds the reading of the MSS. of T. Eliezer (E), he says, holds
that the individual first uses unclean oil and then clean. His
view is that the clean oil forces the unclean out of the leather,
so that it can be wiped off. Sages, on the other hand, hold that
the individual first uses sufficient clean oil to permeate the
leather. When afterwards he uses unclean oil, this oil will exude
from the leather, and so can be wiped off. The problem is that
according to this reading and interpretation, E and F contradict
the positions ascribed to Eliezer and sages at C and D. According
to Lieberman's exegesis, Eliezer, C, should state that the cleanness of the garment depends on the second oil which is applied,
and sages, D, should take the opposite view. I find it very unlikely that T. would so blatantly contradict what is stated in M.,
and in particular in the context of materials which are intended
to give the reasons for views cited by M.'s authorities.[24]

G-I offers a different method by which an individual may use
unclean oil to soften leather. It states that he simply should
wipe the unclean oil off of the surface of the leather.[25] He
must, of course, be careful that more oil does not subsequently
seep out of the leather (I).

> A. (1) [As regards] a pot in which one cooked meat--
> he should not [thereafter] cook in it dairy.
>
> B. (2) [If he cooked in it] dairy, he should not [there-
> after] cook in it meat.
>
> C. (Follow E in deleting: [If he cooked in it] uncon-
> secrated produce, he should not [thereafter] cook in it
> heave-offering.)[26]
>
> D. (3) [If he cooked in it] heave-offering, he should
> not [thereafter] cook in it unconsecrated produce.
>
> E. But if one cooked [food in any of these forbidden
> ways]--
>
> F. lo, this [i.e., what has been cooked second] is for-
> bidden if [the food which was cooked first] imparted to it
> flavor.
>
> T. 8:16 (b. Zeb. 96b, b. Hul. 97a,
> 111b)

The triplet makes a single point, relevant at E-F to the rules
of M. 10:1-6. Food should not be cooked in a pot which may impart
to it the flavor of something which is forbidden. One therefore
does not cook meat in a dish used for dairy, or *vice versa*, and

does not cook unconsecrated food in a pot which had been used for
heave-offering. If this restriction is not followed, E-F, we
apply the criterion of whether or not the food has been flavored
by what previously was cooked in the pot. This is just as
M. 10:1-6 would lead us to expect.

I.   A.   [If] there were before him two pots, one [filled]
with heave-offering and one [filled] with unconsecrated produce,

      B.   and before him [also] was a mortar [filled] with
heave-offering--

      C.   [if] he placed [the heave-offering in the mortar][27]
in one of them [i.e., of the pots], but it is not known in
which of them he placed [it],

      D.   lo, I say, "In the [pot of] (read with MB, HY:)
heave-offering (MSS.: unconsecrated produce) he placed [it].

II.   E.   [If] there were before him two mortars, one [filled]
with unconsecrated produce and the other [filled] with heave-
offering,

      F.   and before him [also] was a pot [filled] with un-
consecrated produce[28]--

      G.   [if] he placed [in the pot at F produce] from one of
them [i.e., of E's two mortars], but it is not known from
which of them he placed [it],

      H.   lo, I say "From the [mortar filled with] unconse-
crated produce he placed [it]."

                              T. 8:17 (see M. 7:5A-C, and
                              T. 6:11b)

III. I.   [If] there were before him two pots, one [filled]
with unconsecrated produce and one [filled] with heave-
offering,

      J.   and before them were two mortars, one [filled] with
heave-offering and one [filled] with unconsecrated produce--

      K.   [if] he placed [in the pots produce] from the two of
them [i.e., put the contents of each of the mortars in one of
the pots], but it is not known whether he placed this in that,
or that in this [i.e., whether he mixed heave-offering with
heave-offering or with unconsecrated produce]--

      L.   lo, I say, "He placed heave-offering with heave-
offering, and unconsecrated produce with unconsecrated
produce."

                              T. 8:18 (see T. 6:14-17)

M. If [the produce in one of the pots mentioned at I
was not heave-offering, but rather] was liable to the separation of tithes, [or had the status of] first tithe or second
tithe, [and it was mixed with either heave-offering or unconsecrated produce, but it is not known which,]--

N. lo, this is forbidden [i.e., none of the produce may
be eaten by a non-priest].

O. For they did not deem permitted [for consumption by
non-priests] produce which might have been mixed with heave-
offering (*spq mdwm*ᶜ) except in a case which can be adjudicated such that all of the produce retains its original
status.

T. 8:19 (O: T. 6:18F; see T. 6:18)

On the surface this discussion is not related to the present
context. At issue is not heave-offering's flavoring unconsecrated
produce, but whether we may declare that heave-offering and unconsecrated produce have not been mixed at all. As we shall see
clearly at T. 8:20-22, however, what T. wishes to do by placing
this discussion in the present context is to treat as a unit the
materials on the problem of mixtures of heave-offering and unconsecrated food which M. covers in diverse chapters. This is a
fine example of T.'s acting as a redactional commentary by re-
organizing M.'s materials in accordance with its own concept of
theme.

The point of cases like these already has been stated above
at T. 6:11-18. This is that in a case in which we can rule that
the heave-offering was mixed with other heave-offering and not
with unconsecrated produce, we do so. In this way we uphold the
prevailing status both of the priestly gift and of the unconsecrated produce (A-L).[29] If the doubt cannot be adjudicated in
such a way that none of the produce involved is deemed to take on
a forbidden status, we must deem all of the produce to be forbidden. This is exemplified at M-O, where a mixture occurs between either heave-offering and unconsecrated produce, or heave-
offering and some different agricultural offering. As O states,
in such cases, neither of the pots of produce may be saved by the
declaration that the heave-offering fell into the other.

A. A forbidden (E lacks: forbidden)[30] piece [of meat]
which was mixed with [other] pieces,

B. even if they are a thousand [in number]--

C. all of them are forbidden.

D.   [*In the case of forbidden*] *broth* [*which was mixed
with pieces of permitted meat*]--
[*the meat is prohibited if the broth*] *imparts* [*to it its*]
flavor [= M. Hul. 7:5C].

E.   If [the piece of meat at A] was dissolved, lo, this
[i.e., all of the meat] is [prohibited if] it imparts flavor
[just like at D].

T. 8:20 (T. Hul. 7:7)

F.   A piece [of meat] from a sin offering which was mixed
with a hundred pieces of unconsecrated [meat],

G.   and so a piece of show-bread which was mixed with a
hundred pieces of unconsecrated [bread],

H.   lo, these are neutralized [such that all of the meat
or bread may be eaten as unconsecrated food].

I.   R. Judah says, "They are not neutralized."

T. 8:21 (y. Or. 2:1; see b. Yeb.

81b)

J.   A piece of unclean sin offering which was mixed with
a hundred pieces of clean sin-offering,[31]

K.   and so a piece of unclean show-bread which was mixed
with a hundred pieces of clean show-bread,

L.   lo, these are neutralized [such that all of the sin
offering or show-bread is deemed clean].

M.   R. Judah says, "They are not neutralized."

N.   And so in the case of meal-offerings,

O.   and so in the case of cakes of thank-offering.

P.   Produce which is liable to the separation of tithes
or wine used for libations [either of which is mixed with
permitted, unconsecrated produce]--

Q.   [if all of the produce in the mixture is] of the
same type [the mixture is forbidden] no matter how little
[forbidden substance it contains].

R.   But [if the produce in the mixture is] not of the
same type [the mixture is forbidden if the prohibited food]
imparts flavor [to that mixture].

S.   And [as to] all other forbidden foods,

T.   whether [the mixture is of foods] of the same kind
or of different kinds,

U.   [it is forbidden if the forbidden food] imparts [its]
flavor [to the mixture].

T. 8:22 (P-U: see M. A.Z. 5:8,

b. A.Z. 73b)

At issue are the conditions under which the rules of neutralization apply and those under which the probative factor is whether or not forbidden food has imparted flavor to permitted food. This problem is stated in terms of cases involving the mixture of meat permitted for consumption by non-priests and forbidden meat. While the unit thus is autonomous of the topic of heave-offering, it ties together the two different types of problems of mixtures discussed in M. Terumot. This material therefore is both pertinent and aptly placed in its context in T.

The point is that in cases in which the forbidden food is of a type different from that with which it is mixed, the other food is rendered prohibited if it is flavored by the forbidden food (D, E, R, S-U). When this happens, even if the forbidden substance is removed from the mixture, the other food remains forbidden, having received the benefit of that which is forbidden. This is not the case if the forbidden and permitted foods are of the same type. In such a case there can be no consideration of whether or not the forbidden food has flavored the permitted. The laws of neutralization therefore are applied, and if the forbidden food is an insignificant proportion of the mixture as a whole, that mixture is deemed permitted (F-H, J-L).[32]

Matters are confused by the view of Judah (I, M), echoed in the anonymous laws of A-C and Q. This view is that the laws of neutralization do not apply in cases in which meat from sacrifices, or show-bread, is involved. The theory here apparently is that these things are of such importance that they never may be disregarded and so never are neutralized (b. Hul. 100a). This is exactly the view attributed to Judah at T. 5:10A-I (pp. 153-154) regarding certain types of produce in the status of heave-offering. S-U is a further source of confusion. It claims a distinction between the types of produce listed at P and all other food. This distinction is contradicted by A-O. I cannot account for it.

10:7

A. [As regards] unconsecrated olives which one pickled with olives in the status of heave-offering--

B. [if it was] (1) crushed, unconsecrated [olives which were pickled] with crushed [olives] in the status of heave-offering,

C. [or] (2) crushed, unconsecrated [olives which were pickled] with whole [olives] in the status of heave-offering,

D.   (3) [or if they were pickled] in brine in the status
of heave-offering (*my trwmh*)--

E.   it is forbidden [i.e., the unconsecrated olives are
rendered forbidden for consumption by a non-priest].

F.   But [if] whole unconsecrated [olives are pickled]
with crushed [olives] in the status of heave-offering--
it is permitted.

M. 10:7

The issue is the circumstances under which unconsecrated
olives are deemed to be flavored by olives in the status of heave-
offering with which they are pickled. If they are so flavored,
they will themselves be deemed to have the status of heave-offering (M. 10:1).[33] According to M. the operative consideration is
whether the unconsecrated olives are crushed or whole at the time
they are pickled with the heave-offering. If they are crushed,
they are asumed to be capable of receiving the flavor of the other
olives. They therefore are deemed forbidden for consumption by a
non-priest (B, C). If they are whole, they are considered im-
pervious to the flavor of the olives in the status of heave-offering, and so retain their unconsecrated status (F). This distinction
is not applied in the case in which the brine itself is in the
status of heave-offering (D). In such a case whether the unconsecrated olives are whole or crushed, they will be flavored by
the forbidden brine.[34]

There is formal evidence that the pericope has undergone a
stage in development beyond the simplest expression of its law.
This simplest statement would consist of the superscription, A,
plus the perfectly balanced, contrasting cases at B+E vs. F. Together these cases make the point of the pericope. C and D appear
to be appended, forming a triplet of cases at B-D. The reason for
the addition of C-D is clear on substantive grounds. I already
have stated the point of D. C stresses that it is irrelevant
whether the olives in the status of heave-offering are crushed or
whole. In either case they are assumed capable of imparting flavor
to the unconsecrated olives.

10:8

A.   [As regards] unclean fish which one pickled with
clean fish--

B.   [in the case of fish pickled in] any keg which holds
two *se'ahs* [= 9600 *zuz*, weight of brine,]

C.   if [in that two *se'ahs*] it contains unclean fish of a
weight of ten *zuz* in Judean measure,

D.   which equals five *sela^{C}s* in Galilean measure,

E.   the brine (*syrw*) is forbidden [i.e., unclean].

F.   R. Judah says, "[It is forbidden if there is] a
quarter [-log, i.e., fifty *zuz*, of unclean fish] in two
se'ahs."

G.   R. Yose says, "[It is forbidden if the unclean fish
is] one sixteenth [of the whole, i.e., 600 *zuz*]."

> M. 10:8 (Sifra, *Shemini*, *parashah*
> 3:9; B: y. R.H. 1:8; see b. Hul.
> 99b)

The pericope carries forward the issue of M. 10:7, problems
of the status of permitted food which is pickled with forbidden
food.   The question now is the minimum quantity of forbidden food--
here, unclean fish--which will flavor, and thereby render prohibited, the food with which it is pickled.   We have a tripartite
dispute on the matter.   The anonymous law of A-E is disputed by
Judah, F, and Yose, G.   As indicated in the translation, the three
positions define progressively greater quantities of unclean fish
to be present in the brine before that brine is rendered unclean.[35]   I find no particular significance in the specific
figures given.

The form of the pericope requires no comment.   Of interest
only is the superscription, A, which is misleading.   Unlike what
A claims, the issue of the pericope is not the status of the clean
fish which is pickled with the unclean, but of the brine.[36]   E
makes this clear.[37]   The reason for this discontinuity is probably
that the superscription here is on the model of M. 10:7A, to which
it is an exact linguistic parallel.   This is a fine example of the
use of a single syntactic pattern for the presentation of materials
which, while on diverse topics, are intended to illustrate a single
underlying problem of law.

A.   [*As regards*] *unclean fish which one pickled with
clean fish*,

B.   and so *a keg* [*in which one pickled fish*] *which contains two se'ahs* [= *9600 zuz, of brine*]

C.   in which *there is unclean fish of a weight of ten
zuz in Judean measure, which equals five sela^{C}s in Galilean
measure*,

D.   *the brine is forbidden* [*i.e., unclean*].

E.   *R. Judah says, "[It is forbidden if there is]* a *quarter [-log, i.e., fifty zuz, of unclean fish] in the two se'ahs."*

F.   *R. Yose says, "[It is forbidden if the unclean fish is] one sixteenth [of the whole, i.e., 600 zuz]* [= M. 10:8].

G.   Said R. Simeon b. Menasia', "You do not find a keg which holds two *se'ahs* in which there is (read *šyš bw*; all MSS.: *š'yn bw*; see Lieberman, TK, I, p. 441) unclean fish of a weight of ten *zuz* in Judean measure, which is five *sela^{c}s* in Galilean measure, which does not contain a quarter [-log of brine]."

H.   Said R. Yose b. R. Judah, "To what case does this apply [i.e., the rule that brine in which is pickled unclean fish may itself be rendered unclean]?

I.   "To the case in which one removes [the fish from the brine] and places it before him and finds it to be of the specified measure.

J.   "But if he takes [pieces of fish from the brine] and tosses [them into a pile] one at a time (*r'šwn r'šwn*),

K.   "even though he [ultimately] found there more than the specified amount—

L.   "[the brine is] permitted."

M.   (Delete the following, which is a marginal gloss that has been copied into the text of T.; see Lieberman, TK, I, p. 442; *His father and his mother did not know that it was from the lord; for he was seeking an occasion against the Philistines* (Jud. 14:4).)

T. 9:1 (I-M: see y. Ter. 10:7)

Important here is the use of "and so" at B, and "in which" at C.   Through these interpolations T. reads M.'s pericope as referring to two different problems.[38]   These are, first, the status of clean fish which is pickled with unclean (A), and, second, the status of the brine in which unclean fish is pickled (B) (Lieberman, TK, I, p. 439).   In T.'s version, these two statements of case share the same ruling, at D.   T. thus resolves the problem of the misleading superscription at M. 10:8A.

G and H-L continue matters by supplementing M.'s rule. Simeon b. Menasia', G, reads B-F as the continuation of A.   The problem for him, thus, is the minimum proportion of unclean brine, derived from the unclean fish in the mixture, which will render unclean the clean fish which is pickled with it.   Thus Judah's

statement, E, of the quantity of unclean fish, is understood to
refer to the quantity of brine derived from that fish. Simeon's
point is that Judah and the anonymous rule are in essential agreement. He says that if the quantity of unclean fish mentioned at
B-D is present, so will there be the quantity of unclean brine
defined by Judah (Lieberman, TK, I, p. 441). I already have
indicated (n. 34) why this reading of matters is not supported by
the language of M. 10:8.

H-L offers a qualification of M.'s rule, separate from G.
Yose b. R. Judah's position is that if the householder removes the
unclean fish a piece at a time, the individual pieces of unclean
fish do not join together to constitute the minimum quantity which
renders the brine unclean. They are, rather, considered separately from each other (Lieberman, TK, I, p. 442).

> I.   A.   [*As regards*] *unclean fish which one pickled with*
> *clean fish* [= M. 10:8A]--
>
> B.   he wipes off [the clean fish], and it is permitted
> [i.e., clean].
>
> II.   C.   [As regards] a salted, unclean fish [which one
> pickled] with unsalted, clean fish, [the clean fish] is for-
> bidden.
>
> III. D.   [As regards] salted clean fish [which one pickled]
> with unsalted, unclean fish, [the clean fish is] permitted.
>
> E.   [As regards] unclean fish which one cooked with clean
> fish--
>
> F.   they consider the matter as if [the unclean fish] is
> a leek or an onion.
>
> G.   If it is of sufficient quantity (*'m yš bw*) to impart
> flavor to the clean fish, [that fish] is forbidden.
>
> H.   But if not, it is permitted.
>
> T. 9:2 (A-D: see y. Ter. 10:8)

T. is in two parts, the triplet at A-B+C+D, and E-H. Both
supplement M. 10:8. The first rule of the triplet, A-B, is
familiar (see T. 8:14). It states that if the householder wipes
the forbidden brine off of clean fish, that fish is considered unaffected by the brine and therefore remains clean. The contrasting cases at C+D explain why this is the case. The point is that
salted fish imparts its flavor to other fish, but unsalted fish
does not. A-B, where, we assume, the unclean fish is unsalted,
the clean fish thus will not have been flavored by it. This is a
consideration unknown to M. 10:8.

E-H stands on its own, offering a criterion for determining
whether or not unclean fish has rendered unclean the clean fish
with which it is cooked. Here there is no issue of brine as an
intermediary between the clean and unclean fish. T. therefore
suggests a method by which the householder simply may determine
whether the unclean fish was sufficient in quantity to flavor the
clean. The method is clear, as stated at F.

10:9

A.   Unclean locusts which were pickled with clean locusts
have not invalidated [i.e., imparted uncleanness to] the brine
[in which they were pickled].

B.   Testified R. Sadoq concerning the brine of unclean
locusts, that it is clean [i.e., that it does not impart
susceptibility to uncleanness; y. Ter. 10:8].

> M. 10:9 (M. Ed. 7:2, Sifra, *Shemini*,
> *pereq* 5:10; B: T. Ed. 3:1)

The pericope is redacted here because of its relevance to
M. 10:8's discussion of the status of brine in which is pickled
a mixture of clean and unclean foods. Unlike M. 10:8, however,
M. 10:9 adds nothing to the laws of M. Chapter Ten. A's rule,
a declarative sentence, is explained by B. Sadoq states that
locust-brine is not considered a liquid which imparts susceptibility to uncleanness to foods it wets down. It therefore does
not impart uncleanness to the mixture of which it is a part.[39]

10:10

A.   All [kinds of unconsecrated produce] which are
pickled together [with heave-offering remain] permitted [for
consumption by non-priests],

B.   except [for unconsecrated produce pickled] with
leeks [in the status of heave-offering].

C.   (1) Unconsecrated leeks [which are pickled] with
leeks in the status of heave-offering,

D.   [or] (2) unconsecrated vegetables [which are pickled]
with leeks in the status of heave-offering

E.   are forbidden [for consumption by non-priests].

F.   But unconsecrated leeks [which are pickled] with
vegetables in the status of heave-offering are permitted [for
consumption by non-priests].

> M. 10:10

A and C-E+F are joined by B, forming a tight little essay. A

states that unconsecrated produce which is pickled with heave-
offering does not take on the status of that offering. The claim,
it appears, is that different types of produce which are pickled
together do not flavor one another. This is not what is assumed
at M. 10:7, a contradiction for which I cannot account.[40] B
states that leeks alone do not fall under A's rule. This introduces C-E+F, on the laws for leeks.[41] C-F states, simply, that
leeks impart flavor to produce with which they are pickled, but
themselves are not flavored by other produce. This point is made
through the contrast between D-E and F. C is added to give the
rule for a case in which both the unconsecrated produce and the
heave-offering with which it is pickled are leeks.

A. These are types of leeks [M. 10:10C-F]:

B. (1) arum (*lwp*),[42] (2) garlic, (3) onions and (4)
porret (*qplwtwt*).[43]

C. R. Judah says, "Porret alone is a type of leek
(*lyn lk myny hwsyt 'l' qplwt blbd*).

T. 9:3 (A-B: b. Ned. 68b)

T.'s contribution is obvious.[44]

A. R. Yose says, "They pickle onions in the status of
heave-offering in unconsecrated vinegar,

B. "but they do not pickle onions in the status of
heave-offering in vinegar in the status of heave-offering.

C. "And there is no need to say [that they do not
pickle] unconsecrated onions in vinegar in the status of
heave-offering."

T. 9:4a

Vinegar which is used for pickling is not thereafter eaten.
For this reason, A-B, vinegar in the status of heave-offering may
not be used for pickling. If it were, the heave-offering could
not afterwards be eaten by the priest. At C, both the unconsecrated onions will be given the status of heave-offering, and the
vinegar in the status of heave-offering will be ruined.[45]

10:11

A. R. Yose says, "All [kinds of unconsecrated produce]
which are boiled with beets [in the status of heave-offering]
are forbidden [for consumption by non-priests],

B. "since they [i.e., beets] impart flavor [to that with
which they are cooked]."

C. R. Simeon says, "[Unconsecrated] cabbage from an
irrigated field [which is boiled] with cabbage [in the status
of heave-offering] from a rain-watered field is forbidden [for
consumption by non-priests],

D. "since it [i.e., the cabbage from the irrigated
field] absorbs [the flavor of the other cabbage]."

E. R. Aqiba (reading with thirteen MSS. and editions;
printed edition reads: Judah) says, "All [kinds of permitted
food] which are cooked together [with forbidden food] are
permitted [for consumption],

F. "except [for that which is cooked] with [forbidden]
meat."

G. R. Yohanan b. Nuri says, "Liver renders [other food]
forbidden, but itself is not rendered forbidden,

H. "for it imparts [flavor], but does not absorb
[flavor]."

M. 10:11

M. 10:11 is in two parts. A-B+C-D provides two Ushan rules
on mixtures of heave-offering and unconsecrated produce. E-H is
Yavnean, on mixtures of a wide range of types of forbidden and
permitted foods. The two units have been redacted together because of the single issue they share.[46] The points both of A and
C, first, are obvious on the basis of the previous rules of the
chapter and in light of the glosses at B and D. Aqiba's statement, E-F, is more difficult, for it is not clear to what type of
forbidden food he refers. I assume that, as its wording claims,
E is intended as a general principle, to be applied to all types
of forbidden foods, including heave-offering.[47] Aqiba thus will
reject all of the laws of M. Chapter Ten. His point, as stated by
F, is that only forbidden meat (i.e., unclean meat, improperly
slaughtered meat, or meat deriving from sacrifices, is of sufficient gravity to render forbidden other foods with which it is
cooked.[48] Yohanan b. Nuri's statement, G, follows upon that of
Aqiba, giving the rule for the specific case of liver. It is
explained by H.

D. *R. Aqiba says, "All [kinds of permitted food] which
are cooked together [with forbidden food] are permitted [for
consumption], except [for that which is cooked]with [for-
bidden meat [= M. 10:11E-F].*

E. "[Permitted] meat [which is cooked] with [forbidden]
meat is prohibited [for consumption].

F.   "And [in the case of] any [two kinds, one permitted
and one forbidden] which were mixed (supply with E: $nt^c rbw$
together and [then] cooked, lo, this is prohibited."

T. 9:4b

F presents an important qualification of Aqiba's position,
cited at D.[49]   According to F, the factor which determines the
status of permitted food which is cooked with forbidden food is
whether or not the permitted and forbidden foods are mixed together to create a single dish before they are cooked.[50]   If they
are, the permitted food is deemed to take on the forbidden status
of the other food.   This is the same notion that is held by
M. 10:1A-D, and which is ignored by the rest of Chapter Ten.   T.
thus shows that view to belong to Aqiba.

A.   R. Eliezer says, *"Liver renders [other food] forbidden, but itself is not* (supply *'ynh* with E) *rendered
forbidden"* [= M. 10:11G].

B.   R. Ishmael b. R. Yohanan b. Beroqah says, "[Liver
which has been boiled renders [other food] forbidden, but is
not itself rendered forbidden.

C.   "[Liver] which has been spiced renders [other food]
forbidden and [also] is itself rendered forbidden [by other
food]."

T. 9:5a (b. Hul. 111a)

What is given in the name of Yohanan b. Nuri in M. is here
attributed to Eliezer.   Ishmael, B-C, qualifies that statement.
Rashi (to b. Hul. 111a, s.v., *mtwblt*) explains that spicing the
liver, C, softens it, such that it will absorb the flavor of that
with which it is cooked.   I can suggest no alternative interpretation.[51]

10:12

A.   [As regards] an egg which was spiced (read with 17
MSS. and editions: *ntblh*; printed editions read: *ntbšlh*)
with forbidden spices [e.g., spices in the status of heave-
offering]--

B.   even its yolk is forbidden [for consumption].

C.   since it [i.e., the yolk] absorbs [the flavor of the
spices].

D.   Liquid in which heave-offering has been boiled or
pickled is forbidden to non-priests.

M. 10:12

Two independent rules, A-C and D, conclude M.'s discussion
of the status of unconsecrated food which is prepared with heave-
offering or other forbidden produce. The theory here again is
that produce which is flavored by heave-offering or other forbidden
food itself takes on a forbidden status. This is explicitly
stated, C, as the reason for the rule of A-B. The basis for the
separate rule at D is the same. The heave-offering imparts its
own flavor to the liquid in which it is boiled or pickled.

D. [As regards] clean eggs which one poached with unclean eggs--

E. if [the unclean eggs] are of sufficient quantity to
impart flavor [to the clean eggs, those eggs are] forbidden.

F. But if not, they are permitted.

G. [As regards] eggs which one boiled and [later] found
a baby bird in one of them--

H. if it is of sufficient quantity to impart flavor [to
all of the eggs, they are] forbidden.

I. But if not, they are permitted.

J. Abortive eggs (Jastrow, p. 241, for *gy^{c}wly bysym*) are
permitted for consumption.

K. [As regards] spoiled eggs (*bysym mwzrwt*; see Lieberman, TK, I, p. 449)--

let a hearty soul (*npš yph*) eat them [i.e., they are
permitted].

L. If one found blood in either of these [i.e., J or K],
he may throw out the blood and eat the rest.

T. 9:5b[52] (y. Ter. 10:10; D-I:

b. Hul. 98a; J-K: b. Hul. 64b)

A. A man (supply *'dm* with E and ed. princ.) may eat
fish and locusts whether they are alive or dead and need not
scruple.

T. 9:6a

T. takes up the discussion of laws regarding eggs, complement-
ing M. 10:12A-C in a most general way. D-I simply applies the
theory of M. Chapter Ten to cases irrelevant to the topic of heave-
offering. In issue, J-M and T. 9:6a are autonomous of M. J-M is
placed here because, like D-I, it gives rules for eggs. T. 9:6a
follows D-I, listing two other foods which are permitted for consumption. The basis of T. 9:6A's rule is that neither fish or
locusts require ritual slaughter (HY).

TERUMOT CHAPTER ELEVEN

The topic of the chapter is the proper preparation and use of
heave-offering by the priest. This forms a logical conclusion to
the tractate as a whole, for it details the rules for the final
disposition of the priestly gift. The central point of the chapter is that produce in the status of heave-offering may not go to
waste. It must, rather, fully be used for the purpose for which it
was designated, the benefit of the priest. This principle is expressed and developed in the chapter's three segments, M. 11:1-3,
M. 11:4-7 and M. 11:8-10. While these units are of diverse
literary forms, they are closely related in substance. Each explains how we are to be certain that heave-offering is used such
that none goes to waste. They constitute, moreover, a fine piece
of redactional organization. Their larger progression of ideas is
from discussion of food, to refuse from food, and finally to what
is not deemed food.

M. 11:1-3 opens the chapter with a statement of the theory
governing all that follows. Produce in the status of heave-offering must be prepared in the manner customary for unconsecrated
produce of its same type. This is to assure that all portions of
the produce which normally are eaten in fact are made available
for consumption by the priest. If the produce were processed in
some manner other than the normal (e.g., if what usually is eaten
fresh were pressed for juice) edible portions of the produce (e.g.,
the skin) would be left to waste. Such processing therefore is
forbidden.

The next logical step is at M. 11:4-7, which refer to produce
that has food value but, nevertheless, normally is not eaten.
Olive pits, for instance, are not customarily used as food. They
are, however, edible, inasmuch as the priest may suck on them for
their juice. The problem is to determine whether or not such produce is to be deemed food, such that it has the consecrated status
of heave-offering and must be eaten by the priest. According to
M., this is determined on the basis of the priest's own attitude
towards the produce. That which he considers worthy as food retains the consecrated status of heave-offering. What he does not
desire to eat is deemed inedible and therefore no longer to have
that status. This is an important application of the notion,
basic throughout Tractate Terumot, that man's own intention

295

determines the status of consecration of produce.

M. 11:8-10 carry forward M. 11:4-7's discussion by referring
to produce of an ambiguous nature. The produce is unclean, and
therefore may not be eaten by the priest, or simply is not desirable to him as food. Unlike at M. 11:4-7, however, here the produce has some alternative use, e.g., as fodder for animals
(M. 11:9), or for kindling in lamps (M. 11:10). Since this produce is not usable as food, the stipulation that heave-offering
be eaten by the priest is relaxed. In order to prevent the heave-
offering's being wasted, it is put to its other purposes. What is
essential, simply, is that the consecrated offering be used to ·
benefit the priest. That is, it must be used to feed *his* cattle
or light *his* way. The delineation of acceptable uses of heave-
offering other than for human consumption is a major aspect of
T.'s extended discussion of this chapter. Its theory, however,
remains exactly the same as that of M.

Attributions to Eliezer and Joshua at M. 11:2 set the basic
principle of this chapter in Yavnean times. Its development and
exemplification, however, take place at Usha, as the other attributed materials in the chapter indicate. In M. attributions
are to Judah (M. 11:1), and to Yose, Simeon, Meir and Judah
(M. 11:10). The picture offered by T. is no different. Important
attributions are to Eliezer b. R. Simeon (T. 9:6b), Simeon b.
Gamaliel (T. 9:17), Dosa' and Jacob (T. 10:2), Meir (T. 10:12) and
Eliezer b. Jacob (T. 10:13).

11:1

I.   A.   They may not put cakes of pressed figs or dried figs
[in the status of heave-offering] in fish-brine [in order to
flavor that brine],

      B.   since this ruins them [i.e., the figs, for use as
food].

      C.   But they may put wine [in the status of heave-offer-
ing] in brine.

II.   D.   And (seven MSS. lack: *w*) they may not perfume oil
[in the status of heave-offering, for it may not thereafter
be eaten].

      E.   But they may make wine [in the status of heave-
offering] into honied-wine (Danby for *yynwmlyn*; see Jastrow,
p. 52, s.v. *'ynwmylyn*).

III. F.   They may not boil wine in the status of heave-
offering,

G. since this diminishes its quantity.

H. R. Judah permits [one to cook wine],

I. for this improves it [i.e., the flavor of the wine].

M. 11:1 (C+E: see T. Dem. 1:24,

T. Sheb. 6:5; D: see M. M.S. 2:1;

H-I: y. Sheb. 8:2, y. Ter. 2:5)

The point of this pericope is that food in the status of heave-offering must be eaten by the priest, and therefore may not be processed in a way that renders it unavailable for consumption (A-B, D, F-G). This point is made in the contrast between rules which apply to figs (A) and oil (D), and those which apply to wine (C, E). F-G+H-I, as we shall see, is cognate, appended here to create what is in all events a poorly balanced triplet.[1] The specifics of the pericope's laws are as follows. Fish brine is consumed as a food. Figs are added to the brine in order to flavor it. Since, as B states, such figs are not thereafter eaten,[2] the priest may not use for this purpose figs in the status of heave-offering. Wine, however, may be added to the brine, in order to sweeten it (b. A.Z. 38b). Unlike the figs, the wine later is drunk along with the brine. The same point is made at D-E. Once oil has been perfumed, it is used as an ointment, but is not eaten. Wine which is mixed with honey (E) still is consumed by the priest (as a medicine, b. Shab. 140a; cf., y. Shab. 14:14 and T. Ter. 9:7).

The theory of F-G is parallel to, and carries forward, that which has preceded. It claims that the volume of consecrated wine may in no way be diminished. Food in the status of heave-offering would thereby be lost. Judah, H-I, disagrees, applying his principle familiar from M. 2:4. He holds that the priest should eat as heave-offering produce of the highest possible quality.[3] It therefore is irrelevant to Judah that in its preparation some of the consecrated wine will evaporate. This simply is part of the process through which the wine is prepared for consumption by a priest.

B. [As regards] wine in the status of heave-offering which fell into [unconsecrated] brine--

[the mixture] is forbidden to non-priests [see M. 11:1C].

C. R. Eliezer b. R. Simeon (E reads: Simeon b. R. Eliezer) permits it to non-priests.

T. 9:6b (T. Sheb. 6:5, see y. Ter. 11:1, y. A.Z. 2:6)

At issue is whether or not being mixed with brine ruins wine.
If it does, then wine in the status of heave-offering which is
mixed with brine would be deemed to lose its consecrated status,
no longer falling into the category of wine. The anonymous rule
of B claims that the wine is not ruined by the brine. It therefore retains its consecrated status and, moreover, imparts that
status to the brine which it flavors. This is in line with
M. 11:1C, which holds that wine in the status of heave-offering
may be mixed with brine. Eliezer b. R. Simeon, C, disagrees with
B, and thus should reject M. 11:1C. He holds that the brine
spoils the wine (see b. A.Z. 38b). It no longer may be considered
heave-offering, and, therefore, the mixture of which it is a part
retains an unconsecrated status.[4]

A. One may put a cake of pressed figs or dried figs [in
the status of heave-offering] in fish-brine in the same way
that he adds spices [cf., M. 11:1A-B].

B. He may not press them in order to squeeze out [their]
juices.

C. In [the case of] spices [in the status of heave-
offering] this is permitted,

D. since this is their normal use ($ml'ktn$).

E. He ties up [in a bundle] spices [in the status of
heave-offering] and puts them in a dish [which is cooking]--

F. if they are left without flavor ($btl\ t^cmn$), they are
[thereafter] permitted [for consumption as unconsecrated
food].

G. But if not, they [remain] forbidden [as heave-
offering].

H. (E lacks H-M). They may not make wine [in the status
of heave-offering] into an unguent, nor oil [in the status of
heave-offering] into spiced-oil.

I. But if he made wine [in the status of heave-offering]
into an unguent, or oil [in the status of heave-offering] into
spiced-oil,

J. [the priest] may anoint [himself] with the oil,

K. but he may not anoint [himself] with wine or vinegar.

L. For [as regards] oil--its normal use ($drkw$) is for
anointing.

M. [As to] wine and vinegar--their normal use is not for
anointing.

T. 9:7 (T. Sheb. 5:6-8; E-M: T.
M.S. 2:2-3)

T. supplements M. 11:1 in two parts, A-B+C-G and H-M. Both
of them make the same point, emphasizing the principle which is
central in M. This is that produce in the status of heave-offering must be used in its normal fashion as a food. This being the
case, A-B claims that the priest may use figs in the status of
heave-offering to flavor fish brine. This is so if he does so in
a way which will not spoil them for his later consumption. T.
thus carries forward M. 11:1A-B, which knows of no way that figs
in the status of heave-offering may be added to brine.[5] C-G, likewise, advances M.'s theory. Since spices normally are used to
flavor foods, but are not eaten, even if they are in the status of
heave-offering, they may be used for that purpose. It follows (F)
that they lose their consecrated status, and may be discarded, when
they no longer serve this usual purpose.

H-M states explicitly the basis for M. 11:1's rule. Wine and
oil in the status of heave-offering should be used in their normal
manner, as foods. As at A-B, T. now adds a point unknown to M.
If, contrary to the law, oil in the status of heave-offering is
perfumed, T. states that it may be used as an ointment. This is
so (L) because this is a normal way in which oil is used. The
point is cognate to the one which T. makes as regards spices in
the status of heave-offering, C-D. This same thinking does not
apply to wine or vinegar, D, since these things are not normally
used as ointments, M.

11:2

A. [As regards any of the following which have the
status of heave-offering:] (1) honey made from dates, (2) wine
made from apples, (3) vinegar made from winter grapes
(*stwnywt*) or (4) any other fruit juice in the status of
heave-offering--

B. R. Eliezer obligates [a non-priest who untentionally
drinks any of these] to [payment of] the principal and [added]
fifth.

C. But R. Joshua exempts.

D. And R. Eliezer declares [that these things render
foods susceptible to] unclean[ness], under the law of liquids
(*mšwm mšqh*).

E. Said R. Joshua, "Sages did not number seven liquids
[which render food susceptible to uncleanness] as do those
who count spices [i.e., imprecisely].

F. "Rather, they said, 'Seven [kinds of] liquids

[render foods susceptible to] unclean[ness], but all other
liquids are clean [i.e., do not render foods susceptible to
uncleanness].'"

                          M. 11:2 (A-C: b. Ber. 38a, b. Hul.
                          120b; F: see M. Mak. 6:4)

We know from M. Chapter Six that a non-priest who untentionally eats heave-offering must replace that heave-offering and give
the priest an additional fifth of the heave-offering's quantity.
This is a penalty for misusing sanctified produce. The issue disputed by Eliezer and Joshua, A-L, is whether or not a non-priest
who unintentionally eats heave-offering which was improperly
processed as fruit juice is obligated to this same restitution.
Objectively, the juice was made from a priestly gift and therefore
has a sanctified status.[6] This being the case, Eliezer holds that
the individual is liable to the usual restitution. This is just
as we would expect on the basis of Eliezer's position in M. Chapter
Eight. Joshua, C, likewise is consistent with his position in that
chapter. He takes into account extenuating circumstances. Although the fruit juice was made from heave-offering, it should not
have been. The non-priest therefore could not have known that it
was heave-offering, and had no reason to suspect that in drinking
it he was doing anything improper.[7] It follows for Joshua that he
is exempt from the penalty.[8] As before, Joshua holds that the
status of an act is determined by the perception of the actor, not
by the objective situation.

D-F is redacted here because, like A-C, it consists of a dispute between Eliezer and Joshua on the topic of fruit juice. It
is however distinct in issue from A-C and from the concerns of
this tractate in general.[9] D-F depends on the law of Lev. 11:34,
38, which states that only foods which have been moistened are
susceptible to uncleanness. M. Makh. 6:4, in turn, lists seven
specific liquids which render foods susceptible to uncleanness.
Eliezer apparently holds that these seven kinds typify larger
categories of liquids (cf., M. Makh. 6:5). He therefore claims
that even though fruit juices are not included in the list, they
render foods susceptible to uncleanness. Joshua's view is clear.
Only the specific liquids listed at M. Makh. 6:4 render foods
susceptible to uncleanness. Fruit juices are not among those
listed.

        A.   [As regards] honey made from dates--

        B.   R. Eliezer declares it liable to [the removal of]
tithes.

C. (E lacks C-G.)[10] Said R. Nathan, "R. Eliezer agrees
that [the honey itself] is exempt from the removal of tithes.

D. "But R. Eliezer used to say ('wmr hyh) that one may
not eat of the honey unless he had tithed the dates [from
which the honey was made].

E. "R. Eliezer agrees that if he tithed the dates here
(kn = k'n; see Jastrow, s.v., k'n, p. 606, Lieberman, TK, I,
p. 456, and Epstein, Mabo', p. 1236) [i.e., in the Land of
Israel] and turned them into honey in Apamaea,[11] that [the
honey] is permitted [for consumption, without further
tithing]."

F. [As regards] honey made from dates--

G. *R. Eliezer declares [that it renders foods susceptible to] unclean[ness], under the law of liquids* [= M. 10:2D].

H. Said R. Nathan, "R. Eliezer agrees that this does
not render [food susceptible] to unclean[ness] under the law
of liquids.

I. "Concerning what did they disagree?

J. "Concerning [the case] in which one put water in it.

K. "For R. Eliezer declares [that it renders foods
susceptible] to unclean[ness] under the law of liquids.

L. "But sages say, 'They rule in accordance with which
is in the majority, [honey or water].'"

T. 9:8 (y. Ter. 11:2; G-L: see

T. Mak. 1:7)

The contribution of each of T.'s two parts (A-B+C-D and F-L)
is the comment of Nathan. This refines Eliezer's position such
that Eliezer is made to agree with the view in M. held by Joshua.
A-B, first, emphasizes Eliezer's notion that honey made from dates
is deemed to be an agricultural produce in the status of the
original dates. Like all produce, the honey therefore is liable
to the separation of tithes, and, it follows, may take on the
status of heave-offering. At C-E+D Nathan restates Eliezer's
opinion, in fact reversing it (MB). He claims that Eliezer holds
that the honey is not an agricultural product which may (C) or
needs to (E) be tithed in its own right. This being the case,
honey will not normally have the status of heave-offering, for
only dates are to be tithed. This is Joshua's position.

Again at G-L Nathan brings Eliezer into line with the view
taken by Joshua in M. 11:2. Nathan states that Eliezer agrees
that honey is not a liquid which renders food susceptible to

uncleanness, Joshua's position at M. 11:2E-F. Nathan then restates the dispute of M. in terms of whether or not honey which is
mixed with water has the status of that water (K). The dispute
is clear as given at K-L, with the opinion we would expect to be
given to Joshua held instead of sages. This shift, along with the
fact that this same dispute appears at T. Mak. 1:7 between Meir
and sages, makes it likely that Nathan's comment reports an
Ushan pericope, recast to mitigate the essential difference between the position of Eliezer and that considered normative in
later times (e.g., at M. Ed. 7:2).

11:3

I.   A.   [Regarding produce in the status of heave-offering
or second tithe:] they may not make (1) dates into honey, nor
(2) apples into wine, nor (3) winter grapes into vinegar, nor
(4) [as regards] all other fruits may they alter their natural
condition if they are in the status of heave-offering or
second tithe,

B.   except [in the case of] olives and grapes.

II.   C.   They do not receive the forty stripes for [drinking
liquids made from produce which is] from the first three
years of growth of a vineyard or orchard (^{c}rlh; Lev. 19:23),

D.   except for [drinking] that which is produced from
olives or grapes.

III. E.   And they may not bring first fruits in the form of
liquids,

F.   except for that which is produced from olives or
grapes.

IV.   G.   And no [fruit juice] imparts [susceptibility to] uncleanness under the law of liquids,

H.   except for that [liquid] which is produced from
olives or grapes.

V.   I.   And they may offer no [liquid] at the altar,

J.   except for that [liquid] which is produced from
olives or grapes.

M. 11:3 (I: b. Pes. 24b; I-J:
b. Hul. 120b)

At A-B the pericope depends on and carries forward the principle of M. 11:1, that produce in the status of heave-offering must
be eaten by the priest. Its particular question is the form in
which produce is to be eaten, whether fresh (A), or, in the case
of olives and grapes, processed (B). The problem for

interpretation is to determine why a distinction is made between
olives and grapes and all other produce. As T. will make clear,
the basis for this distinction is the form in which each type of
produce customarily is eaten. Those things listed at A normally
are eaten in their fresh state, and therefore, if in the status
of heave-offering, must be consumed in that form. This is not the
case for olives and grapes, which M. itself refers to as being
made into wine and oil (cf., e.g., M. 1:8-9). If they have the
status of heave-offering, they therefore may be processed into
wine and oil.[12] The larger consideration, it would follow, is
that of M. 11:1, that food in the status of heave-offering not go
to waste. If produce which normally is eaten fresh is processed,
then parts of the produce which usually are eaten (e.g., the skin)
will be left to waste. For this reason, if such produce is in the
status of heave-offering, it may not be processed. This consideration does not apply in the case of olives and grapes, which
usually are pressed for oil and wine.[13] Those parts of the produce
which are left after pressing (e.g., grape skins) are not normally
deemed the food of the grape or olive, and therefore, even if in
the status of heave-offering, need not be eaten by the priest.

While the four rules at C-D, E-F, G-H and I-J all are formally similar to A-B, only the first two derive from the same reasoning which is operative at A-B. This indicates the unit was probably originally a triplet, A-B, C-D and E-F. G-H and I-J were
added for reasons of form and completeness. The point at C-D and
E-F is that first fruits and produce deriving from a vineyard or
orchard in its first three years of growth, like heave-offering,
are sanctified. For this reason they should be left in the form
in which produce of their type normally is eaten. C-D's particular
consideration is whether or not an individual is deemed culpable
for eating consecrated produce which was improperly processed.
This is the same issue as is disputed by Joshua and Eliezer for
the case of heave-offering, M. 11:2. The anonymous rule here has
the position of Joshua, that the individual is not culpable.
Eliezer, we recall, holds that the individual is culpable, even
though the produce has been misprocessed.

G-H and I-J are separate. G-H goes over the ground of
M. 11:2D-F. Again, the anonymous rule here is in the position of
Joshua at M. 11:2, that fruit juices do not impart susceptibility
to uncleanness. Eliezer, M. 11:2D, holds that they do. I-J simply
refers to the fact that the only liquids used on the altar are

oil, in which cereal offerings are fried (see, e.g., Lev. 2:1-16),
and wine, given as a drink offering (e.g., Ex. 29:40).

A. "[As regards] olives in the status of heave-offer-
ing--

B. "[if they are] clean, let them be made into oil.

C. "[If they are] unclean, let them not be made into
oil.

D. "[As regards] grapes [in the status of heave-offer-
ing]--

E. "whether they are unclean or clean, let them not be
made [into wine]"--the words of R. Meir.

I. F. R. Jacob says (delete following E and ed. princ.:
in his name), "R. Eliezer concedes to R. Joshua in [the case
of] clean olives, that they should be made [into oil].

G. "Concerning what did they disagree?

H. "Concerning [the case of] unclean olives.

I. "For R. Eliezer says, 'Let them not be made [into
oil],'

J. "and R. Joshua says, 'Let them be made [into oil],'

K. "'and clean grapes should be made [into wine], and
unclean grapes should not be made [into wine].'"

II. L. Said R. Judah, "R. Joshua concedes to R. Eliezer
concerning [the case of] clean olives and clean grapes, that
they should be made [into oil and wine].

M. "Concerning what did they disagree?

N. "Concerning unclean [olives and grapes].

O. "For R. Eliezer says, 'They should not be made [into
oil and wine],'

P. "and R. Joshua says, 'They should be made [into oil
and wine].'"

III. Q. Said Rabbi, "R. Eliezer and R. Joshua did not disagree concerning clean olives, that they should be made [into
oil], and concerning unclean grapes, that they should not be
made [into wine].

R. "Concerning what did they disagree?

S. "Concerning unclean olives and clean grapes.

T. "For R. Eliezer says, 'They should not be made [into
oil and wine],'

U. (Ed. princ. lacks:) "and R. Joshua says, 'They should
be made [into oil and wine].'"

T. 9:9 (y. Ter. 11:3)

T. exposes a grey-area in the law of M. 11:3. The problem is
what we are to do in a case in which the processing required for
grapes and olives in the status of heave-offering will leave the
wine or oil in a state of uncleanness. In this state it may not
be eaten by a priest. (We recall that the unclean olives and
grapes themselves may be eaten by the priest, for individually
they are of too small a quantity to render the priest unclean.)
At issue is whether, in such a case, we apply the rule that heave-
offering should be processed as produce of its type normally is,
or the one which states that heave-offering must be eaten. This
question generates four sets of rules, that of Meir, A-D, and
three Ushan versions of an Eliezer-Joshua dispute, F-K, L-P and
Q-U. Since interpretation of the pericope requires a clear statement of the areas of agreement and disagreement among the various
authorities and versions, I offer the following chart. "+" stands
for "may be made into wine or oil," and "-" indicates "may not be
made."

	Meir (A-D)	Jacob Eliezer	(F-K) Joshua	Judah Eliezer	(L-P) Joshua	Rabbi Eliezer	(Q-U) Joshua
clean olives	+	+	+	+	+	+	+
unclean olives	-	-	+	-	+	-	+
clean grapes	-	+	+	+	+	-	+
unclean grapes	-	-	-	-	+	-	-

Seen in this form, it is clear that there is in fact only a small
range of disagreement as to the correct dispute between Eliezer
and Joshua. All three Ushan renditions report the same version of
the dispute for cases concerning clean and unclean olives. Eliezer
and Joshua agree that clean olives in the status of heave-offering
should be made into oil. The reason is as given in M., that olives
normally are consumed in the form of oil. Joshua holds that unclean olives likewise should be made into oil, for this is the
processing they normally undergo. Eliezer, to the contrary, holds
that the priest's eating the produce is central. He therefore requires that the unclean olives be left in their unprocessed form.
This same position is taken by Meir.

When we turn to the question of grapes in the status of heave-
offering, matters are only slightly more complicated. We would

expect that clean grapes in the status of heave-offering should be
made into wine, just as M. states. Only Rabbi's Eliezer, paralleled
by Meir, disagrees with this. I assume that these authorities
hold that grapes are normally consumed, or are more valuable, in
their unprocessed form (HY), contrary to what M. holds. As regards unclean grapes, all of the versions have Eliezer remain consistent with his view concerning unclean olives. The unclean
grapes are not to be processed, for obvious reasons. Meir agrees.
Regarding Joshua, only Judah has him remain consistent with his
position on unclean olives. He says that the unclean grapes should
be processed into wine, even though the priest will not be able to
drink that wine. As before, his view is that proper processing of
the heave-offering is central. For this case, Jacob and Rabbi
have Joshua revert to the position of Eliezer, that the grapes
should not be processed. It is likely that the reason for this
shift is that the unclean wine will go completely to waste. In
this way it is unlike unclean oil in the status of heave-offering,
which may be used to kindle the priest's lamp (M. 11:10). Jacob
and Rabbi thus attribute to Joshua the basic position of Eliezer,
that the rule for processing is not invoked in a case in which, as
a result, the priest will not be able to use the heave-offering.
In doing so, however, they destroy the consistency of Joshua's
position, indicated in Judah's version of matters.

11:4-5

A. The stems of [fresh] figs, dried figs, pods
(*klysym*)[14] and carobs in the status of heave-offering are
forbidden [for consumption] by non-priests.

M. 11:4 (see T. 5:6P-R)

B. [As regards] the pits (*gr^{c}yny*) of produce in the
status of heave-offering--

C. when he [i.e., the priest] keeps them (*mknsn*), they
are forbidden [for consumption by non-priests].

D. But if he throws them out, they are permitted.

E. And so [in the case of] the bones of Holy Things
(*qdšym*) [i.e., animal offerings]--

F. when he keeps them, they are forbidden [to non-
priests].

G. But if he throws them out, they are permitted.

H. Coarse bran (Jastrow, p. 751, for *mwrsn*) [from grain
in the status of heave-offering] is permitted [for consumption
by non-priests].

I.   Fine bran (*swbyn*; Jastrow, p. 360: bran-flour) from
fresh [wheat in the status of heave-offering] is forbidden
[to non-priests].

J.   But [fine bran] from old [wheat in the status of
heave-offering] is permitted.

K.   (Follow O^2, Pa, L, S and K which lack: And) [The
priest] may treat heave-offering just as he treats unconsecrated produce [i.e., he may throw out the parts he does not
normally eat].

L.   One who prepares fine flour (*mslt*) [from wheat in
the status of heave-offering], deriving a *qab* or two from
each *se'ah* [of wheat], may not destroy the residue [which is
edible].

M.   Rather, he places it in a concealed place.

M. 11:5

The several rules of the two pericopae express a single thesis.
This is that only food can have the status of heave-offering; what
is not food cannot. This being the case, those parts of produce
in the status of heave-offering which normally are not eaten are
not deemed consecrated as a priestly gift.[15] They need not be
consumed by the priest and, in fact, are permitted for consumption
by a non-priest who wishes to eat them. In light of this fact,
the problem of the two pericopae is to establish criteria for
determining what is food, such that if it is heave-offering, it
must be eaten by a priest. Two distinct notions are presented.
A, H-J and L-M use an objective standard of what is edible and
what is not. B-C+D, its gloss at E-F+G, and K, to the contrary,
offer cases in which the priest's own attitude towards the heave-
offering is determinative. The claim is that what he deems to be
food is to be treated as such and therefore retains the status of
heave-offering (C). What he does not consider food, indicated by
the fact that he throws it out, is deemed inedible, and so not to
have the status of heave-offering (D). Since A-J is formally unitary[16] we need not expect that these two distinct notions necessarily are contradictory. As we shall see, rather, they simply
are applied in specific cases involving different types of produce.
Each type has its own particular characteristics and, accordingly,
its own rule.

The stems of produce in the status of heave-offering (A) are
forbidden to non-priests because a small portion of food remains
attached to them when the stem is broken off of the piece of

produce (Maimonides, TYY). This same criterion, that a small
quantity of food remains with the waste, is operative at H+I-J and
M-N. Bran, H-J, is the husk of wheat, left over in the production
of flour. Large kernels of bran ("coarse bran," H) will have been
completely emptied of flour-meal, and so are permitted to non-
priests. This is not always the case for fine bran, in which
small amounts of edible flour may adhere, making the husks available for use as food. In the case of fine bran we therefore distinguish between fresh, moist wheat, in the husks of which flour-
meal is likely to have remained, and drier wheat, the husks of
which will easily have emptied of all edible produce. The former
contains food and is forbidden to non-priests; the latter is permitted.

The consideration at L-M is the same. In processing flour of
high quality, much edible grain is left as waste. The priest need
not eat this grain, for it is waste. Since it actually is edible,
however, it may not be consumed by non-priests. It must, therefore, be hidden away (N).

This brings us to B-D+E-G and the question of why the items
mentioned there are subject to a different rule from that which
governs other types of food. In answer to this question it is
notable, first, that pits, B, and bones, E, have in common a
basic characteristic. Whereas they are not themselves edible,
they may be used in the preparation of food, e.g., in making a
broth or flavoring a stew. The status of these things thus is
ambiguous, in that it is unclear whether or not they are to be
deemed foods. It is this problem which interests M. and which
generates the notion that the status of these things is determined
in light of the attitude of the priest. If his actions indicate
that he views the bones or pits as food, they are treated as such.
It follows that they retain their consecrated status.

A.   [*Produce in the status of*] heave-offering *is permitted (ntnh) for (1) eating, (2) drinking and (3) anointing--*
      B.   *(1) to eat that which customarily (drkw) is eaten,
(2) to drink that which customarily is drunk and (3) to anoint
with that which customarily is used for anointing* [=M. Sheb.
8:1, M. M.S. 2:1].

(1) C.   *To eat that which customarily is eaten.* How so?
      D.   They do not obligate him [i.e., the priest] to eat
the peel (*qnybh*) of a vegetable [in the status of heave-
offering], bread [in the status of heave-offering] which has

become mouldy, nor a dish [in the status of heave-offering]
the appearance of which has changed.

E. R. Hanania the Chief of the Priests says, "Heave-
offering which has become unfit for use as food for humans,
but which a dog can eat, imparts uncleanness as a food, yet
(*w*) they burn it in its place [i.e., immediately, and need
not wait for the time of removal; Lieberman, TK, I, p. 458]."

(2) F. *To drink that which customarily is drunk.* How so?

G. They do (Lieberman supplies with E and ed. princ.:
not) obligate him [i.e., the priest] to drink a sauce of oil
and garum (Jastrow, p. 84, for *'nygrwn*) or of vinegar and
garum (Jastrow, p. 64, for *'ksygrwn*), or to drink wine along
with its lees.

> T. 9:10 (A-D, F-G: T. Sheb. 6:1-3;
> E: see b. Pes. 15b, 45b)

H. [A priest] who has a toothache may not rinse them
[i.e., his teeth] in vinegar [in the status of heave-offering, as a cure (b. Shab. 111a)] and [then] spit it out.

I. But he may rinse and swallow.

J. He may dunk [his bread, in any of the liquids mentioned at G, H] and need not scruple [that he has improperly
used a liquid in the status of heave-offering].

> T. 9:11 (T. Sheb. 6:3; see M. Shab.
> 14:4; T. Shab. 12:9, b. Bes. 18b)

K. [A priest] who has a sore throat (Lieberman supplies
hhwšš with E and ed. princ.) may not lubricate it (Lieberman
supplies *y^c r^c nw* with E and ed. princ.) [by gargling] with
oil [in the status of heave-offering].

L. But he may add much [oil] to a sauce of oil and garum
(Lieberman supplies *'nygrwn* with E and ed. princ.) and swallow.

> T. 9:12 (T. Sheb. 6:3, T. Shab.
> 12:10, b. Ber. 36a)

(3) M. *To anoint with that which customarily is used for
anointing.* How so?

N. A person [i.e., a priest] may put oil [in the status
of heave-offering] on his wound,

O. so long as he does not take [the oil] with a rag or
cloth patch [which will absorb some of the oil] in order to
place it on his wound.

> T. 9:13 (T. Sheb. 6:4, T. Shab.
> 9:12)

P.   [A priest] who had a head ache or any [priest] on
whose head there appeared (^{c}lw) scabs may anoint with oil [in
the status of heave-offering], but may not anoint with wine
or vinegar [in that status].

Q.   For [as regards] oil, its normal use is for anointing.

R.   But [as regards] wine and vinegar, their normal use
is not for anointing.

T. 9:14 (T. Sheb. 9:4, T. Shab.
9:11; Q-R: T. Ter. 9:7L-M)

S.   [As regards] wine in the status of heave-offering--
(1) they may not make it into an unguent (*'lntyt*),
and (2) they may not make it into perfumed wine,

T.   and (3) [the priest] may not place in his hand that
which remains in the cup [after he drinks the wine],

U.   (Delete with E and ed. princ.: and he may not take
in his hand that which remains [in the cup])

V.   and (4) a woman may not rinse her son in it.

W.   Rabban Simeon b. Gamaliel says, "[As regards] wine
in the status of heave-offering which became unclean [and so
may not be drunk], or which was left uncovered [and may not
be drunk, lest a snake deposited in it venom (M. 8:4)]--
"[the priest] may pour it out a bit at a time (*sŭpq
wŝwnh*) [in order to enjoy the smell],

X.   "and he need not scruple [that heave-offering is
being misused]."

T. 9:15 (S: see T. Ter. 9:7L-M;
V: see T. Shab. 12(13):13; W:
see b. Pes. 20b, b. B.Q. 116a)

T.'s long construction is formally autonomous of M., placed
here because, at A-B, it states the principle which is operative
at M. 11:1-5. This is that the priest uses produce in the status
of heave-offering in the manner which is normal for produce of its
type. The three part exposition which follows elucidates in turn
each of the three elements of A-B, as indicated in the translation.
The considerations dealt with are (1) that the priest need not eat
food which, were it in an unconsecrated state, would be discarded
(C-E) or used, for example, as a dip (F-G); and (2) that the priest
must actually consume heave-offering. He may not use it for
gargling and then spit it out (H-K), or use it in some other way
which causes some of consecrated produce to go to waste (M-O).
P-X repeats what we already know from T. 9:7.[17]

A. [As regards] the pits of (1) olives, (2) dates and
(3) carobs [in the status of heave-offering]--
    all of these (E lacks: *kwlm*), even though [the priest]
does not keep them [for his own use], are forbidden [for consumption by non-priests].
B. But [regarding] all other pits [from produce in the
status of heave-offering]--
    C. [*if the priest*] *keeps them, they are forbidden,*
    D. [*and if he*] *does not keep them, they are permitted*
[= M. 11:5B-D, with minor variations].

                    T. 10:1 (see T. Uq. 2:10)

T.'s point is clear on the basis of what we already have seen
in M. 11:5. The pits of olives, dates and carobs differ from those
of other produce in that they normally are used as a food, e.g.,
are pressed for their juices.[18] If they come from produce which
is in the status of heave-offering, they therefore also have that
status. This is not the case for pits of other produce (B-D).
These generally are not used as foods.

A. [As regards] the husks (*qlpy*) of fava-beans or
sesame-seeds [in the status of heave-offering]--
    B. [if] they contain food, they are forbidden [to non-
priests].
    C. [If] they do not contain food, they are permitted.
    D. [As regards] peels (*qlpy*) of musk-melons [in the
status of heave-offering]--
    E. even though they do not contain food [from the musk-
melon], they are forbidden [since they may themselves be
eaten (MB, HY)].
    F. The peel of a citron ('*trwg*) [in the status of heave-
offering] is forbidden.
    G. The seeds of a citron [in the status of heave-
offering] are permitted.
    H. The insides (E lacks: *m^ʿy*) of a citron [in the
status of heave-offering] are forbidden,
    I. since those with cravings (*qy'wt*; see Lieberman, TK,
I, p. 464-5, and Jastrow, p. 1321, s.v. *qhh*) eat them.
    J. [As regards] the rind (*qlpy*) of a watermelon and the
insides [i.e., where the seeds are] of a watermelon and [other]
refuse (*qnwbt*) of vegetables in the status of heave-offering--
    K. R. Dosa' permits to non-priests.
    L. But sages prohibit.

M.   R. Jacob says in his [i.e., Dosa's] name, "[If these
are from] early fruits (*hbkrwt*) or late fruits (*syypwt*), they
are forbidden, [but if they are from] the middle of the summer, they are permitted."

N.   The same restrictions which apply to the eating of
[refuse of produce in the status of] heave-offering apply to
untithed produce, (follow E in deleting: $m^c\acute{s}r$ *tbl*), first
tithe from which heave-offering [of the tithe] has not been
separated and second tithe or produce dedicated [to the
Temple] which have not been redeemed.

T. 10:2 (D-E: see T. Uq. 2:10)

O.   Hollow kernels of wheat (*nyswlwt*)[19] and decayed
grain (*rqbwnyt*) in the status of heave-offering are forbidden
[to non-priests, for they still may contain food].

P.   [If] they turned to dust (so MB and HY for: $h^c lw$
'*bq*)[20] they are permitted [for they no longer are food].

T. 10:3

T. further exemplifies M.'s principle that only that which is
edible has the status of heave-offering and must be eaten by a
priest. Waste from produce in the status of heave-offering which
normally is not eaten therefore is deemed unconsecrated and may be
consumed by non-priests.[21] N states that this same principle
applies to produce in the status of other sanctified agricultural
offerings and to untithed produce.

A.   *Fine bran from fresh* [*wheat in the status of heave-
offering*] *is forbidden* [*to non-priests*].

B.   *But* [*fine bran*] *from old* [*wheat in the status of
heave-offering*] *is permitted* [= M. 11:5I-J].

C.   For how long ($^c d$ *mty*) is [fine bran from] fresh
[wheat in the status of heave-offering] forbidden?

D.   For as long as it is normal for people to thresh
(*lhbwt*) at the threshing floors.

E.   R. 'Aha says, "For thirty days [from the harvest]."

F.   [As regards] fenugreek in the status of heave-offering
with which a woman of priestly caste shampooed her hair (*r'*$\check{s}h$)--

G.   an Israelite-woman is not permitted to shampoo after
her [with the same fenugreek].

H.   But she [is permitted afterwards to] rub her hair
against the [priestly woman's] hair.

T. 10:4 (A-F: y. Ter. 11:4; G-I:

T. M.S. 2:1)

A-E's supplement to M. 11:5I-J is clear as stated. F-H is
separate, offering a problem autonomous of M. 11:4-5, yet illustrating the same principle. Fenugreek normally is used as a
shampoo and therefore may be used for this purpose, even if it has
the status of heave-offering. As long as the fenugreek remains
useful as a shampoo, it has the status of heave-offering and may
not be enjoyed by the Israelite-woman (G). Once the fenugreek
has been rinsed out of the priestly woman's hair, however, no
prohibition applies. The law of H follows.

> A.   [As regards] pulse in the status of heave-offering--
> they do not make it into meal.
>
> B.   R. Simeon permits in the case of vetches [a type of
> pulse].

T. 10:5

At issue is the normal manner of preparation of legumes. A
states that pulse in the status of heave-offering may not be
ground, for this is not how such beans normally are eaten.[22]
Simeon, B, exempts vetches from A's rule.

11:6-8

> A.   [As to] a storage bin from which one emptied wheat
> in the status of heave-offering--
>
> B.   they do not obligate him to sit and pick up one at a
> time each kernel of wheat [which remains on the floor of the
> bin].
>
> C.   Rather, he may sweep [the bin] in his normal fashion,
> and [then] may put unconsecrated [wheat in the bin].

M. 11:6

> D.   And so [in the case of] a jug of oil [in the status
> of heave-offering] which was spilled--
>
> E.   they do not obligate him to sit and scoop [it] up
> with his hand (*mtph*; Jastrow, p. 546).
>
> F.   Rather, he treats it as he treats unconsecrated [oil
> which spills; he may wipe it up with a rag, even though the
> rag will absorb some of the consecrated oil].

M. 11:7

> G.   One who pours [wine or oil in the status of heave-
> offering] from one jar to another and [allows] three [last]
> drops to drip [from the jar he is emptying] may [then] put
> unconsecrated [wine or oil] in that [jar, without further
> wiping it out].

H. If [after three drops had fallen] he placed [the jar]
on its side and [more oil or wine] drained [from it]--
    lo, this [wine or oil] is in the status of heave-offering.
I. And what quantity of heave-offering of the tithe
[separated] from produce about which there is a doubt whether
or not it previously was tithed (*dm'y*) need one take to the
priest?
J. One eighth of an eighth *log* [= 1/64 *log*; less than
this quantity is deemed insignificant and need not be given
to the priest].

M. 11:8 (G-H: see M. B.B. 5:8)

An individual may empty a vessel filled with heave-offering
in the same way that he customarily empties a container of unconsecrated produce (A-C). He need not scruple about the small quantity of consecrated offering which remains in the bottom of the
jar and goes to waste when other food is put in it. In the same
way, D-F, one may clean up spilled heave-offering with a rag,
which will absorb and thereby waste some of the consecrated oil.
In each of these cases the small quantity of heave-offering which
goest to waste may be ignored, just as it would be were it unconsecrated food. As at M. 11:3-5 the priest's obligation to eat
produce in the status of heave-offering is determined by whether
or not people normally consider that produce worthy as food. H's
qualification is obvious. By collecting what otherwise would not
be deemed significant as food, the individual indicates that he
desires the produce. As at M. 11:5B-C, this act is determinative
and, if it is in the status of heave-offering, the produce must be
given to a priest.[23]

I-J is separate from the foregoing, referring to heave-offering of the tithe and not to heave-offering. It has been redacted
here because, like A-H, its concern is the householder's obligation
to give to a priest small quantities of consecrated food. Heave-
offering of the tithe separated from the produce about which there
is a doubt whether or not it previously was tithed may not have a
consecrated status. This is because the produce from which it was
separated may already once have been tithed. In such a case of
doubt, insignificant quantities of heave-offering may be destroyed
(T. 10:6J). They need not be given to a priest.[24]

A. *What quantity of heave-offering of the tithe*
[separated] from produce about which there is a doubt whether
or not it previously was tithed need one take to the priest?

One eighth of an eighth log [= M. 11:8I-J].

B. In what case does this apply?

C. [It applies] in the case of produce about which there is a doubt whether or not it previously was tithed.

D. But [as regards] produce which certainly is liable [to the separation of tithes] (*wdyy*), [in the case of] (read with E and ed. princ.:) any quantity [of heave-offering of the tithe, however small, it is forbidden [to destroy the offering; rather, it must be given to the priest].

E. To what case does this [A] apply?

F. [It applies] in the case of clean produce.

G. But in the case of unclean produce, no matter how much [heave-offering of the tithe is separated], it need not be given to the priest.

H. And so you rule (*'wmr*) in [the case of] the heave-offering of the tithe which is in all other produce [i.e., except wine and oil]--

I. if it is of this quantity [i.e., 1/64 *log*] you must give it to the priest.

J. But if it is not of this quantity, one throws it in the fire and burns it.

T. 10:6

T.'s qualification of M. 11:8I-J is in three distinct parts, B-D, E-G and H-J. Each of these clarifies M. by making explicit what previously was hardly subject to doubt.

B-D states that M. 11:8I-J's rule applies only to heave-offering of the tithe separated from produce which may already have been tithed. This is exactly what M. has said. If the heave-offering of the tithe is from produce which certainly never before was tithed, even if it is of insignificant quantity, it must be given to a priest. This is in accordance with the principle of M. 11:8H, that small quantities of consecrated produce which have been collected retain the status of a priestly gift.

F-G is standard. The householder need not give the priest doubtful heave-offering which the priest in all events may not eat, e.g., because it is unclean. This rule is applied no matter how large the quantity of such heave-offering.

H-J, finally, is perplexing. It claims that M. 11:8I-J refers only to some particular kind of produce (e.g., wine and oil, as I have interpolated following Lieberman). M. of course does not know this to be the case. Other than this shift, which I cannot explain, I-J simply repeats M.'s rule.

11:9

A.   [As regards] vetches in the status of heave-offering—

B.   [priests] may feed them to [their] cattle, animals
or fowl.

C.   An Israelite who hired a cow from a priest may feed
it vetches in the status of heave-offering.

D.   But a priest who hired a cow from an Israelite,

E.   even though he is responsible for feeding it
(*mzwnwtyw ᶜlyw*),

F.   may not feed it vetches in the status of heave-
offering.

G.   An Israelite who tended the cow of a priest in return for a share in the value of the animal may not feed it
vetches in the status of heave-offering.

H.   But a priest who tended the cow of an Israelite in
return for a share in its value may feed it vetches in the
status of heave-offering.

M. 11:9

Vetches are a food of an ambiguous type. Since they may be
eaten by humans, they are liable to the separation of heave-offering and tithes. More commonly, however, they are not eaten by
people, but are used as fodder for cattle. In light of this
customary usage, even if vetches have the status of heave-offering,
they may be fed to the priest's animals (A-B).[25] The animals, like
the priest's wife and children, are considered part of the priestly
household.[26] This basic notion, stated at A-B, is the subject of
the little essay at C+D-F and G+H. Each of these cases addresses
the question of the conditions under which animals are deemed to
be under priestly jurisdiction, such that they may eat heave-
offering. C-F states explicitly that the criterion is priestly
ownership. A priest, therefore, may not feed heave-offering to an
Israelite-owned cow, even if he has hired that cow and is responsible for feeding it.[27] An Israelite, however, may feed heave-offering to a priest's animal, just as he would give it to the priest
himself. G-H complicates matters by introducing a case of joint
ownership. One person owns the animal, while another cares for it
in exchange for a share of the profit the mature animal will bring.
In such a case an Israelite may not feed heave-offering to a cow
owned by a priest. The Israelite himself ultimately will profit
from that food, in the form of his share of the increased value of
the animal. Under such terms, however, a priest may feed

heave-offering to an Israelite-owned animal. This is comparable
to a case in which he feeds it to a creature of which he is part
owner.

    A. [As regards] the cow of an Israelite that bore a
first-born [which belongs to the priest, Ex. 13:12]--

    B. [the Israelite] may feed it (follow Lieberman in
reading *m'kylw* for *m'kylh*) vetches in the status of heave-
offering [if these are his to give, e.g., if he inherited
them from his mother's father who was a priest; Lieberman].

    C. Rabban Simeon b. Gamaliel says, "Not only is this
the case (*wl* ^{c}*wd*). Rather, he may [even] take for it vetches
[in the status of heave-offering which he separated from his
own produce]."

    D. A man [i.e., a priest] may place vetches in the
status of heave-offering in his dove-cote and need not scruple
[see M. 11:9B].

T. 10:7

The issue is whether or not a non-priest may feed to an
animal which belongs to a priest heave-offering which he has separated from his own produce but which never has been given to a
priest. One might argue that this heave-offering belongs to the
priestly clan and therefore is not the non-priest's possession to
give away, even to the priest's animal. This is the position of
A-B. It holds that the householder may feed an animal belonging
to a priest only heave-offering which is his rightful property.
Simeon b. Gamaliel disagrees. He states that the non-priest may
take vetches which he has separated from his own produce and give
them to the priest's animal. It appears that Simeon's concern
simply is that the consecrated produce is properly consumed.
Whether or not it at any time is placed in the hands of a priest
is irrelevant.

    D is separate, yet like A-C clarifies M. 11:8. The priest
may feed his doves vetches in the status of heave-offering, even
though he does not benefit from work they perform or from using
them as food. Like his other animals, they are deemed part of the
priestly household.

    A. A priest's slave who fled, or a priest's wife who
rebelled [against him, and ran away], lo, these may eat
heave-offering [under the assumption that the priest still is
alive].

B.   A man guilty of manslaughter should not go outside
of the city of [his] refuge, in the assumption that the high
priest still is alive.

T. 10:8 (T. Yeb. 9:2, T. Git. 2:12)

The same point is made twice. We maintain the prevailing
status of the person who was left behind. In both cases we thus
assume that the priest still is alive, as B states explicitly.

11:10

A.   They kindle [unclean] oil [in the status of heave-
offering] which is fit for burning in (1) synagogues (*bty
knsywt*), (2) houses of study (*bty mdršwt*), (3) dark alleyways
and (4) for sick people,

B.   in the presence of a priest (*bršwt khn*).

C.   [As regards] the daughter of an Israelite who married a priest but is accustomed to visit (supply *lbw'* with
sixteen MSS. and versions; it is lacking in standard printed
editions) her father--

D.   her father may kindle [oil in the status of heave-
offering] in her presence.

E.   "They kindle [oil in the status of heave-offering]
in a house in which there is a wedding feast, but not in a
house of mourning"--the words of R. Judah.

F.   R. Yose says, "[They do so] in a house of mourning,
but not at a wedding feast."

G.   R. Meir prohibits in either case.

H.   R. Simeon permits in either case.

M. 11:10

Unclean oil in the status of heave-offering may not be eaten
by the priest. In line with the laws of M. 11:2, 3 and 9, the oil
may, therefore, be used for one of its other customary purposes,
kindling in lamps.[28] With this as its underlying assumption, the
problem of 11:10 is to determine in what places the oil may be
burned. This is a problem because not only the priest, but also
non-priests who happen to be present, will enjoy the light. Since
non-priests are restricted from benefitting from consecrated
priestly gifts, we should expect that heave-offering-oil should not
be kindled where such individuals are present. A-B and C-D make
the single point that this is not the case. So long as the oil is
used for its designated purpose, the benefit of the priest, it is
irrelevant that non-priests also profit. That is, we take into
account only the oil's intended purpose. Consequences which are

extraneous to that purpose may be ignored. As long as a priest is
present, oil in the status of heave-offering may be kindled either
in public (A),[29] or private (C) places.[30]

E-H carries forward the question of where oil in the status
of heave-offering may be burned. The four-party dispute eludes
interpretation, since its own language offers no grounds for
determining why the rule for a wedding feast should differ from
that governing a house of mourning. A priest may be present in
either place, and therefore it would seem that both locations
should fall under the rule of A-B+C-D.[31]

A. [As regards] a priest's cattle which were standing
[in a barn] next to an Israelite's cattle,

B. and so the garments of a priest which were being
woven near the garments of an Israelite--

C. lo, this one [i.e., the Israelite] may kindle on
their account oil [in the status of heave-offering] which is
fit for burning.

D. [As regards] an Israelite who was sitting in the
shop of a priest--

E. lo, this [priest] may fill for him a lamp with oil
[in the status of heave-offering] which is fit for burning,

F. [and the Israelite] may go up to the attic, or down
to the cellar, in order to do what is needful to the priest,
but not what is needful to the Israelite.

G. If [the Israelite] was a partner in the [ownership
of] the store with him [i.e., the priest], this is permitted
[i.e., the Israelite may use the heave-offering for his own
needs, since this ultimately benefits the priest].

H. And so [in the case of] a priest who was dining (*msb*)
in the home of an Israelite--

I. lo, this [priest] may kindle for him a lamp [filled]
with oil [in the status of heave-offering] which is fit for
burning.

J. Even though the priest [later] got up and left, they
do not obligate him to put out the lamp, until it goes out by
itself.

K. [As regards] an Israelite who entered the home of a
priest to light his [i.e., the Israelite's] lamp and wished
to leave [immediately thereafter]--

[the priest] dips a wick in oil [in the status of heave-
offering] which is fit for burning for him.

L. (E lacks L-M). And so [in the case of] the daughter
of an Israelite who entered [to visit] the daughter of a
priest and wished to leave.

M. [The priest's daughter] dips a wick in oil [in the
status of heave-offering] which is fit for burning for her.

N. [As regards] the daughter of a priest who had in her
hand a lamp filled with oil [in the status of heave-offering]
which was fit for burning, on the eve of the sabbath at the
time of sunset--

lo, this one may add any [small] amount of unconsecrated
oil to the lamp, and may kindle it [for the sabbath].

T. 10:9 (A-N: y. Ter. 11:7; A-G:
y. Shab. 2:1; L-M: y. Sheb. 42;
N: y. Shab. 2:1)

T.'s several rules all repeat the point made by M. 11:10. As
long as the oil in the status of heave-offering is used to the
benefit of the priest, it is irrelevant that non-priests likewise
enjoy the light. What T. adds is that this principle applies even
if the priest benefits from the oil in a most tangential way, e.g.,
in cases in which he is not present (A-C). He may even use the
oil to light the lamp of a passer-by, thereby avoiding the use of
unconsecrated oil which he would have had to purchase (K-M). The
problem at N is that sanctified oil, like any holy thing, normally
is not burned on the sabbath (y. Shab. 2:2, cited by Lieberman, TK,
I, p. 471). To indicate that she does not intend to transgress
this prohibition, but simply to light the lamp required for the
sabbath, the priestly woman adds some unconsecrated oil to the
heave-offering (Lieberman, *ibid.*).

A. A priest may anoint himself with oil in the status
of heave-offering and [afterwards] bring an Israelite member
of his household and roll [the Israelite] around on his [i.e.,
the priest's] back [so that the Israelite is anointed with
the oil].

B. A priest may anoint himself with oil in the status
of heave-offering and enter a bath house,

C. (supply with E: and) a non-priest need not refrain
from rubbing against him (read with E: *mšhw*; V reads:
mšhynw), even though he is anointed by the [oil on the
priest's body].

D.   A priest may not put oil in the status of heave-
offering on a marble table in order to roll on it [and anoint
himself].

E.   Rabban Simeon b. Gamaliel permits.

T. 10:10 (D-E: T. Sheb. 6:9)

T. applies to cases in which the consecrated oil is used as
an ointment M.'s theory on the use of oil in the status of heave-
offering for kindling. This theory is revealed in the contrast between the cases at A+B-C and that at D+E. As long as the oil first
serves its purpose upon the body of the priest, it may be used to
the benefit of non-priests (A-C). Any oil which does not serve
the purpose of the priest, however, is forbidden to non-priests.
For this reason the priest may not put consecrated oil on a marble
table, D. Any oil which is not absorbed by his body will not have
benefitted the priest, yet will be left for non-priests. Simeon b.
Gamaliel, E, does not mind this. His theory is that the consecrated oil left on the table in all events has no further purpose
to the priest, who cannot collect it and use it again. This is
not a rejection of the principle of the pericope, but a qualification of its application.

A.   [As to] oil in the status of heave-offering--

B.   they do not anoint with it with unclean hands.

C.   [But if] it fell on his [i.e., the priest's] skin,
he may rub it in, even with unclean hands (E adds: and need
not scruple).

D.   [As regards] oil in the status of heave-offering--

E.   they do not glaze (ḥsm) an oven or stove with it.

F.   And they do not soften (lit.: anoint) shoes or
sandals with it.

G.   [A priest] may not anoint his foot [with oil in the
status of heave-offering] while (w) it is in a shoe.

H.   He may not anoint his foot while it is in a sandal.

I.   But he may anoint his foot and [then] put on a shoe,

J.   [or] anoint his foot and [then] put on a sandal.

K.   A priest may anoint himself with oil in the status
of heave-offering and [then] roll around on a leather spread
and need not scruple.

T. 10:11 (D-K: T. Sheb. 6:11; F-K:
T. Shab. 3(4):16)

The priest may use oil in the status of heave-offering only

to anoint his own body, a customary use for oil (D-H; cf., T. 9:7).
As at M. 11:10 and T. 10:11, the point here is that once the oil
has served this purpose, it no longer need be treated as a consecrated priestly gift. The priest may thereafter do with it what
previously had been forbidden, i.e., make it unclean (C), or use
it to soften leather (G-K). Since D-E does not make this point,
it must be seen as separate, interpolated because of the con-
guence to A-B of its topic and language. I assume that oil in the
status of heave-offering may not be used for glazing because, unlike anointing, this is not an everyday use of oil.[32]

I.   A. [As regards] the lees of wine in the status of heave-
offering--

B. the first and second times [the priest strains water
through them, the resultant liquid] is forbidden [to non-
priests].[33]

C. But the third time, it is permitted.

D. R. Meir says, "The third time [the liquid is for-
bidden] if [the wine lees] imparted to it flavor."

II. E. [If the lees are in the status of] second tithe--[34]

F. the first time [that someone strains water through
them, the resultant liquid is] forbidden [i.e., has the status
of second tithe].

G. But the second time, [the resultant liquid] is permitted [i.e., unconsecrated].

H. R. Meir says, "The second time, [the liquid is for-
bidden] if [the wine lees] imparted to it flavor."

III. I. And as regards [lees from wine which was] dedicated
[to the Temple]--

J. the first, second and third times [that water is
strained through them, the resultant liquid] is forbidden
[i.e., dedicated to the Temple].

K. But the fourth time, it is permitted [i.e., uncon-
secrated].

L. R. Meir says, "The fourth time, [the liquid is for-
bidden] if [the lees] imparted to it flavor."

                    T. 10:12 (b. B.B. 97a)

M. Lees which derive from the wine of gentiles, which
dried up, [still] are forbidden [to Israelites] for benefit.

N. [As regards] the chamber pot of a *zab* or a *zabah*--

O. the [water of the] first and second [washings of the
pot] conveys uncleanness.

P.   But the [water of the] third [rinsing] is clean.

Q.   Under what circumstances?

R.   When one put water in it [to rinse it].

S.   But when one did not put water into it [but rinsed it with clean urine]--

T.   even up to the tenth [rinsing]--

U.   it conveys uncleanness.

V.   R. Eliezer b. Jacob says, "The third, even though he did not put water into it, is clean."

> T. 10:13 (T. Toh. 5:3; see b. A.Z.
> 34a)

W.   They purchase and borrow urine from any source, and they do not take account of the possibility that it derives from menstruating women,

X.   for the daughters of Israel are not suspected of collecting their urine when they are menstruating.

> T. 10:14[35] (T. Toh. 5:3)

The pericopae explore an ambiguity arising from the law of M. 10:11. The problem is how we determine when produce in the status of heave-offering has served its intended purpose, such that it no longer has the consecrated status of a priestly gift (A-D). The difficulty in interpretation is to discern the theories which underlie the distinct approaches of A-C and Meir, D. In light of the redactional setting of the pericope, I assume that A-C takes into account the number of times which people ordinarily use a batch of lees to prepare a drink. For that same number of times, lees which have the status of heave-offering impart a con- secrated status to the water with which they are mixed. After that number of times, they have fulfilled their usual purpose and so no longer have the status of heave-offering. Meir, on the other hand, applies the criterion of M. Chapter Ten. As long as the lees im- part flavor to the water, they are useful as food and therefore impart to that water the status of heave-offering. E-H are for- mally parallel, carrying out A-D's same exercise for cases of second tithe and produce dedicated to the Temple. The differing number of uses for which the lees impart their own status to the liquid is on the basis of the relative sanctity of the different categories of lees. That which is dedicated to the Temple (i.e., Holy Things) is the most holy, followed by heave-offering (see M. Toh. 2:6) and, finally, second tithe.

Lees from the wine of gentiles, M, fall under the same re- strictions as gentile-wine itself. Since the wine may have been

used for a libation to pagan gods, Israelites may not drink it.
The same applies to a drink made from the lees.

P-V+W-X is redacted here for reasons of its form and underlying theory. Topically, however, it does not belong, its primary
context being in T. Toh. Urine of a *zab* or *zabah* (i.e., an individual who has had a flux and is unclean) or a menstruant, is unclean, like the person from whom it derives. As at A-L, the consideration here is the number of times people ordinarily wash a
bed-pan before they consider it clean. Water from washings prior
to this number is deemed unclean, like the pot itself. Once the
pot is considered clean, water with which it is rinsed likewise is
clean.

A.   They may not mix together grain and pulse in the
status of heave-offering.

B.   But they may mix together sesame-seeds[36] and fava-
beans (*'ypylym*) or fava-beans and lentils,

C.   or any kinds [of produce] which customarily are
sifted (read with V: *lykbr*; E, ed. princ. read: *lykbd*)
[before use, for the different kinds thus will be sifted
apart].

D.   Ever since Judaea was destroyed (Hastily may it be
rebuilt!), they began to mix together different types of
grain, and different types of pulse,

E.   but not grain with pulse, nor pulse with grain.

T. 10:15

F.   [As regards] a priest to whom they gave heave-offering [of produce of one kind] and he found in it produce of a
different kind (*dbrym 'hrym*)--

G.   lo, this [i.e., the other produce] is forbidden
[i.e., assumed to be heave-offering],

H.   since [householders] throw all [of the heave-offering
they separate from various kinds of produce] into the storage
room for heave-offering (*byt hdm^a*).

T. 10:16

T. carries forward M.'s principle that heave-offering is to
be prepared only in ways in which produce of its type normally is
cooked and eaten. D-E describes the way in which people usually
prepare grain and pulse. It therefore provides the key to the
interpretation of A-C. Since people do not customarily mix together grain and pulse, E, it is forbidden to do so if produce of
these kinds has the status of heave-offering (A).[37]   B-C's point

simply is that such mixtures may be created if the produce ultimately will not be cooked together. This hardly is a major
qualification of A's rule.

F-H is not dependent on A-E for meaning. It has been juxtaposed to that unit because it also deals with mixtures of different kinds of produce in the status of heave-offering. Its point
is clear on the basis of its explanatory gloss, H.

> A. They do not bring heave-offering from the threshing
> floor to the city [to be distributed to priests], nor from the
> wilderness to a settlement.
>
> B. However, in a case in which a wild or domesticated
> animal would eat [the heave-offering were it left at the
> threshing floor for a priest to pick up], they ordained that
> the householder should bring it [to the city or settlement],
>
> C. and receive from the priest payment [for his work],
>
> D. to prevent (*mpny*) desecration of the name [of God,
> through the profanation of the heave-offering].
>
> > T. 10:17 (A-B: b. Hul. 134b; A-C:
> > y. Dem. 1:2, see T. M.S. 3:12)
>
> E. There are ten [categories of people] to whom they do
> not distribute [heave-offering] at the threshing floor, and
> these are they:
>
> F. (1) deaf-mutes, (2) imbeciles, and (3) minors,
>
> G. (4) people without sexual traits (*twmtwm*) and (5)
> hermaphrodites,
>
> H. (6) wives [of priests] and (7) slaves [of priests],
>
> I. (8) uncircumcised [priests] and (9) unclean [priests,
> neither of which categories are fit to eat heave-offering],
>
> J. and (10) [priests] who marry women who are not fit
> for them [e.g., divorcees; such priests no longer are ac-
> corded the privileges of the priestly clan, M. Bek. 7:7].
>
> K. But [as regards] all of them, [a householder] may
> give them heave-offering from within [the householder's]
> house,
>
> L. except [in the case of] unclean [priests] and [priests]
> who marry women who are not fit for them.
>
> > T. 10:18 (b. Yeb. 99b)

T.'s final unit is on what individuals are fit to receive
heave-offering and how the offering is distributed to them. While
this topic has been ignored by M., it constitutes a fitting conclusion to the tractate as a whole, paralleling at E-L M. 1:1's

list of individuals who may not separate heave-offering. The point
at A-D is that the expense of transporting heave-offering to the
priest is not incumbent upon the householder. His responsibility
simply is to separate the priestly gift from his produce, thereby
preparing that produce for his table. For this reason, priests
normally receive their due at the threshing floor, where householders separate the heave-offering. Only if the offering is in
danger of being eaten improperly need the householder transport it
to the priest (B-D). The householder does this as a service to
the priest, and therefore the priest must pay him for his labor.

E-J's list is a composite of types of individuals who, for
different reasons, may not be given heave-offering at the threshing floor. The list falls into two major parts, people who are
not fit to eat heave-offering (I-J) and individuals who, while
fit, may not be given the priestly gift in public (F-H). This
latter group consists of individuals who are either intellectually
or physically imperfect (F-G), or who do not themselves have
priestly status (H). Since it would appear improper to give such
people heave-offering, it is forbidden to do so in public. These
people are, however, fit to eat the priestly gift. The householder, therefore, may give it to them in the privacy of his own
home, where appearances are not a consideration (K). The individuals at I-J may not eat heave-offering. They are either per-
manently unfit to serve as priests (e.g., are married to unfit
women, or are uncircumcised), or are temporarily unfit (e.g., are
unclean). A priest who has married an unfit woman no longer has
the right to eat heave-offering, and therefore may not receive it,
even in private. Unclean and uncircumcised priests, on the other
hand, may feed their households with the priestly gift. Still,
they are not given the offering in public. As before, this would
appear a misdeed. An unclean priest, moreover, like the one who
married an unfit woman, is not allowed to receive heave-offering
in private (L). I assume (following b. Yeb. 99b) that the reason
is that he is punished for his lack of care in following the rules
of cleanness.

NOTES TO INTRODUCTION

[1]The other offerings set aside by the Israelite are first
tithe, for the Levite, second tithe, which the householder himself
eats in Jerusalem, poorman's tithe, for the poor, and first fruits,
waved before the altar in Jerusalem. If the householder makes
dough, he further must separate dough-ffering which, like heave-
offering, goes to the priest. The Levite, for his part, takes
from his first tithe an offering for the priest. This is called
heave-offering of the tithe. On the structure and content of the
Order of Agriculture as a whole, see Neusner, *Judaism*, Chapter
Three, part ii, and Chapter Four, part ii. On Mishnah's tithing
system, see Sarason, *Demai*, pp. 1-9, and Sarason, *"Zera*^{c}*im."*

[2]In this way the task of Mishnah Terumot is parallel to that
of the other tractates in the Division of Agriculture which deal
with specific agricultural dues. I refer in particular to Tractate
Pe'ah, on the portion of the unharvested crop which must be left
for the poor, Ma^{c}aser Sheni, on second tithe, Hallah, on dough-
offering, and Bikkurim, on first fruits. Tractate Ma^{c}aserot, for
its part, functions as the introduction to this whole system of
tithes. It does this by indicating exactly what produce is liable
to the separation of tithes, and the point in its ripening or subsequent processing at which it becomes so liable. See the introduction to Jaffee, *Maaserot*.

[3]On this passage, see Eissfeldt, pp. 81-83, Snaith, pp. 266-
67, and Gray, pp. 223-24. The problem of the biblical sources for
Mishnah's system of tithes, and heave-offering in particular, has
been discussed by Sarason, *Demai*, pp. 6-8, and note 8 there, and
in the notes to his *"Zera*^{c}*im."*

[4]Further grounds for Mishnah's identification and description
of this priestly gift is at Neh. 10:37a, which refers to offerings
of "the first of our coarse grain, and our contributions (*trwmtynw*),
the fruit of every tree, the wine and the oil."

[5]It is this concern for the process of sanctification which
in the first place has prompted Mishnah's framers to talk about
heave-offering. This is clear from the fact that the Division of
Agriculture devotes tractates only to those offerings which have
a consecrated status. These are heave-offering, second tithe,
dough-offering and first fruits. There is, on the other hand, no
tractate on first tithe, which is not holy. The inclusion of
Tractate Pe'ah, on poor-taxes, is explained by the fact that the
produce of which it speaks stands completely outside of the system
of tithes. It is not liable to the separation of agricultural
dues. This produce had to be defined if, in its other tractates,
the Division of Agriculture was accurately to detail what produce
is liable and available for payment of the various dues (see,
e.g., M. Ter. 1:5). The whole thus forms a single, indivisible
unit (see Neusner, *Judaism*, Chapter Three, part ii). It appears,
therefore, that a theory of what Mishnah's tithing-tractates were
to discuss preceded and guided all work which actually was done
on these tractates.

[6]This must be qualified. The Israelite's power to designate
as holy applies only to produce which, because it was grown on
God's land is susceptible to sanctification (see Sarason,

"Zera^{c}im"). Note however that even produce grown on the Land of
Israel is not automatically liable to the separation of agricultural offerings. It becomes so liable only in response to certain
desires and intentions on the part of the Israelite householder.
Jaffee, Introduction to *Maaserot*, MS. pp. x-xi, states:

> What is striking...is that the entire mechanism of re-
> strictions and privileges, from the field to home or
> market, is set in motion solely by the intentions of the
> common farmer. Priests cannot claim their dues whenever
> they choose, and God himself plays no active role in
> establishing when the produce must be tithed. Indeed,
> the framers of Maaserot assume a profound passivity on
> the part of God. For them, it is only man who is active
> and whose actions affect the world. God's claims against
> the Land's produce, that is to say, are only reflexes of
> those very claims on the part of Israelite farmers.
> God's interest in his share of the harvest...is first
> provoked by the desire of the farmer for the ripened
> fruit of his labor. His claim to that fruit, further-
> more, becomes binding only when the farmer makes ready
> to claim his own rights to its use, whether in the field
> or at home or market.

Mishnah thus describes the intentions of the common Israelite as
central in all aspects of its system of agricultural dues. This
begins with the circumstances under which produce become liable to
the separation of these dues, and includes the actual separation
and, as we shall see, protection of the offerings.

[7]This is with the provision that the householder does not
violate the taxonomic categories established by God at creation,
for instance, by separating the heave-offering required of a batch
of olives from a batch of grapes. See my discussion of M. 1:4, 8,
9 and, in particular, M. 2:4-6.

[8]The rules for such cases are found at M. 10:1-12.

[9]This is implicit throughout, but is stated quite explicitly
in the position of Judah, M. 10:1H-I, and in Simeon's position in
T.'s correlary material, at T. 8:9b.

[10]In this regard it is possible that Tractate Terumot simply
carries forward and brings to their logical conclusion ideas which
have found their foundation in Scripture. The statement of Moshe
Weinfeld (pp. 214-15, cited by Sarason, *"Zera^{c}im"*) regarding the
Deuteronomic view is pertinent:

> The book of Deuteronomy also contains a less sacral
> conception of the tithes than the other Pentateuchal
> sources. The tithe, which the Priestly document desig-
> nates as 'holy to the Lord' (Lev. 27:30-33), and which
> according to a second tradition accrues to the Levites
> (Num. 18:21-32), remains by deuteronomic legislation
> the property of the original owner (Dt. 14:22-7). Fur-
> thermore, it may be secularized and employed for profane
> purposes on payment of its equivalent monetary value
> (without the addition of the fifth-part required by P
> (cf. Lev. 27:31). This provision seems to be yet another
> expression of the liberation of the cultus from its
> intimate ties to nature. The sanctity of the tithe is
> not conceived as an inherent quality of the grain or

animal, as in the Priestly document (Lev. 27:30-3); for
it is man who consecrates it and may, if he wishes,
secularize it through redemption. In the deuteronomic
view, sanctity is not a taboo that inheres in things
which by nature belong to the divine realm but is rather
a consequence of the religious intentions of the person
who consecrates it.

As is clear, the conception of the sacred described by Weinfeld is
very close to that which is central in Tractate Terumot.

[11]These rules are at M. 9:1-6.

[12]M. makes the same point through cases in which a non-priest
unintentionally eats heave-offering. If that happens, the non-
priest simply sanctifies more produce to replace the heave-offering which he ate. (In this case he also must pay an additional
fifth of the heave-offering's value, as mandated by Lev. 5:16 and
22:14). If, however, the non-priest intentionally eats the priestly gift, he is culpable for destroying the holy thing. He cannot
replace the sanctified produce, and, further, is liable to
extirpation.

[13]The tractate's only attributions to authorities who lived
before A.D. 70 are in three disputes assigned to the Houses of
Hillel and Shammai. As I have argued (in Neusner, *Judaism*,
Appendix I, part iv), only in the case of one of these disputes
are there grounds for holding that the issue actually goes back to
the historical Houses. It therefore is clear that almost all of
the work on Tractate Terumot was done at Yavneh and Ushah.

[14]On the larger statement made by the Order of Agriculture,
see Neusner, *Judaism*, Chapter Four, part ii. I also have used
the introductions to the following commentaries on specific tractates within the order: Sarason, *Demai*, Mandelbaum, *Kilaim*,
Jaffee, *Ma[c]aserot*, Haas, *Ma[c]aser Sheni*, Havivi, *Hallah*.

[15]See Neusner, *Judaism*, Chapter Six, part vi, where he discusses the role of man in Mishnah as a whole. Neusner writes:

So, stated briefly, the question taken up by the Mishnah
is, What can man do? And the answer laid down by the
Mishnah is, Man, through will and deed, is master of
this world, the measure of all things. Since when the
Mishnah thinks of man, it means Israelite, who is the
subject and actor of its system, the statement is clear.
In the aftermath of the two wars, the message of the
Mishnah cannot have proved more pertinent--or poignant
or tragic.

We have seen here clearly that Tractate Terumot corroborates
Neusner's claim.

[16]The original statement of this theory is in Neusner,
Purities, part 21. See in particular pp. 234-46 and 298-302.

[17]This means that in the context of this commentary, no
systematic effort may be made to speak about stages in the development of the law prior to the redaction of the tractate. Such a
picture of the development of the law necessitates a further level
of interpretation. This involves describing the logical unfolding

of the several main principles of the tractate, as these appear in
the mouths of lawyers of different generations. This approach was
developed by J. Neusner and is explicated in "Current Events,"
pp. 410-12. See also the chapters on the "Weaving of the Law" in
his *Purities* (vols. 3, 5, 8, 10, 12, 14, 16-20), vol. 5 of
Appointed Times, vol. 5 of *Women*, vol. 5 of *Damages*, and vol. 6 of
Holy Things.

[18]See Neusner, "Form and Meaning: Mishnah's System and
Mishnah's Language," in J. Neusner, ed., *Method and Meaning in
Ancient Judaism* (Missoula, 1979), pp. 155-81.

[19]MSS. are coded to Latin letters, listed in this volume in
the Abbreviations and Bibliography.

[20]In parentheses below each pericope of Tractate Terumot I
list parallel passages found elsewhere in Mishnah, Tosefta, the
Halakhic Midrashim and in the Talmudim. These are passages to
which I turned for help in interpreting the pericope in question.
An exhaustive list of parallels and other pertinent passages is in
Sacks-Hutner.

[21]In order to facilitate reference, these syntactic units are
designated with the letters of the alphabet.

[22]Neusner calls the statements comprised by these sequences
of syntactic building blocks "cognative units." These are "the
formal result of a single cogent process of cognition, that is,
analysis of a situation and statement of a rule pertaining to it,
observation of a recurrent phenomenon and provision of a general-
ization covering all observations, reflection upon basic rules and
their generation of, or application to, secondary and tertiary
details or situations, in all, again, the product of an act of
thought" (*Purities*, part 21, p. 164; see also "Redaction," p. 10).
It is these cognative units to which I here refer as "pericopae,"
and which constitute the primary foci of my literary analysis.

[23]Neusner, *Purities*, vol. 21, pp. 165-96, presents a full
catalog of Mishnah's forms.

[24]At several points in Tractate Terumot, disparate items have
been brought together at the redactional level, apparently in order
to create lists of five, or a multiple of five, entries. See, for
example, M. 1:1 and M. 1:5. Since in these cases redactional seams
are discernable, they offer the opportunity to examine the meaning
of a particular law outside of its redactional context. While
such cases are informative of the role of the redactional process
in imparting particular meaning to prior laws, they are too
episodic to allow description of sources which might have been used
in the formulation of the tractate.

[25]Neusner, *Purities*, vol. 21, p. 165, defines formulary patterns as "grammatical arrangements of words distinctive to their
subject but in fixed syntactical patterns serviceable for a wide
range of subjects." At pp. 196-246 he catalogs all formulary patterns found in the Division of Purities. See also "Form and Meaning: Mishnah's System and Mishnah's Language," pp. 156-57.

[26]The philological work of modern scholars also has been an
important tool in my examination of the tractate. I make constant
reference to the studies of Feliks, as well as to the brief commentary of Albeck, and to prior translations of the tractate.

These all are important in elucidating the meaning of otherwise obscure words and phrases. Since, however, these studies do not advance the rabbinic treatment of the meaning of the law, I exclude them from the present discussion.

[27]On the following, see Neusner, "Current Events," p. 413. See also, J. Zaiman, "The Traditional Study of the Mishnah," in Neusner, *Modern Study*, pp. 1-12.

[28]See Neusner, "Transcendence," pp. 25-26.

NOTES TO CHAPTER ONE

[1]M. 1:5B-D gives examples of produce from which heave-offering may not be separated, an issue secondary to that of particular methods by which heave-offering is not separated.

[2]Specifically, M. 1:2-3 gloss M. 1:1 by referring to particular individuals listed at M. 1:1. As glosses, these pericopae comprise extensions of M. 1:1, and are not to be viewed as separate entities within the chapter's redactional framework.

[3]Among these pericopae, only M. 1:7 does not evidence the formulaic characteristics I have noted. It lacks the expected statement of the status of heave-offering separated in contradiction to its law. I have explained the redactional placement of this pericope above, p. 12.

[4]Notably, Chapter One's two sub-units both are introduced by formally parallel pericopae (M. 1:1, 6). Each of these lists five individuals who may not separate heave-offering *de jure*.

[5]For other examples of this cliche, see M. R.H. 3:2, M. Git. 2:5, M. B.K. 4:5, *et. al.*, cited in Kasovsky, *Mishnah*, vol. 2, p. 735.

[6]On the variant *ᶜwbd kwkbym* for the term *nkry* found in most MSS., see *JE*, vol. 3, p. 644, Popper, p. 71, and Strack, p. 262, n. 66.

[7]The reading translated here at E-G is supported by Ve, C, K, Sa, T3, the printed edition, the parallel passages and the medieval commentators. The various remaining manuscripts offer three other distinct readings (cited in Sacks-Hutner, p. 101). Two of these do not make good sense. Only the reading of C, M and S remains a viable alternative. It is as follows:

> E. and a gentile who separated heave-offering from [the produce of] an Israelite,

> F. even with permission.

> G. That which these [five individuals] separate is not [valid] heave-offering.

According to this reading, E is introduced with *and* and depends upon A-B for its sense. G then refers back to all of the items of the list. This reading seems to indicate an attempt to harmonize the form of M. 1:1 with that of M. 1:6, and to make M. 1:1 appear less of an artificial construction than it in fact is.

[8]B. Nid. 46b reads: "that which he separates is not [valid] heave-offering." No MS. of the Mishnah supports this reading. Among exegetes, only Rosh argues its veracity.

[9]See M. Makh. 3:8, 6:1, and M. Toh. 8:6. The point of these pericopae is that only the actions of the *heresh* are of consequence; his intention is of no effect.

[10]This exegesis is supported by T. 1:1. Y. Ter. 1:1, followed by all prior exegetes of the tractate, finds Biblical support for the rule of M. 1:1 in Ex. 25:2-3. Its interpretation is as follows: *"Speak to the people of Israel that they make for me an offering; from every man whose heart makes him willing you shall receive an offering for me. And this is the offering which you shall receive from them..."* The reference to "people of Israel" is understood to mean that a gentile may not separate heave-offering. (This is contrary to M. 3:8 and in all events does not explain M. 1:1E-G.) "From every man" excludes the minor from separating heave-offering; "whose heart makes him willing" excludes the deaf-mute and imbecile; "from them" means that each person must separate heave-offering from his own produce.

[11]Sifré Zutta 13:34 (Horovitz, p. 279), b. Kid. 41b, b. Naz. 12b and b. Ned. 72b provide scriptural proof that "a man's agent is like himself." See also Levinthal, p. 25.

[12]Y. 1:1 (= b. Kid. 43b, y. Dem 6:1) derives the rule from Num. 18:22: *"So shall you also present an offering to the Lord."* The word "also" is interpreted to mean that although "you" (=Israelites) may have agents for separating heave-offering, your agents must be like "you," that is, Israelites. See Levinthal, p. 41-2, and b. B.B. 71b, which he cites.

[13]His status thus equals that of the individuals listed at M. 1:6.

[14]Cited by TYT. At y. Meg. 2:4 (cited by Epstein, *Mishnah*, p. 354), R. Hisda states that the inclusion of the *heresh* in M. Meg. 2:4 was caused by *lapsus linguae.*

[15]Both of the Talmudim, and the various commentaries, have noted the contradiction between M. 1:2L and T. 1:2. y. Hag. solves the problem by stating, in reference to M. 1:2L, that "general principles established by Rabbi are not [to be deemed] general principles." This hardly seems to help matters. Isaac de-Treni (*Tosefot RY"D*, b. Git. 71a), alternatively, distinguishes (apparently on the basis of T. Ter. 1:1G-I) between an individual who was a *heresh* (= deaf-mute) from birth, and one who became a *heresh* through disease. The latter is only partially disabled. Others have attempted to discern the specific contexts in which the term *heresh* refers to a deaf-mute or simply to someone who is deaf. Rashi (b. Git. 71a), followed by Serilio (y. Ter. 1:1), states that only the *heresh* mentioned with the imbecile is a deaf-mute. I discern no particular support for this assertion. M. Meg. 2:4 seems to contradict it. Note Jastrow's definition (p. 507) of the *heresh* as either a deaf, dumb, or deaf and dumb person. His only example from M. or T. in which *heresh* means deaf is M. Meg. 2:4. He cites no examples in which the term refers to a dumb person. As regards the meaning deaf and dumb, he cites M. 1:2L and indicates that this is the meaning of the term in a "legal sense." I do not know what he means by that. In all, we are left with no way of discerning the meaning of the term *heresh*

other than context, which, as noted, is almost invariably ambiguous. For convenience sake, unless context requires otherwise, I have rendered the term as *deaf-mute*.

[16]Followed by Sens, GRA, TYY, Bert and Albeck.

[17]Although M. never mentions the requirement of a blessing, T. shows some interest in the issue. Besides the aforementioned T. 3:1-2, T. 3:3 discusses when the blessing on the separation of heave-offering is to be recited. T. Ber. 6:14 gives the actual text of the blessing for the separation of heave-offering.

[18]Since the issue throughout the first chapters of M. is the validity of heave-offering *post facto*, Bert, Sens and TYY state that Yose and Judah agree with M. 1:1 that the minor should not separate heave-offering, and that they dispute only whether heave-offering he has separated is valid. This simply is not what the pericope says.

[19]Albeck, following Maimonides (*Heave-offering* 4:4), solves the problem by rendering M as, "A minor, *even though* he has not produced two pubic hairs." I find no grounds for arguing that this is what Judah means. MR and GRA argue that M refers to a person who has reached the age of majority, but who has not yet produced two pubic hairs. This explanation is not acceptable since Yose, O, refers specifically to someone under the age of majority. Further, if the case were as MR and GRA claim, M should not refer specifically to a minor, but rather, simply to "an individual who has not produced two pubic hairs." In general, the difficulty in interpreting M stems from the fact that no where in M. or T. is there a clear exposition of the relationship between the signs of majority (M. Nid. 6:11) and the age of majority (M. Nid. 5:6). M. Nid. 5:4-6, 9 seem to indicate a distinction between an individual who is chronologically a minor and who has not produced two pubic hairs, and one who, although chronologically a minor, already has produced these signs of majority. The particular obligations and privileges of each are not, however, clear.

[20]At M. Meg. 2:4, cited by TYY, Judah also disputes the grouping of the minor with the deaf-mute and the imbecile. He states there that a minor may read the Scroll of Esther in public.

[21]This view is taken by GRA, MR, Rashi, Maimonides and Albeck. Alternatively, TYY states that the age of vows is the age of majority itself. Although M. Nid. 5:6 is ambiguous on this point, TYY's explanation is not acceptable. According to it, P in no way responds to M, which refers specifically to a minor.

[22]The word *'wtw* is missing in ed. princ. Lieberman suggests reading *'wth*, referring to the heave-offering.

[23]Literally, *pqḥ* has the sense of seeing and hearing. See Jastrow, p. 1208.

[24]Y. Ter. 1:1 and y. Git. 7:1 read *mqyymyn ktb ydw*. This is a scribal emendation (Lieberman, TK, I, p. 294, n. 4) which clarifies Simeon's point. The function of the executors is to witness the document as the deaf-mute's own.

[25]It remains to be noted that C is not stated specifically as a response to B. C refers to a deaf-mute, imbecile and minor, as

well as to both heave-offering and tithes. Judah, B, does not
suggest that his $m^c \check{s}h$ applies to anything but a deaf-mute and
heave-offering.

[26]As concerns Yohanan b. Gudgada, see Neusner, *Pharisees*, vol.
1, pp. 417-19.

[27]Y. Ter. 1:1 finds a biblical basis for the distinction between foods requiring preparation in purity and heave-offering.
Numbers 18:27 reads: *and your offering shall be reckoned to you*
(*wnhšb lkm trwmtkm*). Heave-offering, therefore, requires intention
(*mhšbh*). Leviticus 22:9 states: *They shall therefore keep my*
charge (*wšmrw 't mšmrty*). Accordingly, foods requiiring preparation in purity need only be guarded (*ŠMR*).

[28]This is comparable to sages' understanding of the case of
the son who separates heave-offering under his father's supervision, T. 1:4.

[29]This exegesis takes F-H to be autonomous of D-E. Alternatively, MB holds that F-G explains the distinction between the
deaf-mute of M. 1:1 and the one to which Isaac refers. The deaf-
mute of M. 1:1 is born a deaf-mute. Even under supervision, he
may not separate heave-offering. Isaac, though, refers to an
individual who became a deaf-mute later in life. Since he might
have retained the capacity for intention, he may separate heave-
offering under supervision.

[30]This stich is lacking in the parallels listed.

[31]Y. Ter. 1:1 (= y. Git. 7:1 and b. Hag. 3b) questions whether
an individual must exhibit all of the characteristics listed in
T. 1:3 in order to be considered an imbecile. Both possible
answers are discussed.

[32]GRA, following y. Ter. 1:1, reads *whyh twrm*. The meaning
is the same.

[33]Lieberman, TK, I, p. 295, chooses this reading over that of
the first edition of T., *mqyym*. The meaning of *mdbr* here is like
its meaning at M. 3:4, "to indicate permission." The term *mqyym*
does not make sense here because it would indicate that the
sanctity of the heave-offering depends on the father's validation
(c.f. T. 1:1E), the opposite of Judah's point.

[34]Reading with y. Ter. 1:1 and ed. princ.

[35]The Talmudim disagree as to whether the individual in question picks produce for his own consumption and separates heave-
offering from it or, alternatively, whether he plans only to prepare the produce for the owner's consumption. y. Ter. 1:1 holds
the former position, b. M.B. 22a the latter. Maimonides, *Heave-*
offering 4:3 (followed by HY), offers both possibilities. Neither
view finds particular support in the language of the pericope.

[36]See b. B.M. 22a and y. Ter. 1:1 which question whether the
heave-offering is valid from the time that it is separated or,
alternatively, only from the point at which the feelings of the
householder are revealed.

[37]Literally, "a violent man." See *Aruch*, vol. 1, p. 151, and
Jastrow, p. 86.

[38]In the text of T. in HY and in standard editions of b.,
G-J is numbered T. 1:7.

[39]Cited by Lieberman, TK, I, p. 297.

[40]GRA reads *lhpryš*.

[41]The phrase TRM + *'t hm^c̄ʹsr* appears in the sense of "separate
(e.g., designate) the heave-offering of the tithe" also at T.
M.S. 3:15. The same phrase is used at T. 1:14a (p. 45) and M.
Ned. 4:3 in the sense of "to set aside first tithe."

[42]Y. Ter. 1:1 in fact cites B independently of A.

[43]M. Bik. 2:5 states that heave-offering of the tithe, unlike
heave-offering, may be separated from clean produce on behalf of
unclean produce.

[44]Lieberman, TK, I, p. 300, states that Yose disagrees with
A, his opinion being that the householder may in the first place
separate heave-offering of the tithe and therefore has no need to
set aside a quantity of produce for the Levite to designate. This
interpretation ignores the language of Yose's opinion which--as
Lieberman himself notes--implies that the householder should not
separate heave-offering of the tithe. Lieberman solves this problem by reading B in light of A and asserting that in situations in
which there is a problem of purity, Yose is in favor of the householder's separating heave-offering of the tithe. Since neither A
nor B explicitly refers to problems of cleanness, this appears to
me to be groundless. Lieberman further holds that Yose disputes
T. 1:8B, holding that even the householder's workers may separate
heave-offering of the tithe on behalf of the Levite. Yet T. 1:8
does not know any rule concerning heave-offering of the tithe.
Similarly, Yose says nothing about the rights of workers.

[45]B. Git. 52a adds at A and B: "to provide food for orphans
but not to set aside [i.e., not to put away that which is tithed,
or the funds from that which is sold, in reserve for a later
date]." This appears to be an explanatory comment on the part of
b., and not a variant reading. See however HD.

[46]B. Git. 52a lacks: *in the torah*, at F and H. Rashi, *loc.
cit.*, interprets this reading by stating that the duty of charity
(and presumably the redemption of captives) has no clearly defined
scope, since there are always poor people who need charity (and
captives who must be redeemed). It is therefore detrimental to
orphans to allow their funds to be used for these purposes. Conversely duties such as those listed at C and E apply either one
time a year, or, as in the case of a scroll of the Torah, are one-
time-expenses. These are allowable. Among the exegetes of T., I
find no interpretation of the specific language before us.

[47]B. Git. 52a reads: "to redeem."

[48]HY and HY read: Simeon b. Eleazer.

[49]Ed. princ. reads at E: "If a Levite or priest or poor
person was accustomed [to visit] him [i.e., the householder] (*hyh
lmd 'slw*)--lo, this one [i.e., the householder] provides food for
him from his own [i.e., the householder's own tithed, unconsecrated
produce]." Lieberman, who cites M. Dem. 4:4, states that according

to this reading, the point is that a householder may not use tithes
or heave-offering in entertaining guests.

[50]E-F is missing from T. in standard printings of b. F is
lacking in ed. princ.

[51]It is likely that C, which repeats at F, is secondary.
Without it, the three rules legislated "for the sake of the
social order" (A, B, D) would appear consecutively. This is noteworthy, since, as stated below, D's case fits into this context
primarily because it is a rule required for the "social order."
We would therefore expect it to be juxtaposed to A-B, forming a
nice triplet.

[52]The root *TRM* is used here in the sense of *lhpryš* (HD), that
is, to separate, but not specifically heave-offering. *TRM* in this
sense occurs also at M. Ned. 4:3.

[53]For the use of the infinitive *HYH* + participle in a
"frequentive and iterative sense," see Segal, p. 157.

[54]T. Dem. 7:15 states that the householder may not however
take tithe from other householders as repayment of a loan he has
made to a Levite. In doing so, he arrogates the Levitical right
of receiving tithe.

[55]HD (followed by HY) holds that D refers back to A. Its
sense, he states, is that *even* an individual who always gives
tithes and priestly gifts to a particular priest or Levite may not
take these things for his own use without first asking permission.
The fact that HY interprets the phrase *mkry khwnh wlwyh* as I have
--as referring to the priest or Levite himself--does not affect
his exegesis. He simply interpolates, at D, the joining language
"even in the case of."

[56]This town is mentioned also at T. Yeb. 6:8, M. Par 8:10
(*pwgh*), b. B.B. 74b (*pygh*), b. San. 56a, Yalqut Shemoni Tehillim
#687 and Midrash Tehillim 24:6. On its location and history, see
Press, vol. 4, p. 767.

[57]The rules regarding the status of mixtures of heave-offering and unconsecrated produce are found at M. 4:7-5:9.

[58]Lieberman (TK, I, p. 307-8) states that T. 2:1-3 are
derived from a collection (*qwbṣ*) of rules in which "the measure of
the law was voided for the sake of the social order," or, alternatively, in which the individual is meant "to act more stringently
than is dictated by the measure of the law." He believes that all
pericopae in T. Chapter One which provide rules for the sake of
the social order (including the laws for minors and orphans, loans
to priests and Levites, and lost things) come from this same collection. At no point does Lieberman define what he means by
"collection." The notion that there were organized collections of
pericopae before the final redaction of M. and T. is as yet un-
documented.

[59]While A2-3 do not respond to the superscription at A1,
their meaning is clear. There is no evidence here of a logical
lacuna caused by the redactional juxtaposition of originally
autonomous materials.

[60]On this principle, see b. Ket. 18b.

[61]Lieberman, TK, I, p. 307, suggests that the individual at A may wish to regain possession of property he sold. HY suggests that the persons at D and I hope to grieve the other individuals involved.

[62]According to this interpretation, the pericope refers to olives or grapes which are intended for pressing into oil or wine, such that their preparation for consumption is not yet complete. It does not refer to olives or grapes which are to be eaten whole and which are already fully processed. Cf., Maimonides, *Heave-offering* 5:18 and MS. Note that M. 1:9 explicitly distinguishes between grapes and olives intended for pressing (*zytym*, *[c]nbym*), and those already prepared for consumption (*zytym l'kylh*, *[c]nbym l'kylh*).

[63]In M. Ed. 2:5's version of this Houses-dispute (see also y. Ter. 1:8), the House of Hillel has the position of the anonymous rule of M. 1:10A. The House of Shammai state to the contrary that heave-offering may be separated from olives for oil, or from grapes for wine. The problem of the literary and substantive relationships among these materials has been considered by Epstein (*Mishnah*, p. 399), Lieberman (TK, I, p. 331-2) and Goldberg (*Tarbiz* 38 (1968-9), p. 231-54). Epstein resolves the contradictions among the various versions by asserting that there are two (or three) Yoses, each with a different tradition about the dispute. Lieberman uses a weakly supported variant reading of the statement of Mana at y. Ter. 1:8 in order to harmonize the several pericopae. Goldberg attempts to distinguish in this material among the differing views of five of Aqiba's students. His work, as well as that of Lieberman, has been evaluated by William Green in Neusner, *Modern Study*, pp. 235-41.

[64]M. 1:10D states that heave-offering separated from produce which is not ready for consumption on behalf of produce the preparation for consumption of which is completed is valid *post facto*. Both Houses at M. 1:4 contradict that rule.

[65]On the basis of the Hillelite position, this pericope has been redacted with M. 1:1-3, 5. These pericopae discuss methods of separating heave-offering which even *post facto* do not yield valid heave-offering. Alternatively M. 1:4 could logically have been placed with M. 1:8-9, which provide rules for heave-offering separated from grapes and olives. Lieberman, TK, I, p. 332, n. 54, in fact states that in the recension of M. on which T. is based, M. 1:4 was located after M. 1:8. He supports this statement with the claim that T. 3:14 complements M. 1:4 (and not M. 1:8, as I hold). Even if Lieberman were correct on this point, it would not constitute proof that T. knows a recension of M. ordered differently than the one before us today. As will be seen throughout this commentary, T. often has its own theory of the proper context in which to discuss discrete pericopae of M. On the redactional ordering of T.'s materials, see Neusner, *Purities*, vol. 3, pp. 175-91.

[66]MA notes that the opinions of the Houses here accord with their opinions at M. Ned. 3:2. In that pericope, as in this one, the Shammaites hold that prior intention need not be taken into account in assessing the ultimate effects of a person's actions. The House of Hillel, on the other hand, believe that if a person's original intention cannot be carried out in full, it is null.

[67]C, Pa, O[2] lack: *and*.

[68]B, C, Ca, O[2] lack *and* at G, I and K.

[69]Alternatively, there are ten items prefaced "and not" at
C-D+E-L. For the reason I have given, however, it is apparent
that B and C-D belong together. It therefore is unlikely that
C-L was interpolated as a unit into a prior unit of tradition
consisting of A-B+M-N.

[70]See M. Hal. 1:3 which states that the items at B-D are
exempt from the separation of tithes. Maimonides (followed by
Bert) claims that the point at B is that the householder may not
use gifts of the poor as tithes for his own produce, since these
gifts do not belong to him. This interpretation is rejected by
TYT and Sens. These exegetes, along with TYY, hold, as I do,
that gifts of the poor in no event are subject to the separation
of heave-offering. Cf. y. Ter. 1:5, which deduces the rule of B
from Dt. 14:29.

[71]M. Ma. 1:1 stipulates that only produce which is edible,
grown in the earth and cultivated (*nšmr*) is subject to the separation of heave-offering and tithes. Produce which grows wild,
or which is abandoned does not meet this last requirement. See
Jaffee to M. Ma. 1:1.

[72]At C-D, numerous manuscripts and editions read:

> C. and not from first tithe from which heave-
> offering [of the tithe] has *not* been removed;

> D. and not from second tithe or [produce] dedicated
> [to the Temple] which has *not* been redeemed.

Of these manuscripts and editions only K, G[4] and Z are not influ-
enced by Maimonides. This same reading appears in his Mishnah
commentary and in *Heave-offering* 5:13. This reading is not to be
preferred over that of the printed edition. It has little support
among the exegetes of M. (excluding Maimonides). Further, it
contradicts the rule of first tithe, second tithe and dedicated
produce set out in M. Hal. 1:3, as well as the rule of first tithe
stated at Sifré Zutṭa 18:24 (Horovitz, p. 297, l. 27- p. 298, l.
2). For a complete review of the readings of the various MSS.,
editions and exegetes, see Sacks-Hutner, vol. II, p. 104. In notes
17 and 18, the source of Maimonides error is delineated.

[73]Maimonides, Bert, Sens, TYY and Albeck hold that the items
listed at B-D are both exempt from the separation of heave-offering, and, further, that heave-offering may not be separated from
them for any other produce. Although not intrinsic to B-D, this
exegesis is hardly far-fetched. Through a unitary reading of the
pericope it is easily adduced from E.

[74]MA avoids this multiplication of examples of E-F by stating
that K-L refers to produce grown outside of the Land of Israel
that was brought to the Land before its preparation was completed.
Its status as regards the separation of heave-offering is ambiguous. Alternatively, TYY and TYT explain that according to sages,
even produce grown outside of the Land of Israel is subject to
the separation of heave-offering and tithes. Neither of these
interpretations has a basis in the text before us.

[75] According to MS. E, which reads *grwnwt* at D, T. refers to a field of wheat or other produce, and not to an orchard. This being the case, *kgwn*, at E, follows logically.

[76] Alternatively, T. may refer to produce from a field in Syria owned by an Israelite. The produce from such a field is liable to the separation of heave-offering (T. 2:10). If this is the case, then the point is that produce of Syria and that of Israel is not homogeneous as regards the separation of heave-offering. See Maimonides (*Heave-offering* 1:15) and HY, who distinguish between the source of the obligation to tithe produce of the Land of Israel, and the obligation to tithe produce grown by an Israelite in Syria.

[77] Whereas the operative noun at H, *ship*, is feminine, at I, MS. V shifts into the masculine. E reads the verb *leaving*, I, as masculine, yet has *is not liable* in the feminine. I assume in all events that the referents of the pronouns at I are the same as those at H.

[78] M. 2:6 states that while heave-offering should be separated from the most choice produce, even if it is not, the designation is valid.

[79] "Recite the blessing" at B, all of C and "because he may not" at D have been supplied from E and ed. princ. These words are lacking in V.

[80] I cannot explain why T. has followed neither the order of M.'s list, nor grouped the several individuals in accordance with the reason they may not separate heave-offering.

[81] For the text of the blessing recited over the separation of heave-offering and tithes, see T. Ber. 6:14.

[82] Notably, the pericopae's operative language, the verbal root *PRS* in the causitive stem, remains consistent throughout. This explains the juxtaposition of the two substantively autonomous units.

[83] As regards the designation of heave-offering by oral pronouncement, see M. 3:5. It is apparent from E that such a declaration is not a necessary part of the valid separation of heave-offering. See HY, Lieberman, TK, III, p. 775, and Sifré Bammidbar 121 (Horovitz, p. 147), which Lieberman cites.

[84] Lieberman, TK, I, p. 117, reads the pericope as unitary in issue, equating the recitation of the blessing with the designation of heave-offering by oral pronouncement. This has no grounds in the language of C-E.

[85] Y. Ter. 1:6 (followed by Bert, TYT, MS, GRA) uses Num. 18:27, "And your offering shall be reckoned to you" (*wnhšb lkm trwmtkm*), to prove that the desired quantity of heave-offering may be determined only by estimation and not by exact measure.

[86] TYY, Bert and Albeck hold that E-F refers to a vessel designed for measuring, which has markings to indicate its half-full-point. This seems to me to go beyond the simple sense of E-F.

[87] According to *Aruch* (vol. 6, p. 266) and Jastrow (p. 1114) Ardascus is probably Damascus.

[88]While it is certain that Judah restates the rule of
M. 1:7A-B, his language is somewhat elliptical. It is unclear
exactly what is the force of "brings it into his house." The
phrase is usually used in a technical sense, meaning "to render
produce fully liable to the separation of heave-offering and
tithes." This cannot be the sense of the phrase here, since according to the language of the pericope, we are dealing with produce which already is subject to the removal of tithes. It appears that the phrase is used as a cliche, and thus should not
affect interpretation of Judah's statement.

[89]Lieberman (TK, I, pp. 322-23) states that by first weighing
his produce with the basket, and afterwards calculating the exact
weight of the produce the individual at D never really weighs the
produce itself. He contends that for this reason the man's actions
are agreeable even to Yose.

[90]Lieberman (TK, I, p. 323) reads the pericope as unitary in
issue. He states that since heave-offering is separated by an
estimation only, even if there is more produce than the individual
is conscious of, the heave-offering he designates is valid for all
of the produce. As indicated by F, this is not the point of the
rule.

[91]According to prior exegetes, the issue here is the separation of heave-offering from diverse kinds of produce. They state
that the point made by A is that small and large produce are not
distinct types from which heave-offering must be separated individually. In light of this exegesis, they hold that the force of
bynwny, at B, is that the individual should separate as heave-
offering the quantity of produce which M. 4:3 calls average. I
prefer to read the pericope in the terms suggested by the thematic
unit of which it is a part.

[92]The items at B are refuse of the manufacture of wine. Those
at C result from the manufacture of oil. On this basis, Lieberman
(TK, I, p. 324) follows the reading of ed. princ., viz., *vat* (for
wine) at B and *tank* (for oil) at C. It is not however clear that
T. is at all consistent in distinguishing between the terms *vat*
and *tank*. See, e.g., T. 3:7, which refers to wine in a tank.

[93]What appears as a logical disjunction stems from a technical use of the term *kysd*. This same use is found above, at T. 1:5.

[94]For a discussion of various readings and exegeses of B, see
Lieberman, TK, I, p. 327-28.

[95]This rule is consistent with T. Toh. 11:4, which states that
grapes convey uncleanness as foods only until they are trampled
warp and woof. After this point they are treated as liquids. See
Neusner, *Purities*, vol. 11, p. 234.

[96]Y. Ter. 3:4 reverses the opinions of the Houses of Hillel
and Shammai. In this way it places the Hillelites in the more
lenient position, as is commonplace.

[97]Like the rule of grapes (D-E; above, note 95), this rule is
consistent with T. Toh. 11:4, which states that olives convey uncleanness as foods only until they have been pressed. From that
time on, they are treated as liquids.

[98] I follow Maimonides and Bert. Cf., Albeck.

[99] The use of the root DM^C in the intensive stem to mean "to impose the status of heave-offering" is based on Ex. 22:28's reference to dm^C (= wine) as an agricultural offering given to the Lord. In rabbinic parlance, the term is used specifically in reference to heave-offering. See Jastrow, p. 313. He cites *Yalqut Exodus* 351, M. Ohal. 16:4, and T. Ter. 10:16, all of which refer to heave-offering as dm^C.

[100] The passage reads: *An outsider shall not eat of a holy thing. A sojourner of the priest's, or a hired servant shall not eat of a holy thing...And if a man eats a holy thing unwittingly, he shall add the fifth of its value to it, and give the holy thing to the priest.*

[101] On the various readings at I, see Lieberman, TK, I, p. 331. I follow the reading of MS. E, which holds that tithes alone need be separated from the second heave-offering. Since the first heave-offering was valid, there is no reason that heave-offering need be separated again from this produce, as the readings of V and ed. princ. would require. Heave-offering of the tithe will be separated by the Levite from first tithe. Therefore, the reading offered by Sens and HY is not to be preferred.

[102] Cf., M. 1:4 and T. 3:16F-I.

[103] Following y. Ter. 1:8, Lieberman, HY and MB read U after X. The point then is that while the householder's re-processing of the heave-offering does not affect its consecrated status, he needs to indicate once again that it is heave-offering. He does this by making an oral designation.

[104] E, Sens, Rosh (to M. 1:10), followed by Lieberman (TK, I, p. 334), reverse the names of the Houses at F-I. This puts the House of Hillel in the position of the rule stated anonymously at D, yet in opposition to M. 1:8A-E.

[105] Lieberman, TK, I, p. 334, follows *'Or Sameah* in stating that the Houses here dispute the rule of M. 1:9K-P, and not A-B of this pericope. I see no particular support for this view. It must be rejected since it requires that we ignore the clear structure of T.'s unit.

[106] Note Neusner, *Pharisees*, vol. 2, p. 89. He follows Lieberman in interpreting the Shammaites as stating: "If you say that he has to give Heave-offering a second time, you annul what is already *holy unto the Lord.*" This is plausible, yet has no clear foundation in the language of I.

[107] Lieberman, TK, I, p. 335, states that the term *škšm š* instead of *kšm š* indicates that T. derives this rule from a halakhic midrash. Since no midrashic passage parallel to this one is extant, I do not know the basis for his claim.

NOTES TO CHAPTER TWO

[1]It is possible that this consideration has its source in the Priestly Code itself, which insists that the offering to the priests be given of "the best (hlb) of the oil, and all the best of the wine and of the grain..." (Num. 18:12).

[2]On the equation of this Eliezer with Eliezer b. Hyrcanus, see Neusner, *Eliezer*, vol. 1, p. 43.

[3]Cf., M. Kil. 2:2, M. Shab. 1:3, 10:4, M. Naz. 7:3. See Epstein, *Mishnah*, p. 1263, and Lieberman, TK, II, p. 705, n. 47.

[4]Unclean oil in the status of heave-offering is an exception to this rule. The priest may kindle such oil in a lamp (M. 11:10).

[5]Bert, TYY and MR state that the rule at A was legislated to prevent householders from contaminating all of their produce by bringing the clean and unclean together to form a single batch for purposes of separating heave-offering. This exegesis depends on the contention that M. in fact requires that heave-offering be separated from produce contained in one area for produce contained in the same area (see M. Bik. 2:5). M. and T. however are hardly clear on this point. T. 2:8, for instance, states explicitly that heave-offering may be separated from produce in one city on behalf of produce in a different city. But, cf., T. 3:7. Note also T. Ma. 1:5, which adduces a case in which Rabbi holds that it is preferable that heave-offering be separated from one batch of produce for a different batch.

[6]At b. Yeb. 89a, Hisda and Nathan dispute the sense of the phrase *he has not done anything* (N). Hisda holds that it indicates that the householder has neither separated valid heave-offering nor prepared his produce for consumption. Nathan disagrees. He claims that while the produce must be tithed again, that which was separated from it is considered valid heave-offering and must be given to a priest. While we would have expected M. to use the standard phrase *'yn trwmtw trwmh*, the sense of $l'^{c}\acute{s}h$ $klwm$ is certainly as Hisda states.

[7]This can occur if a portion of the batch has not yet been made wet and therefore is not susceptible to uncleanness. The fig juice which bonds together the figs in a ring does not act as a connector for uncleanness. One of the figs therefore may become unclean without contaminating the rest of the figs in the ring.

[8]Bert holds that the householder at T and W may eat the food he has prepared or make use of the utensils he has immersed only at the conclusion of the Sabbath. TYY states that he need not wait. M. gives no evidence as to which view is correct.

[9]Alternatively, sages' point, G, is that heave-offering was separated from clean produce for unclean produce within a single batch. As M. 2:1C-G states, such a separation of heave-offering is valid. While the sense of *trmw mhn* $^{c}lyhn$ (G) is ambiguous, I prefer the interpretation offered by MB and HY. This interpretation does not attempt to read into T. the issues of M.'s composite pericope at a point at which T. does not clearly intend to offer an exposition of those issues.

[10] On the laws of susceptibility to, and transfer of, uncleanness, see Neusner, *Purities*, vol. 11, p. 23 and vol. 17, pp. 7-12.

[11] Sifré Bammidbar 120 (Horovitz, p. 147, l. 3, and parallels) derives this law from Num. 18:25-26: *And the Lord said to Moses, "Moreover you shall say to the Levites, 'When you take from the people of Israel the tithe which I have given you from them for an inheritance, then you shall present an offering from it, to the Lord...'"* The statement that the offering is to be separated *from it* is interpreted to mean that it must be separated from produce of its same genus.

[12] Albeck states that the case is one in which the produce will be given immediately to the priest, and that Judah and sages simply disagree about which onion is of higher quality. While this is plausible, it seems to me more likely that the dispute concerns the larger issue operative in the pericope, as I have interpreted following TYY and MS.

[13] Alternatively, the term I have translated (following Maimonides, Bert, Sens, MR, TYY) "onions from villages" (*kwpryn*) refers to onions grown in Cyprus. Cf., M. Ned. 9:8 and Albeck to M. Ter. 2:5 and to M. Ned. 9:8. The point is the same in either case.

[14] Bert, TYY, and MR read K-L in light of the preceding. They hold that while onions grown in large towns are more choice, those grown in villages keep for longer periods of time. While this may be the meaning intended by the placement of K-L in its present redactional setting, it is hardly implicit in M. itself. MS, TYY, GRA and Sens, further, read M-P as a continuation of Judah's opinion, as against that of F-G. They state that olives which normally are pickled and wine which has been boiled keep longer than olives used for oil and wine which has not been boiled. While this seems likely in the case of wine which has been boiled, I have found no independent sources which substantiate the possibility (cf., y. Ter. 2:5). On the question of the difference between olives used for oil and those which normally are pickled, see Lieberman, TK, I, p. 332 and Pliny, *Natural History*, xv, 3:10, which Lieberman cites.

[15] The preparation of the olives referred to here has not been completed. This contradicts M. 1:10, which states that heave-offering may not be separated from produce the preparation of which has not yet been completed. On this problem see MS, who contends that while the reference is to olives which normally would be prepared in other ways, in this case they have been prepared to be eaten whole, such that they are ready for consumption. Contextually it is apparent that wine which has not been boiled is held to be of better quality than wine which has been boiled (Bert, MS, TYY). This contradicts the position of Judah, M. 11:1. He holds that the quality of wine is improved through boiling. Y. Ter. 2:5 resolves this difficulty by stating that Judah's point at M. 11:1 is that the wine is improved only insofar as once boiled it keeps longer.

[16] At M. Kil. 1:2 Judah and sages dispute this same issue. Notably, the terminology used in each instance reflects the needs of the dispute's specific redactional context. This is evidence that antecedent materials were available, and that their formulation took place in conjunction with the redactional process.

[17] *Juglans quadrangulata.*

[18] *Amygdalus communis = prunus amygdalus.*

[19] B. Hul. 136b adds: *do not.* Lieberman, TK, I, p. 310, notes that the reading in the printed edition of b. is supported by MS. evidence and by the early exegetes of the Talmud. We have, therefore, divergent versions of the pericope, each of them well attested. T.'s version, which cites the rule as in agreement with M., and with the Hillelites, is preferable in this context.

[20] MS. evidence for b. reads Eleazar, as do the sources for T. See Lieberman, TK, I, p. 310.

[21] T. 2:4-5 appear among the materials in T. pertinent to M. 1:5. On this basis Lieberman suggests that in the recension of M. which was before T., M. 1:5 included the rules we have before us at M. 2:4A-B. This theory ignores the possibility that T. simply has its own theory of the order in which M.'s materials are best presented. It further does not explain why M. 2:4A-B should appear in two different contexts in M.

[22] My translation of G-J follows b. Men. 54b, y. Ter. 2:4, GRA, HY, MB, Maimonides, *Heave-offering* 5:18 and Lieberman, TK, I, p. 338. V and E reverse the terms "volume" and "number" at G-H and I-J. I find no way to interpret that reading.

[23] Cf., T. M.S. 1:18.

[24] Lieberman, TK, I, p. 341, states that the word *'p* occurs in V because of a copyist's error, having been transposed from the line above (J).

[25] Lieberman, TK, I, p. 341, claims that, according to T., Judah's view is that the householder may separate heave-offering either from better produce, or from that which keeps. In light of Judah's statement at G, I cannot concur with this interpretation.

[26] Y. Ter. 8:5 holds that snakes simply will not drink wine which has been boiled. PM (*loc. cit.*, s.v., *'yn bw mšwm glwy*) states that, because it is of very low value, gentiles do not offer as a libation wine which has been boiled.

[27] For a like usage of the phrase *twrmyn ᶜlyw* see T. 1:14aC.

[28] *Cucumis sativus:* Feliks, *Plant World*, p. 168.

[29] *Cucumis melo L:* ibid., p. 164.

[30] *Chicorium endivia:* Lieberman, TK, I, p. 341.

[31] *Lactuc sativa, longifolis:* Feliks, *ibid.*, p. 194.

[32] *Allium porrum:* ibid., p. 174.

[33] *Brassica rapa:* ibid., p. 197-8.

[34] *Allium porrum capitatum.* Note T. Ned. 3:5, (cited by *ibid.*, p. 174) which takes into account locations in which vetches (*kršym*) are called leeks (*qplwtwt*).

[35] *Cucumis sativus*: *ibid.*, p. 168

[36] On the basis of the difference in the terms used to indicate
the concept 'to keep,' we may assume that this pericope was not
formulated specifically in conjunction with M. 2:4F-G. That
pericope uses *QYYM*. Here we have *ŠMR*.

NOTES TO CHAPTER THREE

[1] *Cucumis melo.*

[2] *Cucumis citrullus (vulgaris).* On the identification of M.'s
'btyh with the common watermelon, see Feliks, *Plant World*, p. 164
and Güting, *Terumot*, p. 77. He cites Löw, *Flora*, vol. 1, pp. 550-
53.

[3] According to y. Ter. 3:1, while both quantities of heave-
offering must be given to the priest, the householder should be
remunerated for the greater of the two amounts of the offering.
It bases its conclusion on O, which holds that in cases of mixtures, only the smaller quantity of produce is deemed true heave-
offering.

[4] This follows nicely from Judah's opinion, M. 2:4H, which
holds that the priest's being able to eat heave-offering he is
given is not central.

[5] Cf., M. Miq. 2:3, which reviews problems of doubt in the
status of immersion pools. The principle there is much like that
found here. It holds that in a case in which we can assume that
a pool was not made unfit, we indeed make that assumption.

[6] Bert and TYY note that this should be the second quantity of
produce designated heave-offering. This is so since after separating heave-offering once, the householder will have a smaller
quantity of produce from which to separate heave-offering the
second time.

[7] E, y. Ter. 3:1 and b. B.B. 143a read simply "R. Yose says."
HD makes sense out of V's reading, which I translate, by re-
situating this pericope after T. 4:6E-F, which contains a statement attributed to Yose by his son, Ishmael. In light of the well
supported variant, HD's emendation is hardly a necessary one.

[8] My interpretation follows y. Ter. 3:1. B. B.B. 143a, on the
other hand, holds Yose's point is that each time the householder
separates a chate-melon as heave-offering, he must supply the
priest with an additional amount of produce, as if all chate melons
are part bitter. See Tosafot, *loc. cit.*, s.v. *'yn lk mr bqšwt.*
They follow y.'s exegesis.

[9] Y. Kil. 1:1 omits F-G entirely, adding after E: "If he
transgressed and separated heave-offering in that way, that which
he has separated is [valid] heave-offering." Y., then, reads the
rule as in accord with M. 2:6, which holds that if heave-offering
is separated from produce of worse quality for produce of better
quality, *post facto* it is considered valid heave-offering.

[10] So y. Ter. 3:1 (*s.v., r ḥyyh bšm r ywḥnn dr ḥy'*).

[11]I follow Lieberman, TK, I, p. 344, who reads *twrm* as a
passive construction (*pual*). Sens and Rosh (to M. 3:1) and MB
read *trwm*.

[12]Lieberman has supplied C-D on the basis of E and ed. princ.
It is missing in V.

[13]In supplying E, I follow Maimonides, *Heave-offering* 5:21,
Sens and Rosh (to M. 3:1), Rašba' and Ritba' (to b. Yeb. 89a).

[14]G is lacking in ed. princ.

[15]Alternatively the point of *ᶜd slwšh ymym* (I) is that the
keg is considered certainly to have contained wine for three days
from the last time it was examined. After these three days and
until the examination in which the wine is found to have turned
sour, it is held to be in doubt whether the wine had already become vinegar. Both this interpretation and the one I have given
in the body of the text are suggested at y. B.B. 6:1, b. Qid. 79a
and parallels.

[16]A comparable problem is at M. Ned. 5:1.

[17]Y. Ter. 3:5 (cited by GRA; followed without citation by TYY,
Bert and Albeck) interprets matters somewhat differently. It holds
that Aqiba's view is that half of the heave-offering separated by
each of the partners is considered valid heave-offering, and half
retains the status of unconsecrated food. Between them, then, the
two partners will have separated exactly the required quantity of
heave-offering. Since, however, a householder who wishes may give
much more than the quantity of produce normally separated as
heave-offering (M. 4:5), y.'s view is neither implied nor necessi-
tated by Aqiba's statement.

[18]B. Tem. 13a reports a variant version of the dispute. It
assigns Aqiba's opinion to Eliezer, and that of sages to Aqiba.
On that version, and on b. and y.'s interpretation of the laws before us, see Primus, *Aqiva*, pp. 53-4.

[19]Yose's view here is comparable to that of T. 4:16. According to that pericope, a householder who separates less than the
required quantity of heave-offering may separate heave-offering
from the same produce a second time.

[20]Albeck states that Yose, E, holds that if the first individual did not separate the required quantity of heave-offering,
only that which is separated by the second is valid heave-offering. The wording of Yose's statement hardly requires this interpretation. I see no reason that the first separation of heave-
offering should not be valid, and therefore find this exegesis
unacceptable.

[21]Albeck notes the discontinuity in operative verbs--*dbr*, at
G; *hršh* at I--and states that the text at H-I originally read
'bl dbr 'w hršh... On p. 388 he claims that the word *dbr* eventually was omitted because it was understood simply to repeat the
sense of *hršh*. While Albeck seems to indicate that this corruption
occurred at the time of y.'s interpretation of this pericope, the
exact sense of his statement is unclear. Albeck, moreover, holds
that F-J refers to Yose's statement at E. This interpretation is
based on his claim (see above, note 20) that at E Yose holds that
the heave-offering separated by the first partner is not valid.

Albeck states that the point of F-J is that this separation of
heave-offering is not valid only if the partners had not beforehand agreed to separate less than the usual amount of heave-
offering. If however they had agreed to do so, that which the
first partner separates is considered valid heave-offering. Since
it is based on an incorrect understanding of E, Albeck's view is
highly implausible.

[22]Lieberman, TK, I, p. 300 suggests reading at I a disjunctive
w and *məmšym*, thus "a small tank, or a tank which others touch."
In this way he sees the issue here to be cultic cleanness, as at
M. 3:4/O-P.

[23]Lieberman, TK, I, p. 229, offers no interpretation of his
own for this rule. He notes however that Maimonides, *Heave-
offering* 4:10 omits this stich. HD claims the point is that while
the sharecropper may separate heave-offering and tithes for the
householder, he may not go ahead and give these things to the
priest or Levite. That is the right of the householder. HY claims
that D refers to Dt. 14:28-9's requirement that at the end of every
three years, all tithes be removed from one's household and given
to their proper recipient. The point, he says, is that a sharecropper may not perform this obligation on behalf of the householder. Neither of these interpretations is acceptable because
they are not attentive to the usual sense of the term *lḥwsy' mᶜšr*,
found at D, or to the legal context in which D is redacted.

[24]Note that T. 3:3 claims that heave-offering may be separated without a prior designation. From the materials presented
within M., it is impossible to establish whether or not the tractate shares this same view. From the present pericope, it appears
that it does not.

[25]According to Albeck, Eleazar Hisma' differs from Simeon in
that Eleazar does not even require the householder to state that
the offering is within the batch from which he plans to separate
it. While this is the case, the important point, which Albeck
misses, is that Eleazar's underlying theory is the same as Simeon's.

[26]Rabbi's point in T. 4:9 may be that, having yet properly to
designate heave-offering, the householder should perform an additional designation of the offering. At this time he would
specify more exactly in which portion of the batch he wishes the
heave-offering to be located. This interpretation is compelling
in that it prevents us from concluding that Rabbi views half of
the produce as having the status of heave-offering. The notion
that problems in mixtures of heave-offering and unconsecrated
produce are resolved through an additional designation of heave-
offering, however, is foreign to the texts before us, and, therefore, is not a defensible exegetical possibility.

[27]Y. Ter. 3:5 holds that by *špwn špwnw* Simeon states that one
eighth of the produce has been designated heave-offering. Y. thus
understands the pericope to be formulated as a numerical progression, with Rabbi's one half followed by sages' one fourth and
Simeon b. Gamaliel's one eighth.

[28]Albeck notes that Sifré Debarim #64 (Finkelstein, p. 130,
ls. 12-14) understands the term *trwmt ydkm* (Dt. 12:6) to refer to
first fruits. See also Mekhilta D'Rabbi Ishmael, Mishpatim #17.

[29]On the biblical sources for the various agricultural offerings referred to in M., see Sarason, *Demai*, pp. 3-10.

[30]On the basis of the biblical description, M. holds that in the first, second, fourth, and fifth years of the sabbatical cycle, second tithe is separated and eaten in Jerusalem by the householder himself. In the third and sixth years poor man's tithe is separated by the householder and distributed to the poor of the community of Israel.

[31]Note M. Naz. 5:1, in which the Houses dispute whether or not a dedication to the Temple made in error is valid. The House of Hillel states that it is not, comparable to the anonymous rule of M. 3:8. The Shammaites disagree.

[32]V, and ed. princ. read: first tithe. I follow the reading of E. See Lieberman, TK, I, p. 348.

[33]GRA, HY emend to read: He did not say anything.

[34]Lieberman, TK, I, p. 348, holds that in each of T.'s cases at A-I the individual literally "was going" to separate one offering, but, at the time of his designation, changed his mind and intentionally designated a different offering. For this reason, he states, the designation is valid. The language of the pericope does not support this reading of the law.

[35]Printed editions read $h^cwbd\ kwkbym$ here at C and E. Almost all MSS. have *nwkry*. See above, p. 331, n. 6.

[36]That these rules are autonomous of each other is shown by the fact that they each may be fully understood apart from the others. Further, while A+B refers both to a gentile and to a Samaritan, the subsequent materials deal only with a gentile.

[37]Bert, TYY, Sens, GRA, Albeck state that Simeon holds heave-offering separated by a gentile to be exempt only from payment of the added fifth. None of these exegetes offers a reason for this view. Both this possibility and the one I have accepted are discussed at y. Ter. 3:9. Note Sifra Emor 6:8, which cites Lev. 22:2 and proves from it that the law of the added fifth applies only to that which is consecrated by Israelites.

[38]Alternatively T. simply knows a different version of the dispute. I see no way to verify either this possibility, or the one presented in the text.

NOTES TO CHAPTER FOUR

[1]E-G assumes that heave-offering already has been separated, presumably at the threshing floor (T. 3:11).

[2]In his commentary and code (*Heave-offering* 3:7) Maimonides states that heave-offering separated from a batch of produce does not take on a sanctified status until all of the heave-offering required of that produce has been designated and removed. I do not know the source of this notion. It is not hinted at in the language of M. 4:1-2 and clearly is precluded by Meir's position at M. 4:2B.

[3]Lieberman, TK, I, p. 352, emends to read *mwddt*, "measured."
For the reason that he makes this emendation, see below, n. 5.

[4]Note y. Hal. 3:5, cited by Lieberman, TK, I, p. 354, which
questions whether or not Rabbi holds that the presence both of
heave-offering and untithed produce in a single piece of fruit
causes the piece of fruit as a whole to take on the status of
heave-offering. Y. suggests both the possibility that Rabbi as-
sents to this position and that he disagrees with it.

[5]According to Lieberman, TK, I, p. 355, Meir's point (A) is
that a householder who has yet to determine the quantity of produce he owns anyway may separate tithes and give them to their
proper recipient, Levite or poor person. Lieberman continues
(following Maimonides to M. 4:1) by stating that the produce the
householder designates takes on the actual status of the offering
only after he determines the quantity of produce contained in the
whole batch and separates gifts sufficient for all of it. In
light of this interpretation, Lieberman, TK, I, p. 352, emends
T. 4:15aA (above, p. 133) to refer to a heap of produce which has
been measured, and which he claims, may validly have heave-offering and tithes separated from it. Lieberman's perspective is not
acceptable because it reads into the law notions which these texts
themselves do not evince.

[6]Lieberman, TK, I, p. 355, states that at issue is whether or
not that which was separated as tithes has been burned. He chooses
this interpretation because of his view (see above, n. 5) that the
produce given to the Levite or poor person does not have the status
of tithes until such time as the whole quantity of offerings required of the produce is separated. We would not expect the Levite
or poor person to eat what he receives until that point. I follow
Maimonides. Neither HD nor HY commit themselves on the matter.

[7]Lieberman follows Maimonides, *Tithes* 3:7, in stating that
sages' point, E, is that the individual may eat without further
tithing a quanity of produce commensurate with the amount of
tithes which still exist in the hand of the Levite or poor person.
According to this interpretation M. in fact knows the consideration
suggested by T. There is no evidence that this is the case.

[8]Note M. 1:7 which states that the householder must estimate
the quantity of produce he separates as heave-offering. M. 4:3A-E
seems to assume that the individual will derive the proper quantity
by measuring the quantity of produce he takes. F-M on the other
hand is clear that the individual should separate heave-offering
by an estimation, in agreement with M. 1:7. It is in light of F-M
that the redactor clearly wishes A-E to be read.

[9]I have excluded here the possibility that M.'s rule is intended to ensure that the priestly cast is adequately maintained.
This is because M. in general is surprisingly uninterested in the
priest's receiving and eating produce separated as heave-offering.
This is abundantly clear in M. 2:1A's rule, which forces the householder to separate as heave-offering produce which is unclean and
therefore may not be consumed by a priest.

[10]This additional produce is in no way comparable to doubtful
heave-offering (see e.g., M. 3:1-2), which, since it might be true
heave-offering, is not subject to the separation of tithes.

[11]MR distinguishes between cases in which the householder

intends to separate the required quantity of heave-offering and
fails to do so, and cases in which he had no such intention in
the first place. He states that only in a case in which the individual desired to separate one-sixtieth or more of his produce and
failed to do so must he separate heave-offering a second time.
MR's point, of course, is that since there is no quantity of heave-
offering set by Scripture, as long as the individual separates all
that he intends to, he has fulfilled his obligation. This interpretation, however, has no support in the language of the pericope
itself.

[12]For the interpretation of Judah's statement, cf., M. Bik.
2:5, T. Ma. 1:5 and T. Ter. 2:8.

[13]M. 1:7 does not state whether or not *post facto* heave-
offering separated according to a set measure is to be considered
valid.

[14]Cf., Lieberman, TK, I, p. 353.

[15]C-D is lacking in E.

[16]It is logical to assume that in a case such as this the
householder is required to separate heave-offering again, in order
to remove from the produce all that he originally intended as
heave-offering. T., however, is not clear on this point.

[17]If C-D and E-F are read independently of each other, C-D
makes no point of any weight, and E-F simply cites M.

[18]While the logic of this view is clear, M. 4:3A-E, which
holds that the quantity of heave-offering contained in a batch of
produce is determined by the disposition of the householder, need
hardly agree.

[19]That heave-offering is of low market value is hinted at in
M. 5:1 and is stated explicitly in both of the Talmudim. It
follows, further, from the laws of supply and demand. Heave-
offering is of value only to priests. Yet these individuals need
not purchase such produce. Being little in demand, heave-offering
should be of low market value compared to other produce, which may
be purchased and used by the whole community.

[20]See in particular T. 2:9. Lieberman, TK, I, p. 360-61,
holds that the rabbis declared these things subject to the separation of heave-offering. Since the laws governing these categories of produce thus are not scriptural in provenance, Lieberman
states that only a minimal separation is required. M. itself at
no point distinguishes between scriptural and rabbinic law. This,
therefore, is not a viable approach to the interpretation of the
text before us.

[21]According to y. Ter. 4:4 the agent should separate the percentage he knows the householder normally to separate, whether or
not that individual has told him specifically to do so.

[22]TYY, GRA, Sens, Bert, Albeck hold that G refers only to the
case in which the agent knows the quantity of heave-offering
normally separated by the householder. Since the issue here
clearly is that of the agent's carrying out the terms of his ap-
pointment--as is shown by the contrast between F and G--I do not
believe that this is the case. The rules of F-G should apply
equally to the case of B and to that of C.

[23] I assume that if the agent intentionally separated less than he should, the separation is valid. This is because, in such a case, all that the agent separated was intended by the house-holder to be heave-offering.

[24] Sacks-Hutner, p. 131, n. 26, notes that MS. Oxford 671 simply reads "heave-offering." Since heave-offering may not be taken from produce which no longer is liable to that offering on behalf of other produce (M. 1:5F), this reading is not viable.

[25] Ca, L and M read "but not for a different batch." See MS, GRA, and Sens (all cited by Sacks-Hutner, *loc. cit.*) who discuss the problem of the reading here. I follow the well supported reading of the printed edition.

[26] According to T. 1:7 (above, p. 111) a householder may sepa-rate heave-offering of the tithe in place of the Levite.

[27] In its own redactional context, T. 5:3b glosses M. 4:3's rules on the quantity of heave-offering normally separated from a batch of produce.

[28] Maimonides, Bert, TYY and MR claim that A-B refers to the case of a householder who habitually counts his produce. Since the size of the produce varies from beginning to end of the har-vest, such a householder must be careful to separate heave-offer-ing from produce of a given point in the harvest on behalf of produce of that same time. This is not intrinsic to the language of A-B.

[29] This same rule appears at M. Or. 2:1.

[30] According to both A and Simeon, B, ^{c}*orlah* and produce grown in a field in which were grown diverse kinds of seeds thus are much more potent than heave-offering in their ability to impose their own status upon produce with which they are mixed.

[31] Lieberman, TK, I, p. 306, follows HD in claiming that the point is that if someone takes produce from the mixture, we assume that it was forbidden produce which he took and therefore declare the rest of the produce to have become permitted. I do not see how this interpretation follows from the language of T.

[32] For instance, one who might have eaten this doubtful heave-offering need not repay its value and the added fifth required in the case of holy things (M. 6:1). If, however, it is certain that an individual ate the possibly forbidden mixture, he is liable to all penalties incurred by one who improperly uses that which cer-tainly is forbidden.

[33] Lieberman, TK, I, p. 366, n. 56, notes that sweet pomegran-ates are one of the five types of pomegranates mentioned by Pliny, *Natural History*, book 13, #113.

[34] Lieberman follows Rashi, b. Yeb. 74a, in claiming that the produce in the last batch is deemed to have the status of un-consecrated produce. This is not what H states.

[35] Lieberman (TK, I, pp. 366-7) notes that shoots of beets are a type of produce which M. Or. 3:7 states never is neutralized from the status of ^{c}*orlah*. Lieberman concludes that during Judah b. Baba's time, or in his particularly dwelling place, shoots of beets

were no more prized than any other type of produce. On the basis
of T. 5:10L he states that in the same way, over a period of time,
people's love (ḥbybwt) for all other types of produce waned.
Lieberman's reasoning is not sound, since it reads into Judah b.
Baba's opinion considerations which are extraneous to it.

[36]See Primus, pp. 57-8, who offers a more complete formal
analysis.

[37]Primus, p. 56.

[38]Note M. 2:4D, which states specifically that all types of
figs and pressed figs are deemed a single species.

[39]So Neusner, *Eliezer*, vol. 1, p. 50, cited also by Primus,
pp. 56-7.

[40]K and L are fully aware of and point out this shift. I am
unable to account for the reversal of the positions of the two
authorities. See Neusner, *op. cit.*, pp. 52-3.

[41]The words "but he does not know which [jar]" at M. 4:10M,
are included to allow for Joshua's opinion, O. They are irrelevant to, and in fact confuse, Eliezer's statement, N.

[42]Neusner, *op. cit.*, pp. 51-2. Neusner also cites the interpretation offered by prior exegetes of M. for the pericope as
it stands before us.

[43]For Lieberman's explanation, see n. 44.

[44]Lieberman, TK, I, pp. 369-70, states that Meir, T. 5:10,
reverses the opinions of Eliezer and Joshua for the case of
M. 4:8, and that Judah does the same here for M. 4:10's dispute
in order to make the opinions of each authority consistently
stringent or lenient.

[45]See y. Dem. 4:1 (s.v., *ᶜl r ḥgy 'mryn*), cited by Lieberman,
TK, I, p. 370.

[46]In the case cited here, all of the heave-offering of the
tithe separated from the batch of produce falls into that same
produce. Since heave-offering of the tithe is a full tenth of the
produce, it is not neutralized but, rather, imparts the status of
heave-offering to the produce with which it is mixed.

[47]Lieberman, TK, I, p. 371, cites M. Or. 2:1, which claims
that heave-offering of the tithe separated from *demai* is neutralized under the same conditions as is other heave-offering. Only
sages, at F, would agree.

[48]This pericope is both formally and substantively autonomous
of its redactional context in T. I am unable to account for its
positioning.

[49]Maimonides, Bert and TYY state that the issue here is
whether or not produce which takes on the status of heave-offering
by being mixed with that offering itself has the power to impart
the status of heave-offering to produce with which it is mixed.
According to this interpretation Yose's point is that although the
half *se'ah* of heave-offering will have imparted its status to the
bundle with which it initially is mixed, all of the produce in

this bundle does not impart the status of heave-offering to unconsecrated produce with which it subsequently is mixed. While
this exegesis can be supported on the basis of C, it does not take
into account the redactional juxtaposition of M. 4:12 and 4:13.

NOTES TO CHAPTER FIVE

[1]I argue this in Neusner, *Judaism*, Appendix I, part iv, as
well as below, p. 173-74.

[2]O^1, B, C and O^2 read "[The heave-offering] is neutralized
and eaten...." Since heave-offering which is mixed with less than
a hundred times its quantity in unconsecrated produce is not
neutralized (M. 4:7), this reading clearly is in error. See on
this point Sacks-Hutner, p. 140, n. 6, who cites MS.

[3]See above, p. 350, n. 19.

[4]These same rules should apply to a case in which unclean
heave-offering is mixed with first tithe, second tithe or produce
dedicated to the Temple, A-B. In those cases the priest simply
may not eat the heave-offering which he finally receives.

[5]The printed edition reads *ltwk m'h*. Eleven MSS. have *lm'h*.
There is, of course, no difference in meaning.

[6]B. Bek. 22b reads: let rot. On the problem of the reading
here, see Sacks-Hutner, p. 141, n. 10. The distinction made between heave-offering which is left to rot (e.g., M. 5:1A-D) and
that which is burned (as in the present case) is based on a distinction between produce which may be unclean, and that which
surely is unclean. Since the former might be clean, it may not be
destroyed. Yet since it may be unclean, it likewise may not be
eaten by a priest. It therefore is left to rot. Heave-offering
which certainly is unclean, on the other hand, is disposed of
through burning, as M. Tem. 7:3 states.

[7]Sifré Bammidbar #121 proves from Num. 18:29 that heave-
offering imposes its own status upon unconsecrated produce with
which it is mixed.

[8]I interpolate "unclean" at A and B, as is required by the
sense of E and F. It is of course possible that the pericope is
not unitary, and that A-D deals with the neutralization of clean
heave-offering in clean unconsecrated produce. If this is the
case, however, Judah is left to reject the basic premise that
heave-offering is neutralized, an unlikely situation. The glosses
at E-F, further, would be left with no antecedent rule. Y. Ter.
4:13, in fact, cites A+C, inclusive of the word "unclean."

[9]Lieberman, TK, I, p. 374, follows Jonah b. Judah Gershon and
states 1) that D should read Yose instead of Judah, and 2) that
the case is one in which the unclean heave-offering has not been
mixed with the clean produce, as at T. 5:13E-F. There is, however, no MS. support for the emendation. There is little likelihood that this pericope knows the issue of T. 5:13.

[10]Lieberman, *loc. cit.*, states that the pericope is a continuation of T. 5:13, and that the case is one in which unclean
heave-offering has been mixed with clean heave-offering. Judah

holds that since the produce is susceptible to uncleanness, as E
makes clear, the priest will be careful not to allow the unclean
heave-offering to become lost in the clean, and so to impart uncleanness to it. For this reason Judah (or Yose; see n. 9) holds
that the unclean heave-offering simply can be recovered from the
mixture. Since invalid heave-offering, F, does not impart a
status of uncleanness to produce which it touches, the priest is
not careful with such a mixture, and so the heave-offering is
neutralized. While Lieberman's reference to the question of
whether or not the householder (or priest) is careful with the
mixture is given some support at y. Ter. 4:13, it seems unlikely
from the language before us that this issue is known to T.

[11]See Neusner, *Eliezer*, vol. 1, pp. 56-7.

[12]E reads "unclean heave-offering." This is a scribal error.

[13]Lieberman, TK, I, p. 379, states that this rule implies
that the priests were not themselves trusted as regards observance
of the law of the ${}^{c}omer$. If this were not so, the householder
could give the priest his share immediately and expect him to refrain from eating it until the proper time arrived. This is not
a point intended by the framers of the pericope.

[14]In sages view, at the time that the second *se'ah* of heave-
offering falls into the batch, that batch already contains almost
a full *se'ah* of heave-offering. The batch therefore takes on the
sanctified status of a priestly gift.

[15]E reads "less than a hundred." The reading self-evidently
is incorrect, since according to it, no replacement offering
should be taken.

[16]*Lolium temulentum*, a kind of weed which grows among wheat.
See Feliks, *Agriculture*, p. 120, n. 42 and Lieberman, TK, p. 387,
n. 42.

[17]My interpretation of the preceding follows Lieberman and
HD, as indicated in the translation. Neither of these commentators refers to this problem.

[18]These rules assume the view of Eliezer and sages, M. 5:5-8,
that even after heave-offering is neutralized or imparts its own
status to produce with which it is mixed, we take into account the
quantity of true heave-offering found in the mixture.

[19]This same distinction is made by Yose, T. 5:10aP-R.

[20]*Vigna sinensis*: Feliks, *Agriculture*, p. 152 and p. 152,
n. 284, listed as *fwl hmṣry*. Löw, *Planzennamen*, p. 312, gives:
Vicia faba for *fwl hlbn*.

[21]*Lathyrus cicera*: Lieberman, TK, I, p. 389.

[22]M. Or. 2:11 refers to a case like that of A-B. Eliezer
there states that the heave-offering imparts a sanctified status
to the dough only if it is mixed with it after the unconsecrated
leaven, such that it completes the leavening process (Albeck).
Sages hold that unless the leaven in the status of heave-offering
is of sufficient quantity by itself to leaven the dough, it is
neutralized. Neither of these positions agrees with T. 6:11B's

view that the status of the dough is judged by whether or not the leaven in the status of heave-offering imparts its own taste to the mixture.

NOTES TO CHAPTER SIX

[1]The syntax of the Hebrew text is difficult here. I follow Bert and Albeck in supplying the words "since" and "even." Danby offers a comparable translation: "[therefore] even if the priest would remit he may not."

[2]The case of a non-priest who intentionally eats heave-offering is discussed at M. 7:1.

[3]See Martin Noth, *Leviticus*, pp. 46 and 162, and J.R. Porter, *Leviticus*, pp. 45 and 174. Porter likens the fifth to a guilt offering. MR suggests a different view. See his comments to M. 6:2 and, in particular, to M. 3:1.

[4]First tithe is not usually referred to as consecrated. The reference here, however, is to first tithe from which heave-offering of the tithe has not yet been separated. This produce does have a sanctified status. See Lieberman, TK, I, p. 364, and, in particular, Sifré Korah, #119, Horovitz, p. 146, which Lieberman cites.

[5]This refers us back to M. 4:7's dispute about the quantity of unconsecrated produce required to neutralize heave-offering. Yose's position, K, is the same as that of Eliezer, M. 4:7A; Simeon's has no counterpart in M. 4:7. It is on the basis of this debate that T. 5:8b has been redacted in its context in T., with other materials supplementary to M. 4:7. H-K, however, is out of place in that context.

[6]Lieberman and HY state that the basis of Simeon's opinion is the fact that Lev. 22:14 refers specifically only to the eating of heave-offering, and does not explicitly prohibit using it as a lotion.

[7]This interpretation of B-C follows b. Pes. 32b's version of the pericope, cited also by MB, HY and Lieberman.

[8]Reference to this rule is made at Sifra, *'Emor*, *pereq* 6:3, cited by Lieberman, TK, I, p. 397.

[9]The meaning of *hmyšt hmynym* ("the five kinds") is not clear. It is usually taken to refer to the five species of grain for which the Land of Israel was known, i.e., wheat, barley, rye, oat and spelt (Jastrow, p. 775-6, s.v. *myn*).

[10]This same emendation is accepted by HY and Lieberman, TK, I, p. 399. The ruling would be the same if the second act of eating involved produce of a different kind.

[11]I follow Lieberman in deleting six words from the text of V. These occur in that MS. through dittography.

[12]My translation of T. 7:4b-6 relies upon that of Sarason, *Demai*, p. 98.

[13]The rule that heave-offering must be given to a priest who is scrupulous about cleanness is assumed here, but neither stated nor adduced elsewhere in the tractate.

[14]I read with V (*^{c}wnh 'wtn dmym*) and ed. princ. (*nwtn lhn dmym*). E reads: "And the [priest who is a] *haber* does not give them its monetary equivalent." The reason for this choice of reading is made clear in my exegesis of the pericope.

[15]The printed edition and the text in Albeck read *lkl my šyrṣh*. Eleven MSS. have *lmy šyrṣh*. There is no difference in meaning.

[16]See M. 8:1, which deals with the right of a priest's wife to eat heave-offering.

[17]Bert, TYY and Sens state that the woman has eaten heave-offering which she separated from her own produce but did not give to a priest. This being the case, the heave-offering is hers to give to whichever priest she wishes. I see no reason that the rule should be restricted to such a case.

[18]So GRA. Bert, TYY and TYT conclude that, according to Meir, the householder gives the priest the monetary equivalent of the heave-offering, as if he had stolen, but not eaten, that offering (see M. 6:4). I do not understand how they reach this conclusion since, according to M. 6:4, a person who steals heave-offering pays twice its monetary equivalent. This is not Meir's view here. Further, the language of M. 6:4 distinguishes explicitly between cases in which the non-priest pays the principal (*qrn*), and those in which he pays the value of the heave-offering (*dmy trwmh*).

[19]The verse reads, *If a man delivers to his neighbor money or goods to keep, and it is stolen out of the man's house, then, if the thief is found, he shall pay double.*

[20]Such a dedication of heave-offering to the Temple is carried out by the priest who owned the heave-offering (Albeck). Cf., Y. Ter. 1:1.

[21]See Lev. 5:16, which refers to "holy things of the Lord" and states, *He shall also make restitution for what he has done amiss in the holy thing, and shall add a fifth to it and give it to the priest.*

[22]See M. B.M. 4:9,and T. Ter. 7:8A-D which explains from Scripture why this is the case. Cf.,Maimonides, *Commentary.*

[23]In E the word "that" is written between the lines of the text.

[24]Lieberman suggests reading here: "This [added] fifth is liable to the law of sacrilege." While this statement surely is in keeping with the law, there is no textual evidence supporting such an emendation of T.

[25]On the laws of sacrilege, see Neusner, *Holy Things,* vol. 5, chapter 8, pp. 79-84.

[26]Lieberman, TK, I, p. 401, states that the reference here is to heave-offering which the non-priest has received as an inheritance or in payment of a debt, as at T. 7:7G-K. While this solves

the difficulty presented by L, it depends on a unitary reading of several formally and substantively distinct pericopae of T.

[27]The reading with "not" (here and at B) clearly is secondary, poorly attested in MSS. and among the exegetes of M. For a complete discussion, see Sacks-Hutner, vol. 2, p. 151.

[28]Sifra cites the whole of the pericope and proves Meir's position on the basis of Lev. 22:14. Scripture's statement that the non-priest must *give the holy thing to the priest* is taken to mean that restitution must be paid with produce which is fit to take on a sanctified status.

[29]We recall however that the produce must be fully tithed at the time it is given as restitution (M. 6:1E). The reason for this is explained above, p. 194.

[30]For a complete discussion, see my treatment of M. 1:5, above, pp. 50-52. That pericope contains the same list of items that is found here.

[31]If the first tithe still is liable to the separation of heave-offering of the tithe, it may not be given as restitution. The priest already has a claim on it.

[32]I assume that the reference is to produce which was dedicated to the Temple before it became liable to the separation of tithes. Even when it is redeemed, it does not take on such liability (see above, p. 52).

[33]My view is that of Sifra (*'Emor*, *pereq* 6:5). Yoḥanan (y. Ter. 6:5) and Maimonides. Simeon b. Laqish (y. Ter. 6:5), Bert and TYY hold that sages dispute only C.

[34]Eight MSS. designate D-I as M. 6:7.

[35]Note Primus, p. 61, who follows Neusner, *Eliezer*, vol. I, p. 59, in stating, "The case in D [my D-E] in fact provides a common ground for Aqiba and Eliezer in so far as the opinion of the latter is limited by B. If the sixth-year cucumbers are available, but not acceptable, as for instance, if they have hardened, then, according to B, Eliezer would agree that they cannot be used (see Bert., TYY)." He continues, p. 62, "The limitation of Eliezer's view in B would not be inferred from the exegesis in F [my G-H].... Since B brings Eliezer over to Aqiba's opinion, it seems that Aqiban editors have transmitted this tradition." The exegesis at F-I, we presently see, is further evidence for Primus' theory. It attributes to Eliezer what clearly is the Aqiban view regarding the restitutions' taking on a sanctified status.

[36]HD and HY suggest reading "heave-offering." See below, n. 37.

[37]HD, HY and Lieberman are troubled by the fact that T. M.S. 3:11 and b. Ḥul. 130b state explicitly that restitution may not be paid for untithed produce which is eaten. T. M.S. 3:11 states that the offender's only recourse is to beg forgiveness from heaven. This being the case, HD and HY emend A to read "heave-offering." Lieberman, TK, I, p. 403, offers a more complicated emendation, allowing for a citation of M. 6:6A and a separate rule on unconsecrated produce. There are, however, no textual variants on which to base such emendations. It is more likely that we simply have contradictory rules.

NOTES TO CHAPTER SEVEN

[1]See, e.g., M. Miq. Chapter One.

[2]Maimonides, TYY and Bert note that Lev. 22:14 refers only to an individual who unintentionally eats a holy thing, thereby excluding from the requirement to pay the added fifth a person who intentionally eats heave-offering.

[3]My interpretation of this pericope follows Maimonides.

[4]The pericope is formally and substantively parallel to T. Miq. 2:3-4. My translation and comment, accordingly, follow the model offered by Neusner, *Purities*, vol. 13, pp. 54-55.

[5]Lieberman, TK, I, p. 392, offers a different and more complicated interpretation of the pericope. I follow GRA, cited by MB.

[6]Notably, the pericope assumes that non-priests eat unconsecrated food in a state of cleanness.

[7]Lieberman, (TZ, I, p. 141) cites Jonah b. Judah Gershon (who states that it is permitted to measure the heave-offering (see M. 4:6) since, at the time of the measuring, the offering already has been designated and separated.

NOTES TO CHAPTER EIGHT

[1]For a review of approaches to this problem in moral theory, see the chapter on Consequentialism in Donagan, pp. 172-209. In particular, see pp. 182-83, where Donagan discusses the implications for moral theory of the rules of M. 8:12 and T. 7:20.

[2]My interpretation of this pericope carries forward that offered by William Green, "Techniques," pp. 1-11. See also Neusner, *Eliezer*, vol. 1, pp. 61-62.

[3]On this point, see Green, p. 4.

[4]My interpretation differs from that of prior exegetes of M., who simply claim a distinction between the biblical injunction concerning priests of impaired lineage and that regarding priests who are blemished (see e.g., Bert). Their interpretation does not explain why Joshua and Eliezer disagree on the law of the priest of impaired lineage and agree on the case of the blemished priest.

[5]See Albeck, p. 390, who discusses the way in which the wife of a priest (A-B) may be deemed divorced before she actually is informed of her husband's actions.

[6]The case of the priest (E-F) is different only in that it turns out that he never had the right to eat heave-offering. He must pay the principal and added fifth for all the priestly gifts he ever had eaten.

[7]MR differs from the other exegetes of M. and from y.'s view in stating that the issue here is the proper disposal of heave-offering which has become unfit for consumption. Eliezer's position, he says, is that even in its present condition, the

heave-offering may not be allowed to be ruined. The individual
therefore swallows it, and does not spit it out onto the ground.
Joshua, however, holds that once the heave-offering is unfit for
consumption (in this case, consumption by another person), the
individual may do anything necessary to dispose of it. While, as
MR notes, these positions are comparable to those views held by
Eliezer and Joshua at M. 8:8, this interpretation is unacceptable
in light of the authorities' agreement at S-V and the cases at
M. 8:3.

[8]TYY and Bert state that M. 8:2M-O refers only to the case of
the woman or slave. Since the priest never had the right to eat
heave-offering, they state that his case is just like that at S-V.
As at S-V, Eliezer should hold that the priest of impaired lineage
must spit out the heave-offering, which he never had the right to
eat. While TYY and Bert's reasoning surely is correct, their interpretation cannot be upheld on the basis of the language at
M. 8:2M. This further inconsistency in Eliezer's thought is additional evidence for my view (p. 231) that the pericope is formulated with Joshua's point of view in mind.

[9]Alternatively, Eliezer's view is that since the individual
already is liable for his actions, he may complete them without
added culpability (TYY, TYT, Maimonides). If this is his view,
however, I do not understand why Eliezer should agree that in the
case of S-V the individual must stop eating. This interpretation
also is unacceptable in light of the cases at M. 8:3. There the
individual will incur liability only upon swallowing the food in
his mouth.

[10]Green, p. 6.

[11]Bert and TYY read this pericope into their interpretation
of M. 8:3.

[12]Lieberman, "Light," p. 395, states that the term "different path" refers to heterodoxy. See below, n. 15.

[13]See also HD. Lieberman, TK, I, p. 406, cites Rashi to
b. Ket. 60a, who states that the loaf here is in the status of
heave-offering, and that the problem is whether or not the individual may waste some of the sanctified produce by scraping it
away. One need hardly assume from the language of T., however,
that we deal here with produce in the status of heave-offering.
This surely is not the concern in the continuation of the pericope.

[14]The six cases are not a unitary construction, as is evidenced by the shift in language, *culpable/exempt*, at C-F,
permitted/forbidden, at G-H. It is possible that this is an
original triplet of C, D and F, three cases beginning with (or
assuming) the words "If he ate," glossed by E and augmented by G-H.
In all events, the redactor's intent is clear, as I have numbered
the cases in the translation.

[15]According to Lieberman, "Light," I implies that certain
ultra-pious Jewish sects of Judah's time deemed all tiny insects
forbidden as food. They thus were scrupulous about removing all
creatures from liquids they drank. Judah therefore considers
straining liquids a heterodox practice. Prayers said to the sun
(J), which are not ordained by rabbinical authority, are in the
same category. Since we know of no such sects in Judah's time,
and since the very meaning of "a different path" is unclear, this

view is highly conjectural. Lieberman goes on to argue from statements in the Damascus Covenant and Josephus that Judah's statements are directed against the Essenes. The difference between
the time in which Judah lived and the documented existence of the
Essene community makes this unlikely.

[16]This interpretation is given by Maimonides, Bert, TYY, MR
and Albeck. Alfasi (to b. A.Z. 30a; cited by Albeck) Sens and
Tur Yoreh De^{c}ah #116 (cited by MR) hold the opposite view. These
authorities state that large quantities of liquid are subject to
the law, since venom which they contain will be diluted and therefore invisible to the eye. Small quantities, on the other hand,
normally are permitted, for if they contain venom, it will be
visible. This latter view surely is incorrect. According to it,
most major sources of water (wells, ponds, cisterns) would be forbidden, for they contain large quantities of water. T., moreover,
assumes that water in jugs and small jars is liable. According
to the view just cited, it would not be.

[17]None of the exegetes cited in the previous footnote offers
an explanation of Yose's view.

[18]Y. Ter. 8:6 (cited by Lieberman, TK, I, p. 415 and HY) adds
that at the time Johanan came upon the pond it was raining. Y.'s
point clearly is that Johanan deemed the pond permitted because
of the flow of rain-water into it (so Lieberman, *loc. cit.*; cf.,
PM), comparable to the flow of water in a spring.

[19]Bert and TYY state that by way of the moisture in the produce the venom becomes spread throughout the vegetable. If there
is a snake bite on dry produce, the individual simply may cut off
that part of the piece of produce and eat the rest. Maimonides
has this same view when he states that a piece of produce is forbidden on account of snake bites only if the bites pierce the
vegetable down to its moist insides. Cf. y. Ter. 8:7.

[20]My interpretation follows Albeck. Alternatively, Bert and
Maimonides read at B *kkr* ("loaf") and state that even if the produce is very large, such that a single person does not eat a whole
piece, it still is forbidden. A third explanation is offered by
TYY and MS, who state that *kkr* refers to a large quantity of produce (TYY: sixty *maneh*). According to this view, even though it
is unlikely that a snake could have bitten and deposited venom in
all of the produce, that produce still is forbidden. MR, finally,
states that *kkr* refers to a loaf of pressed figs (*kkr dbylh*), and
that the point is that even though there is a bite only on one
fig, the whole loaf is forbidden. I find none of these interpretations convincing, and therefore have chosen to uphold the best
attested reading at B.

[21]Maimonides, Bert, MR and Albeck ignore this lemma. TYY
claims that it indicates that Yose (M. 8:5D) concedes that produce
still on a tree, unlike water contained in pools in the ground, is
subject to the law. There are however no substantive or formal
grounds on which to claim that M. 8:6 was formulated with M. 8:5
in mind. TYY presupposes a unitary text in which every rule knows
and interacts with every other rule.

[22]In six MSS. the pericope appears as a continuation of
M. 8:6. Except for the common issue addressed, I see no formal or
substantive reasons for reproducing it as such. I therefore have
followed the division of pericopae found in standard editions of M.

[23]Albeck cites MS, who states that this pericope is lacking
from most of the editions of M. known to him. In the extant MSS.,
however, it is missing only from K and G[7]. In both of these it
has been copied by a later hand into the margin. Epstein, *Mabo'*,
p. 950, cites a MS. (which I am unable to identify from the reference he gives) which indicates M. 8:7 to be an interpolation, according to Epstein, from the Tosefta. The pericope, however, appears in the form it has in M. neither in T. nor in any other
rabbinic document. The evidence adduced thus is not sufficient
to show the pericope to be an interpolation.

[24]E reverses the order of P and Q-R.

[25]HY and MB do not comment. Y. Ter. 8:6 (followed by HD)
reverses the order of A and B-D. It thus claims that the wine in
the vat at A is wine which still is fermenting, and so in no case
is liable. That however is not what is suggested in T.'s version,
as Lieberman, TK, I, p. 416 points out. Lieberman proposes that
the reason for Judah b. Baba's ruling is that there was in the vat
sufficient wine for it not to be subject to the law of uncovered
liquids. Lieberman thus sees the *ma*^{a}*seh* as standing in dispute
with the rule given at T. 7:14/O-P (above, p. 235), that wine
always is subject to the law. This is not suggested by the facts
of the case as given in T. 7:15. It is possible that the vat here
was in fact covered. But if this is the case, it is unclear how
the dead snake got into it.

[26]Lieberman, TK, I, p. 418, suggests that the words "in the
case of dried foods" have dropped out of the text. There are no
grounds for this proposal except the assumption that Simeon b.
Menasia should not disagree with the law as stated in M.

[27]Lieberman, TK, I, p. 418 is troubled by the fact that elsewhere mushrooms are indicated as a kind of food. (Lieberman offers
no citations and does not state to which documents he refers.) On
this basis he suggests that the mushrooms referred to here are
those mentioned at b. Shab. 108a, which grow in jugs of water.
Lieberman states that since these mushrooms are nourished from
uncovered water we would expect them to be forbidden. Neither the
pericope before us, nor b. Shab. 108a, knows this consideration.
It therefore is more likely that we simply have contradictory
notions about whether or not mushrooms are fit for consumption.

[28]See above, p. 331, n. 6.

[29]So Neusner, *Eliezer*, p. 64, and Green, *Joshua*, p. 77.

[30]On M. 8:10P see Neusner, *Eliezer*, p. 63, and MR.

[31]Bert, MR and Albeck state that in order to save the heave-
offering in cleanness the householder must go to bring a clean
jug. In the meantime some of the heave-offering will flow down
into unclean, unconsecrated wine (or, oil) in the lower vat and
render that batch forbidden (see M. 5:1). The point of M. 8:9H
and M. 8:10M is that Joshua agrees with Eliezer that even so, if
the householder can save a fair quantity of the heave-offering in
cleanness, he must do so, and allow the rest of the heave-offering
and the unconsecrated wine to be ruined. The householder cannot,
however, use his hands to prevent all of the wine from running
down into the lower vat, thereby making unclean a great deal more
heave-offering than otherwise would have been rendered unclean. I

agree with Neusner, *Eliezer*, p. 64, that this is reading too much
into the pericope, especially M. 8:10, which knows nothing of a
lower vat.

[32]The formulation here is that of Green, *Joshua*, p. 79. According to Joshua's view, the householder may stop the heave-
offering from running down into the lower vat and mixing with the
unconsecrated wine there. By doing so, he salvages the oil for
use, for example, in lighting the lamp of a priest (M. 11:10).
Cf., Neusner, *Eliezer*, p. 65.

[33]Maimonides, followed by Bert and Albeck, states that Joshua
also agrees to the rule given at M. 8:12. They suggest no reason
for which Joshua would not simply apply to this case his previously
held position.

[34]T. 1:14a is above, p. 45. This pericope is formally and
substantively autonomous of its context in T. Chapter One.

[35]A better reading would be Eliezer, that is, the authority
cited in M. There is however no MS. evidence for such a reading.

[36]Lieberman, TK, I, p. 306, states that at H the householder
has no place in which to hide the heave-offering. This is not
indicated in the text of T., and, further, does not resolve the
contradiction between Eleazar's view here and his previous contention that the householder may not allow a gentile to render the
heave-offering unclean.

[37]My view here is supported by M. Pes. 1:7, which has Joshua
state that heave-offering which might be unclean may be burned
with heave-offering which certainly is unclean. This does not
agree with T. 7:18A. In M. Pes. 1:7 Eliezer, on the other hand,
holds that unclean heave-offering may not be burned with that which
is in doubt, a position which is compatible with that of T. 7:18A.
This being the case, I find no basis for Lieberman's view, TK, I,
p. 418, that both Eliezer and Joshua agree to the rule of A.

[38]T. Toh. 8:14 gives the case of E, but rules that the heave-
offering is deemed clean. Neusner, *Purities*, vol. 11, p. 178,
states that this is the case because in going to ask of its status,
the householder shows concern for, and willingness to protect, the
heave-offering. While the point thus surely is the same as that
made by T. 7:18D-E, I find no way to explain the contradictory
texts.

[39]Lieberman, TK, I, p. 420, suggests that the version of M.
known to T. contained only the dispute between Eliezer and
Gamaliel, M. 8:8A-C+F, and included no reference to the opinion of
Joshua. T. 7:19, then, provides what should be acceptable to both
Eliezer and Gamaliel. The householder must allow the heave-offering to impart its own status to the wine in the lower vat and to
be made unclean at the same time. The householder himself, however, may not render the heave-offering unclean. Lieberman's
theory depends on the unproven assumption that T. knows a version
of M. different than the one extant today. It also disregards
the fact that T. commonly records opinions different from those
cited in M.

[40]On this rule, see Donagan, pp. 182-83.

[41]F-H, further, interrupts the progression of ideas from C-E
to I-J+K, both of which refer to Sheba the son of Bichri. F-H,
thus, would be better placed before C-E.

NOTES TO CHAPTER NINE

[1]M. 9:4 applies this principle to a case of doubt whether or
not a garden-bed is planted with heave-offering. As we shall see,
however, that case serves to emphasize the disjuncture between
the principle governing this part of the chapter and the principle
of M. 8:1-4.

[2]Ca, N, Sa, T[3] add: *and poorman's tithe*. This is a scribal
error. Cf., M. 9:3/O.

[3]See M. 9:4A. Cf., Primus, *Aqiva*, pp. 66-68, and Gereboff,
Tarfon, p. 27.

[4]See "Flax," *Encyclopaedia Brittanica*, (Chicago, 1968), vol.
9, p. 430. The seeds of flax are the source of linseed oil, used
in ancient times as food.

[5]Gereboff, *Tarfon*, p. 27, is correct in stating that "Tarfon
can admit to the validity of this [i.e., Aqiba's] argument and
still maintain the reasoning attributed to him." Gereboff goes
on to note, "Thus as is common throughout the entire Tarfon-
corpus, Aqivan redactors have attempted to portray Aqiva as the
wiser of the two masters. But in the present pericope, they have
not given Aqiva a good argument."

[6]MS. E lacks the attribution at C and all of D. This is a
scribal error, homoeoteleuton.

[7]The usual translation of the Hebrew "*hwlyn*" is "unconsecrated produce." This refers to produce which is properly tithed
and ready for consumption by an Israelite. This clearly is not
what is intended here, for crops grown from the types of produce
listed at C do need to be tithed before they are eaten (as T.
8:5-6 will state explicitly). I therefore have translated "common
food," which both captures the sense of the Hebrew "*hwlyn*" and
allows for the meaning which the term must elicit.

[8]R reads: at the value of the seed. This reading does not
change the point of E. See Sacks-Hutner, p. 174, ns. 129-130.

[9]Bert, TYY and MR follow b. Shab. 17b in stating that this
rule was enacted in order to encourage householders not to leave
heave-offering in their homes until the point at which the produce
goes to seed. M. knows no such consideration.

[10]This is analogous to the rules governing the Substitutes
and offspring of animal offerings. The offspring or Substitute
of an offering has the same status as the original animal. The
Substitute of an offspring, or the Substitute of a Substitute,
however, retains an unconsecrated status (see M. Tem. 1:5 and 2:3
on Substitutes of Substitutes, and M. Tem. Chapter Three, on the
offspring of animal offerings). Judah, however, should not agree
with the present law, for he holds (M. Tem. 1:5) that the offspring of an animal offering does in fact produce a Substitute.
This is comparable to a claim that a crop grown from heave-offering

in turn produces a crop which has the status of heave-offering.
Cf., y. Bik. 2:2, which reads into the exegesis of our pericope
the consideration of whether or not the seed is of a type which
is integral to the crop which it produces.

[11]Only the heave-offering of the tithe contained in first
tithe is consecrated. T. 8:5 (below, p. 259) relates to the
problem posed by this offering.

[12]My understanding of the term "added quantity of heave-
offering (*twspt trwmh*)," at A, equals that of MB, HY and Lieberman. For B, see MB, HY and HD.

[13]This interpretation follows MB and HY. Cf., Lieberman, TK,
I, p. 428, who follows HD (and Shiṭṭah Mequbeṣet to b. Ned. 48b)
in claiming that T. refers to a crop grown from first or second
tithe of a kind the seed of which does not disintegrate (see
M. 9:5). While according to this view the point of the pericope
remains substantially the same as I have stated it, it seems to
me that this interpretation reads more than is necessary into the
language of T.

[14]Cf., y. Ter. 9:4, followed by TYY, which reads the considerations of this pericope into the interpretation of M. 9:4.

[15]On the rule governing the consumption of untithed produce
as a chance meal, see Jaffee, Introduction.

[16]This is the view of Rabah (b. Pes. 34a), Sens, Rabad (on
Maimonides, *Heave-offering* 11:23), and Albeck. Maimonides, Bert
and TYY hold that the produce is forbidden both to priests and
non-priests. This law, they say, was enacted in order to prevent
individuals from planting produce in the status of heave-offering.
Such a consideration, however, is not known to M.

[17]Judah's view is in keeping with his statement at M. Tem.
1:5 (see above, n. 10), where he holds that, in the case of animal
offerings, the Substitute of a Substitute has the same status as
the original offering.

[18]As noted in the translation, I follow the reading of b. Ned.
58b, followed also by HY and Shiṭṭah Mequbeṣet (cited by Lieberman,
TK, I, p. 427). Cf., Lieberman, *ibid*., who prefers the reading
of E and V (i.e., "he may not make a chance meal of it"). This
reading is not to be preferred for, as Lieberman himself notes,
it makes the phrase "even though" (at B) nonsensical. It also
creates a tension between A-C and Simeon's gloss at D. Cf., GRA,
who has simply created a composite of the version of the pericope
found in M., and that of MSS. E and V.

[19]Lieberman correctly notes that T. 8:8b would more logically
be redacted before T. 8:8a. It thus would follow directly upon
T. 8:7, which likewise supplements M. 9:6-7, and not upon T. 8:8a,
which belongs with the rules of M. Chapter Ten. While it is possible that the redactor of T. has his own theory of the logical
ordering of these materials, or sees some connection between
T. 8:8a and T. 8:8b, this is not apparent to me.

[20]An onion set is an area heavily planted with onions, which
will produce a crop for several years. See "Onion," *Encyclopaedia
Brittanica*, (Chicago, 1968), v. 16, p. 967.

NOTES TO CHAPTER TEN

[1]Maimonides, Bert, TYY and Albeck follow y. Ter. 10:1, which states that the present law applies only if the heave-offering and unconsecrated produced are placed together after the unconsecrated produce has been cooked, but not if they actually are cooked together. Y.'s point, unknown to M., is that in the process of cooking, the heave-offering invariably imparts its flavor to the unconsecrated produce.

[2]Maimonides, Bert, and Albeck state that the point of the pericope is the same whether it is the lentils or the onions which are in the status of heave-offering. These exegetes make this claim because they incorrectly read the issue of whether or not the heave-offering imparts flavor to the other food as central at A-D, as well as at E-I. The pericope, however, clearly assumes that the onion is heave-offering, as Judah's opinion, H-I, proves. The view I take in reference to this matter is the same as that of TYY.

[3]I find no reason that the rule for lentils, A-E, should be different from the rule for any other food. Presumably E has been formulated simply to harmonize the contradictory rules at A-D and E-G. Cf., MR.

[4]MR states that Judah permits the mixture even if the heave-offering imparts its flavor to it, because the flavor of the onion spoils the taste of the brine. It therefore is not taken into account (see T. 8:9J-M, above, p. 269). This simply is not what M. 10:1I suggests.

[5]M. Or. 2:4 is cited by TYT and referred to by Maimonides.

[6]The rule self-evidently does not refer to the criterion expressed by M. 10:1 and assumed by M. 10:2D-F, of whether or not the heave-offering imparts flavor to the other food. The present rule does not however seem to me to contradict that principle, but only to offer a consideration pertinent to its particular case.

[7]So T. 8:9I-M, followed by TYY, TYT and Sens. Albeck cites M. A.Z. 5:2, which states that a dish flavored by wine used for libations is prohibited only if the flavoring benefits the Israelite who wishes to eat the dish. The point here clearly is the same.

[8]Lieberman has followed ed. princ. in supplying the words "wine," at B, through "oil," at C.

[9]For variant readings of T. 8:10A-C, see Lieberman, TK, I, p. 431.

[10]Ed. princ. mistakenly reads: permitted. See Lieberman, TK, I, p. 432.

[11]We recall that according to the law of neutralization, if heave-offering or other produce of special status is mixed with unconsecrated produce so as to comprise an insignificant proportion of the mixture as a whole, it is neutralized, and the mixture is permitted for consumption as unconsecrated food. I have interpolated the problem of neutralization into T. 8:11-12 on the basis of the phrases "and one lifted it out," at A, and "if he knew about it," at D. That these phrases constitute references to

cases of neutralization is proven by parallel usage at T. 5:9 and
T. 6:5, 8-9. This same interpretation of the pericope is given
by Lieberman, *loc. cit.*, and HD.

[12]On the reading of the printed edition, see Sacks-Hutner,
p. 180, n. 8. It appears that the word "bread" dropped out
through haplography.

[13]MR asks why the status of the bread is not determined by
whether or not the bread has taken on the taste of the heave-
offering. He concludes that the issue here simply is the status
the bread is deemed to have until a priest tastes it in order to
ascertain whether it has indeed been flavored by the heave-offering. While MR's interpretation is plausible it does not seem to
me to touch the deeper point of this dispute, as I state it in the
continuation of my comment.

[14]Bert and TYY hold, as I do, that Judah agrees that the bread
absorbs the wine vapor. They state that Judah's position is that
the vapor is immaterial, and therefore is not deemed to render the
bread forbidden. While this is an accurate restatement of Judah's
view, it ignores the question, which I answer, of why Judah deems
the vapor insignificant.

[15]Note in particular M. Makh. 3:3 (also M. Makh. 3:1), which
offers the present pericope in the context of the question of
whether or not the wine vapor renders the hot bread susceptible to
uncleanness. My interpretation is the same as that which Neusner,
Purities, vol. 17, pp. 57-58, gives for Judah's position there.
Neusner states that according to Judah, "we adjudge the matter
according to the man's deed.... He could and would have done
exactly what he wanted to indicate his intention, and not having
done so, has not made the wine capable of imparting susceptibility
to uncleanness to the bread which happens to be subject to its
fumes." I cannot determine whether the pericope is primary to
Tractate Terumot, or to its context in M. Makh. In both cases it
carries forward the point of the materials with which it is redacted. In each instance it likewise instantiates a view of Judah
evidenced by other materials in its same redactional unit.

[16]*Trigonella Foenum-graecum* (Feliks, *Agriculture*, p. 125,
n. 87). See "Fenugreek," *Encyclopaedia Britannica*, (Chicago,
1968), vol. 4, p. 176.

[17]G and L read: water. This same reading in K has been corrected to read "wine," as I have translated. The point of the
pericope is the same no matter which reading is accepted.

[18]On the basis of this problem the present unit has been redacted in Chapter Ten of Tractate Terumot.

[19]T. 8:9b is found above (p. 269), with M. 10:2, to which it
is supplementary. I cannot account for the fact that T. 8:9a has
been redacted before that pericope, instead of after T. 8:13. I
have placed it where it clearly belongs, as a redactional element
joining the issues of M. 10:3-4 and M. 10:5.

[20]According to Lieberman, TK, I, p. 440, at issue between
Meir and Judah is whether or not the stalks of the fenugreek are
deemed to have the status of heave-offering. Judah, he says, has
the position of M. 10:5, that they do not, while Meir, to the contrary, holds that they do. While Lieberman clearly is correct in

reading this pericope as supplementary to M. 10:5, he ignores the fact that T. knows nothing of M.'s distinction between seed and stalks. Lieberman likewise does not take into account the positions of Meir and Judah which M. 10:3 already has provided.

[21]Cf., Lieberman, *loc. cit.*, and y. Ma. 1:3, which he cites. I do not see the relevance of b. Erub. 81b and b. San. 25a, which Lieberman cites in his n. 35.

[22]See Neusner to T. Miq. 1:4 (*Purities*, vol. 13, p. 25). The pericope deals with problems related to heave-offering and so has its primary location in Tractate Terumot. As Neusner notes it is not pertinent to its context in T. Miq.

[23]Neither Lieberman, MB, HD or HY comments on this problem.

[24]An alternative to the solution I have offered is given by Sens (to M. Or. 2:13, cited by Lieberman). Sens reads at E and F, "A man should *not* lubricate...."

[25]Lieberman, MB and HY assume that the individual also will immerse the garment in an immersion pool in order to render it ritually clean.

[26]This lemma must be removed because it is nonsensical. There is no reason that a priest may not eat heave-offering which was flavored by unconsecrated produce. C has been added in V as the formal corollary to D, but surely is not primary to the pericope before us. On the basis of the text of E and the parallel passages in b., Lieberman, TK, I, p. 435, draws this same conclusion.

[27]E reads: If the heave-offering fell... It has this same locution for each point at which V reads: If one placed... There is no difference in meaning.

[28]E reads: And before him were [also] two mortars, one filled with heave-offering and one filled with unconsecrated produce. This appears to be a scribal error on the basis of T. 8:18J.

[29]Lieberman, TK, I, p. 435, upholds the reading of the MSS. at D. He states that in each of T.'s cases the pots are filled with produce and the mortars contain spice, the taste of which can be discerned if it is mixed with the produce. In the first case, A-D, the spice is in the status of heave-offering, and it is not known whether it was mixed with other heave-offering or with unconsecrated produce. According to Lieberman, since here we can determine on the basis of taste with which of the produce the heave-offering-spice was mixed, we initially deem it to have been mixed with the unconsecrated produce, as the MS. reading at D states. A priest later can taste that produce to see if that indeed is so. This is not the case in T.'s two other cases, in which either spice in the status of heave-offering or unconsecrated spice is mixed with produce. Since in these cases it cannot be determined on the basis of taste whether or not spice in the status of heave-offering was mixed with unconsecrated produce, we maintain the prevailing status of all of the produce, as I have explained in my commentary. This interpretation is interesting in that it both upholds the MS. reading at D, and explains the connection of these pericopae to the laws of M. Chapter Ten. It seems to me, however, that Lieberman reads more into the text of T. than is acceptable. That this is the case is highlighted by the fact that Lieberman does not explain why D does not read simply "if it imparts flavor,"

expected in cases dealing with the problem as Lieberman sees it. There is, further, no basis for the assumption that the term "mortar" refers specifically to a container of spices.

[30]Lieberman, TK, I, p. 437, follows E in deleting the word "forbidden," stating that the reference is to meat of sin offerings. The point in all events is the same, and I prefer to follow the reading of the parallel passage at T. Hul. 7:7, as well as the reading of V and ed. princ.

[31]At J-K, MS. E repeats F-G. This is a scribal error.

[32]The claim of J-L, that the status of uncleanness of food is neutralized when the food is mixed with clean edibles is in line with the position of the House of Hillel, M. 5:4. The Shammaites will not agree.

[33]In each of these cases olives in one condition, crushed or whole, are pickled with olives in a different state of preparation. The laws of neutralization therefore do not apply.

[34]My interpretation of the pericope follows y. Ter. 10:7, accepted likewise by Maimonides, Bert and TYY. Note MR, who reads M. 10:7 in light of M. 10:1's distinction between produce which is cut up when it is prepared with heave-offering and that which is whole.

[35]Maimonides and Bert interpret matters differently. They hold that what I take to be references to quantities of unclean fish, at C and in the opinions of Judah and Yose, indicate, rather, quantities of brine derived from unclean fish. The issue, then, is the proportion of unclean brine which must be present in the mixture in order to render unclean the clean fish pickled in that brine. While this interpretation attempts to take seriously the contention of A, that at issue here is the status of the clean fish, and not of the brine (see the continuation of my comment in the text), it does not take seriously M.'s own reference, at C, to the quantity of unclean fish in the mixture and, at E, to the status of the brine. Cf., T. 9:1H, which may be the source of Maimonides' and Bert's exegesis.

[36]As is clear from M. 10:7D, the unclean brine will in all events render unclean the clean fish which is pickled in it. So the force of B-G is to make the point called for by A. See, however, T. 9:2, which will not agree with this claim.

[37]Cf., Sens, who also refers to the problem of the superscription of this pericope. It appears from his comment that he adopts the reading of T. 9:1A, which claims that this superscription is comprised of two separate rules.

[38]HY states that on the basis of M., T. should be corrected to read *any keg*. This is a good example of the traditional harmonization of M. and T., which misses the point of T.'s function as critical commentary to M.

[39]Bert, TYY and Albeck state that Sadoq disputes A. A, they say, holds that brine from unclean locusts is itself unclean, but, as I have said (following y. Ter. 10:8), does not impart susceptibility to uncleanness. Sadoq, they claim, holds that the brine of unclean locusts neither is unclean itself, nor imparts

susceptibility to uncleanness. This interpretation must be rejected, since the pericope is not set in the form of a dispute.

[40]TYY notes that M. Sheb. 7:7 and 9:5, as well as M. Ter.
10:7, all are contradictory to A. He resolves the contradiction
by stating that M. 10:10 refers to cases involving vegetables.
He claims that the requirement to separate heave-offering from
these is rabbinic in origin, and not biblical. TYY further states
that the rules governing mixtures of heave-offering and unconsecrated produce are rabbinic. He thus concludes that the reason
for the rule of A is that a rabbinic prohibition, in this case,
the rule for mixtures, does not extend to agricultural offerings
which themselves are rabbinic in origin. While this reasoning is
common in the two *Talmudim*, it is not a viable interpretation of
M. That document itself knows no distinction between rabbinic and
biblical law. A different approach is taken by MR, who notes the
contradiction posed by the rule of M. 10:7. He states that as
regards the law, olives, which have a strong flavor, are comparable
to leeks. This does not seem to me to solve the problem. Note
also GRA and TYT. They follow y. Ter. 10:9 in claiming that here
the term pickling actually refers to boiling (see M. 10:11).
There is, self-evidently, no basis for this in the text before us.

[41]A different approach is that B was formulated at the time
of the redaction of the pericope, in reaction to the juxtaposition
of the otherwise contradictory rules at A and C-F.

[42]See Feliks, *Agriculture*, p. 118. He cites Löw, *Flora*, I,
p. 214.

[43]*Allium porrum capitatum*; Feliks, *Plant World*, p. 174.

[44]Feliks, *Agriculture*, p. 118, n. 18, states that Judah's
point is that of the things listed, porret alone has such a strong
flavor that it falls under the law of M. 10:10C-F. I do not see
how the language of T. supports this interpretation. For further
discussion of Judah's position, see Lieberman, TK, I, p. 444.

[45]My interpretation follows HD and Maimonides, *Heave-offering*
11:4. See Lieberman, TK, I, p. 445, who cites these same authorities and discusses the issue in terms of whether or not pickling
improves the taste of the onions in the status of heave-offering.
Since T. phrases matters in terms of the status of the vinegar,
this issue seems to me to be irrelevant to the point of the
pericope.

[46]For a more complete formal description of M. 10:11, including a statement of the differences in formulation between Aqiba's
opinion and A-B+C-D, see Primus, *Aqiba*, p. 69.

[47]Bert, TYY and Maimonides state that the several laws of
this pericope comprise qualifications of the rule of M. 10:10.
Yose in particular, they say, disputes the anonymous authority of
that pericope, claiming that beets in the status of heave-offering,
not leeks, render forbidden the unconsecrated produce with which
they are cooked. Since M. 10:10 and Yose here refer to different
methods of preparation, however, I see on the surface no dispute
between the two rules. The source of Bert, TYY and Maimonides'
view probably is y. Ter. 10:9's statement that M. 10:10 actually
refers to the case of foods which are boiled together, the same
method of cooking mentioned here (see above, n. 40).

[48]My interpretation of Aqiba's position follows Sens and Bert.
Maimonides states that Aqiba refers to a case in which permitted
meat is cooked with, and so flavored by, produce in the status of
heave-offering. This approach, based on a unitary reading of the
pericope, is not called for by the language of Aqiba's statement.
See MR, cited at length by Primus, p. 68. MR gives an overview
of the two traditions of exegesis of this pericope.

[49]In explaining this pericope, Lieberman, TK, I, p. 445,
follows Maimonides' interpretation of Aqiba's position. See above,
n. 47.

[50]Lieberman, *loc. cit.*, states that Aqiba's view holds only
for the case of vegetables, the separation of heave-offering from
which is ordained by rabbinic law, but not by Scripture. I already have discussed the problematic nature of this approach to
the exegesis of M., above, n. 40.

[51]On variant readings and interpretations of the pericope,
see Lieberman, TK, I, p. 446.

[52]E orders the laws of the pericope differently than V, the
order of which I have preserved. E places J first, followed by
G-I, K-L and finally D-F. There is no difference in meaning. For
a complete list of other sources which follow the order of E, see
Lieberman, TK, I, p. 447. Lieberman also discusses the implications of this ordering for b. Hul. 98a's interpretation of D-I.

NOTES TO CHAPTER ELEVEN

[1]The pericope probably originates as a doublet, A-B+C
paralleled at D+E. The third case then was appended for reasons
of substance. This case breaks the prevailing form. It lacks a
clause which balances C and E, and provides, rather, Judah's
dispute.

[2]See MR and b. A.Z. 38b.

[3]Judah's "for it improves it (*mšbyhw*)" is not set in contrast
to B's "since this ruins them (*m'bdn*)." The technical opposite
of the root *ŠBH* is *PGM* (T. 8:9bK-M), not *'BD*. This being the case,
A-E should not be interpreted in light of Judah's principle, as if
A and D simply offer cases in which the flavor of the food is
spoiled. This is not what is suggested by the language of B.

[4]My interpretation follows Lieberman, TK, I, pp. 451-2, MB
and HD. HY claims the issue here is whether the wine improves or
spoils the flavor of the brine. Eliezer, HY holds, says that it
spoils the flavor of the brine, and therefore does not impart to
that brine its status (see T. 8:9bK-M). I prefer to read the
pericope in terms of the issue of M. 11:1.

[5]Bert, TYY and Sens interpret M. 11:1A in light of this
pericope. See Lieberman, TK, I, p. 454, who refers to the question of whether T. agrees or disagrees with M., but who reaches
no conclusion of his own.

[6]See Green, "Techniques," p. 8.

[7]Maimonides, Bert, TYY and Albeck follow y. Ter. 11:2 in taking the logical view that Joshua exempts the individual only from the added fifth. Thus the non-priest must replace that which he wrongly ate. Since he is not culpable for eating consecrated food, however, he need not pay the penalty of the added fifth.

[8]According to the commentators cited in the previous note, Joshua's position is that the fruit juice is not equal to the original fruit, and therefore, while deemed to be heave-offering, does not have a consecrated status at all (cf., MR). The distinction seems to me to be artificial. It is more likely that Joshua and Eliezer agree on basic facts, and dispute the correct interpretation of those facts. The viability of this approach to exegesis is indicated by the fact that in M. Chapter Eight and here, Eliezer and Joshua are shown to have cogent legal positions.

[9]The discontinuity between the two parts of the pericope is highlighted by the fact that it is irrelevant to D-F that the produce is in the status of heave-offering. This is, however, a fact necessary to A-C. See Green, p. 9.

[10]C-G apparently was left out in E through homoeoarchton.

[11]Apamaea is a town in Syria. See Smith, *Historical Atlas of the Holy Land*, p. 24. See also *Aruch*, I, p. 188, and Maimonides to M. Hal. 4:11.

[12]Both Albeck, p. 211, and Lieberman, TK, I, p. 457, state that the consideration here is the form in which the various types of produce normally are consumed. See MS, who notes that processing diminishes the quantity of the consecrated produce. This seems to me to be the basic consideration here, as I indicate in the continuation of my comment.

[13]Bert states that this rule has scriptural basis. He cites Num. 18:12, in which God designates for the sons of Aaron the best of the oil and wine of the people of Israel. Bert's point is that since wine and oil are specifically referred to as priestly dues, grapes and olives may be given in this form to the priest. As is usually the case, however, M. knows of no basis in Scripture for its rule.

[14]*Prosopis stephaniana*; Albeck, p. 211, and Lieberman, TK, I, p. 359.

[15]This same notion has been illustrated for the case of fenugreek, M. 10:5-6, above, p. 274-275. See also M. Ma. 5:8, which refers to parts of produce which, because they are not eaten, are not subject to the separation of heave-offering and tithes.

[16]Each of the rules at A, B-C+D, E-F+G, H and I-J is based on the pattern *substantive + permitted/forbidden*. A is a fitting introduction to all of these rules, for it adds "to non-priests" required for the sense of the other rules, yet not explicitly stated in them. As we shall see, the expansion of the form at C-D and E-F is in light of the particular substance of those cases. K and L-M, on the other hand, do completely break the basic form. They are included here because they make the same point as A-J.

[17]For a more complete discussion, see Lieberman, TK, I, pp. 458-63.

[18]For a full discussion of this point, see Lieberman, TK, I,
pp. 463-64. MB, followed by HY, simply states that these types
of pits are "valuable." I assume that MB means "valuable as food,"
such that the point is as I have explained it.

[19]See Lieberman, TK, I, p. 466, who offers an extended discussion of this term.

[20]The exact sense of the phrase is obscure. Lieberman does
not comment.

[21]T. Uq. 2:10 states that even if the peels of musk-melons
contain food, they are not susceptible to uncleanness as foods.
This is contradictory to T. 10:2D-E, which assumes that the peels
of musk-melons are themselves food. I cannot account for this
contradiction. Lieberman likewise notes the problem, yet offers
no explanation.

[22]See Lieberman, TK, I, p. 467. On the cultivation and use
of legumes in ancient times, see White, pp. 189-90.

[23]MR states that this qualification applies also in the case
of A-C. His reason is the one I have given.

[24]Heave-offering of the tithe normally is separated from
first tithe by the Levite. It is given to the priest. In the
case of produce purchased from an individual who is not trust-
worthy as regards the separation of tithes, we assume that first
tithe was not separated from the produce. The householder who
wishes to tithe the produce, therefore, himself takes from the
produce heave-offering of the tithe and gives it to the priest.
See Sarason, pp. 8-9.

[25]On the liability of vetches to the separation of heave-
offering and tithes, see Bert, MS and TYY. On the cultivation and
consumption of vetches in the Roman world, see Pliny, *Natural
History*, XVIII, 37, and Theophrastus, *Enquiry*, II, iv, 2. These
authors bear out M.'s notion of the two possible uses for vetches.

[26]Maimonides cites Lev. 22:11, which states, *If a priest buys
a slave as his property for money, the slave may eat of it* (i.e.,
holy things). The priest's beast is comparable to the slave.

[27]This is in line with Lev. 22:11, which reads, *A sojourner
of the priest's or a hired hand shall not eat of a holy thing.*
The rules of this pericope in general thus derive from a simple
reading of Scripture.

[28]Another common use for oil is anointing (T. 9:7H-M). This
is not permissible in the case of unclean oil, which would render
the priest unclean.

[29]"For sick people," (A4) is discontinuous with the first
three items in A's list, which refer to public places. I assume
that A4 is included because in this case again, oil will benefit
not only the priest, but also the sick person and others who might
visit.

[30]This interpretation depends on my rendering of *bršwt* (B and
D) as "in the presence of," and not as "with the permission of"
(see Jastrow, p. 1499, s.v. *ršwt*). In this I follow Bert, Sens

and TYY (who suggests that the priest must both be present and
offer permission). I disagree with Maimonides who states that
only the permission of the priest is required. This seems in-
sufficient, since the heave-offering is consecrated for the priest's
own use.

[31]Y. Ter. 11:7 interprets the pericope by reading into it the
question of the likelihood that non-priests will dirty themselves
with the consecrated oil, e.g., by adjusting the lamp. This would
constitute an improper waste of the heave-offering. According to
y., Judah (F) holds that at a wedding feast, at which people wear
fine clothes, it is unlikely that they will dirty themselves with
the oil. The heave-offering therefore may be kindled in that
place. This is not the case for a house of mourning, where people
are not well dressed and are likely to adjust the lamp. Yose (G),
on the other hand, takes into account the fact that the people at
the wedding feast are active, and therefore likely to knock over
the lamp and waste the oil. This is not the case in a house of
mourning. For this reason, heave-offering may be kindled there.
Meir (H) and Simeon (I) take intermediate positions, based on the
considerations offered by Judah and Yose. While y.'s interpretation is plausible, it has no grounding in the language of M.,
and there cannot be shown to represent the sense intended by the
redactor who formulated the dispute. Since M.'s own language
offers no clues to the meaning of the dispute, its correct interpretation must be left in question.

[32]Neither Lieberman, HY, HD or MB explains the rule.

[33]MS. E and ed. princ. have at B-D the reading that V (which
I translate) gives for F-H.

[34]E and ed. princ. read "in the case of tithe," and continue
at F-H with what V has at B-D. This is the version of the
pericope found at b. B.B. 97a.

[35]The translation of N-X is that of Neusner, *The Tosefta*,
vol. 6, p. 273.

[36]*Sesamum indicum* (Lieberman, TK, I, p. 477, citing Löw,
Flora, vol. 3, p. 1f.).

[37]Lieberman, TK, I, p. 479, follows RiDBaZ (to Maimonides,
Heave-offering 11:4) in stating that the reason for A is that
pulse is of low quality and therefore ruins the grain with which
it is cooked. (This is forbidden on the basis of the rule of
M. 11:1.) While reasonable, this interpretation is not acceptable
because it has no basis in the specific language of the pericope
before us, and indeed ignores D-E.

BIBLE

MISHNAH

BABYLONIAN TALMUD

JERUSALEM TALMUD